Adobe® Dreamweaver® CS6

ILLUSTRATED

Sherry Bishop

COURSE TECHNOLOGY
CENGAGE Learning®

Australia • Brazil • Japan • Korea • Mexico • Singapore • Spain • United Kingdom • United States

COURSE TECHNOLOGY
CENGAGE Learning·

Adobe® Dreamweaver® CS6—Illustrated

Sherry Bishop

Editor-in Chief: Marie Lee

Executive Editor: Marjorie Hunt

Associate Acquisitions Editor: Amanda Lyons

Senior Product Manager: Christina Kling Garrett

Product Manager: Kimberly Klasner

Editorial Assistant: Brandelynn Perry

Director of Marketing: Cheryl Costantini

Developmental Editor: Marj Hopper

Senior Content Project Manager: Cathie DiMassa

Art Director: GEX Publishing Services

Print Buyer: Fola Orekoya

Cover Designer: GEX Publishing Services

Cover Artist: Mark Hunt

Text Designer: GEX Publishing Services

Proofreader: Kim Kosmatka

Indexer: BIM Indexing

QA Manuscript Reviewers: Jeff Schwartz, Danielle Shaw, Susan Whalen, Ashlee Welz Smith, Serge Palladino

Composition: GEX Publishing Services

For product information and technology assistance, contact us at
Cengage Learning Customer & Sales Support, 1-800-354-9706

For permission to use material from this text or product, submit all requests online at **www.cengage.com/permissions**
Further permissions questions can be emailed to
permissionrequest@cengage.com

Library of Congress Control Number: 2012943661

ISBN-13: 978-1-133-52602-5
ISBN-10: 1-133-52602-0

Course Technology
20 Channel Center Street
Boston, MA 02210
USA

Cengage Learning is a leading provider of customized learning solutions with office locations around the globe, including Singapore, the United Kingdom, Australia, Mexico, Brazil, and Japan. Locate your local office at:
international.cengage.com/region

Cengage Learning products are represented in Canada by Nelson Education, Ltd.

To learn more about Course Technology, visit **www.cengage.com/coursetechnology**

To learn more about Cengage Learning, visit **www.cengage.com**

Purchase any of our products at your local college store or at our preferred online store
www.cengagebrain.com

Adobe product screen shot(s) reprinted with permission from Adobe Systems.

Adobe®, Dreamweaver®, Flash®, InDesign®, Illustrator®, and Photoshop® are either registered trademarks or trademarks of Adobe Systems Incorporated in the United States and/or other countries. THIS PRODUCT IS NOT ENDORSED OR SPONSORED BY ADOBE SYSTEMS INCORPORATED, PUBLISHER OF ADOBE® DREAMWEAVER®, FLASH®, INDESIGN®, ILLUSTRATOR®, AND PHOTOSHOP®.

Printed in the United States of America
1 2 3 4 5 6 7 18 17 16 15 14 13 12

Contents

Preface

Welcome to *Adobe® Dreamweaver® CS6—Illustrated*. The unique page design of the book makes it a great learning tool for both new and experienced users. Each skill is presented on two facing pages so that you don't have to turn the page to find a screen shot or finish a paragraph. See the illustration on the right to learn more about the pedagogical and design elements of a typical lesson.

This book is an ideal learning tool for a wide range of learners—the "rookies" will find the clean design easy to follow and focused with only essential information presented, and the "hotshots" will appreciate being able to move quickly through the lessons to find the information they need without reading a lot of text. The design also makes this book a great reference after the course is over!

Coverage

Ten units offer thorough coverage of basic to intermediate skills for working with Adobe Dreamweaver, including setting up a Web site, using CSS for page layout, inserting media objects, using Live view, and publishing a Web site. Best practices covered include designing accessible Web sites, using CSS to separate content from presentation, and managing Web site files.

New features of this book include:

- New coverage of Web 2.0 tools
- New chapter on Adding Media and Interactivity
- Expanded appendix coverage of Using Templates and Presenting and Publishing a Web Site
- Redesigned and updated Data Files—HTML files, text files, images, Flash content, and video content—engage students and give them the tools they need to develop Web sites from start to finish

Each two-page spread focuses on a single skill.

Introduction briefly explains why the lesson skill is important.

A case scenario motivates the steps and puts learning in context.

UNIT D
Dreamweaver CS6

Setting Text Properties

After you place text on a page, you format it to enhance its appearance. Text formatting attributes such as paragraph formatting, heading styles, fonts, size, color, alignment, indents, and CSS styles are easy to define by using the CSS Styles panel, the HTML Property inspector, or the CSS Property inspector. Some formatting options are available with both the HTML and CSS Property inspectors, while some are specific to each. Using standard fonts is wise because those set outside the default range may not be available on all computers. Global formatting applied with styles is much preferred over formatting applied directly to text. Styles applied across a website promote a clean and consistent look. As you format your pages, it is important to read the code for each element to see how it is written. The more fluent you are with code, the easier it will be when you have to debug the site (correct coding errors). HTML code is built from a series of **tags** surrounded by < and > symbols. Tags instruct the browser how to display each page element. You want to format the new text on the spa page to improve its appearance. You also want to examine the code for the formatting commands to understand the HTML tags that are generated.

STEPS

QUICK TIP
To apply character formats such as bold and italic, you must select the paragraph rather than click within the text.

1. **Click the HTML button [◇ HTML] on the Property inspector if necessary, scroll up if necessary, then click anywhere within the words** *The Sea Spa Services*
   The words *The Sea Spa Services* are classified as a paragraph; even a single word is considered a paragraph if there is a hard return or paragraph break after it. Paragraph commands are applied by clicking the insertion point within the paragraph text. The Property inspector shows the settings for the paragraph with the insertion point placed inside of it; Paragraph appears in the Format text box.

2. **Click the Format list arrow on the Property inspector, then click** Heading 1
   The Heading 1 format is applied to the Sea Spa Services paragraph. The HTML code for a Heading 1 tag is <h1>. The tag is then closed with </h1>. The level of the heading tag follows the h, so the code for a Heading 2 tag is <h2>.

3. **Repeat Steps 1 and 2 to add the Heading 2 style to** Massages, Facials, and Body Treatments **right under the logo**
   The Heading 2 format is applied, as shown in Figure D-6. The H1 and H2 tags make the text a little large for the page, but is more in keeping with semantic markup to begin with level 1 headings and work down. **Semantic markup** means coding to emphasize meaning. You can change the size of the text for each heading using style sheets.

TROUBLE
Mac users may notice that the insertion point does not match when viewing Code and Design view.

4. **Click after the word "Treatments", insert a line break, click the** Show Code and Design views button [Split] **on the Document toolbar**
   The HTML code for the headings displays in the left window, as shown in Figure D-7. The first tag in each pair begins the code and the last tag ends the code.

5. **Click the Show Design view button [Design] on the Document toolbar, then save your work**
   The spa page redisplays in Design view with its changes saved.

Dreamweaver 78   Working with Text and Cascading Style Sheets

Tips and troubleshooting advice, right where you need it–next to the step itself.

Written by Sherry Bishop, a digital media instructor at North Arkansas College in Harrison, Arkansas, Dreamweaver CS6 Illustrated offers a real-world perspective with exercises designed to develop the practical skills and techniques necessary to work effectively in a professional Web development environment.

Assignments

The lessons use The Striped Umbrella, a beach resort in Florida, as the case study. The assignments on the light yellow pages at the end of each unit increase in difficulty. Additional case studies provide a variety of interesting and relevant exercises for students to practice skills.

Assignments include:

- **Concepts Reviews** consist of multiple choice, matching, and screen identification questions.

- **Skills Reviews** provide additional hands-on, step-by-step reinforcement.

- **Independent Challenges** are case projects requiring critical thinking and application of the unit skills.

- **Design Quest Independent Challenges** direct students to the Internet to critique selected Web sites with regard to the features and design principles learned in each unit.

- **Real Life Independent Challenges** are practical exercises to help students with their everyday lives by creating a personal Web site of their own design. Students maintain and update this site using the skills they learn in each unit.

- **Advanced Challenge Exercises** set within the Independent Challenges provide optional steps for more advanced students.

- **Visual Workshops** are practical, self-graded capstone projects that require independent problem solving.

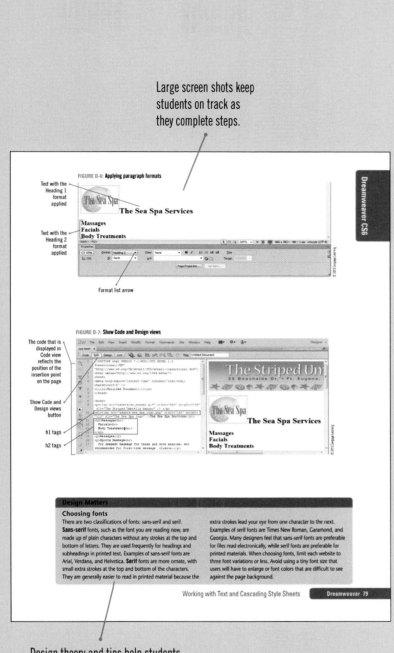

Large screen shots keep students on track as they complete steps.

Design theory and tips help students integrate basic design principles with Web site development skills.

Read This Before You Begin

Frequently Asked Questions

What are Data Files?

A Data File is a partially completed Web page, Web site, image, or other type of file that you use to complete the steps in the units and exercises to create the final document that you submit to your instructor. The Data Files that you need for each unit are listed in the back of the book.

Where are the Data Files?

Your instructor will provide the Data Files to you or direct you to a location on a network drive from which you can download them. As you download the files, select where to store them, such as a hard drive, a network server, or a USB storage device. The instructions in the lessons refer to "the drive and folder where your Data Files are stored" when referring to the Data Files for the book.

What software was used to write and test this book?

This book was written and tested on a computer with a typical installation of Microsoft Windows 7. The browsers used for any steps that require a browser are Mozilla Firefox and Internet Explorer 8. If you are using this book on Windows Vista, your dialog box title bars will look slightly different, but will work essentially the same.

This book is written for the Windows version and the Macintosh version of Adobe Dreamweaver CS6. The two versions of the software are virtually the same, but there are a few platform differences. When there are differences between the two versions of the software, steps written specifically for the Windows version end with the notation (Win) and steps for the Macintosh version end with the notation (Mac). In instances when the lessons are split between the two operating systems, a line divides the page and is accompanied by Mac and Win icons.

Also, in this book, Macintosh commands instruct users to press the [return] key to enter information. On some newer Macintosh keyboards, this key may be named [enter] or the keyboard may include both [return] and [enter]. On the newest Mac OS X, the F-keys are assigned to system functions: F1=monitor brightness and F4=widgets. You can change this in your system preferences. Newer keyboards have an "FN" or "fn" key that can be used in conjunction with the F-keys so that they function "normally."

Do I need to be connected to the Internet to complete the steps and exercises in this book?

Some of the exercises in this book assume that your computer is connected to the Internet. If you are not connected to the Internet, see your instructor for information on how to complete the exercises.

What do I do if my screen is different from the figures shown in this book?

This book was written and tested on computers with monitors set at a resolution of 1280 × 1024. If your screen shows more or less information than the figures in the book, your monitor is probably set at a higher or lower resolution. If you don't see something on your screen, you might have to scroll down or up to see the object identified in the figures. In some cases, the figures will not match your screen because the Dreamweaver windows have been resized or cropped in an effort to make the figures as easy to read as possible. The Application bar (Win) or Menu bar (Mac) may be displayed as two bars when a lower resolution is used or when the application window is sized down.

How do I create Web sites that have not been built through previous consecutive units? (Windows)

If you begin an assignment that requires a Web site that you did not create or maintain earlier in the text, you must perform the following steps:

1. Copy the Solution Files folder from the preceding unit for the Web site you wish to create onto the hard drive or USB storage device. For example, if you are working on Unit E, you need the Solution Files folder from Unit D. Your instructor will furnish this folder to you.
2. Start Dreamweaver.
3. Click **Site** on the Application bar, then click **Manage Sites**.
4. Click **New**.
5. Type the name you want to use for your Web site in the Site Name text box. Spaces and uppercase letters are allowed in the Site name.
6. Click the **Browse for folder icon** next to the Local Site Folder text box.
7. Navigate to the location of the drive and folder of your newly copied folder to set the local site root folder. The local site root folder contains the name of the Web site you are working on. For example, the local site root folder for The Striped Umbrella Web site is called striped_umbrella.
8. Double-click the local site root folder, then click **Select**.
9. Click **Advanced Settings** in the category list in the Site Setup dialog box, click the **Browse for folder icon** next to the Default Images folder text box. A message appears stating that the site cache is being updated. This scans the files in your site and starts tracking links as you change them.
10. Double-click the assets folder in your site root folder, then click **Select**.
11. Verify that the **Links relative to: Document option** is checked.
12. Click **Save** to close the Site Setup dialog box.
13. Click **Done** to close the Manage Sites dialog box.

How do I create Web sites that have not been built through previous consecutive units? (Macintosh)

If you begin an assignment that requires a Web site that you did not create or maintain before this unit, you must perform the following steps:

1. Copy the Solution Files folder from the preceding unit for the Web site you wish to create onto the hard drive, or USB storage device. For example, if you are working on Unit E, you need the Solution Files folder from Unit D. Your instructor will furnish this folder to you.
2. Start Dreamweaver, click **Site** on the Menu bar, then click **New Site**.
3. Click **Site** in the category list in the Site Setup dialog box (if necessary).
4. Type the name you want to use for your Web site in the Site name text box.
5. Click the **Browse for folder icon** next to the Local Site Folder text box, and then navigate to the location of the drive and folder of your newly copied folder to set the local site root folder.
6. Click the local site root folder, then click **Choose**.
7. Click **Advanced Settings** in the category list in the Site Setup dialog box, then click **Local Info** if necessary.
8. Click the **Browse for folder icon** next to the Default Images folder text box. If necessary, click the drive and folder of your newly copied folder to locate the assets folder.
9. Click the assets folder, click **Choose**, then click **Save** to close the Site Setup dialog box.
10. Click **Done** to close the Manage Sites dialog box.

How do I use Dreamweaver on multiple computers?

If you are using Dreamweaver on multiple computers, such as one in the classroom and one at home or in a lab, you must set up each Web site on each computer before you can access your Web site files on each computer. You only have to do this once for each Web site, but the site root folder must be accessible from both machines. For instance, if you are storing your Web sites on a USB storage device and using it on a computer in a lab and your computer at home, you must set up the Web site on each machine. Once you tell Dreamweaver where to find the files (the USB drive), it will find them automatically from that point forward.

What if I can't find some of the information in the exercises on the Internet?

This book uses the Internet to provide real-life examples in the lessons and end-of-unit exercises. Because the Internet is constantly changing to display current information, some of the links used and described in the book may be deleted or modified before the book is even published. If this happens, searching the referenced Web sites will usually locate similar information in a slightly modified form. In some cases, entire Web sites may move. Technical problems with Web servers may also prevent access to Web sites or Web pages temporarily. Patience, critical thinking, and creativity are necessary whenever the Internet is being used in the classroom.

What if my icons look different?

Symbols for icons, buttons, and pointers are shown in the steps each time they are used. Icons may look different in the Files panel depending on the file association settings on your computer.

What if my screen fonts look different?

Your screen fonts may be larger or smaller than they appear in figures. The figures were captured using the default Windows display setting of Smaller - 100% (default). Use the Control Panel to compare your settings in the Appearance and Personalization, Display window.

What if I can't see my file extensions?

The learning process will be easier if you can see the file extensions for the files you will use in the lessons. To do this in Windows, open Windows Explorer, click Organize, click Folder and Search Options, click the View tab, then uncheck the box Hide Extensions for Known File Types. To do this on a Macintosh, go to the Finder, click the Finder menu, then click Preferences. Click the Advanced tab, then select the Show all file extensions check box.

What if I can't see Flash content in my browser?

To view objects such as Flash movies, you must set a preference in your browser to allow active content to run. Otherwise, you will not be able to view objects such as Flash buttons. To set this preference in Internet Explorer, click Tools, click Internet Options, click the Advanced tab, then check the box Allow active content to run in files on My computer (under Security). Your browser settings may be slightly different, but look for similar wording. When using Windows Internet Explorer 7, you can also click the information bar when prompted to allow blocked content.

What do I do if I see a Server Busy dialog box?

You may see a message that says "This action cannot be completed because the other program is busy. Choose 'Switch To' to activate the busy program and correct the problem." when you are attempting to import Word content. This is probably a memory problem. If it happens, click Word when the Start menu opens. Repeat again if necessary, then switch back to Dreamweaver. You should see the imported text.

Acknowledgements

Author Acknowledgements

It is so difficult to fully express my appreciation to the many dedicated members of the Illustrated team. Christina Kling-Garrett, the Senior Product Manager, was at the helm and did a wonderful job guiding the process. It was amazing to be a part of such a wonderful team with so many talented professionals.

This was my first time working with Marj Hopper, our Developmental Editor. Her sharp eye, keen perspective, and sense of humor were so appreciated by all of us. Thank you, Marj! Cathie DiMassa, the Senior Content Project Manager, and Louise Capulli, the Project Manager, moved the units along smoothly, ensuring that this book would be ready for each of you. We thank them for keeping up with the many details and deadlines. I am always so appreciative of the work so many do to ensure that the book is technically accurate: Kim Kosmatka, our Proofreader; and Jeff Schwartz, Danielle Shaw, Susan Whalen, and Ashlee Welz Smith, QA Manuscript Reviewers.

Thank you, Adobe, for giving us this outstanding web development tool. It is an exciting program that is easy to use whether you are a professional web developer or a beginning design student. I hope each of you enjoy exploring its many exciting features.

Thanks to the Beach Club in Gulf Shores, Alabama, for being such a delightful place to visit. Several photographs of their beautiful property appear in The Striped Umbrella website.

Thanks, also, to my encourager and sounding board, my husband Don. Our travels with our children and grandchildren provide happy memories for us and content for each website.

Advisory Board Acknowledgements

We would like to thank our Advisory Board for their honest feedback and suggestions that helped guide our development decisions for this edition. They are as follows:

Rich Barnett, Wadsworth High School

Lisa Cogley, James A. Rhodes State College

Trudy Lund, Smoke Valley School District

Diane Miller, James A. Rhodes State College

Charles Schneider, Red Clay Consolidated School District

CourseMate

CourseMate

ENGAGING. TRACKABLE. AFFORDABLE

Cengage Learning's CourseMate for Adobe Dreamweaver CS6 Illustrated brings course concepts to life with interactive learning, study, and exam preparation tools that support the printed textbook. Watch student comprehension soar as your class works with the printed textbook and the textbook-specific website. CourseMate goes beyond the book to deliver what you need!

FOR STUDENTS:

Interactive eBook that you can read, highlight, or annotate on your computer.

Total Training videos with audio-visual, step-by-step instructions reinforce concepts you learn about Adobe Dreamweaver.

Glossary and Flashcards to help you master key terms.

Interactive exercises give you immediate feedback to help you learn.

FOR INSTRUCTORS:

Engagement Tracker, a first-of-its-kind tool that monitors student engagement in the course.

Instructor Resources

The Instructor Resources CD is Course Technology's way of putting the resources and information needed to teach and learn effectively into your hands. With an integrated array of teaching and learning tools that offer you and your students a broad range of technology-based instructional options, we believe this CD represents the highest quality and most cutting edge resources available to instructors today. The resources available with this book are:

- **Instructor's Manual**—Available as an electronic file, the Instructor's Manual includes detailed lecture topics with teaching tips for each unit.

- **Sample Syllabus**—Prepare and customize your course easily using this sample course outline.

- **PowerPoint Presentations**—Each unit has a corresponding PowerPoint presentation that you can use in lecture, distribute to your students, or customize to suit your course.

- **Figure Files**—The figures in the text are provided on the Instructor Resources CD to help you illustrate key topics or concepts. You can create traditional overhead transparencies by printing the figure files. Or you can create electronic slide shows by using the figures in a presentation program such as PowerPoint.

- **Solutions to Exercises**—Solutions to Exercises contains every file students are asked to create or modify in the lessons and end-of-unit material. Also provided in this section, there is a document outlining the solutions for the end-of-unit Concepts Review, Skills Review, and Independent Challenges.

- **Data Files for Students**—To complete most of the units in this book, your students will need Data Files. You can post the Data Files on a file server for students to copy. The Data Files are available on the Instructor Resources CD-ROM, the Review Pack, and can also be downloaded from cengagebrain.com. For more information on how to download the Data Files, see the inside front cover of this book.

- **ExamView**—ExamView is a powerful testing software package that allows you to create and administer printed, computer (LAN-based), and Internet exams. ExamView includes hundreds of questions that correspond to the topics covered in this text, enabling students to generate detailed study guides that include page references for further review. The computer-based and Internet testing components allow students to take exams at their computers, and also saves you time by grading each exam automatically.

Other Adobe® CS6 Titles

Adobe® Dreamweaver® CS6—Illustrated
Sherry Bishop (9781133526025)

Eleven units provide essential training on using Adobe Dreamweaver CS6 to create websites. Coverage includes creating a web site, developing web pages, formatting text, using and managing images, creating links and navigation bars using CSS to layout pages, and collecting data with forms.

Adobe® Flash® Professional CS6—Illustrated
Barbara M. Waxer (053847789X)

Eight units provide essential training on using Adobe Flash Professional CS6 including creating graphics and text, using the Timeline, creating animation, creating buttons and using media, adding interactivity, and integrating with other programs.

Adobe® Illustrator CS6—Illustrated
Chris Botello (1111221960)

Eight units cover essential skills for working with Adobe Illustrator CS6 including drawing basic and complex shapes, using the Pen tool, working with blends, compound paths and clipping masks, creating pattern fills and gradient fills for objects, and designing stunning 3D effects.

Adobe® InDesign® CS6—Illustrated
Ann Fisher (0538477873)

Eight units provide essential training on using Adobe InDesign CS6 for designing simple layouts, combining text, graphics, and color, as well as multi-page documents, layered documents, tables, and InDesign libraries.

Adobe® Photoshop® CS6—Illustrated
Chris Botello (0538477814)

Eight units offer thorough coverage of essential skills for working with Adobe Photoshop CS6 from both the design and production perspective, including creating and managing layer masks, creating color effects and improving images with adjustment layers, working with text and combining text and imagery, and using filters and layer styles to create eye-popping special effects.

Adobe® Creative Suite 6 Web Tools: Dreamweaver, Photoshop, Flash Illustrated (9781133629740)

Covers essential skills for working with Adobe Dreamweaver CS6, Adobe Flash CS6, and Adobe Photoshop CS6 with ten Dreamweaver units, one Bridge unit, four Photoshop units, five Flash units, and one unit on integration.

Adobe® Creative Suite 6 Design Tools: Photoshop, Illustrator, InDesign Illustrated (9781133562580)

Covers essential skills for working with Adobe Photoshop CS6, Adobe Illustrator CS6, and Adobe InDesign CS6 with seven Photoshop units, seven Illustrator units, six InDesign units, and one unit on integration.

 For more information on the Illustrated Series, please visit:
www.cengage.com/ct/illustrated

Using Adobe Bridge to Manage Assets

Files You Will Need:

To view a list of files needed for this unit, see the Data Files Grid in the back of the book.

Adobe Bridge is a media content manager integrated with many Adobe products for quic access to project files. Bridge is very easy to use as a "bridge" between your library of asset and the project files you are developing in programs such as Dreamweaver, Photoshop Fireworks, Flash, Illustrator, and InDesign. In Bridge, you can open and preview any fil format that Adobe recognizes such as JPGs, SWFs, PNGs, PDFs, MP3s, and MP4s. Althoug the most common use of Bridge is to organize and view media, it has many powerful features that you will find useful, such as adding metadata and keywords to files. **Metadat** is file information you add to a file with tags (words) that are used to identify and describ the file. **Keywords** are words you add to a file to identify, group, and sort files. Yo work for a marketing firm that designs and maintains websites for several business client. They include a beach resort, a nursery, a travel agency, a canoe outfitter, and a caterin business. You will use Bridge to manage all of the media files that will be used to create th sites, so you begin by looking at the organizational functions Bridge has to offer.

OBJECTIVES

Start Adobe Bridge CS6
Explore the Bridge workspace
Use metadata

Starting Adobe Bridge CS6

Adobe Bridge is packaged with the Adobe Creative Suite. There are several ways to access the program: by opening it directly from your Applications or Program Files folder on your computer's hard drive, or within Adobe Illustrator, Photoshop, or InDesign either with the Bridge button on the Menu bar (in Windows, it's next to Help), or by choosing File on the Menu bar, then Browse in Bridge within the program. In Flash, the Bridge button is on the Document toolbar. A streamlined version of Bridge called **Mini Bridge** is also available in Photoshop and InDesign; it appears as a panel that opens directly within the Photoshop and InDesign programs. You use Bridge as your primary tool for viewing, copying, and moving media files similar to the way you use Windows Explorer or Macintosh Finder. You can also configure Bridge to start automatically each time you log in or start your computer or device by choosing Start Bridge At Login on the Advanced tab in the Adobe Bridge Preferences dialog box. To access the Preferences dialog box, click Edit on the Menu bar, then choose Preferences. You begin your work by starting Bridge and locating your media files.

STEPS

Win

TROUBLE
f a dialog box opens
asking if you want
to activate a Flash
add in, check with
your instructor.

1. Click the Start button ⊕ on the taskbar
2. Point to All Programs (if necessary), click Adobe Bridge CS6, then proceed to Step 3

Mac

QUICK TIP
Once Bridge is run-
ning, you can add it
to the Dock perma-
nently by [control]-
clicking the Bridge
con, clicking
Options, then click-
ng Keep in Dock.

1. Click Finder in the Dock, then click Applications
2. Click the Adobe Bridge CS6 folder, double-click the Adobe Bridge CS6 application, then proceed to Step 3

From an Adobe Creative Suite 6 component that is integrated with Bridge

1. Click File, click Browse in Bridge, then proceed to Step 3

Or

1. Click the Adobe Bridge button 🖼 on the Standard toolbar (Dreamweaver), then proceed to Step 3

Or

1. Press [Ctrl][Alt][O], then proceed to Step 3

All users

3. Verify that you are in the Essentials workspace (the default workspace), as shown in Figure BR-1

   Your panels probably show a darker background than the panels in Figure BR-1. To increase the readability, the Bridge interface was lightened for the figures. See Editing Bridge Preferences on page 3.

4. Use the breadcrumb trail across the top of the Bridge window on the Path bar or use the Folders panel to navigate to and select the Bridge_data folder from the drive and folder where you store your Bridge data files, as shown in Figure BR-1

   Thumbnails of each file in the Bridge Data Files folder appear in the Content panel. These are the same media data files you will use to complete each of the lessons in Dreamweaver.

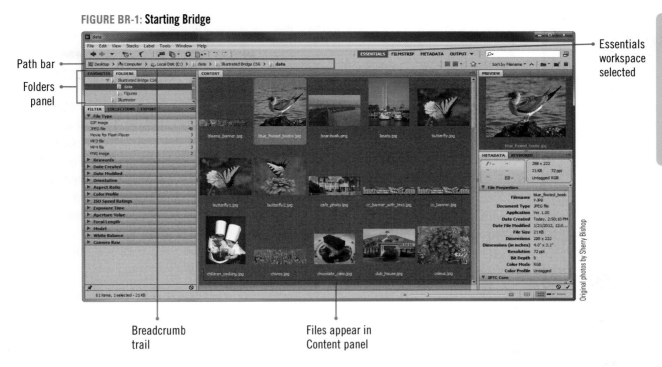

FIGURE BR-1: Starting Bridge

Path bar

Folders panel

Essentials workspace selected

Breadcrumb trail

Files appear in Content panel

Original photos by Sherry Bishop

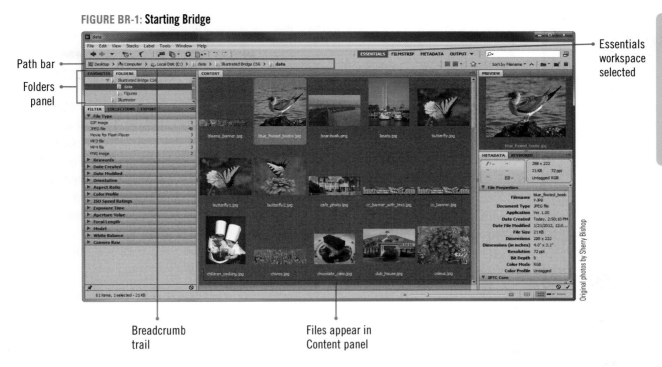

Editing Bridge Preferences

The panels in the Bridge CS6 interface have dark gray backgrounds that help you focus better on the images displayed in the Content panel. You can lighten the Bridge interface if you prefer by choosing a different color theme. To do this, click Edit on the Menu bar (Win) or click Bridge CS6 on the Menu bar (Mac), choose Preferences, then view the General tab in the Preferences dialog box. Four color boxes ranging from a dark gray to a light gray appear next to Color Theme. Click one of these boxes to select a different color theme or use the User Interface Brightness slider to create your own color theme. You can also enable (or disable) a script that enables other applications to communicate with Bridge when you start Bridge by checking the Adobe Bridge CS6 check box on the Startup Scripts tab in the Preferences dialog box.

Exploring the Bridge Workspace

When you start Bridge, you see the Bridge **Essentials workspace**, the default workspace that includes all of the menus, panels, buttons, bars, and panes that you use to organize your media files. Other workspace choices are the Filmstrip, Metadata, Output, Keywords, Preview, Light Table, and Folders workspaces. You can change workspaces by using the Window menu or by clicking one of the Workspace buttons on the Application bar. You can also arrange the panes and panels to create a custom workspace and then assign it a unique name using the Window > Workspace > New Workspace command. You can work in **Compact mode**, which is a mode with a smaller, simplified workspace window, as shown in Figure BR-2. Press [Ctrl][Enter] (Win) or [command][return] (Mac) to switch back and forth between your workspace and Compact mode. You spend some time exploring the Bridge workspace.

DETAILS

Use Figure BR-3 to locate the workspace components listed below.

- The Essentials workspace is divided into three panes, which are arranged in columns and further divided into panels. Each panel can be expanded or collapsed by double-clicking the panel title bar. You can also hide panels using the Windows > (panel name).

- The left pane includes the Favorites, Folders, Filter, Collections, and Export panels. You can use the **Favorites panel** to quickly access folders that you designate as folders you use frequently. The **Folders panel** is used to navigate through your folders to select a folder to view the folder contents. The **Filter panel** is used for filtering files to view in the Content panel. The **Collections panel** is used to group assets into collections. The **Export panel** is used to optimize images by saving them as JPEGs for use on the web.

- The center pane is the **Content panel**, where thumbnails of the files from the selected drive and folder in the Folders panel appear. You can change the size of the thumbnails by using the **Thumbnail slider** at the bottom of the workspace.

- The right pane includes the Preview, Metadata, and Keywords panels. The **Preview panel** is where a preview of a selected file appears. The **Metadata panel** lists the metadata for a selected file. You use the Metadata panel to assign new metadata to a file. The **Keywords panel** lists the keywords assigned to a file. You use the Keywords panel to add new keywords to a file.

- The **Menu bar** with the program commands is at the top of the Bridge workspace. Below the Menu bar is the **Application bar** that contains navigation buttons, the Workspace buttons, and the Search text box. Under the Application bar is the **Path bar**, where you see the path for the selected folder in the Folders panel that you are currently viewing. The Path bar makes it easy to navigate quickly from folder to folder.

FIGURE BR-2: Bridge in compact mode

Content panel is the only panel displayed

Menu bar
Application bar
Path bar

Favorites and Folders panels

Filter, Collections, and Export panels

FIGURE BR-3: The Bridge Essentials workspace

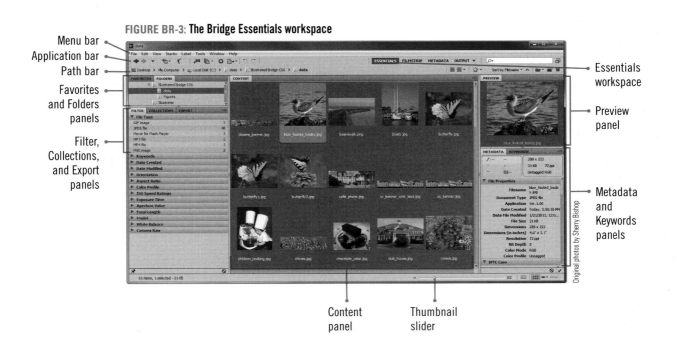

Essentials workspace

Preview panel

Metadata and Keywords panels

Content panel

Thumbnail slider

Using Metadata

The Metadata panel is a rich source of information about a file, including the camera settings used (descriptive information that you cannot change) and copyright information (additive data that you can change). You can view and edit the copyright information in the IPTC (International Press Telecommunications Council) Core section of the Metadata panel. Image resolution, author name, and keywords are also examples of metadata you can view in the Metadata panel. Metadata is saved using the **Extensible Metadata Platform (XMP) standard**. XMP metadata is used by Adobe products, such as Illustrator, InDesign, Flash, and Photoshop, and is usually stored with the file name. If a file contains metadata, XMP allows the metadata to stay with the file when the file is converted to a different file type or placed in a project. You can add metadata using the File > File Info command.

You use the Keywords panel to view and add keywords to a file to help group, organize, and sort files. There are two types of keywords: **parent keywords** and **child keywords**. Child keywords are also referred to as **sub keywords**. Child keywords are subcategories of parent keywords. For instance, you could have a parent keyword "food" and a child keyword "desserts." After you have added keywords to files, you can use the Filter panel to sort files by their keywords. You have added keywords to each of the media files you will use in your websites. You view each group separately to quickly verify that you added the correct keywords to each file.

STEPS

QUICK TIP
You cannot add metadata to .gif files.

1. **Click the Metadata panel tab to open the Metadata panel, click the first file listed in the Content panel, blooms_banner.jpg, then click File Properties (if necessary) to expand the panel to view the file size, dimensions, and resolution of the selected file, as shown in Figure BR-4**

QUICK TIP
Your other keywords will vary as keywords are deleted or added as you use Bridge or as files are selected with additional keywords associated with them.

2. **Click the Keywords panel tab, double-click the parent keyword Unit to expand it if necessary, then view the keywords for the selected file, as shown in Figure BR-5**
   Keywords let you search for and quickly locate files with common characteristics. Each file is assigned one or more chapter numbers that correspond to the unit or units the file is used in. The blooms_banner.jpg file is used in Units A, B, E, and F. Each file also includes a keyword that corresponds to the website the file is associated with.

QUICK TIP
If the files are not listed in alphabetical order, click View > Sort > By Filename.

3. **Double-click the Filter panel tab to expand the panel if necessary, click Keywords, if necessary to expand it, then click to select striped_umbrella under the Keywords criteria**
   Fourteen files appear in the Content panel, as shown in Figure BR-6.

4. **Click to select blooms under the Keywords criteria, then click to deselect striped_umbrella**
   The Content panel now shows seventeen files listed for the Blooms & Bulbs website.

5. **Click to deselect blooms under the Keywords criteria**
   All sixty-one files appear in the Content panel.

Using Metadata to label and rate files

You use the Keywords panel to view and add keywords to a file to help group, organize, and sort files. There are two types of keywords: parent keywords and child keywords. Child keywords are also referred to as sub keywords. Child keywords are subcategories of parent keywords. For instance, you could have a parent keyword "animal" and a child keyword "dog." After you have added keywords to files, you can use the Filter panel to sort files by their keywords. You can also identify groups of files by using labels.

Labels allow you to assign a file a color or a star rating from zero to five stars. The stars will appear under the thumbnail and above the filename in the Content panel and Preview panel. This is an easy way to mark the files you want to keep and others you may want to delete. You can also add labels such as "Approved" to indicate art that has been approved for a project. After you have entered labels for files, you can filter them with their labels in the Filter panel. To remove a label, use the Label > No Label command.

FIGURE BR-4: Viewing the metadata for the blooms_banner.jpg file

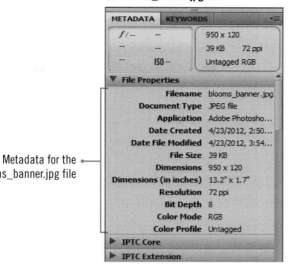

Metadata for the blooms_banner.jpg file

FIGURE BR-5: Viewing the keywords for the blooms_banner.jpg file

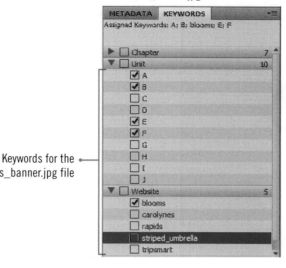

Keywords for the blooms_banner.jpg file

FIGURE BR-6: Viewing files with the striped_umbrella keyword

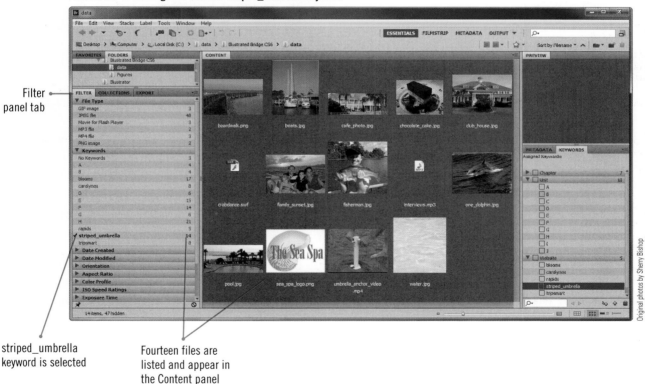

Filter panel tab

striped_umbrella keyword is selected

Fourteen files are listed and appear in the Content panel

Adding and applying keywords

To add a keyword to the Keywords panel, click the **New Keyword button** in the Keywords panel, then enter the keyword. To add a new sub keyword, click the **New Sub Keyword button** in the Keywords panel, then enter the sub keyword. To apply a keyword or a sub keyword to a file, select the file, then click the check box by the keyword or sub keyword you want to apply.

Practice

Concepts Review

Label each element in the Bridge window, as shown in Figure BR-7.

FIGURE BR-7

Original photos by Sherry Bishop

1. _____
2. _____
3. _____
4. _____

5. _____
6. _____
7. _____
8. _____

Match each of the following terms with the statement that best describes its function.

9. **Keyword**

10. **Breadcrumb trail**

11. **Metadata**

12. **Content panel**

13. **Folders panel**

14. **Menu bar**

15. **Application bar**

16. **Metadata panel**

a. File information added to a file with tags (words) that are used to identify and describe the file, such as keywords

b. The center pane, where thumbnails of the files from the selected drive and folder in the Folders panel appear

c. The bar that contains navigation buttons, the Workspace buttons, and the Search text box

d. The bar at the top of the Bridge workspace where program commands are listed

e. The path used to access a selected file; listed on the Path bar

f. Used to assign new metadata to a file

g. The panel used to navigate and select a folder to view the folder contents

h. Words you add to a file to identify, group, and sort files

UNIT
A
Dreamweaver CS6

Getting Started with Adobe Dreamweaver CS6

Adobe Dreamweaver CS6 is a web design program used to create media-rich web pages and websites. Its easy-to-use tools let you incorporate sophisticated features, such as animations and interactive forms. In this unit, you learn to start Dreamweaver and examine the workspace. Next, you open a web page and learn how to use the Help feature. Finally, you close the web page and exit the program. You have recently been hired as a manager at The Striped Umbrella, a beach resort in Florida. One of your main responsibilities is to develop the resort's website using Dreamweaver. You begin by familiarizing yourself with the Dreamweaver program.

OBJECTIVES

Define web design software

Start Adobe Dreamweaver CS6

View the Dreamweaver workspace

Work with views and panels

Open a web page

View web page elements

Get help

View a web page in a browser

Close a web page and exit Dreamweaver

Defining Web Design Software

Adobe Dreamweaver CS6 is a powerful **web design program** that lets you create interactive web pages with text, images, animation, sounds, and video. You can create web page objects in Dreamweaver as well as import objects created using other programs. Although you can create several different types of files with Dreamweaver, you will be saving files with the .html file extension throughout this book. **HTML** is the acronym for **Hypertext Markup Language**, the language web developers use to create web pages. You need to learn some basic Dreamweaver features for your new position.

DETAILS

Using Dreamweaver you can:

- **Create web pages or websites**

  You can use Dreamweaver to create individual web pages or entire websites, depending on your project needs. **Web pages** are pages of text in HTML format combined with images in various image formats. **Websites** are collections of related web pages. Websites are stored on **servers**, which are computers connected to the Internet. Users can view websites using a **web browser**, which is software used to display pages in a website; some of the most popular browsers are Internet Explorer, Mozilla Firefox, Google Chrome, Opera, and Safari. You can also import web pages created in other programs, edit them in Dreamweaver, and then incorporate them into an existing website. Dreamweaver provides predefined page layouts called **templates** that you can apply to existing pages or use as a basis for designing new ones.

- **Add text, images, tables, and media files**

  You can add text, images, tables, and media files to a web page by using the Insert panel. The **Insert panel** (also referred to as the **Insert bar**) contains buttons for creating or inserting objects, such as tables, images, forms, and videos. Using the Insert panel, you can also insert objects made with other Adobe software programs, including Fireworks, Flash, and Photoshop. Table A-1 describes the Insert panel categories.

- **Display web pages as they will appear to users**

  Dreamweaver is a **WYSIWYG** ("What You See Is What You Get") program. As you design a web page in Dreamweaver, you see the page exactly as it will appear in a browser window.

- **Use the Property inspector to view and edit page elements**

  The **Property inspector** (also referred to as the **Properties panel**) is a panel that displays the characteristics of a page's currently selected object. Figure A-1 shows a web page open in Dreamweaver. Note that the properties of the selected text appear in the Property inspector. The Property inspector changes depending upon the type of page object selected. For example, when an image is selected, the Property inspector displays image properties. When text is selected, the Property inspector displays text properties with either the HTML Property inspector or the CSS Property inspector.

- **Manage websites**

  Dreamweaver lets you manage website pages to ensure that all the **links**, or connections among the pages, work properly. The importance of proper site management increases as new pages are added to a website. Part of managing a website involves identifying problems or challenges as content is added and the site becomes more complex. There are several types of reports that you can run to check for problems across the website. Dreamweaver also has special tools that help you manage a site when you are working as part of a team on a project.

FIGURE A-1: Web page open in Dreamweaver

Tab displays filename of open file (Macintosh users will not see tabs unless multiple pages are open.)

Web page

Insert panel

Property inspector showing properties for selected text

Selected text

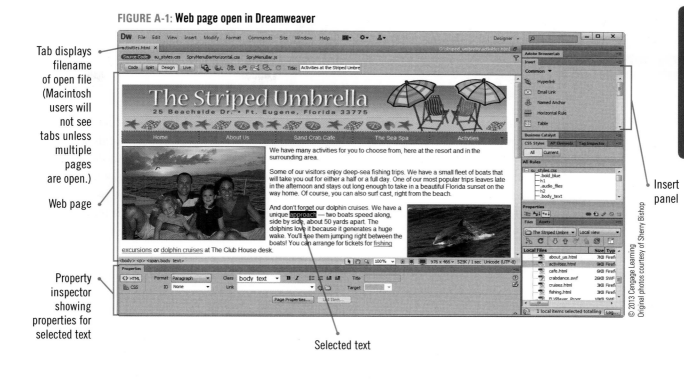

© 2013 Cengage Learning
Original photos courtesy of Sherry Bishop

TABLE A-1: Insert panel categories and corresponding buttons

category	buttons
Common	Commonly used buttons, such as images, media, and hyperlinks
Layout	Buttons for inserting divs, tables, Spry objects, and frames
Forms	Buttons for inserting form objects, such as check boxes and radio buttons
Data	Buttons for inserting Tabular Data, Dynamic Data, and Recordsets
Spry	Buttons for inserting Spry data sets, Spry validations, and Spry panels
jQuery Mobile	Buttons for inserting widgets in jQuery Mobile Pages
InContext Editing	Buttons for creating editable regions to allow others to add content
Text	Buttons for formatting text; for example, strong, headings, and lists
Favorites	Buttons you can customize; Dreamweaver will add those you use most frequently

Starting Adobe Dreamweaver CS6

There are several ways to start Dreamweaver, depending on the type of computer you are using and the type of installation you have. Although the steps below start the program using the Start menu (Win) or the hard drive icon (Mac), the fastest way to start Dreamweaver is to place a shortcut (Win) or an alias (Mac) for Adobe Dreamweaver CS6 on your desktop or add it to the taskbar (Win) or Dock (Mac). **Shortcuts** and **aliases** are icons that represent a software program stored on your computer system. When you double-click a shortcut (Win) or an alias (Mac), you do not need to use the Start menu (Win) or open submenus (Mac) to find your program. When you initially open Dreamweaver, the Welcome Screen appears. The Welcome Screen provides shortcuts you can click to open files or to create new files or websites. You are given your first web-related assignment and begin by starting Dreamweaver.

STEPS

WIN

QUICK TIP
Your Start button may look different, depending on your version of Windows and your Windows settings.

1. **Click the Start button ⊕ on the Windows taskbar**
   The Start menu opens, which lists the names of the software programs installed on your computer.

2. **Point to All Programs, click Adobe Web Premium CS6 or Adobe Design Premium CS6 (if you have one of these suites of Adobe products), then click Adobe Dreamweaver CS6**
   Dreamweaver opens and the Welcome Screen appears, as shown in Figure A-2.

3. **Click HTML in the Create New column on the Dreamweaver Welcome Screen**
   A new blank HTML document named Untitled-1 opens.

MAC

TROUBLE
Your Adobe Dreamweaver folder may be in a folder other than Applications. See your instructor or technical support contact if you have trouble locating Dreamweaver.

1. **Click Finder in the Dock, then click Applications**

2. **Click the Adobe Dreamweaver CS6 folder, then double-click the Adobe Dreamweaver CS6 program**
   Dreamweaver opens, and the Welcome Screen appears, as shown in Figure A-2.

3. **Click HTML in the Create New column on the Dreamweaver Welcome Screen**
   A blank document named Untitled-1 opens.

Using Dreamweaver layouts

Dreamweaver has several preset workspace layouts that you can choose between. In the **Designer layout**, the panels are docked on the right side of the screen, and Design view is the default view. In the **Coder layout**, the panels are docked on the left side of the screen, and Code view is the default view. The **Dual Screen layout** is used with two monitors: one for the Document window and Property inspector and one for the panels. Other layouts include App Developer, App Developer Plus, Business Catalyst, Classic, Coder Plus, Designer Compact, Fluid Layout, and Mobile Applications. You can change the workspace layout by using a feature called the **Workspace switcher**. The Workspace switcher allows you to quickly change between different preset workspace layouts. You can also create and name your own custom layout with the New Workspace command on the Workspace switcher menu. You can reset your workspace back to the preset Designer layout after you have moved, opened, or closed panels with the 'Reset Designer' command.

FIGURE A-2: The Dreamweaver Welcome Screen (Win)

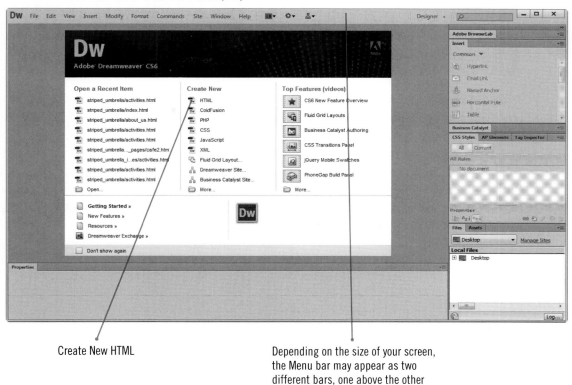

Create New HTML

Depending on the size of your screen,
the Menu bar may appear as two
different bars, one above the other

FIGURE A-2: The Dreamweaver Welcome Screen (Mac)

Create New HTML

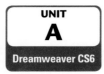
Viewing the Dreamweaver Workspace

The Dreamweaver **workspace**, shown in Figure A-3, consists of the Document window, the Application bar (Win) or Menu bar (Mac), toolbars, Property inspector, and panels. The default layout in Dreamweaver is called the Designer layout. Other layouts include the Coder and Dual Screen layouts. The Designer and Coder layouts are built with an integrated workspace using the **Multiple Document Interface (MDI)**. This means that all Document windows and panels are positioned within one large application window. **Panel Groups** are sets of related panels that are grouped together. The Property inspector, or Properties panel, is a panel that changes to display the properties of the currently selected web page object. It contains text boxes, shortcut menus, and buttons that allow you to make formatting changes without having to open menus. Its contents vary according to the object currently selected. In order to continue with your website project, you want to spend some time familiarizing yourself with the Dreamweaver workspace.

DETAILS

Use Figure A-3 to find many of the elements detailed below.

- When a document is open, the filename, path, and document type appear in the **Browser Navigation toolbar**. This toolbar, located directly above the Document window contains navigation buttons you use when following links on your pages in Live view. **Live view** displays an open document with its interactive elements active and functioning, as if you were viewing the document in an actual browser window.

- The **Application bar** (Win) or **Menu bar** (Mac), located at the top of the Dreamweaver workspace, includes menu names, a Workspace switcher, and other program commands. The Application bar (Win) or Menu bar (Mac) appears as one bar or two bars, depending on your screen size and resolution. You use commands by using shortcut keys or by clicking corresponding buttons on the various panels. We will simply refer to this as the Menu bar from this point forward.

TROUBLE

If you don't see the Insert panel, click Window on the Menu bar, then click Insert.

- The Insert panel contains buttons that allow you to insert objects, such as images, tables, and horizontal rules. The buttons on the Insert panel change depending on the category you select using a drop-down menu. Each category contains buttons relating to a specific task. When you insert an object using one of the buttons, a dialog box opens, letting you choose the object's characteristics. The last button selected becomes the default button for that category. The Insert panel's drop-down menu also has an option to show the program icons in color.

TROUBLE

To see hidden toolbars, click View on the Menu bar, point to Toolbars, then click the toolbar name. The Standard and Style Rendering toolbars do not appear by default.

- The **Document toolbar** contains buttons for changing the current web page view, previewing and debugging web pages, and managing files. The Document toolbar buttons are listed in Table A-2.

- The **Standard toolbar** contains buttons for some frequently used commands on the File and Edit menus, such as the Copy and Paste commands.

- The **Style Rendering toolbar** contains buttons that can be used to display different media types.

- The **Coding toolbar** is useful when you are working with HTML code; it can only be accessed in Code view.

- The **Related Files toolbar** displays files related to an open and active file.

- The **Document window** is the large area under the Document toolbar that encompasses most of the Dreamweaver workspace. Web pages that you open in Dreamweaver appear in this area.

- The **Status bar** appears under the Document window. The left side displays the **tag selector**, which shows the HTML tags being used at the insertion point location. The right side displays window size data and page download time estimates.

QUICK TIP

To make an open panel active and display its contents, click the panel tab. To expand or collapse a panel, double-click the panel tab.

- **Panels** are small windows containing program controls. Related panels appear together in panel groups, such as the CSS Styles panel and the Files panel. You display a panel by choosing its name from the Window menu. You can dock panel groups to the right side of the screen, or undock them by dragging the panel tab. When two or more panels are docked together, you can access the panel you want by clicking its tab name to display its contents.

FIGURE A-3: The Dreamweaver CS6 workspace

Menu bar (Application bar)

File tab with file name

Related Files toolbar

Document toolbar

Style Rendering toolbar

Standard toolbar

Document window

Status bar

Property inspector

Tag selector

Workspace switcher (The Workspace switcher on a Mac is in the middle of the Menu bar.)

Insert panel

Expanded Panel group

Collapsed panel group

© 2013 Cengage Learning

TABLE A-2: Document toolbar buttons

button	name	function
Code	Show Code view	Displays only the Code view in the Document window
Split	Show Code and Design views	Displays both the Code and Design views in the Document window
Design	Show Design view	Displays only the Design view in the Document window
Live	Switch Design View to Live View	Displays the page with interactive elements active and functioning
	File management	Displays file management options
	Preview/Debug in browser	Activates the browser for viewing the page
	Multiscreen	Displays the page in three devices in one integrated window; list arrow lets you select options
	W3C Validation	Submits the page to the W3C service for validation
	Check browser compatibility	Checks the page for problems when viewed in browsers
	Visual Aids	Displays options for visual display of information
	Refresh Design View	Reloads the page to reflect any changes made in Code view

Working with Views and Panels

Dreamweaver has three working views. **Design view** shows a page within the entire Document window and is primarily used when designing and creating a web page. **Code view** fills the Document window with the underlying HTML code for the page and is primarily used when reading or directly editing the code. **Code and Design views** (Split view) is a combination of Code view and Design view; each layout displays in a separate window within the Document window. This view is a good choice for debugging or correcting errors because you can see both the Design and Code views simultaneously. No matter which view you are using, panels and panel groups appear on the right side of the screen by default in the Designer workspace, although you can move them and use them as "floating panels." Panels are individual windows that display information on a particular topic, such as Reference or History. Panel groups, sometimes referred to as Tab groups, are sets of related panels that are grouped together. Panels are listed by groups on the Window menu and are separated by horizontal lines. As part of your Dreamweaver exploration, you want to learn how to work with views and organize your screen by opening and closing panels.

STEPS

QUICK TIP

The icons shown in the figures are in color, although the icons by default are not in color. To change to color icons, click the Insert panel drop-down menu, then click Color Icons.

1. **In the Dreamweaver workspace, click the Show Code view button `Code` on the Document toolbar**

    The HTML code for the untitled, blank document appears, as shown in Figure A-4. The code for a blank, untitled page is very limited since the page has no content. As content is added, the number of lines of code will increase as well. Notice in the first line of code that this is an XHTML document type, although the file extension is .html.

2. **Click the Show Code and Design views button `Split` on the Document toolbar**

    A split screen appears. The left side displays the HTML code, while the right side displays the open page. The open page is blank because the current document, Unitled-1, doesn't have any content.

3. **Click the Show Design view button `Design` on the Document toolbar**

    A blank page appears again because there is no page content to view.

TROUBLE

If you don't see the CSS Styles panel, click Window on the Menu bar, then click CSS Styles.

4. **Click the CSS Styles panel tab, if necessary, to expand the panel group.**

    The CSS panel group expands so you can see the contents of the active panel. The CSS Styles panel is the active panel in the default Designer workspace when the program is opened initially. An **active panel** is displayed as the front panel in an expanded panel group with the panel options displayed. Panels open in the position they held when the program was last closed. The CSS Styles panel contains two buttons, All and Current, which are used to view specific information in the panel. When two or more panels are docked together, you can access the panel you want by clicking its tab to display its contents.

QUICK TIP

If you want to restore your workspace to the original settings, click Window on the Menu bar, point to Workspace Layout, click Reset 'Designer'; click View on the Menu bar, scroll down, if necessary, then click Color Icons if you want to view your icons in color.

5. **Click the AP Elements panel tab on the CSS Styles panel group**

    AP Elements becomes the active panel with the panel contents displayed. As you click each panel tab, the panel tab changes color and the panel contents are displayed. See Figure A-5.

6. **Click the CSS Styles panel tab to display it, then double-click the CSS Styles panel tab**

    The panel group collapses. When a panel is collapsed, you click the panel tab to expand it. If a panel group is expanded, you simply click the panel tab to make the panel active.

7. **Click File on the Menu bar, click Close to close the untitled document, then click No if necessary if you are asked about saving the untitled page**

FIGURE A-4: **Code view for a blank document**

Show Design view button

Show Code view button

Show Code and Design views button

Code for blank document

Document type code

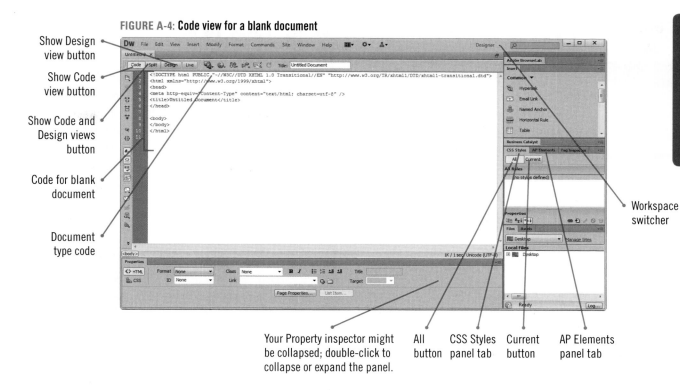

Your Property inspector might be collapsed; double-click to collapse or expand the panel.

All button

CSS Styles panel tab

Current button

AP Elements panel tab

Workspace switcher

Dreamweaver CS6

FIGURE A-5: **Viewing a panel in an expanded panel group**

AP Elements panel tab

CSS Styles panel tab

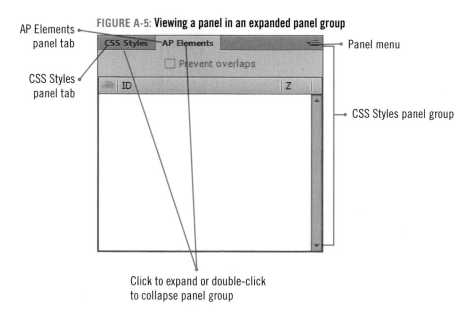

Panel menu

CSS Styles panel group

Click to expand or double-click to collapse panel group

Using panel groups

By default, the Adobe BrowserLab panel, Insert panel, CSS Styles panel group, Business Catalyst panel, and Files panel group open when you first start Dreamweaver in Windows. The panels will retain their arrangement from one session to the next. For instance, if you open the Files panel and do not close it before exiting Dreamweaver, it will be open the next time you start Dreamweaver. To close a panel group, right-click (Win) or [control]-click (Mac) its title bar, then click Close

Tab Group. The **panel group title bar** is the dark gray bar at the top of each panel group. The Panel menu lets you choose commands related to the currently displayed panel. You can also rearrange the workspace using your own choices for panel placement and save the workspace with a unique name using the "New Workspace" and "Manage Workspaces" commands on the Workspace switcher. The Workspace switcher is shown in Figure A-4.

Opening a Web Page

After opening Dreamweaver, you can create a new website or page, or open an existing website or page. The first web page that appears when you access a website is called the **home page**. The home page sets the look and tone of the website and contains a navigation structure that directs the user to the rest of the pages in the website. The resort's marketing firm has designed a new banner for The Striped Umbrella. You begin by opening The Striped Umbrella home page to view the new banner.

STEPS

TROUBLE

If you do not have your preferences set to show file extensions, you will not see the file extensions for each file. To show file extensions, open Windows Explorer, click Organize, click Folder and search options, click the View tab, then uncheck Hide extensions for known file types.

1. **Click File on the Menu bar, then click Open**

   The Open dialog box opens.

2. **Click the Look in list arrow ⏷ (Win) or click the Current file location list arrow ⬍ (Mac), navigate to the drive and folder where you store your Unit A Data Files, then double-click (Win) or click (Mac) the unit_a folder**

   The list of the data files in the unit_a folder, along with an assets folder where the image files for this unit are stored, appear in the Name column. See Figure A-6.

QUICK TIP

You can also double-click a file in the Open dialog box to open it. Or click File on the Menu bar, then click one of the recently opened files listed in the Open Recent submenu.

3. **Click the dwa_1.html file, then click Open**

   The document named dwa_1.html opens in the Document window in Design view. Since you are in Design view, all of the page elements appear as if you were viewing the page in a web browser. The interactive elements, however, will not work unless you change to Live View. Since you opened this page as a single page without access to the accompanying pages, the links will not work in Live View or in a browser.

4. **If necessary, click the Maximize button ▢ (Win) or ⊕ (Mac) on the Document window title bar**

5. **Click the Show Code view button ⌗Code⌗ on the Document toolbar**

   The HTML code for the page appears.

6. **Scroll through the code, click the Show Design view button ⌗Design⌗ on the Document toolbar to return to Design view, then, if necessary, scroll to display the top of the page**

Design Matters

Opening or creating different document types with Dreamweaver

You can use either the Welcome Screen or the New command on the File menu to open or create several types of files. For example, you can create HTML documents, XML documents, style sheets, and text files. You can create new documents from scratch, or base them on existing pages. The predesigned CSS page layouts make it easy to design web pages based on

Cascading Style Sheets without an advanced level of expertise in writing HTML code. Predesigned templates save you time and promote consistency across a website. As you learn more about Dreamweaver, you will find it worthwhile to explore each category to understand what is available to you as a designer.

FIGURE A-6: Open dialog box (Windows and Mac)

dwa_1.html data file

Look in list arrow

Displaying and docking panel groups

You can move panel groups to a different area on the screen by dragging the panel group title bar. To dock a panel group, drag the panel group to the right side of the screen. A heavy blue bar indicates the position it will take when you release the mouse button. This position is called the **drop zone**. You can also minimize all panels to icons by clicking the Collapse to Icons button in the top-right corner of the top panel. You can hide and show all panels by pressing the F4 key (Win).

Viewing Web Page Elements

There are many elements that make up web pages. Web pages can be very simple, designed primarily with text, or they can be media-rich with text, images, sound, and videos. You can use the programs shown in Table A-3 to create many of the more common web page elements. Web page elements can be placed directly on the page, or pages can be designed with elements placed in defined areas called **divs** to format and position page elements. Differences in monitor size and settings affect the size of the program and Document windows so your screen may show a larger or smaller area of the document than the figures in this book. To familiarize yourself with web page elements, you examine the various elements on the Striped Umbrella page.

Compare your screen to Figure A-7 as you examine the following:

- **Text**

  Text is the most basic element on a web page. Most information is presented with text. You type or import text onto a web page and then format it with the Property inspector so it is easy to read. Text should be short and to the point so that users can easily skim through it as they browse through websites.

- **Images**

  Images add visual interest to a web page. However, the adage "less is more" is certainly true with images. Too many images cause the page to load too slowly and discourage users from waiting. Many web pages contain **banners**, images that appear across the top of the screen. Banners can incorporate information, such as a company's logo and contact information.

- **Hyperlinks**

  Hyperlinks, also known as **links**, are graphic or text elements on a web page that users click to display another location on the page, another web page within the same website, or a web page in a different website.

- **Divs and AP Divs**

  Divs and AP divs are important page layout options because they allow you to "draw" or insert blocks of content on a page. These content containers can then be used to hold page elements, such as text or images. Because AP divs can "float" over any page element, they are easy to reposition and can be programmed to display according to set criteria. Most designers use divs formatted with Cascading Style Sheets (CSS) for page design. You will learn more about CSS in Unit D.

- **Tables**

  Tables, grids of rows and columns, can be used to hold tabular data on a web page. When used as a design tool, the edges of the table (table borders) can be made invisible to the user. Elements are then placed in table cells to control the placement of each element on the page. Div tags, however, are the best way to display general information that you want to place in columns and rows.

- **Flash movies**

  Flash movies are low-bandwidth animations and interactive elements created using Adobe Flash. These animations use a series of vector-based graphics that load quickly and merge with other graphics and sounds to create short movies. Some websites are built entirely by using Flash, while others may have Flash content in defined areas on individual pages. Most current browsers include Flash player as part of the software. **Flash player** is an Adobe program that is free to download and use. It is required to play Flash animations.

- **Flash video**

  Flash videos are videos that have been converted from a digital video file format to an .flv file using Adobe Flash. The big advantage to Flash videos is that they can be **streamed**, which means that they begin playing before the entire file has been downloaded.

FIGURE A-7: Viewing web page elements

Banner •

Links to other pages in the website •

Text •

Image •

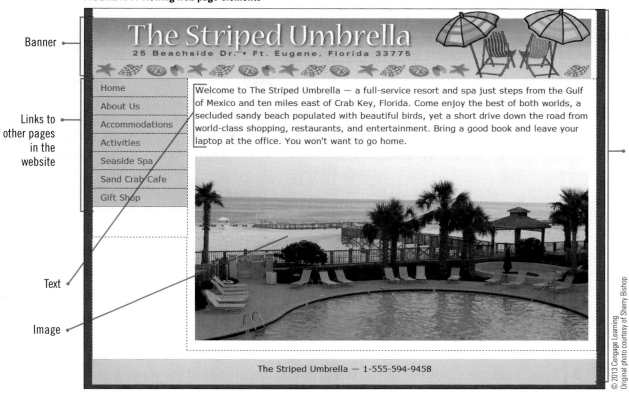

Page layout based on divs •

© 2013 Cengage Learning
Original photo courtesy of Sherry Bishop

TABLE A-3: Programs used to create web page elements

source program	elements created
Adobe Edge	Used to create animation and interactive content
Adobe Fireworks	Used to create and optimize images for the web
Adobe Flash	Used to create animation and vector graphics
Adobe Illustrator	Used to create and edit vector graphics
Adobe Photoshop	Used to edit and enhance bitmap images

Getting Help

Dreamweaver has an excellent Help feature that is comprehensive and easy to use. When questions or problems arise, you can use the Adobe Community Help window. This window contains two tools that you can use to search for answers in different ways: the link to the PDF and a Search box. Clicking the link to the PDF opens the Dreamweaver Help PDF file that is saved locally on your computer and that contains a list of topics and subtopics by category. The Search box at the top-left corner of the window enables you to enter a keyword to search for a specific topic. You can see context-specific help by clicking the Help button in the Property inspector (Win). The Help feature in Dreamweaver CS6 is based on Adobe Air technology. **Adobe AIR** is an Adobe product used for developing content that can be delivered with a browser or as a desktop application. Context-specific help can be accessed by clicking the Help button on the Property inspector (Win). You decide to access the Help feature to learn more about Dreamweaver.

STEPS

1. **Click Help on the Menu bar**

   The Help menu appears, displaying the Help categories. See Figure A-8.

2. **Click Dreamweaver Help**

   The Dreamweaver Help/Help and tutorials window opens. Since the help feature is online content, you must have Internet access to use it. This also means that since it is Web content, the pages are live pages subject to change. Your screens will probably not match the figures exactly.

3. **Type "workspace switcher" in the search box on the left side of the window under the words Adobe Community Help, click the drop-down menu next to the search text box, click Dreamweaver if necessary, then press [Enter]**

   A list of topics related to the workspace switcher appears.

4. **Click the option button next to "Only Adobe content" as shown in Figure A-9 then read the information in the Content pane**

   The list repopulates to show only content from the Adobe website. Community content includes content that has been posted from other approved sources outside of Adobe.

5. **Click one of the links listed**

6. **Scroll through and read some of the information, as shown in Figure A-10, then close the Dreamweaver Help window**

Using Adobe Help

When you access the Help feature in Dreamweaver, you have the choice of downloading a PDF for offline help (which is similar to searching in a Dreamweaver manual) or using online help. The online help feature is called Adobe Community Help.

Adobe Community Help is a collection of materials such as tutorials, published articles, or blogs, in addition to the regular help content. All content is monitored and approved by the Adobe Community Expert program.

FIGURE A-8: **Help menu**

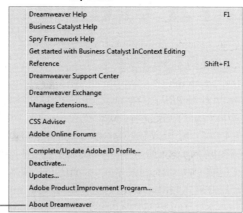

Dreamweaver Help   F1
Business Catalyst Help
Spry Framework Help
Get started with Business Catalyst InContext Editing
Reference   Shift+F1
Dreamweaver Support Center

Dreamweaver Exchange
Manage Extensions...

CSS Advisor
Adobe Online Forums

Complete/Update Adobe ID Profile...
Deactivate...
Updates...
Adobe Product Improvement Program...

Macintosh users will see this on ———— About Dreamweaver
the Dreamweaver menu

FIGURE A-9: **Displaying the Help topics**

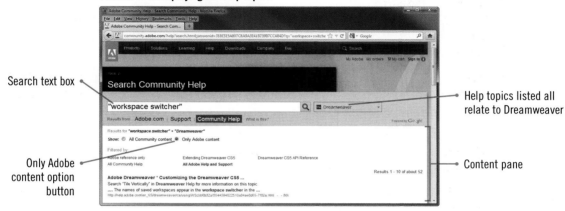

Search text box

Help topics listed all
relate to Dreamweaver

Only Adobe
content option
button

Content pane

FIGURE A-10: **Displaying Help content**

Viewing a Web Page in a Browser

During the process of creating and editing a web page, it is helpful to frequently view the page in a web browser. Dreamweaver also has a view called Live view that displays the page as if it were being viewed using a browser. In Live view, the Browser Navigation toolbar above the Document window becomes active. The **Browser Navigation toolbar** allows you to follow links in Live view as if you were viewing the pages in the browser. Viewing the page in a browser provides visual feedback of what the page will look like when it is published on the Internet. It is best to view a web page using different browsers, screen sizes, and resolutions to ensure the best view based upon your computer's capabilities. It is important to remember that you cannot print a web page in Dreamweaver except in Code view. You use the Print command on your browser toolbar or menu to print the page. ▟▟▟▟ You decide to view The Striped Umbrella home page in your default browser.

STEPS

TROUBLE
If the status bar is out of view, then resize and reposition the Document window as necessary for it to be visible. Drag a corner to resize the window and drag the title bar to reposition it.

1. **In Design view, click the Maximize button 🔲 (Win) or ⊕ (Mac) on the Menu bar, then click the Window Size pop-up menu on the right side of the status bar**

   The Window Size pop-up menu appears, as shown in Figure A-11. The Window Size pop-up menu lists several options for simulating commonly used screen sizes. You may need to double-click the right side of the Property inspector to collapse it in order to see the Window Size pop-up menu.

2. **Click 1000 × 620 (1024 × 768, Maximized)**

   The screen size is set to 1000 × 620, which translates to a monitor set at a 1024 × 768 screen resolution. When you choose your screen size, it is important to consider the equipment your users may have when they view your page in their browser. You need to consider how your pages will look, not only with different size desktop monitors, but also on tablets and other mobile devices. The Status bar also has Mobile size 📱, Tablet size 📱, and Desktop size 🖥 buttons you can use to view pages with these device sizes. See Table A-4 for window size options.

QUICK TIP
You can change the browser list by using the Edit > Preferences > Preview in Browser command, then using the Add or Remove Browser buttons to add or remove browsers from the list.

3. **Click the Preview/Debug in browser button 🌐 on the Document toolbar, then click Preview in [browser name]**

   The browser opens, and the Striped Umbrella web page previews in the browser, as shown in Figure A-12.

TROUBLE
If you don't see a menu bar, press [Ctrl] [P] to print.

4. **Click File on the browser Menu bar, then click Print**

   The Print dialog box opens.

5. **Click Print**

   A copy of the web page prints. The black background that appears on the web page will not print unless you have selected the Print background colors and images option in your printer settings.

FIGURE A-11: Window size pop-up menu

© 2013 Cengage Learning
Original photo courtesy of Sherry Bishop

Your panel
arrangement
may differ

Window Size
pop-up menu

Mobile size
button

Tablet size
button

Desktop size
button

Current Window
size dimensions

FIGURE A-12: Web page previewed in a browser window

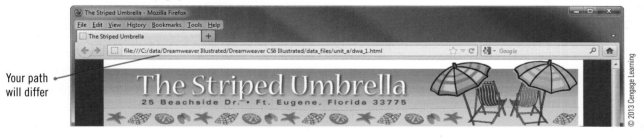

Your path
will differ

© 2013 Cengage Learning

TABLE A-4: Window size options

window size (inside dimensions of browser window without borders)	corresponding resolution
240 × 320	Feature Phone
320 × 480	Smart Phone
480 × 800	Smart Phone
592w	
768 × 1024	Tablet
1000 × 620	(1024 × 768, Maximized)
1260 × 875	(1280 × 1024, Maximized)
1420 × 750	(1440 × 900, Maximized)
1580 × 1050	(1600 × 1200, Maximized)

Getting Started with Adobe Dreamweaver CS6

Closing a Web Page and Exiting Dreamweaver

When you are ready to stop working with a file in Dreamweaver, it is a good idea to close the current page or pages you are working on and exit the program. This should prevent data loss if power is interrupted; in some cases, power outages can corrupt an open file and make it unusable. You are finished working for the day so you want to close the web page and exit Dreamweaver.

STEPS

1. **In the browser, click File on the Menu bar, then click Exit (Win), or click [Browser name] on the Menu bar, then click Quit [Browser name] (Mac)**

   The browser closes, and The Striped Umbrella Web page reappears in the Dreamweaver window, as shown in Figure A-13. In this book, screen shots of finished projects feature enlarged windows to display as much content as possible. You may have to scroll to see the same amount of content.

   QUICK TIP
   You may need to click the Dreamweaver CS6 title bar to activate the program.

2. **In the Dreamweaver workspace, click File on the Application bar, then click Exit (Win) or click Dreamweaver on the Menu bar, then click Quit Dreamweaver (Mac)**

   Dreamweaver closes.

Saving and closing Dreamweaver files

It is wise to save a file as soon as you begin creating it and to save frequently as you work. A quick glance at the title bar shows whether you have saved your file. If you haven't saved the file initially, the filename shows "Untitled" rather than a filename. This does not refer to the page title, but the actual filename. After you save the file and make a change to it, an asterisk appears at the end of the filename until you save it again. It is always wise to save and close a page on which you are not actively working. Keeping multiple files open can cause confusion, especially when you are working with multiple websites which have similarly named pages. Each open page has a tab at the top of the page with the filename listed. You use these tabs to switch between each open page to make it the active page. You can also press [Ctrl] [Tab] (Win) or [command][tab] (Mac) to move between open documents.

FIGURE A-13: The finished project in Dreamweaver

Design Matters

Designing for multiple window sizes

It is not enough today to simply design for several different screen resolutions and sizes for prospective users using desktop monitors. Although desktop sizes are probably your main focus, you should have a design plan in place for tablet sizes and mobile phone sizes in both portrait and landscape modes. Your first thought may be that your users can just enlarge their screens using gestures. **Gestures** are interactions with a touchscreen, usually with a combination of fingers and a thumb. Gestures can be used to enlarge or reduce a screen. When users pinch their thumb and finger together, the screen zooms out. When users move their thumb and finger apart (a reverse pinch), the screen zooms in. Although most people are familiar with how to use gestures, you should not make them use them in order to read your content. Dreamweaver can help you develop a design plan for multiple window sizes with the new Fluid Grid Layout, a system for designing an adaptive website based on a single fluid grid. Another option is to use Media Queries, a tool that uses CSS3 and HTML5 to identify the device a page is being displayed in and apply the appropriate styles for optimum viewing. We will learn more about Media Queries in Unit J.

Practice

Concepts Review

Label each element in the Dreamweaver window as shown in Figure A-14.

FIGURE A-14

1. _____
2. _____
3. _____
4. _____

5. _____
6. _____
7. _____
8. _____

Match each of the following terms with the statement that best describes its function.

9. **Standard toolbar**
10. **Document toolbar**
11. **Code view**
12. **Tag selector**
13. **Workspace**
14. **Design view**
15. **Insert panel**
16. **Menu bar**

a. The Document window, the menu bar, toolbars, inspectors, and panels

b. Allows you to choose program commands

c. Shows the page layout

d. Contains buttons that allow you to insert objects, such as images

e. Contains buttons for some of the more commonly used options under the File and Edit menus

f. Shows the HTML code

g. Contains buttons for changing the current Dreamweaver view

h. Shows the HTML tags being used at the current insertion point

Select the best answer from the list of choices.

17. You display panels using the _____ menu.
a. Window
b. Edit
c. Panel
d. View

18. The tool that allows you to show the properties of a selected page element is called the:
a. Tool inspector.
b. Element inspector.
c. Insert panel.
d. Property inspector or Properties panel.

19. Most information on a web page is presented in the form of:
a. text.
b. images.
c. links.
d. video.

20. The view that is best for designing and creating a web page is:
a. Code view.
b. Design view.
c. a combination of both Code and Design views.
d. any of the above.

21. Which of the following is one of the Dreamweaver default panel groups?
a. History
b. Design
c. Application
d. Files

Skills Review

1. Define web design software.
a. Write a short paragraph describing at least three features of Dreamweaver.
b. Add another paragraph describing three views that are available in Dreamweaver, then describe when you would use each view.

2. Start Adobe Dreamweaver CS6.
a. Start Dreamweaver and create a new HTML page.
b. Write a list of the panels that currently appear on the screen.

3. View the Dreamweaver workspace.
a. Locate the document title bar.
b. Locate the Menu bar.
c. Locate the Document toolbar.
d. Locate the Insert panel.
e. Locate the Property inspector.

4. Work with views and panels.
a. Switch to Code view.
b. Switch to Code and Design views.
c. Switch to Design view.
d. Expand the CSS Styles panel group.
e. Collapse the CSS Styles panel group.

5. Open a web page.
a. Open dwa_2.html from the drive and folder where you store your Unit A Data Files. Maximize the window, if necessary. (*Hint*: The file will open in the window size last selected. You can change it by using the Window Size menu.)
b. Display the page in Code view.
c. Display the page in Design view.
d. Display the page in Live view, as shown in Figure A-15.
e. Return to Design view.

6. View web page elements.
a. Locate a banner.
b. Locate text.
c. Locate an image.

FIGURE A-15

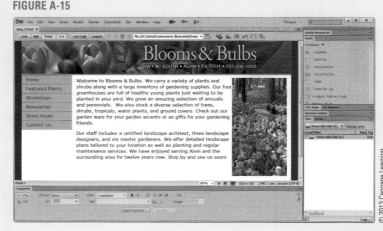

Skills Review (continued)

7. Get Help.

   a. Use Dreamweaver Help to search for topics relating to the Assets panel.

   b. Display Help information on one of the topics.

   c. Print the topic information.

   d. Close the Help window.

8. View a web page in a browser window.

   a. Note the window size that is currently selected in Dreamweaver.

   b. Change the window size to a different setting.

   c. Preview the page in your web browser.

   d. Print the page.

   e. Close the browser.

9. Close a web page and exit Dreamweaver.

   a. Close the web page.

   b. Exit Dreamweaver.

Independent Challenge 1

You have recently purchased Adobe Dreamweaver CS6 and are eager to learn to use it. You open a web page and view it using Dreamweaver.

   a. Start Dreamweaver.

   b. Open the file dwa_3.html from the drive and folder where you store your Unit A Data Files. Your screen should resemble Figure A-16. (*Hint*: The file will open in the window size last selected. You can change it by using the Window Size menu.)

   c. Change to Code view.

   d. Change back to Design view.

   e. Collapse the Files panel group if necessary.

   f. Expand the Files panel group.

   g. Change the window size, then preview the page in your browser.

   h. Close the browser, close the file, then exit Dreamweaver.

FIGURE A-16

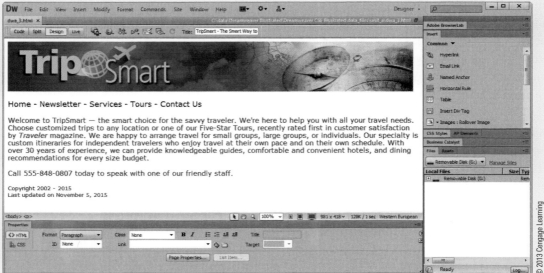

Independent Challenge 2

When you work in Dreamweaver, it is important to organize your panels so that you have the information you need where you can access it quickly.

a. Start Dreamweaver.

b. Use Dreamweaver Help to locate information on how to collapse or expand panel groups.

c. Read and print the information.

d. Close the Help window, then exit Dreamweaver.

Independent Challenge 3

The Adobe website has a feature called Customer Showcase, which includes links to websites that were created using Adobe software such as Dreamweaver, Flash, and Fireworks. The Customer Showcase feature includes the Site of the Day and Customer Showcase Features. The Customer Showcase Features links provide information about spotlighted companies, the challenges that were presented to the design team, the solution, and the resulting benefits to the companies. You visit the Adobe website to look at some of the featured websites to get a feel for what constitutes good page design.

a. Connect to the Internet, then go to the Adobe website at adobe.com.

b. Click the Company link at the top of the screen, then click Customer Showcase. Scroll down and click one of the examples.

c. Read the success story, then print the page from the browser.

d. Close your browser.

e. Using a word processing program or paper, write a short summary (two paragraphs) of the success story, then list three things that you learned about the Adobe software that was used. For example: "I learned that the Adobe Digital Publishing Suite can be used to develop tablet applications."

Real Life Independent Challenge

You are about to begin work on an original website. This site can be about anything you are interested in developing. It can be about you and your family, a hobby, a business, or a fictitious website. There will be no data files supplied. This site will build from unit to unit, so you must do each Real Life Independent Challenge to complete your website.

a. Decide what type of website you would like to build.

b. Find sites on the Internet that are similar to the one you would like to design to gather some ideas.

c. Evaluate what works on these sites and what doesn't work.

d. Write down at least three ideas for your new site.

e. Write down the screen resolutions you will use for designing your pages.

Visual Workshop

Open Dreamweaver, create a new HTML file using the Welcome screen, then use the Window menu to open the panels and document, as shown in Figure A-17. If necessary, collapse or expand the panels into the position on the screen shown in Figure A-17. Exit (Win) or Quit (Mac) Dreamweaver.

FIGURE A-17

UNIT B
Dreamweaver CS6

Creating a Website

Creating a website requires lots of thought and careful planning. Dreamweaver CS6 has many tools to help you plan, create, and manage your sites. In this unit, you use these tools to plan and design a new website. The owners of The Striped Umbrella meet with you to discuss their ideas for a new and improved website. You assure them that you can create a great site for them with Dreamweaver.

OBJECTIVES

Plan a website

Create a folder for website management

Set up a website

Add a folder to a website

Save a web page

Copy a new image to a website

Add new pages to a website

Planning a Website

Developing a website is a process that begins with careful planning and research. You should plan all development phases before you begin. Figure B-1 illustrates the steps involved in website planning. Your plan should include how you will organize and implement your site. It should also encompass testing your pages on different types of computers and modifying the pages to handle challenges such as page elements appearing inconsistently in different devices or browsers. Careful planning of your website may prevent mistakes that would be costly and time-consuming to correct. ░░░░░ After consulting with the lead member of the web development team, you review the steps described below to help you create a plan for The Striped Umbrella site.

DETAILS

- ### Research site goals and needs
  When you research your website, you determine the site's purpose and requirements. Create a checklist of questions and answer them before you begin work. For example: "What are the company's or client's goals for the website? What tools will I need to construct the site? Will the site require media files? If so, who will create them?" The more questions that you can answer about the site, the more prepared you will be to begin development. Once you have gone through your checklist, create a timeline and a budget for the site.

- ### Create a wireframe
  A **wireframe** can range from a small sketch that represents the relationship between every page of a website to a complex prototype of each page's content on a website, including filenames, navigation, images, text, and link information. Like a flowchart or storyboard, a wireframe shows the relationship of each page to the other pages on the site. Wireframes are used throughout the development process. Consult your wireframe before beginning work on a new page to use as your "blueprint" and compare each completed page to its prototype to make sure you met the specifications. The wireframe example shown in Figure B-2 is helpful during the planning process as it allows you to visualize how each page on the site is linked to the others.

- ### Create folders
  Before you create your website, you can plan for your file storage needs by creating a system of folders for all of the elements you will use in the site. Decide where on your computer you will store your site. Start by creating a folder for the website with a descriptive name, such as the name of the company. Then create a subfolder to store all of the files that are not web pages—for example, images, audio files, and video clips. An organized folder system makes it easier to find files quickly as you develop and edit your website. Figure B-3 shows the folder structure of the Striped Umbrella site.

- ### Collect the page content and create the web pages
  This is the fun part! After studying your wireframe, gather the files you need to create the pages—for example, text, images, buttons, videos, and animations. Some of these elements will be imported from other software programs, and some will be created in Dreamweaver. For instance, you can create text either directly in Dreamweaver or in a word processing program and then import it into Dreamweaver.

- ### Test and modify the pages
  It is important to test your web pages using a variety of web browsers. The four most common browsers are Microsoft Internet Explorer, Apple Safari, Google Chrome, and Mozilla Firefox. You should also test your website using different versions of each browser, a variety of screen resolutions (as discussed in Unit A), and various connection speeds (dial-up modems are considerably slower than cable or DSLs (Digital Subscriber Lines). Your web pages will need to be updated on a regular basis as new information is released and older information becomes outdated. Each time you modify a website element, it is wise to test the site again.

- ### Publish the site
  To publish a website means to make it available for viewing on the Internet or on an **intranet**, an internal website without public access. Many companies have intranets to enable them to share information within their organizations. You publish a website to a **web server**, a computer that is connected to the Internet with an **IP (Internet Protocol) address** and has software that enables it to make files accessible to anyone on the internet or an intranet. Until a website is published, you can only view the site if you have the files stored on a hard drive, USB disk, or other storage device connected to your computer.

FIGURE B-1: **Steps in website planning**

FIGURE B-2: **The Striped Umbrella website wireframe**

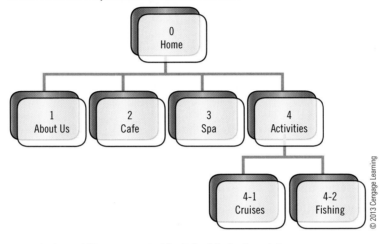

FIGURE B-3: **Folder and file structure for The Striped Umbrella website**

Design Matters

IP addresses and domain names

To make a website accessible over the Internet, you must publish it to a web server with a permanent IP (Internet Protocol) address. An **IP address** is an assigned series of four numbers, each between 0 and 255 and separated by periods, that indicates the address of a specific computer or other piece of hardware on the Internet or an internal computer network. To access a web page, you enter either an IP address or a domain name in the address box of your browser window. A **domain name** is expressed in letters instead of numbers, and usually reflects the name of the business, individual, or other organization represented by the website. For example the domain name for the Adobe website is adobe.com, but the IP address (at the time of this writing) is 192.150.18.200. Because domain names use descriptive text instead of numbers, they are much easier to remember.

Creating a Folder for Website Management

After composing your checklist, creating wireframes, and gathering the files and resources you need for your website, you then set up the site's folder structure. The first folder you create for the website is called a local site folder, sometimes referred to as the **root folder**. A **local site folder** is a folder on your hard drive, USB disk, or network drive that contains all the files and folders for a website. You can create this folder using Windows Explorer (Win), the Finder (Mac), or the Files panel in Dreamweaver. The **Files panel** is a file management tool similar to Windows Explorer (Win) or Finder (Mac), where Dreamweaver stores and manages your website files and folders. Avoid using spaces, special characters, or uppercase characters when naming files or folders to prevent problems when you publish your website. When you publish the website, you transfer a copy of the local site folder contents to a remote computer, usually hosted by an Internet Service Provider (ISP). ████ You want to create the local site folder (root folder) for The Striped Umbrella website and name it striped_umbrella.

STEPS

1. **Start Dreamweaver**

   The Dreamweaver Welcome Screen opens. If you don't want the Dreamweaver Welcome Screen to open each time you start Dreamweaver, click the "Don't show again" check box on the Welcome Screen. If you change your mind later, select the Show Welcome Screen check box in the General category of the Preferences dialog box.

QUICK TIP

Determine the location where you will store your new folders and files. Check with your instructor or technical support person if you need assistance.

2. **Click the Files panel tab or expand the Files panel, if necessary, to view its contents**

   The Files panel displays a list of the drives and folders on your computer.

3. **Click the Files panel Site list arrow**

   The drop-down menu displays the list of drives on your computer. See Figure B-4.

TROUBLE

If you see a drive or folder in the list box in the drop-down menu, you do not have a website open.

4. **Click to select the drive, folder, or subfolder in the list where you want your local site root folder to reside**

   The name of the selected drive or folder appears in the Files panel list box. Dreamweaver will store all of the folders and files you create for your websites in this drive or folder.

5. **Right-click (Win) or control-click (Mac) the drive, folder, or subfolder that you selected in Step 4, then click New Folder**

QUICK TIP

From this point forward, Mac users should know that "right-click" means they should control-click.

6. **Type striped_umbrella, then press [Enter] (Win) or [return] (Mac)**

   The local site root folder is named striped_umbrella, as shown in Figure B-5. All of the folders and files for The Striped Umbrella website will be saved in this folder.

FIGURE B-4: Selecting a drive in the Files panel

Files panel
Site list arrow

The drive or folder
that you select to
store your files
might differ

Files panel

FIGURE B-5: Creating a local site root folder using the Files panel

striped_umbrella root
folder; the file folder is
yellow because you have
not created a website
yet (the folder will be
blue on a Mac)

Design Matters

Managing files

It is imperative that you understand the basics of good file management before you can master Dreamweaver. You should be able to create new folders and new files in a specified location. You should also learn the basic file naming conventions for web content. To ensure that your files are available to all users regardless of their operating system, do not use uppercase letters or spaces in filenames. Although files with uppercase letters or spaces in their names may look fine on your screen, they might not when they are published on a web server and might appear as broken links. If you do not have a basic understanding of file management, a quick review on how to use your operating system will pay big dividends and shorten your Dreamweaver learning curve.

Setting Up a Website

After you create a local site folder, the next step is to define, or set up your website. When you set up a website, you specify the site's local site root folder location to help Dreamweaver keep track of the links among your web pages and related files. After you set up the site, the program displays the local site root folder in the Files panel. The Files panel commands also help you publish your website to a remote computer. See Unit J for more information on publishing your site. ▰▰▰▰ You are ready to define The Striped Umbrella site.

STEPS

QUICK TIP
If you have created another new site since you have opened Dreamweaver, your Unnamed Site number might be different.

1. **Click Site on the Application bar (Win) or Menu bar (Mac), then click New Site**

    The Site Setup dialog box opens, as shown in Figure B-6. (From this point forward, we will refer to "Application bar (Win) or Menu bar (Mac)" as "Menu bar" to simplify the instructions.)

QUICK TIP
You can also create a new site by clicking Dreamweaver Site under Create New on the Welcome Screen.

2. **Type The Striped Umbrella in the Site Name text box**

    The site is renamed The Striped Umbrella.

QUICK TIP
It is acceptable to use uppercase letters in the site name because it is not the name of a file or folder.

3. **Click the Browse for folder button 📁 to the right of the Local Site Folder text box, click the Select list arrow ▾ (Win) or the Current file location list arrow ⬍ (Mac) in the Choose Root Folder dialog box, navigate to the drive and folder where you created your Local Site Folder, double-click (Win) or click (Mac) the striped_umbrella folder, then click Select (Win) or Choose (Mac)**

    The Choose Root Folder dialog box closes and the Site Setup dialog box reappears with "The Striped Umbrella" as the new name, confirming that you have defined The Striped Umbrella website with the name "The Striped Umbrella". The local site folder, striped_umbrella, is designated as the location for the website files and folders. See Figure B-7.

4. **Click Save in the Site Setup dialog box**

    The Site Setup dialog box closes. Your Files panel should resemble Figure B-8. You can use the Site Setup dialog box at any time to edit your settings. Notice that the striped_umbrella folder is green. In Dreamweaver, this indicates that it is a website folder. Other types of folders are displayed in yellow.

Design Matters

Using the web as your classroom

Throughout this book, you are asked to evaluate real websites. You learn basic design principles parallel to the new skills you learn using Dreamweaver. Learning a new skill, such as inserting an image, will not be very useful if you do not understand how to use images efficiently and effectively on a page.

The best way to learn is to examine how live websites use page elements such as images to convey information. Therefore, you are encouraged to complete the Design Quest Independent Challenges to gain a practical understanding of the skills you learn.

FIGURE B-6: **Site Setup dialog box**

Your default
Site number
might differ

Default
name for a
new site that
has not yet
been named

FIGURE B-7: **Site Setup for The Striped Umbrella dialog box**

Site Name

The Striped
Umbrella local
site folder
(your path
might differ)

Browse for
folder button

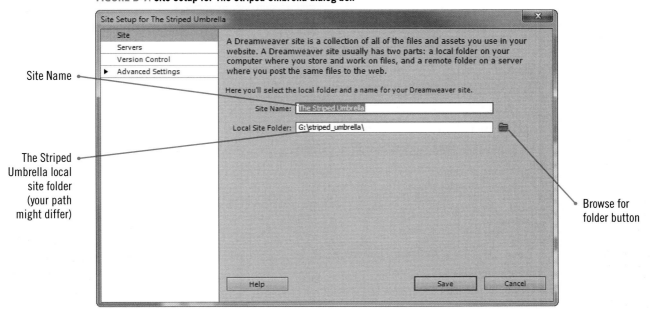

FIGURE B-8: **Files panel**

The Striped Umbrella local
root folder—your path might
differ—the file folder is now
green, rather than yellow,
indicating that a website has
been created

Mac Files panel
will vary slightly

Adding a Folder to a Website

After defining your website, you need to create folders to contain the non-HTML files that will add content to the site. Creating a folder called "assets" or "images" is a good beginning. Complex websites with many types of media or text files may have organizing subfolders within this folder—for example, separate folders for text files, image files, sound files, and video clips. It is better to create these folders in Dreamweaver rather than in Windows Explorer or Macintosh Finder; once you have defined a site, it is much easier to avoid errors if you let Dreamweaver perform all of the file management tasks. ▓▓▓▓ You want to create a folder called assets for The Striped Umbrella website and set this as the default folder for the images you save in the website.

STEPS

1. **If necessary, click the Files panel tab to expand the Files panel, then click the striped_umbrella folder in the Files panel if necessary**
   The striped_umbrella folder is highlighted, indicating that the site is selected.

2. **Click the Panel menu button ▣ on the Files panel, then point to File**
   See Figure B-9.

3. **Click New Folder, as shown in Figure B-9**
   A new untitled folder appears beneath the striped_umbrella folder in the Files panel.

TROUBLE
If you are using a Mac, you may not see the new folder if the striped_umbrella folder is collapsed. To expand it, click the triangle to the left of the striped_ umbrella folder.

4. **Type assets in the folder text box, then press [Enter] (Win) or [return] (Mac)**
   The Files panel displays the assets subfolder indented under the site root folder, as shown in Figure B-10. You will use the assets folder to store images and other elements used in the website. But first the assets folder has to be set as the default folder.

5. **Click Site on the Menu bar, click Manage Sites, then click the Edit the currently selected site button ✎**
   The Site Setup for The Striped Umbrella dialog box opens with The Striped Umbrella website selected.

6. **Click Advanced Settings from the category list in the left column, click the Browse for folder button ▣ next to the Default Images folder text box, then click the Select list arrow ▾ (Win) or the Current file location list arrow ⬍ (Mac) if necessary to display the striped_umbrella folder in the Select text box**

7. **Click the assets folder**
   The Choose Image Folder dialog box shows the assets folder listed in the Select text box.

8. **Click Select (Win) or Choose (Mac), click Save in the Site Setup for The Striped Umbrella dialog box, then click Done in the Manage Sites dialog box**
   The new folder called "assets" for The Striped Umbrella website is created and established as the default location for saving all images. This will save steps when you copy image files to the website because you will not have to browse to the assets folder each time you save an image. Dreamweaver will save all images automatically in the assets folder. The Files panel shows the assets folder listed under the local site root folder, as shown in Figure B-10.

Design Matters

Why name the folder "assets"?

There is no particular significance to the word *assets* for the name of the folder you will use to store non-HTML files in your websites. Many web designers use the term *images* instead. You can name the folder anything you want, but the term *assets* is a good descriptive word for a folder that can be used to store other types of graphic or media files besides images for your site, such as sound files. The main idea is to organize your files by separating the HTML files from the non-HTML files by using a folder structure with appropriately named folders to reflect the content that they store.

FIGURE B-9: Creating a new folder in the Files panel

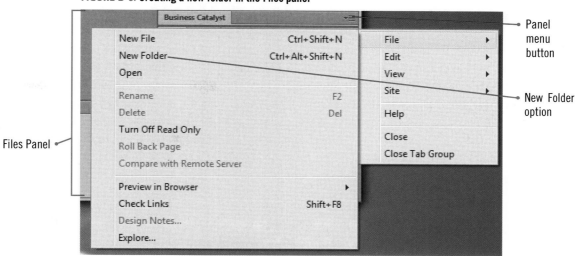

Files Panel

Panel menu button

New Folder option

FIGURE B-10: Files panel with the assets folder added

assets folder

Using the Files panel for file management

You can use the Files panel to add, delete, move, or rename files and folders in a website. *It is very important that you perform these file maintenance tasks in the Files panel rather than in Windows Explorer (Win) or the Finder (Mac). If you make changes to the folder structure outside the Files panel, you may experience problems.* If you move or copy the site root folder to a new location, you must define the website again in Dreamweaver, as you did in the lesson on defining a website.

Saving a Web Page

It is wise to save your work frequently. A good practice is to save every five or ten minutes, before you attempt a difficult step, and after you successfully complete a step. This ensures that you do not lose any work in the event of a power outage or computer problem. In this book, you are instructed to use the Save As command after you open each Data File. The Save As command duplicates the open document and allows you to assign the new document a different name. By duplicating the Data Files, you can repeat an exercise or start a lesson over if you make a mistake. ▗▚▞▞ You are ready to create the first draft of the home page. You want to open a copy of the existing home page from a folder outside the new website, rename it, and then save it in the site root folder for the Striped Umbrella website.

STEPS

1. **Click** File **on the Menu bar, click** Open, **navigate to the drive and folder where you store your Unit B Data Files, then double-click** dwb_1.html

   The Striped Umbrella home page opens in the Document window in Design View. This is the home page that users will see when they first visit The Striped Umbrella website.

QUICK TIP

The file extension php stands for PHP: Hypertext Preprocessor. It is a server-side scripting language.

2. **Click** File **on the Menu bar, click** Save As, **click the** Save in list arrow ⊡ **(Win) or the** Current file location list arrow ⬍ **(Mac) to navigate to the** striped_umbrella **local site root folder, then double-click (Win) or click (Mac) the** striped_umbrella folder

   The home page will be saved in the Striped Umbrella website root folder, striped_umbrella. Because it will be the home page for your site, you save the file using the name "index.html", the conventional name for a site's home page. Web servers are programmed to search for files named "index.html" or "default.html" to display as the initial page that opens in a website, as well as other file types such as index.php.

QUICK TIP

You can just type the filename "index"; the program automatically adds the .html file extension to the filename after you click Save.

3. **Click in the** File name **text box (Win) or** Save As **text box (Mac) if necessary, select the existing file name (**dwb_1.html**), type** index.html, **as shown in Figure B-11, click** Save, **click** No **in the Update Links dialog box, maximize the Document window if necessary, then click the** Show Design view button ▭Design▭ **if necessary**

   The Striped Umbrella home page displays in the Document window, as shown in Figure B-12. If you are not viewing the page in a separate window (Win), the path to the site root folder and the filename is displayed to the right of the document tab. If you are viewing the page in a separate window, this information appears on the document title bar. Mac users point to the file tab to see this information. The drive designator, folder name, subfolder names, and filename is called the **path**, or location of the open file in relation to any folders in the website. The page banner does not appear and is replaced by a gray box, indicating the link is broken. This means the program cannot link to the image, which currently resides in the Data Files folder. In the next lesson you will repair the link so that the image appears.

TROUBLE

If you don't see the index.html file listed in the Files panel, click the Refresh button ⟳.

4. **Click the** Close button ✖ **on the** dwb_1.html **file tab, click the** Insert panel drop-down menu, **then click** Color Icons **if necessary to show the icons in color**

   The dwb_1.html page closes. You leave the index.html page open to correct the link to the banner image.

Design Matters

Choosing filenames

When you name a file, you should use a descriptive name that reflects the file's contents. For example, if the page is about a company's products, you could name it "products." You must also follow some general rules for naming web pages. For example, the home page should be named "index.html" or "default.html". You can also use the file extension "htm" instead of "html." Do not use spaces, special characters, regular or back slashes, or punctuation in web page filenames or in the names of any images that will be inserted in your website. Another rule is not to use a number for the first character of a filename. To ensure that everything loads properly on all platforms, including UNIX, assume that filenames are case sensitive and use lowercase characters. A good practice is to limit filenames to eight characters.

FIGURE B-11: The Save As dialog box (Windows and Mac)

The striped_umbrella
local site root folder

index.html is the name of
the new home page

FIGURE B-12: The Striped Umbrella home page

Close button

Banner link
is broken
because the
image file
has not been
copied into
the website
assets folder

Path of
index.html
(Mac title bar
placement
differs)

Name of
open file

Name of local
site root folder

index.html
file is saved
in local site
root folder

Copying a New Image to a Website

When you open a web page in one folder and then save a copy of it in a different folder, you must take care to copy each image on the page from the original folder into the new folder. If you don't do this, the links to each image will be broken when the page is published to a web server and subsequently viewed in a web browser. ████ You want to identify The Striped Umbrella banner source file and copy it to the website's assets folder.

STEPS

TROUBLE
If your index.html page does not appear in the Files panel, click the Refresh button ⟳ on the Files panel toolbar.

1. **Click the gray box representing the broken image on the index page**

   Selection handles appear on the lower and right edges of the broken image and the Property inspector displays the banner's properties. The Src (Source) text box in the Property inspector displays the location: assets/su-banner.gif, but it is referencing the assets folder in the unit_b Data Files folder, not the assets folder in the website folder. The Striped Umbrella banner, which is the source file, currently resides in the unit_b assets folder. You navigate to the Data Files and select the source file. The concept of broken links will become clearer upon completing Unit F which explores the relationship between absolute and relative links.

TROUBLE
If the path for an image or a link begins with the word *file*, you will have linking problems. Delete all extraneous path information in the Src text box or the browser will not be able to find the image when the website is published. A good practice is to go to Code view and search for the word *file*. If you find *file* in your code, you must evaluate each occurrence to see if you need to remove unnecessary code.

2. **If necessary, double-click the right side of the Property inspector to expand it, click the Browse for File button 🗀 next to the Src text box, click the Look in list arrow ▾ (Win) or the Current file location list arrow ⬍ (Mac) if necessary to navigate to the drive and folder where you store your Data Files, double-click the unit_b folder, double-click the assets folder, then double-click the su_banner.gif file**

   The correct source file is selected from the Data Files folder. Dreamweaver copies the file to the assets folder in the website automatically because you designated the website assets folder as the default location for images when you set up the site. The Src text box in the Property inspector displays the path "assets/ su_ banner.gif" without any extra path designation in front of it. If you see a path in front of the word *assets*, Dreamweaver is trying to link the image file to the Data Files folder.

3. **Click anywhere on the page outside of the banner, if necessary, to display the image, select the image again to display the image settings in the Property inspector, click File on the Menu bar, click Save, then compare your screen to Figure B-13**

   The banner now displays correctly on the page which indicates that the source file has been successfully copied to the website assets folder. The Property inspector displays the properties of the selected image.

Design Matters

Making a good first impression

Since the home page is the first page users see as they enter a website, it is important to make a good first impression. When you enter a store, you immediately notice the way the merchandise is displayed, whether the staff is accessible and friendly, and the general overall appearance and comfort of the interior. The same is true of a website. If you see pleasing colors and images, friendly and easy-to-understand text, and a simple navigation system, you are favorably impressed and want to explore the site. If you see poorly organized content, misspelled words, and confusing navigation, you will probably leave the site. It is much faster and easier to leave a website than to leave a store, so you have less time to correct a bad first impression. Have others evaluate your home page before you finalize it so you understand how others see your page.

FIGURE B-13: Property inspector showing properties of The Striped Umbrella banner

Selected Striped Umbrella banner

Lower Selection handles

Property inspector provides details about the selected image

Source is pointing to assets folder

Browse for File button

© 2013 Cengage Learning

Planning the page layout

When you begin developing the content for your website, you must decide what to include and how to arrange each element on each page. You must also design the content with the audience in mind. Who is your target audience? What is your audience's age group, sex, race, and residence? What reading and computer literacy level is appropriate? Should pages be simple, containing mostly text, or rich with images and media files? To ensure that users do not get "lost" in your website, make sure all the pages have a consistent look and feel. This can be accomplished easily through the use of templates. **Templates** are web pages that contain the basic layout for each page of a site. You can create original templates with the File menu in Dreamweaver or download them from the Internet. See the Appendix for more information on templates.

Adding New Pages to a Website

Websites may be as small as one page or contain hundreds of pages. In Dreamweaver, you can add new pages to a website, and then add content such as text and images. The blank pages serve as placeholders for pages that you anticipate designing. That way you can set up the navigation structure of the website and test the links between the pages. When you are satisfied with the overall structure, you can then create the content for the pages. You add new pages by using the Files panel. After consulting your wireframe, you decide to create new web pages to add to The Striped Umbrella website. You create new pages called about_us, spa, cafe, activities, cruises, and fishing, and place them in the site root folder.

STEPS

1. **Click the Refresh button 🔄 on the Files Panel, then click the plus sign (Win) or the triangle (Mac) to the left of the assets folder in the Files panel to expand the folder if necessary**

   The assets folder expands to display its contents, as shown in Figure B-14. The su_banner.gif file is located in the assets folder.

   > **TROUBLE**
   > Be careful not to delete the .html file extension when you name the file.

2. **Click the site folder under the Local Files column to select it, right-click the site folder, click New File, click in the filename text box to select untitled if necessary, type about_us, then press [Enter] (Win) or [return] (Mac)**

   The about us page is added to the website. You can also click the Files panel menu button 📋, point to File, then click New File to create a new file.

3. **Repeat Step 2 to add five more blank pages to The Striped Umbrella website, and name the new files spa.html, cafe.html, activities.html, cruises.html, and fishing.html**

   The new pages appear in the striped_umbrella root folder.

   > **TROUBLE**
   > If you accidentally create your new files in the assets folder rather than the site root folder, select and drag each one to the site root folder.

4. **Click the Refresh button 🔄 on the Files panel toolbar**

   The file listing is refreshed and the files are now sorted in alphabetical order, as shown in Figure B-15.

5. **Click File on the Menu bar, click Close, click File on the Application bar, click Exit (Win) or click Dreamweaver on the Menu bar, then click Quit Dreamweaver (Mac)**

Managing a project with a team

When working with a team, it is essential that you define clear goals for the project and a list of objectives to accomplish those goals. Your plan should be finalized after conferring with both the client and team to make sure that the purpose, scope, and objectives are clear to everyone. Establish the **deliverables**, or products that will be provided to the client upon project completion, such as creation of new pages or graphic elements, and a timeline for their delivery. You should present the web pages to both your team and client for feedback and evaluation at strategic points in the development process. Analyze all

feedback objectively, incorporating both the positive and the negative comments to help you make improvements to the site and meet everyone's expectations and goals. A common pitfall in team management is scope creep. **Scope creep** occurs when impromptu changes or additions are made to a project without accounting for corresponding increases in the schedule or budget. Proper project control, resource allocation, and communication between team members and clients can minimize scope creep and achieve the successful and timely completion of a project.

FIGURE B-14: Files panel showing su_banner.gif in the assets folder

assets folder ●

su_banner.gif file in the
assets folder

FIGURE B-15: New pages added to The Striped Umbrella website and sorted

Refresh icon ●

Your image icon for
su_banner.gif
might differ

New pages added to the
striped_umbrella site folder
and sorted after the Files
panel is refreshed

A Mac Files panel will differ
slightly in appearance

Practice

Concepts Review

Label each element in Figure B-16.

FIGURE B-16

1. _____
2. _____
3. _____
4. _____

5. _____
6. _____
7. _____

Match each of the following terms with the statement that best describes its function.

8. **Domain name**
9. **Wireframe**
10. **Assets**
11. **IP address**
12. **web server**
13. **Local site folder**
14. **Intranet**
15. **Home page**
16. **Publish a website**

a. An address on the web expressed in numbers

b. Computer connected to the Internet with an IP address and software that enables it to make files accessible for viewing on the Internet

c. An internal website without public access

d. To make a website available for viewing on the Internet

e. A folder that holds all the files and folders for a website

f. Usually the first page users see when they visit a website

g. A folder that contains non-HTML files

h. A diagram of a website's folder structure showing links and placement of main page elements

i. An address on the web expressed in letters

Select the best answer from the following list of choices.

17. An internal website without public access is called a(n):
    - **a.** Internet
    - **b.** Intranet
    - **c.** Domain
    - **d.** Extension

18. The first step in designing a website should be:
    - **a.** Setting up web server access
    - **b.** Testing the pages
    - **c.** Planning the site
    - **d.** Creating the pages and developing the content

19. Which icon or button do you click to refresh the Files panel after you have changed files listed there?
    - **a.** 🖿
    - **b.** ↻
    - **c.** Code
    - **d.** 🌐

20. Web pages that contain the basic layout for each page in a website are called:
    - **a.** Templates
    - **b.** Examples
    - **c.** Shells
    - **d.** Forms

Skills Review

1. **Plan a website.**
   - **a.** Create a wireframe with five pages for a company called Blooms & Bulbs.
   - **b.** Name the pages **index**, **plants**, **workshops**, **newsletter**, and **tips**. (The plants, workshops, newsletter, and tips pages will be linked to the index page.)

2. **Create a folder for website management.**
   - **a.** Start Dreamweaver, then open or expand the Files panel if necessary.
   - **b.** Select the drive or folder in the Site list box where you will store your website files.
   - **c.** Create a new folder with the name **blooms** to store your website files.

3. **Define the website.**
   - **a.** Create a new site using the Site > New Site command. Name the site **Blooms & Bulbs**.
   - **b.** In the Site Setup dialog box, browse to select the root folder you created for the website.
   - **c.** Save the site definition and exit the site setup.

4. **Add a folder to the website.**
   - **a.** Use the Files panel to create an assets folder for the website.
   - **b.** Use the Site Setup dialog box to set the assets folder as the default images folder for storing your image files.

5. **Copy a new image to a website.**
   - **a.** Open dwb_2.html from the drive and folder where your unit_b Data Files are stored.
   - **b.** Save the file as **index.html** in the blooms folder in the Blooms & Bulbs website, and do not update the links.
   - **c.** Close the dwb_2.html file.
   - **d.** Select the gray box representing the broken link to the banner image on the page.
   - **e.** Using the Browse for File button next to the Src text box on the Property inspector, navigate to the assets folder inside the unit_b folder where you store your Data Files, then select blooms_banner.jpg.
   - **f.** Refresh the Files panel, click on the page to deselect the banner, then verify that the banner was copied to the assets folder in your Blooms & Bulbs site, then save the index.html file.

Skills Review (continued)

6. Add new pages to a website.

    a. Using the Files panel, create a new page called **plants.html**.

    b. Create three more pages, called **workshops.html**, **tips.html**, and **newsletter.html**.

    c. Use the Refresh button to sort the files in alphabetical order, then compare your screen to Figure B-17.

    d. Close the index page, then exit Dreamweaver.

FIGURE B-17

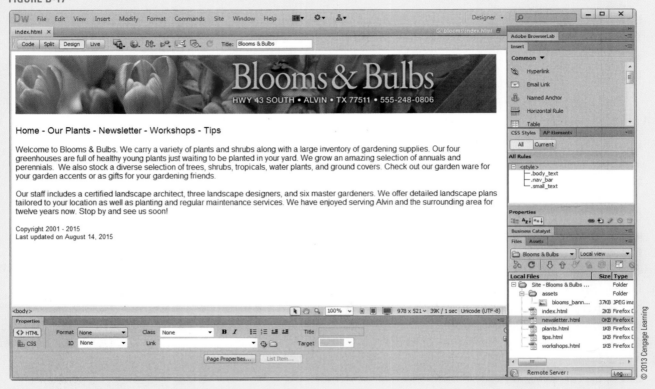

Independent Challenge 1

You have been hired to create a website for a river expedition company named Rapids Transit, located on the Buffalo River in Arkansas. In addition to renting canoes, kayaks, and rafts, they have several types of cabin rentals for overnight stays. River guides are available, if requested, to accompany clients on float trips. The clients range from experienced floaters to beginners. Refer to Figure B-18 as you work through the following steps:

a. Create a website plan and wireframe for this site.

b. Create a folder named **rapids** in the drive and folder where you save your website files.

c. Define the site with the name **Rapids Transit**, setting the rapids folder as the site root folder for the website.

d. Create an **assets** folder, then set it as the default images folder.

e. Open dwb_3.html from the drive and folder where your Unit B Data Files are stored, then save it in the site folder as **index.html**. Do not update the links.

f. Close dwb_3.html.

g. Save the rt_banner.jpg image in the assets folder for your site and save the index.html file. (*Hint*: Use the Browse for File button next to the Src text box to navigate to the unit_b assets folder to locate the image.) Refresh the Files panel and verify that the rt_banner.jpg image was copied to the site assets folder.

h. Create four additional files for the pages in your site plan, and give them the following names: **guides.html**, **rates.html**, **lodging.html**, and **before.html**. Refresh the Files panel to display the files in alphabetical order.

i. Close the index page, then exit Dreamweaver.

FIGURE B-18

Independent Challenge 2

Your company is designing a new website for a travel outfitter named TripSmart. TripSmart specializes in travel products and services. In addition to selling travel products such as luggage and accessories, they organize trips and offer travel advice. Their clients range from college students to families to vacationing professionals. The owner, Thomas Howard, has requested a dynamic website that conveys the excitement of traveling. Refer to Figure B-19 as you work through the following steps:

a. Create a website plan and wireframe for this site to present to Thomas.

b. Create a folder named **tripsmart** in the drive and folder where you save your website files.

c. Define the site with the name **TripSmart**, then set the tripsmart folder as the site root folder.

d. Create an assets folder, then set it as the default images folder.

e. Open the file dwb_4.html from the drive and folder where you store your Unit B Data Files, then save it in the site root folder as **index.html**. Do not update the links.

f. Close dwb_4.html.

g. Save the tripsmart_banner.jpg image in the assets folder for the site, save the index.html file, then refresh the Files panel to display the image file in the assets folder.

h. Create four additional files for the pages in your plan, and give them the following names: **catalog.html**, **newsletter.html**, **services.html**, and **tours.html**. Refresh the Files panel to display the files in alphabetical order, then compare your screen to Figure B-19.

i. Close the index page, then exit Dreamweaver.

FIGURE B-19

Independent Challenge 3

Patsy Broers is interested in a national program that encourages high school students to memorize and recite poetry. This program is sponsored by the National Endowment for the Arts (NEA), so she goes to the NEA website, shown in Figure B-20, to look for information on the program. (As this is a live site, your figure may differ due to content changes.) Record your answers to the questions below.

FIGURE B-20

National Endowment for the Arts website (nea.gov)

a. Connect to the Internet and go to the NEA website at nea.gov.

b. Click the Site Map link at the bottom of the page. What do you think is the purpose of the site map?

c. How has the NEA organized its information to help you navigate its website?

d. Can you find the information that Patsy needs?

e. Did you feel that the site map helped you navigate the website?

f. Do you feel that the site map link is beneficial for users?

g. Close your browser.

Real Life Independent Challenge

In this assignment, you create a personal website entirely on your own. There will be no Data Files supplied. These Independent Challenges will build from unit to unit, so you must do each unit's Real Life Independent Challenge assignment to complete your website.

a. Decide what type of website you would like to build. It can be a personal website about you and your family, a business website if you have a business you would like to promote, or a fictitious website. Your instructor may direct your choices for this assignment.

b. Create a wireframe for your website and include at least four pages.

c. Create a site root folder where you store your website files and name it appropriately.

d. Define the site with an appropriate name, using the site root folder that you created.

e. Create an assets folder and set it as the default location for images.

f. Begin planning the content you would like to use for the home page and plan how you would like to organize it on the page.

g. Use the Files panel to create the pages you listed in your wireframe.

h. Collect information to use in your website, such as images or text. Store these in a folder (either electronic or paper) that you can bring with you to class as you develop your site.

i. Exit Dreamweaver.

Visual Workshop

Your company has been selected to design a website for a catering business called Carolyne's Creations. In addition to catering, Carolyne's services include cooking classes and daily specials available as take-out meals. She also has a retail shop that stocks gourmet treats and kitchen items. Create the website pictured in Figure B-21, using **Carolyne's Creations** for the site name and **cc** for the site root folder name. Use the files dwb_5.html for the index (home) page and cc_banner.jpg for the banner. These files are located in the drive and folder where you store your Data Files. Next, add the files **catering.html**, **classes.html**, **recipes.html**, and **shop.html** to the local site root folder.

FIGURE B-21

Developing a Web Page

When you begin developing web pages, you should choose the page content with the purpose of the website and the target audience in mind. A website designed for a large professional corporation should be designed quite differently than an educational website for children. You can use colors, fonts, and images to set a formal or casual tone. In this unit, you learn about planning a website, modifying a web page, and linking it to other pages. Finally, you'll use Code view to modify some of the page code, and test the links to make sure they work. The Striped Umbrella website should appeal to families, singles, and maturing baby boomers with leisure time and money to spend. You improve the design and content of the home page to attract this broad target audience.

OBJECTIVES

Plan the page layout

Create the head content

Set web page properties

Create and format text

Add links to web pages

Use the History panel

View HTML code

Test and modify web pages

Planning the Page Layout

When people visit your website, you want them to feel at home, as if they know their way around the pages in your site. You also want to ensure that users will not get lost on the site due to layout inconsistencies. To help maintain a common look for all pages, you can use templates. Templates are web pages that contain basic layouts you can apply to your website pages, standardizing elements, such as the location of a company logo or a menu of buttons. As you will learn in Units D and G, the use of **Cascading Style Sheets (CSS)** provides a way to easily position and format objects or entire pages by providing common formatting characteristics that can be applied to multiple objects. And, as you will learn in Unit G, many designers use tables, simple grids of cells in rows and columns, as a page layout tool to position lists of tabular data on the page easily. Before you begin working on The Striped Umbrella home page, you want to identify key concepts that govern good page layout.

When planning the layout of your web pages, remember the following guidelines:

- **Keep it simple**

  Often the simplest websites are the most appealing. Websites that are simple in layout and design are the easiest to create and maintain. A simple website that works is far superior to a complex one with errors.

- **Use white space effectively**

  Too many text blocks, links, and images can confuse users, and actually make them feel agitated. Consider leaving some white space on each page. **White space** is the area on a web page that is not filled with text or graphics. (Note that white space is not necessarily white in color.) Using white space effectively creates a harmonious balance on the page. Figure C-1 shows how white space can help emphasize strong visual page elements, yet still achieve a simple, clean look for the page.

- **Limit media objects**

  Too many media objects—such as graphics, video clips, or sounds—may result in a page that takes too long to load. Users may tire of waiting for these objects to appear and leave your site before the entire page finishes loading. Placing unnecessary media objects on your page makes your website seem unprofessional.

- **Use an intuitive navigation structure**

  A website's navigational structure should be easy to use. It can be based on text links or a combination of text and graphic links. Users should always know where they are in the website, and be able to find their way back to the home page easily. If users get lost on your website, they may leave the site rather than struggle to find their way around.

- **Apply a consistent theme using templates**

  A theme can be almost anything, from the same background color on each page to common graphics, such as buttons or icons that reflect a collective theme. Common design elements such as borders can also be considered a theme. Templates are a great way to easily incorporate consistent themes in websites.

- **Use CSS for page layout**

  When you use CSS as the basis for page layout, you can control both how the entire page appears in browser windows and how the various page elements are positioned on the page in relation to each other. This allows a page to look the same, regardless of the size of a user's screen.

- **Be conscious of accessibility issues**

  There are several techniques you can use to ensure that your website is accessible to individuals with disabilities. These techniques include using alternate text with images, avoiding certain colors on web pages, and supplying text as an alternate source for information that is presented in audio files. Dreamweaver can display Accessibility dialog boxes to prompt you to insert accessibility information for the page objects, as shown in Figure C-2.

FIGURE C-1: An example of an effective web page layout

First Federal Bank website used with permission from First Federal Bank (ffbh.com)

FIGURE C-2: Accessibility attributes for inserting objects on a page

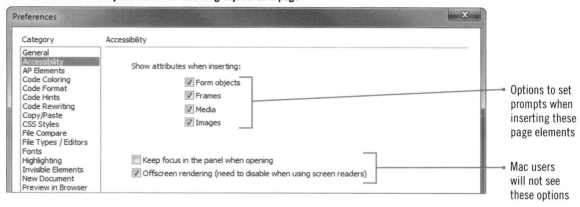

Options to set prompts when inserting these page elements

Mac users will not see these options

Design Matters

Designing for accessibility

It is extremely important to design your website so that individuals with disabilities can successfully navigate and read its web pages. In fact, government websites must be made accessible pursuant to Section 508 of the Workforce Investment Act of 1998, based on the Americans with Disabilities Act (ADA). On May 5, 1999, the first Web Content Accessibility Guidelines (WCAG) were published by the World Wide Web Consortium (W3C). The levels of accessibility are grouped into three priority level checkpoints. Although all websites should comply with the Priority 1 checkpoints, government websites *must* comply with them, such as providing a text equivalent for every non-text element. For more

information about priority level checkpoints, go to w3.org. Adobe's Accessibility Resource Center (adobe.com/accessibility); this site provides specific information about website compliance with Section 508 guidelines, such as suggestions for creating accessible websites, an explanation of Section 508, and information on how people with disabilities use assistive devices to navigate the Internet. These guidelines are based on four principles called the POUR principles: websites should be Perceivable, Operable, Understandable, and Robust. For more information about the POUR principles (Putting People at the Center of the Process) for website accessibility, go to webaim.org.

Creating the Head Content

A web page consists of two sections: the head section and the body. The **body** contains all the page content users see in their browser window, such as text, graphics, and links. The **head section** contains the **head content**, including the page title that is displayed in the browser title bar (not to be confused with the filename which is used to save the page), as well as some very important page elements that are not visible in the browser. These items are called meta tags. **Meta tags** are HTML codes that include information about the page such as keywords and descriptions. **Keywords** are words that are representative to the content of a website. Search engines find web pages by matching the title, description, and keywords in the head content of web pages with keywords users enter in search text boxes. A **description** is a short summary of website content. ▓▓▒▒▓ Before you work on page content for the home page, you modify the page title and add a description and keywords that will draw users to The Striped Umbrella website.

STEPS

TROUBLE
If you don't see the index.html file listed, click the plus sign (Win) or triangle (Mac) next to the striped_umbrella folder to expand the folder contents.

1. **Start Dreamweaver, click the** Site list arrow ▼ **(Win) or** ▼ **(Mac) on the Files panel, then click** The Striped Umbrella **if it isn't already selected**
   The Striped Umbrella website opens in the Files panel.

2. **Double-click** index.html **in the Files panel, make sure the Document window is maximized and you are in either Design view or Split view, click** View **on the Menu bar, then if necessary click** Head Content **to select it**
   The head content section appears at the top of The Striped Umbrella home page, as shown in Figure C-3. The head content section includes the Meta tag icon 🖼, the Title tag icon ⇥🔲, and the CSS icon 🔲.

QUICK TIP
You can also change the page title using either the Title text box on the Document toolbar or the Page Properties dialog box.

3. **Click the** Title icon ⇥🔲, **place the insertion point after The Striped Umbrella in the Title text box in the Property inspector, press [spacebar], type** beach resort and spa, Ft. Eugene, Florida, **then press [Enter] (Win) or [return] (Mac)**
   The new page title appears in the Title text box. See Figure C-4. The new title uses the words *beach* and *resort*, which potential guests may use as keywords when using a search engine.

4. **Expand the Insert panel if necessary, click the** Insert panel list arrow, **then click the** Common category **(if necessary), scroll down if necessary to locate the Head object, then click the** Head button list arrow, **as shown in Figure C-3**
   Some buttons on the Insert panel include a list arrow, indicating that there is a menu of choices beneath the current button. The button that was selected last appears on the Insert panel until you select another.

QUICK TIP
Multiple keywords should always be separated by commas.

5. **Click** Keywords, **type** The Striped Umbrella, beach resort, spa, Ft. Eugene, Florida, Gulf of Mexico, fishing, dolphin cruises **(including the commas) in the Keywords text box, as shown in Figure C-5, then click** OK
   The Keywords icon 🔑 appears selected in the head section, indicating that keywords have been created for the page.

6. **Click the** Head button list arrow **on the Insert panel, click** Description, **type** The Striped Umbrella is a full-service resort and spa just steps from the Gulf of Mexico in Ft. Eugene, Florida. **in the Description dialog box, as shown in Figure C-6, then click** OK
   The Description icon 🔲 appears selected in the head section, indicating that a description has been entered.

TROUBLE
You may see embedded style tags above the title, keywords, and description. Scroll down to see the rest of the head content code.

7. **Click the** Show Code view button ▭Code▭ **on the Document toolbar, click anywhere in the code, then view the head section code, as shown in Figure C-7**
   The title, keywords, and description appear in the head section of the HTML code. The title is surrounded by title tags, and the keywords and description are both surrounded by meta tags.

8. **Click the** Show Design view button ▭Design▭ **on the Document toolbar, click** View **on the Menu bar, then click** Head Content
   The Striped Umbrella home page redisplays without the head content section visible above the Document window.

FIGURE C-3: Viewing the head content section

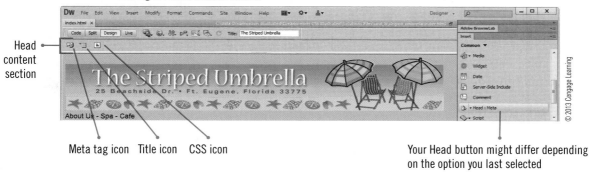

Head content section

Meta tag icon   Title icon   CSS icon

Your Head button might differ depending on the option you last selected

FIGURE C-4: Property inspector displaying new page title

New page title

FIGURE C-5: Keywords dialog box

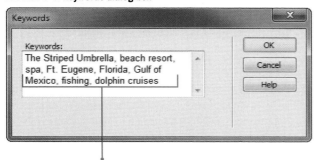

Keywords separated by commas

FIGURE C-6: Description dialog box

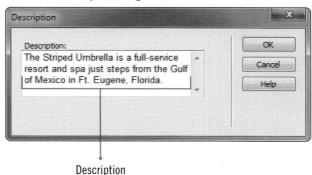

Description

FIGURE C-7: Code view displaying the code for the head content

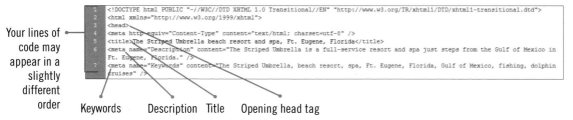

Your lines of code may appear in a slightly different order

Keywords   Description   Title   Opening head tag

Design Matters

Entering titles, keywords, and descriptions

Search engines use titles, keywords, and descriptions to find pages after the user enters search terms. It is therefore important to anticipate what your potential customers will use for search terms, and to try to include those in the keywords, description, or title. Many search engines print the page titles and descriptions when they list pages in their search results. Some search engines limit the number of keywords that they will index, so again keep your keywords and description to a minimum. It is usually sufficient to enter keywords and a description only for the home page or any other page you want users to find, rather than for every page on the website. To choose effective keywords, many designers use focus groups to learn which words potential customers or clients might use. A **focus group** is a marketing tool that asks a group of people for feedback about a product, such as the impact of a television ad or the effectiveness of a website design.

© 2013 Cengage Learning

Setting Web Page Properties

One of the first design decisions that you should make is the background color of your web page. This color should complement the colors used for text, links, and images you place on the page. A strong contrast between the text and background colors makes it easier for users to read the text. You can choose a light background color and a dark text color, or a dark background color and a light text color. A white background, though not terribly exciting, is the easiest to read for most users, and provides good contrast in combination with dark text. The next decision is to choose the default text color. The **default text color** is the color the browser uses to display text when a color is not specified. Settings such as the page background color and the default text color are specified using CSS. You want to set the background color and choose a default text color for The Striped Umbrella home page.

STEPS

1. **Click Modify on the Menu bar, then click Page Properties**

   The Page Properties dialog box opens. You use this dialog box to set page properties, such as the background color and default text color.

2. **Click the Background color box 🔲, as shown in Figure C-8**

   The color picker opens, and the pointer changes to an eyedropper 🖊. When Dreamweaver is first installed, the Background color box appears gray, which represents the default color. This does not mean that the color gray will be applied *unless* gray has previously been selected as the default color for the selected page element. Once you select a color from the color picker, the Background color box changes accordingly.

3. **Click the blue color swatch, #9CF (the fifth color in the last row), as shown in Figure C-8**

   Each color is assigned a **hexadecimal value**, a numerical value that represents the amount of red, green, and blue in the color. For example, white, which is made of equal parts of red, green, and blue, has a hexadecimal value of FFFFFF. Each pair of numbers represents the red, green, and blue values. The hexadecimal number system is based on 16, rather than 10 as in the decimal number system. Since there aren't any digits after reaching the number 9, letters of the alphabet are then used. The letter A represents the number 10, and F represents the number 15 in the hexadecimal number system. The hexadecimal values can be entered in the code using a form of shorthand that shortens the six characters to three characters. For instance: 99CCFF becomes 9CF and FFFFFF becomes FFF. The number value for a color is preceded by a pound sign (#) in HTML code.

4. **Click Apply in the Page Properties dialog box**

   The background color of the web page changes to a different shade of blue while the text color remains the default color, which is black. The Apply button allows you to see changes that you have made to the page without having to close the Page Properties dialog box. The blue background does not provide the best contrast between the page background and the text.

5. **Click 🔲 next to Background color, click the white color swatch (the rightmost color in the bottom row), then click Apply**

   The white page background provides a better contrast.

6. **Click the Text color box 🔲, shown in Figure C-9, use the eyedropper 🖊 to select a light shade of blue, then click Apply**

   The light blue text color on the home page is not quite as easy to read as the black text.

7. **Click 🔲 next to Text color, then click the Default Color icon ⊘ at the top of the color picker**

   The Page Properties dialog box shows the text color setting restored to the default color. See Figure C-9. The Default Color button restores the default color setting after either the Apply button is clicked or the dialog box is closed.

8. **Click OK**

   The Page Properties dialog box closes and The Striped Umbrella web page redisplays with the default black text color and new white background color.

FIGURE C-8: **Page Properties dialog box**

Background color box

Blue color #9CF

White color #FFF

Default Color button

Color picker

These buttons are in a different order on a Mac

FIGURE C-9: **Page Properties dialog box**

Text color restored to the default color

Background color set to white

Apply button

Design Matters

Choosing Colors to Convey Information

Prior to 1994, colors appeared differently on different types of computers. In 1994, Netscape developed the first **web-safe color palette**, a set of colors that appears consistently in all browsers and on Macintosh, Windows, and UNIX platforms. The evolution of video cards has made this less relevant today, although understanding web-safe colors may still be a factor when you are designing for some devices, such as cell phones and PDAs. The use of appropriate colors is an important factor in creating accessible pages. Be sure to only use colors that provide good contrast on your pages. Dreamweaver has two web-safe color palettes: Color Cubes and Continuous Tone. Each palette contains the 216 web-safe colors. Color Cubes is the default color palette; however, you can choose another one by clicking Modify on the Menu bar, clicking Page Properties, clicking the Appearance (CSS) or (HTML) category, clicking the color box next to the Background or Text color boxes, clicking the color palette list arrow, then clicking the desired color

palette. Figure C-10 shows the list of color palette choices. Another WCAG guideline states that color should never be the only visual means of conveying information. For instance, don't say "Refer to the brown box"; rather, say something like "Refer to the box immediately below this paragraph."

FIGURE C-10: **Color palettes**

Click list arrow to choose a color palette

Web-safe palettes

Creating and Formatting Text

Text is an important part of any web page. You can enter text directly in Dreamweaver, import it (Win only), or copy and paste text from another document. When you are entering text, each time you press [Enter] (Win) or [return] (Mac), you create a new paragraph in the HTML code. Each paragraph is surrounded by <p> tags. Once you enter or import text, you can format it in Dreamweaver by changing the font, size, and color, just as in other programs. **Headings** are six different HTML text sizes that you can apply to text: Heading 1 (the largest size) through Heading 6 (the smallest size). Using a heading format is a way of showing the importance level of selected text in relation to other text on the page. Examples of tags that show emphasis are the bold tag, <strong>, and the italic tag, <em>. While you can set some formatting characteristics with HTML tags, the preferred practice is to use CSS for most formatting. The current menu bar does not include links to all of the main pages so you decide to replace it with a link to each main page and format it using an HTML heading format, then apply the italic setting to the contact information.

STEPS

QUICK TIP
Make sure the text is selected properly—the next keystroke will replace the selected items. If you have difficulty selecting text, try [Backspace] or [Delete].

1. **Position the insertion point to the left of A in About Us, then drag to select About Us - Spa - Cafe, as shown in Figure C-11**

   The current menu bar is selected. A small icon may appear next to the selected text. If you click this icon, you will bring up the **Code Navigator**, a small window that opens with code for the selected page element. You will learn more about the Code Navigator in Unit D.

2. **Type Home - About Us - Spa - Cafe - Activities, using spaces on either side of the hyphens**

   This text becomes the page's new menu bar. A menu bar is a set of text or graphic links that is used to navigate to other pages in your website.

3. **Position the insertion point at the beginning of the first paragraph, type Welcome to our beach! then, press [Enter] (Win) or [return] (Mac)**

   Pressing [Enter] (Win) or [return] (Mac) creates a paragraph break represented by a <p> tag. Even a single character is considered a paragraph if it is preceded and followed by a paragraph break. Paragraphs can share common formatting, such as alignment settings.

QUICK TIP
Line breaks are useful when you want to apply the same formatting to text but place it on separate lines. The HTML code for a line break is <br />.

4. **Click anywhere in the "Welcome!" text you just entered, click the HTML button `<> HTML` on the Property inspector to open the HTML Property inspector if necessary, click the Format list arrow in the HTML Property inspector, then click Heading 1**

   The Heading 1 format is applied to the text "Welcome to our beach!" as shown in Figure C-12.

5. **Position the insertion point after the period following "...want to go home", as shown in Figure C-12, press [Enter] (Win) or [return] (Mac), then type The Striped Umbrella**

6. **Press and hold [Shift], press [Enter] (Win) or [return] (Mac) to create a line break**

   You can create separate lines within a paragraph by entering a line break after each line. A **line break** places text on separate lines without creating a new paragraph, which enables you to apply common formatting attributes to separate lines of text.

QUICK TIP
The Italic button is located in both the CSS and HTML Property inspectors, but each one produces different results. The HTML Italic button formats selected text and the CSS Italic button will ask you to create a new CSS rule to use to format the text.

7. **Enter the following information, repeating the instructions in Step 6 to place a line break at the end of each line: 25 Beachside Drive; Ft. Eugene, Florida 33775; (555) 594-9458**

   The semicolons indicate where the line breaks go.

8. **Position the pointer to the left of The Striped Umbrella, click and drag to select it and all of the information you entered in Step 7, click the Italic button `I` in the Property inspector, then click anywhere to deselect the text**

   The contact information appears as italicized text. See Figure C-13.

FIGURE C-11: Replacing the current menu bar

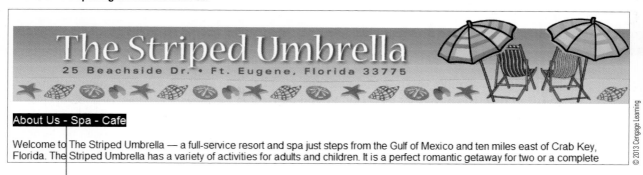

Selected text

FIGURE C-12: Formatting the new heading

New heading with Heading 1 format applied

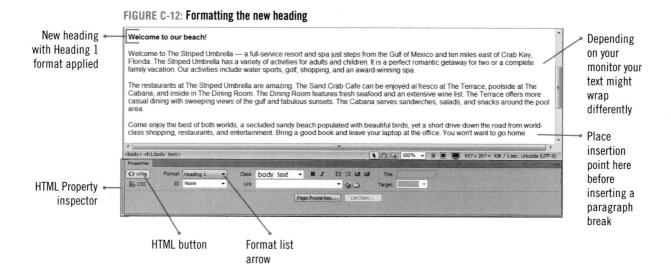

Depending on your monitor your text might wrap differently

Place insertion point here before inserting a paragraph break

HTML Property inspector

HTML button

Format list arrow

FIGURE C-13: Adding and formatting the contact information

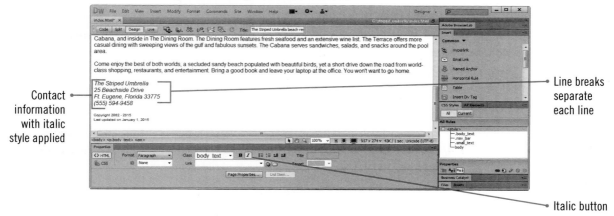

Contact information with italic style applied

Line breaks separate each line

Italic button

Developing a Web Page   **Dreamweaver 55**

Adding Links to Web Pages

Links, or hyperlinks, are specially formatted text or images that users click to navigate through and between websites. Users are more likely to return to sites that have a user-friendly navigation system and interesting links to other web pages or sites. After a link has been clicked in a browser window, it is called a **visited link**, and it changes by default to a purple color in the browser window. The default color for links that have not yet been clicked is blue. When creating web pages, it is important to avoid **broken links**, which are links that are unable to access the intended destination file. In addition to the links that you create to enable users to move from page to page, a helpful link to include is a **point of contact**, a place on a web page that gives users a means of contacting the website if they have questions or problems. A **mailto: link**, an email address for users to contact the website's headquarters, is a common point of contact. You create links for each of the menu items to their respective web pages in The Striped Umbrella website. You also create an email link to the club manager at The Striped Umbrella.

STEPS

1. **Double-click Home in the menu bar**
   You use this selected text to make a link.

2. **Click the Browse for File button ▢ next to the Link text box in the HTML Property inspector, as shown in Figure C-14, then navigate to the striped_umbrella site root folder if necessary**
   The Select File dialog box opens. The contents of the striped_umbrella site root folder are listed.

3. **Click index.html, as shown in Figure C-15, verify that Document is selected in the Relative to pop-up menu then click OK (Win) or Open (Mac)**
   The Select File dialog box closes.

4. **Click anywhere on the home page to deselect Home**
   Home is underlined and blue, the default color for links, indicating that it is a link. When users click the Home link in a browser, the index.html page opens.

5. **Repeat Steps 1–4 to create links for About Us, Spa, Cafe, and Activities, using about_us.html, spa.html, cafe.html, and activities.html as the corresponding files, then click anywhere on the page**
   All five links are now created for The Striped Umbrella home page. See Figure C-16.

6. **Position the insertion point immediately after the last digit in the telephone number, press and hold [Shift], then press [Enter] (Win) or [return] (Mac)**
   A line break is created.

7. **Click the Insert panel list arrow on the Insert panel, click Common if necessary, then click Email Link**
   The Email Link dialog box opens.

8. **Type Club Manager in the Text text box, press [Tab], type manager@thestripedumbrella.com in the Email text box, as shown in Figure C-17, then click OK**
   The email link to the Club Manager appears under the telephone number.

9. **If the email link does not appear in italics, position the pointer to the left of Club Manager, click and drag to select the text, click the Italic button _I_ in the HTML Property inspector, then click anywhere to deselect the text**
   The Club Manager link appears in italics to match the rest of the contact information.

FIGURE C-14: **Creating a link using the Property inspector**

Link text box   Browse for File button

FIGURE C-15: **Select File dialog box**

striped_umbrella
local site
root folder

index page

Relative to
drop-down
menu shows
"Document"

FIGURE C-16: **Links added to menu bar items**

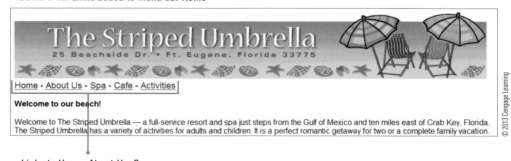

© 2013 Cengage Learning

Links to Home, About Us, Spa,
Cafe, and Activities pages

FIGURE C-17: **Email Link dialog box**

Text for email link
that will appear
on the web page

Email address

Using the History Panel

The **History panel** shows the steps that you have performed while editing and formatting a document in Dreamweaver. To **edit** a page means to insert, delete, or change content by, for example, inserting a new image, adding a link, or correcting spelling errors. Remember that formatting, in contrast, means to change just the appearance of page elements. The History panel records all of the tasks that you perform and displays them in the order in which you completed them. If you make a mistake while editing or formatting a page, you can undo your previous steps. Simply drag the slider up next to the step you want to revert to, as shown in Figure C-18. This is a more efficient way to undo steps than using the Edit, Undo command. 🔩 You want to add a horizontal rule to divide the banner and menu bar from the rest of the page as well as use the History panel to undo the changes as you experiment.

STEPS

1. **Click Window on the Menu bar, then click History**

   The History panel opens, and the steps you have already performed during this session, such as Make Hyperlink and Line Break, display in the panel window.

QUICK TIP
A horizontal rule can also be inserted by clicking Horizontal rule in the Common category on the Insert panel.

2. **Click the Panel menu ▤ on the History panel title bar, click Clear History, as shown in Figure C-18, then click Yes in the Dreamweaver warning box**

   The steps that were previously listed in the History panel are cleared and the panel is empty.

3. **Position the insertion point to the left of the words Welcome to our beach! heading, click Insert on the Menu bar, point to HTML, then click Horizontal Rule**

   A horizontal rule, or line, appears on the page above the first paragraph and remains selected.

QUICK TIP
The preferred way to format horizontal rules is with CSS. After you learn how to use CSS, you will use styles to format your horizontal rules.

4. **If "pixels" is not displayed in the width pop-up menu, click the width list arrow in the Property inspector, click pixels, type 950 in the W text box, then press [Enter] (Win) or [return] (Mac)**

   The width of the horizontal rule changes to 950 pixels wide and the step is recorded in the History panel.

5. **Click the Align list arrow in the Property inspector, then click Left**

   The horizontal rule is left-aligned on the page. Compare your Property inspector settings to Figure C-19.

6. **Select 950 in the W text box, type 80, click the Width list arrow, click %, click the Align list arrow, then click Center**

   The horizontal rule is set to 80% of the width of the window and is center-aligned. When you set the width of a horizontal rule as a percentage of the page rather than in pixels, it resizes itself proportionately when viewed on different-sized monitors and resolutions. You prefer the way the rule looked when it was wider, a set width, and left-aligned.

7. **Drag the slider on the History panel up until it is pointing to Set Alignment: left, as shown in Figure C-20, then release it**

   The bottom three steps in the History panel appear gray, indicating that these steps have been undone, and the horizontal rule returns to the left-aligned, 950-pixel width settings.

8. **Click File on the Menu bar, then click Save**

Using the History panel

Dragging the slider up and down in the History panel is a quick way to undo or redo steps. However, the History panel offers much more. It can "memorize" certain steps and consolidate them into one command. This is a useful feature for steps that you need to perform repeatedly. However, some Dreamweaver features, such as steps performed in the Files panel, cannot be recorded in the History panel. The default number of steps that the History panel will record is 50, unless you specify otherwise in the General Preferences dialog box. Setting this number higher requires additional memory, and may affect the speed at which Dreamweaver functions.

FIGURE C-18: **History panel**

FIGURE C-19: **Property inspector settings for horizontal rule**

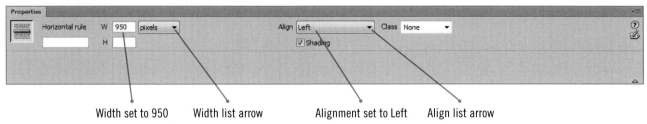

Width set to 950   Width list arrow   Alignment set to Left   Align list arrow

FIGURE C-20: **Resetting horizontal rule properties using the History panel**

Slider

Selected steps
to undo

Left alignment, 950-pixel
settings remain

Checking your screen against book figures

To show as much of the Document window as possible, most figures appear with the Standard toolbar hidden. Keep in mind that Dreamweaver will "remember" the screen arrangement from the last session when it opens each time. This may mean that you would have to open, close, collapse, or expand the various panels, toolbars, and inspectors to match your screens to the figures in the book. This is not really necessary unless you need a panel that is not open to complete a step. The rulers may also be displayed in figures in Design view. To turn this feature on or off, use the View > Rulers > Show command.

Viewing HTML Code

XHTML is the newest standard for HTML code. Although the default files created in Dreamweaver are XHTML files, the file extension is .html, and the code is referred to as "HTML." It is often helpful to view the code while editing or formatting a web page to understand how the code is working. You can use the **Reference panel** to find answers to coding questions covering topics such as HTML, JavaScript, and accessibility. The built-in electronic reference books supplied with Dreamweaver are available using the Book pop-up menu on the Reference panel. Dreamweaver also has a feature that tells you the last date that changes were made to a web page. ████ Although you are satisfied with the placement of the horizontal rule on the page, you decide to use the Reference panel to research how to change its color. You also want to add a code so that the date will automatically update each time the page is saved.

STEPS

1. **Click Window on the Menu bar, click History to close the History panel, then click the horizontal rule**

   The horizontal rule is selected.

2. **Click the Show Code view button** `Code` **on the Document toolbar**

   The highlighted HTML code represents the selected horizontal rule on the page. The Coding toolbar is docked along the left side of the Document window.

3. **If necessary, click to select the Line Numbers and Word Wrap option buttons on the Coding toolbar, as shown in Figure C-21**

   The option buttons on the Coding toolbar appear with a black border when they are selected. The Line Numbers and Word Wrap options make it easier to navigate code. **Line numbers** provide a point of reference when locating specific sections of code. **Word wrap** keeps all code within the width of the Document window so you don't have to scroll to read long lines of code. It is easier for you to read and select the lines of code as you research the <hr> tag using the Reference panel.

4. **Click Window on the Menu bar, point to Results, click Reference, if necessary click the Book list arrow in the Reference Panel to select O'REILLY HTML Reference, click the Tag list arrow to select HR if necessary, as shown in Figure C-22**

   The HR tag appears in the Tag text box in the Reference panel menu bar; HR is the HTML code for horizontal rule tag.

5. **Read the information about horizontal rules**

   The color of rules can be changed by using CSS; this will be covered in Unit D.

6. **Click the Panel menu** ▼ **on the Results panel title bar, then click Close Tab Group**

   The Results tab group closes.

7. **Scroll down if necessary in the Document window, select January 1, 2015, then press [Delete]**

   The date is deleted.

8. **Scroll down the Common category on the Insert panel until the Date object button appears, click Date to open the Insert Date dialog box, click March 7, 1974, in the Date format options list, click the Update automatically on save check box if necessary to select it, as shown in Figure C-23, then click OK**

   The Insert date dialog box closes and the JavaScript code for the date is added to the page. The current date will be placed on the page each time the page is opened and saved.

9. **Click the Show Design view button** `Design` **on the Document toolbar, then save your work**

   The index page appears in Design view in the Document window.

FIGURE C-21: **Code view options**

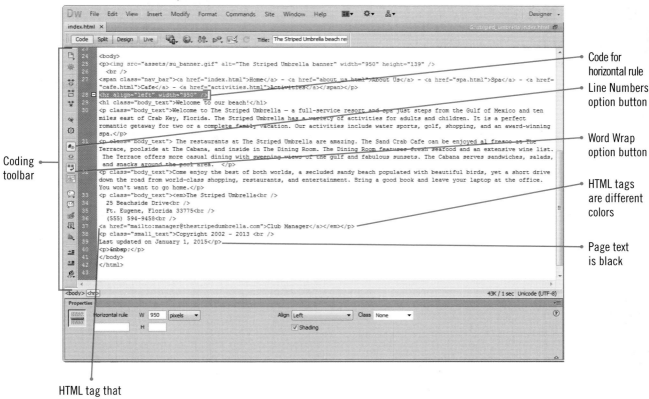

Coding toolbar

Code for horizontal rule

Line Numbers option button

Word Wrap option button

HTML tags are different colors

Page text is black

HTML tag that begins a link

FIGURE C-22: **<HR> tag information displayed in the Reference panel**

Information about the <HR> tag (Horizontal Rule)

O'REILLY HTML Reference

Book drop-down menu

HR tag in Tag drop-down menu

FIGURE C-23: **Insert Date dialog box**

Selected date format

Examples of date formats

Update automatically on save check box

Design Matters

Using Code view to edit pages

Some designers prefer to make changes to their pages by typing directly into the code, rather than working in Design view, because they feel that this gives them more precise control. Some features, such as JavaScript functions, are often added to pages by copying and pasting code into the existing page's HTML code. **JavaScript** is code that adds interaction between the user and the web page,

such as rollovers or interactive forms. **Rollovers** are screen elements that change in appearance as the pointer rests on them. You can view the HTML code in Dreamweaver by using Code view or Code and Design view. This enables you to view the HTML code and the page content in different colors, highlight HTML code that contains errors, and **debug**, or correct, HTML errors.

Testing and Modifying Web Pages

As you develop your web pages, you should test them frequently. The best way to test a web page is to preview it in a browser window to make sure it appears the way you expect it to. You should also check to see that the links work properly, that there are no typographical or grammatical errors, and that you have included all of the necessary information for the page. Dreamweaver has a preview feature that allows you to see what a page would look like if it were viewed on a mobile hand-held device, such as a phone or tablet. This is a feature called the **Multiscreen Preview**. The Multiscreen button 🔲 is located on the Document toolbar. This button allows you to see the page in three different sizes in the same window, or you can choose one size to preview in the whole Document window. You can also use the Mobile size 🔲, the Tablet size 🔲, or the Desktop size 🔲 buttons on the Status bar to simulate page size. ▰▰▰▰ You decide to view The Striped Umbrella home page in Dreamweaver to check its appearance in a simulated window size, preview it using your default browser, make adjustments to the page, then preview the changes in the browser.

1. **Click the Tablet size button 🔲 on the Status bar to see how the page would appear on a tablet using the default tablet settings, as shown in Figure C-24**

   The page is resized to simulate what it would look like in the default Tablet size, (768 × 1024). The Mobile size 🔲 and Desktop size 🔲 buttons are on either side of the Tablet size button 🔲 and are used to view a page in a simulated mobile and desktop screen.

2. **Click the Desktop size button 🔲, scroll down if necessary and highlight the period after the "...go home" text, then type !**

   An exclamation point replaces the period after "...go home".

3. **Click File on the Menu bar, click Save, click 🌐 on the Document toolbar, then click Preview in [your default browser]**

   The Striped Umbrella home page displays in your browser window. See Figure C-25. You can also press the F12 key (Win) to preview a page in the default browser.

4. **Click the About Us link on the menu bar to display one of the blank pages you created in Unit B, then click the Back button on the Address bar (Win) or the Navigation toolbar (Mac)**

   The index page reappears in the browser window.

5. **Repeat Step 4 to test the Spa, Cafe, and Activities links**

   Each link opens a corresponding blank page in the browser window since you haven't placed any text or images on them yet.

6. **Click the Club Manager link**

   The default mail program on your computer opens with a message addressed to manager@thestripedumbrella.com.

7. **Close the email message dialog box, close the browser window, close the index page, then click Exit on the File menu (Win) or Quit on the Dreamweaver menu (Mac) to close the Dreamweaver program**

FIGURE C-24: Using Tablet size to view the page

Multiscreen button

Page viewed in default tablet size

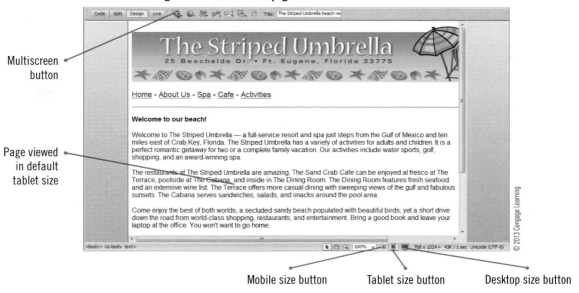

© 2013 Cengage Learning

Mobile size button   Tablet size button   Desktop size button

FIGURE C-25: The finished page

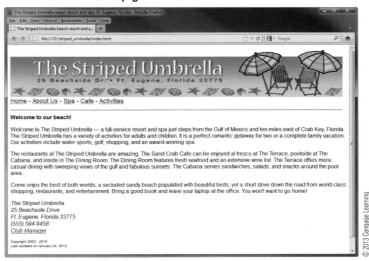

© 2013 Cengage Learning

Design Matters

Using smart design principles

As you view your pages in the browser, take a critical look at the symmetry of the page. Is it balanced? Are there too many images for the amount of text, or too few? Does everything "heavy" seem to be on the top or bottom of the page, or do the page elements seem balanced, with the weight evenly distributed between the top, bottom, and sides? Use design principles to create a site-wide consistency for your pages. **Horizontal symmetry** means that the elements are balanced across the page. **Vertical symmetry** means that they are balanced down the page. **Diagonal symmetry** balances page elements along the invisible diagonal line of the page. **Radial symmetry** runs from the center of the page outward, like the petals of a flower.

These principles all deal with balance; however, too much balance is not good, either. Sometimes it adds interest to place page elements a little off center to have an asymmetrical layout. Color, white space, text, lines, shapes, forms, textures, and images should all complement each other and provide a natural flow across and down the page. The **rule of thirds**—dividing a page into nine squares like a tic-tac-toe grid—states that interest is increased when your focus is on one of the intersections in the grid. The most important information should be at the top of the page where it is visible without scrolling— "above the fold," as they say in the newspaper business. Other design principles include the use of emphasis, movement, unity, proximity, and repetition to place elements attractively on a page.

Practice

Concepts Review

Label each element in the Dreamweaver window shown in Figure C-26.

FIGURE C-26

1. _____
2. _____
3. _____
4. _____
5. _____
6. _____
7. _____
8. _____
9. _____
10. _____

Match each of the following terms with the statement that best describes its function.

11. Style
12. Head section
13. Body section
14. Page Properties dialog box
15. Heading 1
16. Heading 6
17. Edit a page
18. Format a page

a. The part of a web page that includes text, graphics, and links

b. A named group of formatting characteristics

c. Includes the default web page settings

d. The smallest heading size

e. Make adjustments in the appearance of page elements

f. Insert, delete, or change page content

g. The largest heading size

h. The part of a web page that includes the page title and meta tags

Select the best answer from the following list of choices.

19. **The head section of a web page can include:**
    a. keywords.
    b. descriptions.
    c. Meta tags.
    d. all of the above.

20. **Links that have been previously clicked are called:**
    a. active links.
    b. links.
    c. visited links.
    d. broken links.

21. **The button that is used to display a web page in Design view in three different sizes is the _____ button.**
    a. Multiscreen
    b. Mobile display
    c. Simulated screens
    d. Media

22. **The _____ on the History panel is used to undo or redo several steps.**
    a. scroll bar
    b. pointer
    c. slider
    d. Undo/Redo tool

23. **An example of a point of contact is a:**
    a. heading.
    b. title.
    c. mailto: link.
    d. keywords.

24. **The Dreamweaver default color palette is the:**
    a. Continuous Tone.
    b. Color Cubes.
    c. Windows OS.
    d. Mac OS.

Skills Review

Important: *If you did not create the websites used in the preceding exercises in Unit B, you need to create a local site root folder for each website and define the websites using files your instructor provides. See the "Read This Before You Begin" section for more detailed instructions.*

1. **Plan the page layout.**
   a. Using a word processor or a piece of paper, list three principles of good page design that you have learned, then list them in order of most important to least important, based on your experiences.
   b. Explain why you chose these three concepts and why you selected the order you did.

2. **Create the head content.**
   a. Start Dreamweaver.
   b. Use the Files panel to open the Blooms & Bulbs website.
   c. Open the index page, then view the head content.
   d. Use the Head button list arrow to insert the following keywords: **Blooms & Bulbs, garden, plants, nursery, flowers, landscape design**, and **greenhouse**.
   e. Insert the following description: **Blooms & Bulbs is a premier supplier of garden plants and trees for both professional and home gardeners.**
   f. Switch to Code view to view the HTML code for the head section.
   g. Switch to Design view.
   h. Save your work, then hide the head content.

3. **Set web page properties.**
   a. View the page properties.
   b. Change the background color to a color of your choice, then apply it to the page, leaving the dialog box open.
   c. Change the background color to white.
   d. Save your work.

4. **Create and format text.**
   a. Replace the hyphens in the current menu bar with a split vertical bar (the top of the backslash key) to separate the items.
   b. Place the insertion point at the end of the last sentence in the second paragraph, then add a paragraph break.
   c. Type the following text, inserting a line break after each line.
   Blooms & Bulbs
   Hwy 43 South
   Alvin, Texas 77511
   555-248-0806
   d. Delete the date in the "Last updated" line, then replace it with a date that will update automatically each time the page is saved, using the March 7, 1974 format.
   e. Using the HTML Property inspector, italicize the copyright statement and last updated statement.
   f. Save your work.

5. **Add links to web pages.**
   a. Link the word *Home* on the menu bar to index.html.
   b. Link *Our Plants* to plants.html.
   c. Link *Newsletter* to newsletter.html.
   d. Link *Workshops* to workshops.html.
   e. Link *Tips* to tips.html.
   f. Using the Insert panel, create an email link under the telephone number with a line break between them; type **Customer Service** in the Text text box and **mailbox@blooms.com** in the Email text box.

Skills Review (continued)

6. **Use the History panel.**
   a. Open and clear the History panel.
   b. Using the Insert menu, insert a horizontal rule right before the first paragraph.
   c. Using the Property inspector, left-align the rule and set the width to 950 pixels.
   d. Edit the horizontal rule to center-align it with a width of 70%.
   e. Use the History panel to change the horizontal rule back to left-aligned with a width of 950 pixels.
   f. Close the History panel.
   g. Save your work.

7. **View HTML code.**
   a. Use Code view to examine the code for the horizontal rule properties, the email link, and the date in the "Last updated" statement.
   b. Return to Design view.

8. **Test and modify web pages.**
   a. Using the Preview buttons on the status bar, view the page at two different preview sizes.
   b. Preview the page in your browser.
   c. Verify that all links work correctly, then close the browser.
   d. Add the text **We are happy to deliver or ship your purchases.** to the end of the first paragraph.
   e. Save your work, preview the page in your browser, compare your screen to Figure C-27, then close your browser.
   f. Close the page, then exit Dreamweaver.

FIGURE C-27

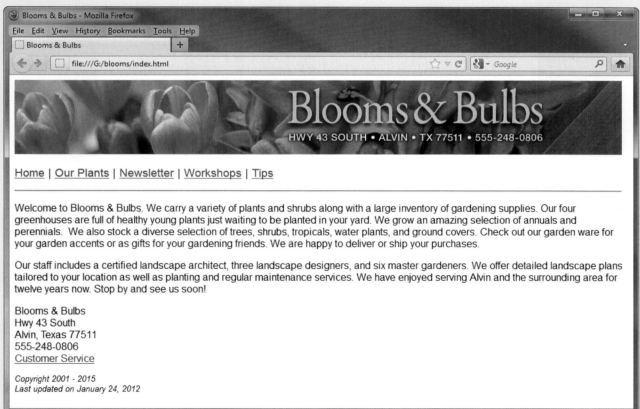

Important*: If you did not create the websites used in the exercises in Unit B, you need to create site root folders for each website and define the websites using files your instructor provides. See the "Read This Before You Begin" section for more detailed instructions.*

Independent Challenge 1

You have been hired to create a website for a river expedition company named Rapids Transit, located on the Buffalo River in Arkansas. In addition to renting canoes, kayaks, and rafts, they have several types of cabin rentals for overnight stays. River guides are available, if requested, to accompany clients on float trips. The owner's name is Mike Andrew.

a. Use the Files panel to open the Rapids Transit website.

b. Open the index page.

c. Create the following keywords: **Rapids Transit, river, rafting, Buffalo River, Arkansas, kayak, canoe,** and **float**.

d. Create the following description: **Rapids Transit is a river expedition company located on the Buffalo River in Arkansas.**

e. Change the page title to **Rapids Transit – Buffalo River Outfitters**.

f. Edit the menu bar below the Rapids Transit banner by changing **Our Guides** to **River Guides**.

g. Enter a line break under the address, then enter the telephone number **(555) 365-5228**.

h. Italicize the company copyright and last updated statements, then, after the phone number, enter a line break and create an email link, using **Mike Andrew** for the text and **mailbox@rapidstransit.com** for the email link.

i. Add links to the entries in the menu bar, using the files index.html, guides.html, rates.html, lodging.html, and before.html in the rapids site root folder. (Recall that these files don't have any content yet, but you can still link to them. You will add content to the pages as you work through the remaining units of the book.)

j. Delete the horizontal rule.

k. Delete the date in the last updated statement and change it to a date that will be automatically updated when the page is saved, using the March 7, 1974 data format. Reformat the date to match the rest of the line if necessary.

l. View the HTML code for the page, noting in particular the code for the head section.

m. View the page in Design view in two different screen sizes, save your work, then test the links in your browser, as shown in Figure C-28.

n. Close the browser, close the page, then exit Dreamweaver.

FIGURE C-28

Independent Challenge 2

Your company is designing a new website for a travel outfitter named TripSmart. TripSmart specializes in travel products and services. In addition to selling travel products such as clothing, luggage, and accessories, they promote trips and offer travel advice. Their clients range from college students to families to vacationing professionals. The owner, Thomas Howard, has requested a dynamic website that conveys the excitement of traveling. Refer to Figure C-29 as you work through the following steps.

a. Open the TripSmart website, then open its index page.

b. Create the following keywords: **TripSmart, travel, traveling, tours, trips, vacations**.

c. Create the following description: **TripSmart is a comprehensive travel store. We can help you plan trips, make the arrangements, and supply you with travel gear.**

d. Change the page title to read **TripSmart: Serving all your travel needs**.

e. Change the menu bar below the banner to read **Home - Tours - Newsletter - Services - Catalog**.

f. Add links to the menu bar entries, using the files index.html, tours.html, newsletter.html, services.html, and catalog.html. (Recall that these files don't have any content yet, but you can still link to them. You will add content to the pages as you work through the remaining units of the book.)

g. Replace the date in the "Last updated" statement with a date that will update automatically when the file is saved.

h. Add the following contact information between the last paragraph and copyright statement using line breaks after each line: **TripSmart**, **1106 Beechwood**, **Fayetteville**, **AR 72604**, **555-848–0807**.

i. Immediately beneath the telephone number, place an Email link using **Contact us** as the text and **associate@tripsmart.com** for the link.

j. Insert a horizontal rule that is 950 pixels wide and left-aligned above the contact information.

k. View the HTML code for the page, noting in particular the head section code.

l. View the page in two different screen sizes, save your work, then test the links in your browser window.

m. Close the page and exit Dreamweaver.

FIGURE C-29

Independent Challenge 3

Angela Lou is a freelance photographer. She is searching the Internet for a particular type of paper to use in printing her digital images. She knows that websites use keywords and descriptions to increase traffic from search engines such as Google and Bing. She is curious as to how keywords and descriptions work with search engines. Write your answers to these questions on paper or using your word processor.

a. Connect to the Internet, then go to snapfish.com to see the Snapfish website's home page, as shown in Figure C-30.

b. View the page source by clicking View on the menu bar, then clicking Source (Internet Explorer) or Tools > Web Developer > Page Source (Mozilla Firefox). (*Hint*: Press the Alt key if the menu is hidden.)

c. Can you locate a description and keywords?

d. How many keywords do you find?

e. How many words are in the description?

f. In your opinion, is the number of keywords and words in the description about right, too many, or not enough?

g. Use a search engine such as Google (google.com), type the words **photo quality paper** in the Search text box, then press [Enter] (Win) or [Return] (Mac).

h. Choose a link in the list of results and view the source code for that page. Do you see keywords and a description? Do any of them match the words you used in the search? (You may have to scroll down quite a bit to find the keywords. Try using the Find feature to quickly search the code.)

i. If you don't see the search words in keywords or descriptions, do you see them in the body of the pages?

j. Save your work, then exit all programs.

FIGURE C-30

Real Life Independent Challenge

This assignment will continue to build on the personal website that you created in Unit B. In this lesson, you will work with your home page.

a. Insert a brief description and a list of meaningful keywords for your home page in the appropriate locations.

b. Insert an effective title for your home page.

c. Format the home page attractively, creating a strong contrast between your page background and your page content.

d. Add links from the home page to your other pages.

e. Insert an email link.

f. Insert a "Last updated" statement that includes a date that updates automatically when you save the file.

g. Preview the home page in your browser, verifying that each link works correctly.

h. Check the page for errors in content or format and edit as necessary.

i. Save your work, close the page, and exit the program.

Visual Workshop

Your company has been selected to design a website for a catering business named Carolyne's Creations. You are now ready to add content to the home page and apply formatting options to improve the page appearance, using Figure C-31 as a guide. Open your Carolyne's Creations website and modify the index page to duplicate Figure C-31. You can use **carolyne@carolynescreations.com** as the email link. (*Hint*: Remember to add an appropriate description and keywords, and revise the last updated statement so it will automatically update when the page is saved.)

FIGURE C-31

Working with Text and Cascading Style Sheets

Files You Will Need:

To view a list of files needed for this unit, see the Data Files Grid in the back of the book.

The content of most web pages is text-based. Because text on a computer screen can be more tiring to read than text on a printed page, you should strive to make your web page text attractive and easy to read. Dreamweaver has many options for enhancing text, including HTML properties for paragraphs and lists, as well as Cascading Style Sheets (CSS). CSS are used to assign sets of common formatting characteristics to page elements, such as paragraph text, lists, and table data. You decide to group content on the spa page for The Striped Umbrella website using lists to make the page more readable. Using lists to format text is also considered to be more accessible for users using screen readers. You want to use CSS to make these types of formatting changes consistent throughout the website.

OBJECTIVES

Create a new page

Import text

Set text properties

Create an unordered list

Understand Cascading Style Sheets

Create a rule in a new Cascading Style Sheet

Apply and edit a rule

Add rules to a Cascading Style Sheet

Attach a Cascading Style Sheet to a page

Check for spelling errors

Creating a New Page

You use the New Document dialog box to create a new page in Dreamweaver. You can create a blank page, a blank template, a fluid grid template, a page from a template, or a page from a sample layout. You have the option of several page types you can create, for example, HTML, CSS, XML, and ASP. Each page type has layout option choices. The HTML page type layouts include one column, two columns, and three columns. The new HTML5 layouts include two or three column layouts. You are ready to create a new page that will replace the placeholder spa page. You decide to use the HTML page type with no preset layout. After you create the page you insert the banner and the spa logo.

STEPS

1. **Start Dreamweaver, click the Site list arrow (Win) ▼ or ▼ (Mac) on the Files panel, then click The Striped Umbrella, if it isn't already selected**
   The Striped Umbrella website opens in the Files panel.

2. **Click File on the Menu bar, click New, click Blank Page (if necessary), click HTML in the Page Type column, click <none> in the Layout column, click the DocType list box, click HTML 5, as shown in Figure D-1, click Create, then click the Show Design view button** Design **if necessary**
   A new blank page opens in the Document window.

3. **Click File, click Save As, navigate to your Striped Umbrella local site root folder, then save the file as spa.html, overwriting the existing (blank) spa.html file**

4. **Click the Insert bar menu, click Common, click the Images list arrow, then click Image**
   The Select Image Source dialog box opens, as shown in Figure D-2.

5. **Browse to and open the website assets folder, double-click su_banner.gif, type The Striped Umbrella banner in the Alternate text box in the Image Tag Accessibility Attributes dialog box, then click OK**
   The banner appears at the top of the new page. You will learn more about the Image Tag Accessibility Attributes dialog box in Unit E.

6. **Click to the right of the banner to deselect it, press [Enter] (Win) or [Return] (Mac), repeat Step 4 to open the Select Image Source dialog box, then navigate to the assets folder in your unit_d Data Files folder**

7. **Double-click sea_spa_logo.png, type The Sea Spa logo in the Alternate text box in the Image Tag Accessibility Attributes dialog box, then click OK**

8. **Click to the right of the logo to place the insertion point on the spa.html page**
   The Sea Spa logo appears under the banner, as shown in Figure D-3.

FIGURE D-1: **Creating a new HTML document with the New Document dialog box**

HTML Page Type

Blank Page

<none>Layout

DocType list arrow

Create button

FIGURE D-2: **Selecting the source for the banner**

Double-click the filename to select the file and close the dialog box

Path for image

FIGURE D-3: **Image file added to the Striped Umbrella assets folder**

Images placed on page

Images listed in assets folder

© 2013 Cengage Learning

Working with Text and Cascading Style Sheets

Importing Text

Entering text in Dreamweaver is as easy as entering text in a word processing program. The Dreamweaver text editing features, listed in Table D-1, are similar to those in word processing programs. If you have existing text to place on a page, you can either copy and paste it, or import it from the source program, such as Microsoft Word or Excel. To ensure that text is readable, you can use CSS to set alignment, indentation, headings, and lists to organize the content on the page. Your manager has given you a list of services to include on The Striped Umbrella spa page. The document, which contains a list of spa services and descriptions, was created in Microsoft Word, then saved as a Word document. You open the spa page, import the text, and use the Clean Up Word HTML command to remove any unnecessary tags.

STEPS

1. **Click File on the Menu bar, point to Import, click Word Document, browse to the folder where you store your Unit D Data Files, then double-click spa.doc (Win); or using Finder, navigate to spa.doc stored in your unit_d data files folder, open spa.doc, select all, copy, close spa.doc, then paste the copied text on the spa page in Dreamweaver (Mac)**

   Mac users cannot use the Import > Word command. The text from the Word file is placed beside and wraps under the logo, as shown in Figure D-4. Although you may not see evidence of unnecessary code on the page, it is always a good idea to remove any unnecessary tags that are added by Microsoft Word.

QUICK TIP

If a dialog box opens stating that Dreamweaver was unable to determine the version of Word used to generate this document, click OK, click the Clean up HTML from list arrow, then select Word 2000 and newer, if necessary.

2. **Click Commands on the Menu bar, then click Clean Up Word HTML**

   The Clean Up Word HTML dialog box opens, as shown in Figure D-5.

3. **Click to select each check box in the Clean Up Word HTML dialog box if necessary, click OK, then click OK again**

   The Clean Up Word HTML dialog box closes.

Importing and linking Microsoft Office documents

Adobe makes it easy to transfer data between Microsoft Office documents and Dreamweaver web pages. To import a Word or Excel document with a PC, click File on the Menu bar, point to Import, then click either Word Document or Excel Document. Select the file you want to import, then click the Formatting list arrow to choose among importing Text only; Text with structure (paragraphs, lists, and tables); Text, structure, basic formatting (bold, italic); or Text, structure, full formatting (bold, italic, styles) before you click Open. The option you choose depends on the importance of the original structure and formatting. Always use the Clean Up Word HTML command after importing a Word file.

On a Mac, open the file you want to import, copy the text, then paste it to an open page in Dreamweaver in Design view.

You can also create a link to a Word or Excel document on your web page. Simply drag the Word or Excel document from its current location to the place on the page you want the link to appear; if the document is located outside the site, you can browse for it using the Site list arrow on the Files panel, Explorer (Win), or Finder (Mac). Next, select the Create a link option button in the Insert Document dialog box, then save the file in your local site root folder so it will be uploaded when you publish your site. If it is not uploaded, the link will be broken.

FIGURE D-4: Spa page with text imported

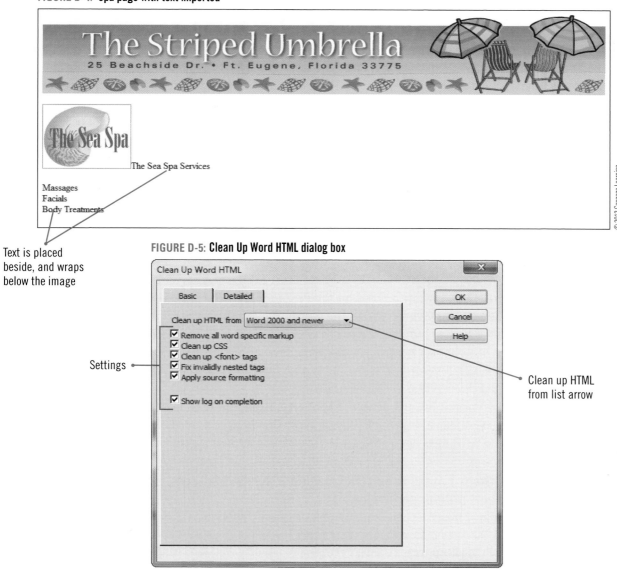

© 2013 Cengage Learning

Text is placed beside, and wraps below the image

FIGURE D-5: Clean Up Word HTML dialog box

Settings

Clean up HTML from list arrow

TABLE D-1: Dreamweaver text editing features

feature	menu	function	feature	menu	function
Find and Replace	Edit	Finds and replaces text on the current web page, the entire website, or in selected files	**Font families**	Modify	Selects font combinations for a browser or allows you to create custom font combinations
Indent and Outdent	Format	Indents selected text to the right or left	**Style**	Format	Sets various styles, such as bold and italic
Paragraph Format	Format	Sets paragraph, H1 through H6, and preformatted text	**CSS Styles**	Format	Provides options for applying a rule, creating a new CSS rule, attaching a style sheet, converting or moving rules, and applying Design-Time Style Sheets
Align	Format	Aligns text with the left or right margin, justifies it, or centers it on the page	**Color**	Format	Sets text color
List	Format	Creates unordered, ordered, or definition lists	**Check Spelling**	Commands	Runs a spell check on the page

Setting Text Properties

After you place text on a page, you format it to enhance its appearance. Text formatting attributes such as paragraph formatting, heading styles, fonts, size, color, alignment, indents, and CSS styles are easy to define by using the CSS Styles panel, the HTML Property inspector, or the CSS Property inspector. Some formatting options are available with both the HTML and CSS Property inspectors, while some are specific to each. Using standard fonts is wise because those set outside the default range may not be available on all computers. Global formatting applied with styles is much preferred over formatting applied directly to text. Styles applied across a website promote a clean and consistent look. As you format your pages, it is important to read the code for each element to see how it is written. The more fluent you are with code, the easier it will be when you have to debug the site (correct coding errors). HTML code is built from a series of **tags** surrounded by < and > symbols. Tags instruct the browser how to display each page element. **You want to format the new text on the spa page to improve its appearance. You also want to examine the code for the formatting commands to understand the HTML tags that are generated.**

STEPS

1. **Click the HTML button** `<> HTML` **on the Property inspector if necessary, scroll up if necessary, then click anywhere within the words** *The Sea Spa Services*

   The words *The Sea Spa Services* are classified as a paragraph; even a single word is considered a paragraph if there is a hard return or paragraph break after it. Paragraph commands are applied by clicking the insertion point within the paragraph text. The Property inspector shows the settings for the paragraph with the insertion point placed inside of it; Paragraph appears in the Format text box.

2. **Click the Format list arrow on the Property inspector, then click Heading 1**

   The Heading 1 format is applied to the Sea Spa Services paragraph. The HTML code for a Heading 1 tag is <h1>. The tag is then closed with </h1>. The level of the heading tag follows the h, so the code for a Heading 2 tag is <h2>.

3. **Repeat Steps 1 and 2 to add the Heading 2 style to Massages, Facials, and Body Treatments right under the logo**

   The Heading 2 format is applied, as shown in Figure D-6. The H1 and H2 tags make the text a little large for the page, but is more in keeping with semantic markup to begin with level 1 headings and work down. **Semantic markup** means coding to emphasize meaning. You can change the size of the text for each heading using style sheets.

4. **Click after the word "Treatments", insert a line break, click the Show Code and Design views button** `Split` **on the Document toolbar**

   The HTML code for the headings displays in the left window, as shown in Figure D-7. The first tag in each pair begins the code and the last tag ends the code.

5. **Click the Show Design view button** `Design` **on the Document toolbar, then save your work**

   The spa page redisplays in Design view with its changes saved.

FIGURE D-6: **Applying paragraph formats**

Text with the Heading 1 format applied

Text with the Heading 2 format applied

Format list arrow

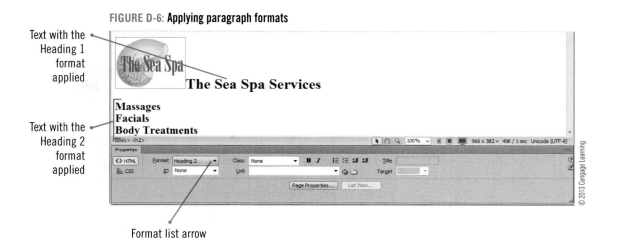

FIGURE D-7: **Show Code and Design views**

Show Code and Design views button

The code that is displayed in Code view reflects the position of the insertion point on the page

h2 tags   h1 tags

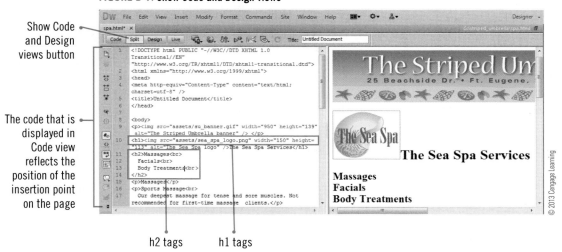

Design Matters

Choosing fonts

There are two classifications of fonts: sans-serif and serif. **Sans-serif** fonts, such as the font you are reading now, are made up of plain characters without any strokes at the top and bottom of letters. They are used frequently for headings and subheadings in printed text. Examples of sans-serif fonts are Arial, Verdana, and Helvetica. **Serif** fonts are more ornate, with small extra strokes at the top and bottom of the characters. They are generally easier to read in printed material because the

extra strokes lead your eye from one character to the next. Examples of serif fonts are Times New Roman, Garamond, and Georgia. Many designers feel that sans-serif fonts are preferable for files read electronically, while serif fonts are preferable for printed materials. When choosing fonts, limit each website to three font variations or less. Avoid using a tiny font size that users will have to enlarge or font colors that are difficult to see against the page background.

Creating an Unordered List

You can break up the monotony of large blocks of text by dividing them into smaller paragraphs or by organizing them as lists. Dreamweaver utilizes three types of lists: unordered lists, ordered lists, and definition lists. **Unordered lists**, also called bulleted lists, are lists of items that do not need to be placed in a specific order. Each item is usually preceded by a small filled circle (known as a **bullet**) or a similar icon. Numbered lists, or **ordered lists,** are lists of items that must be placed in a specific order, and each item is preceded by a number or a letter. **Definition lists** are similar to unordered lists, but do not use numbers or bullets. They are displayed with a hanging indent and are often used with terms and definitions, such as in a dictionary or glossary. You decide to organize the types of services into logical groups to make them easier to read. You want to create an unordered list for each of the spa service items.

STEPS

1. **Select the three spa service items and their descriptions under the Massages heading**
   Sports Massage, Swedish Massage, and Hot Stone Massage and their descriptions are selected.

2. **Click the Unordered List button** ▤ **on the HTML Property inspector, then deselect the text**
   The spa service items redisplay as an unordered list, as shown in Figure D-8.

3. **Repeat Steps 1 and 2 to create unordered lists of the spa service items under the Facials and Body Treatments headings**
   Each group of services redisplays as an unordered list.

4. **Click to place the insertion point before the first item in the first unordered list, then click the Show Code view button** `Code` **on the Document toolbar**
   The page displays in Code view. The HTML tags surrounding the unordered list are <ul> and </ul>. Each of the list items is surrounded by <li> and </li> tags, as shown in Figure D-9.

5. **Click the Show Design view button** `Design` **on the Document toolbar to return to Design view, then save your work**

FIGURE D-8: Creating an unordered list

Massages

- Sports Massage
  Our deepest massage for tense and sore muscles. Not recommended for first-time massage clients.
- Swedish Massage
  A gentle, relaxing massage. Promotes balance and wellness. Warms muscle tissue and increases circulation.
- Hot Stone Massage
  Uses polished local river rocks to distribute gentle heat. Good for tight, sore muscles. Balances and invigorates the body muscles. Advance notice required.

Facials

Revitalizing Facial

Unordered list items

FIGURE D-9: Viewing an unordered list in Code view

```
16  <ul>
17    <li>Sports Massage<br>
18      Our deepest massage for tense and sore muscles. Not recommended for first-time massage  clients.</li>
19    <li>Swedish Massage<br>
20      A gentle, relaxing massage. Promotes balance and wellness. Warms muscle tissue  and increases circulation.</li>
21    <li>Hot Stone Massage<br>
22      Uses polished local river rocks to distribute gentle heat. Good  for tight, sore muscles. Balances and invigorates the body muscles. Advance  notice required. format,</li>
23  </ul>
24  <p>Facials</p>
25  <ul>
```

Beginning unordered list tag

Closing unordered list tag

Beginning list item tag

Closing list item tag

Design Matters

Coding for the semantic web

You read several pages back about semantic markup and have previously heard the term *semantic* web. The word *semantics* refers to the study of word or sentence meanings. So the term **semantic web** refers to the way page content, such as paragraph, text, or list items, can be coded to emphasize their meaning to users. HTML tags such as the <p> tag, used for marking paragraphs, and the <ul> tag, used for marking unordered lists, provide a clear meaning of the function and significance of the paragraphs or lists. **Semantic markup**, or coding to emphasize meaning, is a way to incorporate good accessibility practice. CSS styles affect the appearance of web page content while semantic markup enhances the meaning of the content. Both techniques work together to provide well-designed web pages that are attractive and easy to understand.

Using ordered lists

Ordered lists contain numbered or lettered items that need to appear in a particular order, such as listing the steps to accomplish a task. For example, if you followed directions to drive from point A to point B, each step would have to be executed in order or you would not successfully reach your destination.

For this type of sequential information, ordered lists can add more emphasis than bulleted ones. Dreamweaver uses several options for number styles, including Roman and Arabic. The HTML tags that surround ordered lists are <ol> and </ol>.

Understanding Cascading Style Sheets

Cascading Style Sheets (CSS) consist of sets of formatting rules that create styles. You create CSS when you want to apply the same formatting attributes to web page elements, such as text, images, and tables. A style sheet can contain many different rules, such as heading or body text, saved within a descriptive name. You can apply rules to any element in a document or, if you choose, to all of the documents in a website. If you edit an existing rule, all the page elements you have formatted with that rule will automatically update. 🖱️ You decide to research the ways CSS can save you time and provide your site with a more consistent look.

As you plan to use CSS in a website, keep in mind the following:

QUICK TIP
Pages formatted with CSS comply with current accessibility standards better than pages that have not used CSS.

- **Advantages of using CSS**

  CSS are made up of individual **rules**, or sets of formatting attributes, such as font-family and font-size. These rules create styles that are applied to individual page elements including text, headings, images, and horizontal rules. CSS are great time-savers and provide continuity across a website by applying the same style to all elements of a given type. After you apply rules, you can edit the rules definition. Once you complete the definition, every item to which you've applied that rule will then be automatically updated to reflect the changes. CSS separate content from layout, which means that you can make editing changes without affecting formatting and vice versa.

QUICK TIP
While internal styles are useful for creating a quick style that you do not expect to use on other pages, external styles are still preferred because they can be attached to other pages.

- **CSS classified by location**

  One way to categorize styles is by the location where they are stored. An **external style sheet** is a single, separate file with a .css file extension that can be attached to one or all pages in a website. This type of style sheet determines the formatting for various page elements and can contain many individual styles. If you have an external style sheet with 10 styles, you would only need to create one file with 10 styles defined within it, rather than 10 separate style sheet files. You can then attach this style sheet file to all of the pages in the same website (or to pages in other websites) to apply all of the specific styles. **Internal style sheets** are in the code for an individual web page and can either be embedded or inline styles. An **embedded style** consists of code that is stored in a page's head content while an **inline style** is stored in a page's body content. While you are learning, you will create styles of each type. In a work environment, however, you will probably use external styles.

- **CSS classified by function**

  Another way to classify CSS is by their function. A **Class style** can be used to format any page element, such as a paragraph of text or an image. An **HTML style** is used to redefine an HTML tag, such as changing the color of a horizontal rule or the font size for a heading tag. An **Advanced** or **Compound style** is used to format combinations of page elements. For example, you could define an Advanced style that determines how all images are displayed inside a div tag.

- **The CSS Styles panel**

  You use the CSS Styles panel to create, edit, and apply rules. The panel has two views: All (Document) Mode and Current Selection Mode. Figure D-10 shows the CSS Styles panel in All (Document) Mode, which lists all attached and embedded styles. When you select a rule in the All Rules pane, that rule's properties appear in the Properties pane at the bottom of the panel. Figure D-11 shows the CSS Styles panel in Current Selection mode, which shows the properties for the page element at the current position of the insertion point. You can edit the properties for the rule in the Properties pane. The small pane between the Summary for Selection pane and the Properties pane in Current mode is called the Rules pane, which shows the location of the current selected rule in the open document.

FIGURE D-10: **CSS Styles panel in All (Document) Mode**

Switch to All (Document) Mode button

External CSS styles

All Rules pane

Properties for selected style are displayed in Properties pane

FIGURE D-11: **CSS Styles panel in Current Selection Mode**

Switch to Current Selection Mode button

The insertion point on the page is in a paragraph with the body_text rule applied

Summary for Selection pane

Rules pane

Properties for selected rule are displayed in Properties pane

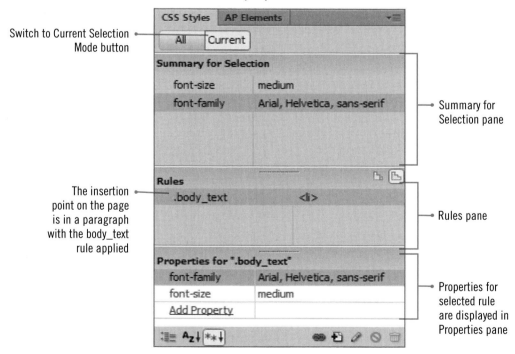

Using the CSS and HTML Property inspector

You apply CSS rules using either the CSS or HTML Property inspectors. You first select the element on the page, then apply a rule from the Property inspector. In the HTML Property inspector, you select a rule from the Class list box. In the CSS Property inspector, you select a rule from the Targeted Rule list box. You change back and forth between the two Property inspectors by clicking the HTML button <> HTML or CSS button ᗷ CSS.

Creating a Rule in a New Cascading Style Sheet

The steps for creating the first rule in a new style sheet are different from the steps for creating additional rules in an existing style sheet. Creating the first rule in a new style sheet is a two-step process. When you create the first rule, you have not yet created the style sheet, so you must first name the style sheet file in which you want to save the first rule. Once you have named and saved the style sheet file, you can then add new rules to it. If you decide to change a rule later, you only have to change the CSS rule and all the items will be updated automatically. ▉▉▞▞▞ You decide that the same formatting style should be applied to each of the spa service headings. You want to use CSS to apply the same rule to each item.

STEPS

1. **Click** Window **on the Menu bar, click** CSS Styles **if necessary, then click the** Switch to All (Document) Mode **button** [All] **under the CSS Styles panel tab**

   The CSS Styles panel opens in the CSS Styles tab group. This panel is where you can add, delete, edit, and apply styles. All (Document) Mode displays all styles in the open document.

   QUICK TIP

   If you do not create a style before you begin formatting page elements, Dreamweaver will prompt you to create a new rule after you make your first formatting choice.

2. **Click the** New CSS Rule **button** ⊞ **in the Properties pane on the CSS Styles panel, click the** Selector Type list arrow **in the New CSS Rule dialog box, if necessary, to select** Class (can apply to any HTML element), **then type** bold_blue **in the Selector Name text box**

   The Class option creates a new custom rule that can apply to any HTML tag.

3. **Click the** Rule Definition list arrow, **click** (New Style Sheet File), **compare your screen to Figure D-12, then click** OK

   The Save Style Sheet File As dialog box opens, prompting you to name the Cascading Style Sheet file and store it in the website's root folder. The name of the new rule is bold_blue. The New Style Sheet File option makes the CSS style available for use in the entire website, not just the current document.

   QUICK TIP

   You can also create a new rule using the New CSS Rule command in the CSS Property inspector.

4. **Type** su_styles **in the File name text box (Win) or the Save As text box (Mac), then click** Save

   The CSS Rule Definition for bold_blue in su_styles.css dialog box opens. This dialog box allows you to choose attributes, such as font color and font size, for the CSS rule.

5. **Click the** Font-family list arrow, **click** Arial, Helvetica, sans-serif; **click the** Font-size list arrow, **click** 14, **leave the size measurement unit as px, click the** Font-style list arrow, **click** normal; **click the** Font-weight list arrow, **then click** bold

   The font-family, size, style, and weight settings are updated. Keeping the measurement at pixels (px) in the size measurement drop-down menu ensures that the text will be an absolute size when viewed in the browser.

   TROUBLE

   If the CSS rule does not appear, click the plus sign (Win) right-pointing triangle (Mac) next to the CSS file in the CSS Styles panel to expand it and see the styles listed in the file. If the styles do not appear, click [All].

6. **Click the** Color box ▦ **to open the color picker, type** #006, **as shown in Figure D-13, click** OK, **then click the** Refresh button ⟳ **on the Files panel**

   The CSS rule named bold_blue appears in the CSS Styles panel, preceded by a period in the name. The Related Files toolbar displays under the file tab (Win) or file title bar (Mac) listing the style sheet filename su_styles.css. The Related Files toolbar, which displays the names of files related to the open document file, is used to quickly access files that are linked to the open document. The su_styles.css file appears in the file listing for the website, as shown in Figure D-14, with a different file extension from the HTML files. You may have to scroll down to see the su_styles.css file listed.

7. **Click the** Show Code view button [Code] **on the Document toolbar**

   The HTML code linking to the su_styles.css file appears in the Head section, as shown in Figure D-15. The bold_blue rule appears indented under the file su_styles.css in the CSS Styles panel.

8. **Click** File **on the Menu bar, then click** Save All

FIGURE D-12: Adding a new CSS Rule in the New CSS Rule dialog box

Selector
list arrow

Selector
Name
text box

Rule
Definition
list arrow

FIGURE D-13: CSS Rule Definition for .bold_blue in su_styles.css dialog box

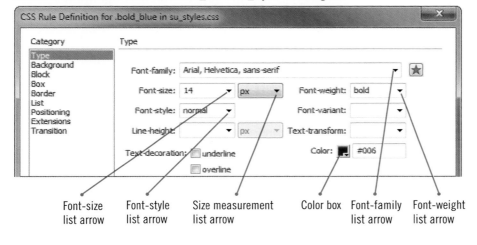

Font-size
list arrow

Font-style
list arrow

Size measurement
list arrow

Color box

Font-family
list arrow

Font-weight
list arrow

FIGURE D-14: The Striped Umbrella site
with the su_styles.css file listed

su_styles.css
style sheet file

FIGURE D-15: Code view showing link to style sheet file

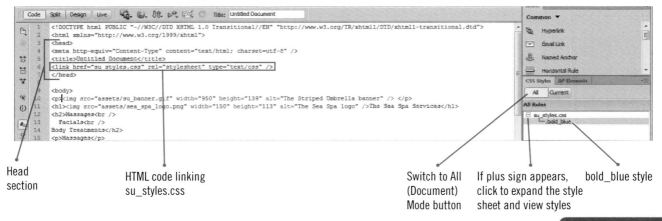

Head
section

HTML code linking
su_styles.css

Switch to All
(Document)
Mode button

If plus sign appears,
click to expand the style
sheet and view styles

bold_blue style

Working with Text and Cascading Style Sheets

Applying and Editing a Rule

After creating a style sheet, it is easy to apply its rules to page elements. If you are not satisfied with the results after applying a rule, you can edit the rule to change the formatting of all elements to which that rule applies. To apply a rule, you select the text or page element to which you want to apply the rule, remove any manual formatting, and then select the rule from the Property inspector. ⬛⬛⬛⬛⬛ You want to apply a color style to each unordered list heading as well as increase their size to make them stand out.

STEPS

QUICK TIP
You can also click the Class list arrow in the HTML Property inspector to apply the bold_blue rule.

QUICK TIP
You can press [Ctrl][Y] (Win) or [command] [Y] (Mac) to redo (repeat) an action.

QUICK TIP
If a rule is not selected, the Edit Rule button becomes the Edit Style Sheet button and opens the css file for editing.

1. **Click the Show Design view button** `Design` **on the Document toolbar, then click the CSS button** `⯗ CSS` **to switch to the CSS Property inspector**
   The spa page redisplays in Design view.

2. **Select the unordered list heading Massages, click the Targeted Rule list arrow on the CSS Property inspector, then click bold_blue, as shown in Figure D-17**
   The bold_blue style is applied to the Massages heading. The Font-family, Font-size, Font-weight, Color, and Font-style text boxes on the Property inspector all reflect the bold_blue settings.

3. **Repeat Step 2 to apply the bold_blue style to the Facials and Body Treatment unordered list headings**
   The bold_blue style is applied to each unordered list heading.

4. **Click the bold_blue rule in the CSS Styles panel, then click the Edit Rule button** ✎ **on the CSS Styles panel**
   The CSS Rule Definition for bold_blue in su_styles.css dialog box opens. This same dialog box that you used to create the original rule is used to edit a .css file.

5. **Click the Font-size list arrow, click 16, as shown in Figure D-18, click OK, then deselect the text**
   The unordered list headings appear on the page with a larger text size applied, as shown in Figure D-19.

6. **Click File on the Menu bar, then click Save All**
   The changes to both the spa document file and the style sheet file are saved.

Understanding CSS code

You can also use CSS rules to format page content other than text. For example, you can use CSS to format backgrounds, borders, lists, and images. A CSS rule consists of two parts: the selector and the declaration. The **selector** is the name or the tag to which the style declarations have been assigned. The **declaration** consists of the property and the value. An example of a property would be font-family. An example of a value would be Arial. Figure D-16 shows the coding for three CSS rules in a style sheet.

FIGURE D-16: Code for three rules in the su_styles.css file

Code for heading rules

Code for .body_text rule

```
9  h1 {
10     font-family: Arial, Helvetica, sans-serif;
11     font-size: 24px;
12     font-weight: bold;
13  }
14  h2 {
15     font-family: Arial, Helvetica, sans-serif;
16     font-size: 18px;
17     font-weight: normal;
18  }
19
20  .body_text {    font-size: medium;
21     font-family: Arial, Helvetica, sans-serif;
22  }
```

FIGURE D-17: Applying a rule to text

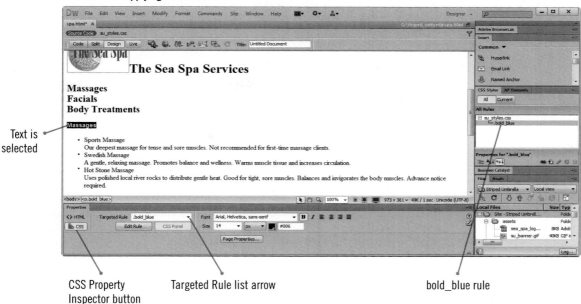

Text is selected

CSS Property Inspector button

Targeted Rule list arrow

bold_blue rule

FIGURE D-18: Editing the bold_blue rule

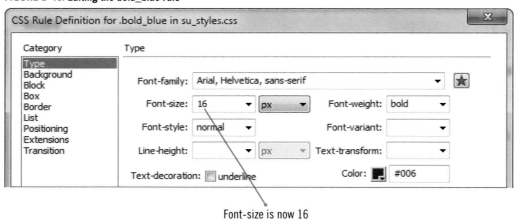

Font-size is now 16

FIGURE D-19: Viewing text after editing the Font-size property

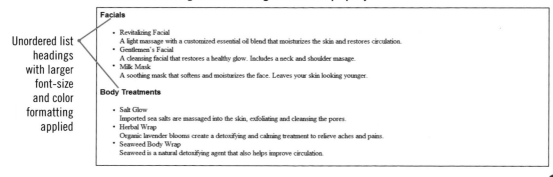

Unordered list headings with larger font-size and color formatting applied

Adding Rules to a Cascading Style Sheet

Once you have created a style sheet, it is easy to add additional rules to it. Generally, the more rules you have defined in a Style Sheet, the more time you can save. Ideally, you should create rules for all page elements. You add rules by using the New CSS Rule button in the CSS Styles panel. You should use the same style sheet for each page to ensure that all your elements have a consistent appearance. You decide to add two new rules in the su_styles.css file, one to modify the <h1> tag and one to modify the <h2> tag. These rules will be Tag selector types, rather than class selector types.

STEPS

1. **Click the New CSS Rule button 🗗 on the CSS Styles Panel**
   The New CSS Rule dialog box opens.

2. **Click the Selector Type list arrow, click Tag (redefines an HTML element), type h1 in the Selector Name text box, click the Rule Definition list arrow, click su_styles.css, as shown in Figure D-20, then click OK**
   The CSS Rule Definition for h1 in su_styles.css dialog box opens.

3. **Click the Font-family list arrow, click Arial, Helvetica, sans-serif, click the Font-size list arrow, click 24, click the Font-weight list arrow, then click bold, as shown in Figure D-21, then click OK**
   The font is set to a 24px, bold, Arial, Helvetica, sans-serif font-family. Notice that the heading "The Sea Spa Services" has changed appearance. Since it was originally formatted with the Heading 1 paragraph format, the new <h1> rule properties have been automatically applied to this heading.

> **QUICK TIP**
> If you click the insertion point within text or select text that has an applied rule, that rule appears in the Class list box in the HTML Property inspector, or the Targeted Rule list box in the CSS Property inspector.

4. **Repeat Steps 1 through 3 to create a rule to modify the <h2> tag using the following settings: Font-family: Arial, Helvetica, sans-serif; Font-size: 18; Font-weight: normal**
   The headings "Massages", "Facials", and "Body Treatments" have changed appearance. Since they were formatted with a Heading 2 paragraph format, the new <h2> rule properties have been automatically applied, as shown in Figure D-22.

5. **Click File on the Menu bar, then click Save All**
   The changes are saved to both the spa document file and the style sheet file.

Using font combinations in styles

When you are setting rule properties for text, it is wise to apply font combinations. That way, if one font is not available, the browser will apply a similar one. For instance, with the font family "Arial, Helvetica, sans-serif," the browser will first check the user's system for the Arial font, then, if it can't find the Arial font, it will look for the Helvetica font, and so on. If you prefer to use a different set of fonts than the ones Dreamweaver provides, click the Font list arrow on the CSS Property inspector, click Edit Font list, then choose from the available fonts listed. This is also known as a custom font stack. You can also select font combinations in any dialog box with a Font-family option.

Another option for specifying fonts is to use external font libraries. Font libraries are fonts that are downloaded with your page content when viewed in a browser so you are assured that your users will have the correct font applied. Use the @font-face CSS rule to specify fonts from a font library. Go to typekit.com and google.com/webfonts#HomePlace:home for examples of font libraries.

FIGURE D-20: Creating a new CSS rule to define the <h1> rule

Selector Type list arrow

Selector Name text box

Rule Definition list arrow

FIGURE D-21: Setting the properties for the <h1> rule

Font-family = Arial, Helvetica, sans-serif

Font-weight = bold

Font-size = 24px

FIGURE D-22: New <h1> and <h2> properties applied to headings

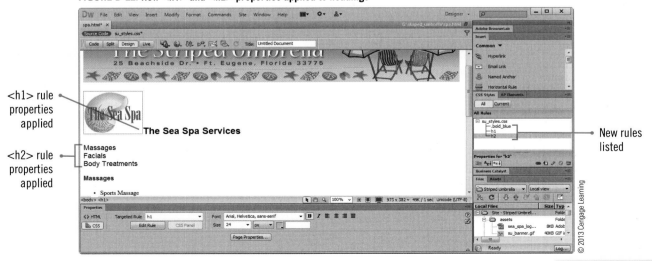

<h1> rule properties applied

<h2> rule properties applied

New rules listed

Working with Text and Cascading Style Sheets

© 2013 Cengage Learning

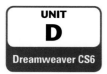
Attaching a Cascading Style Sheet to a Page

After creating an external style sheet, you should attach it to the rest of the pages in your website to utilize the full benefit. Being able to define a rule and apply it to page elements across all the pages of your site means that you can make hundreds of formatting changes in a few minutes. Style sheets create a more uniform look from page to page and lead to cleaner code. ▨▨▨ You decide to attach the su_styles.css file to the home page and use it to format the paragraph text. Since you already have an internal style on the index page, you want to delete it so the external style will be used to format the paragraph text instead.

STEPS

QUICK TIP

(Win) To switch between open documents, click the tab for the document you wish to view, or press [Ctrl][Tab].

QUICK TIP

If you don't see your styles listed, click the plus sign (Win) or right-pointing triangle (Mac) next to su_styles.css in the CSS Styles panel.

1. **Open the index.html page**

   Since an external style sheet has yet to be linked to the index page, the external style sheet is not listed in the CSS Styles panel. In order to use an external style sheet with other pages in the website, you must first attach the style sheet file to each page.

2. **Click the Attach Style Sheet button 🔗 on the CSS Styles panel**

   The Attach External Style Sheet dialog box opens.

3. **Click Browse next to the File/URL text box, click su_styles.css in the Select Style Sheet File dialog box if necessary, click OK (Win) or Open (Mac); compare your screen to Figure D-23, then click OK**

   The Attach External Style Sheet dialog box closes and the su_styles.css style sheet file appears in the CSS Styles panel, indicating that the file is attached to the index page. In addition to the su_styles.css external style sheet, some internal styles are also listed in the CSS Styles panel: body_text, nav_bar, small_text, and body.

4. **Right-click the body_text rule under <style> in the CSS Styles Panel in the internal style sheet, click Move CSS Rules, verify that su_styles.css displays in the Move to External Style Sheet dialog box, as shown in Figure D-24, then click OK to close the Move to External Style Sheet dialog box**

   The internal body_text style is moved to the external style sheet, so it can now be used to format the text on all other pages in the website.

5. **Repeat Step 4 to move the nav_bar, small_text, and body rules to the external style sheet, compare your screen to Figure D-25, delete the remaining <style> tag in the CSS Styles panel, save all files, then close the index page**

6. **Select the first unordered list on the spa page, click the Targeted Rule text box on the CSS Property inspector, then click body_text.**

7. **Repeat Step 6 to apply the body_text rule to the rest of the text on the page that does not have a rule applied, click File on the Menu bar, then click Save All**

   The three unordered lists and the last paragraph are now formatted with the body_text rule.

FIGURE D-23: **Attaching the su_styles.css file to the index page**

Name of external style sheet to attach to the page

Browse button

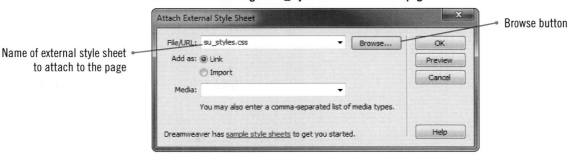

FIGURE D-24: **The Move to External Style Sheet dialog box**

su_styles.css is selected for the destination file

FIGURE D-25: **The internal rules moved to the external style sheet**

Select and delete this tag in Step 5

Internal rules are moved to the external style sheet

Design Matters

The evolution of CSS3

The use of Cascading Style Sheets has evolved over the years from CSS Level 1 to the present CSS Level 3. Cascading Style Sheets revisions are referenced by "levels" rather than "versions." Each new level builds on the previous level. CSS Level 1 is obsolete today. CSS Level 2 is still used, but CSS Level 3 is the latest W3C (World Wide Web Consortium) standard. With CSS3, several properties are available that promote website accessibility such as the @font-face rule. This rule in CSS2 provided the ability to embed fonts in documents using the WOFF format. WOFF stands for Web

Open Font Format and was proposed to the W3C to be a standard format for all web browsers to use. Currently, Firefox Version 3.6 and up, Internet Explorer Version 9 and up, Google Chrome Version 5 and up, and Safari Version 5.1 and up support the WOFF format. The @font-face rule now is used to download a specific font from a font library to render text on a web page if the user does not have that font installed on their system. Examples of font libraries are typekit.com. and google.com/webfonts. For more information about CSS3, go to w3.org/TR/CSS/.

Checking for Spelling Errors

Dreamweaver has a feature for checking spelling errors that is similar to those you have probably used in word processing programs. It is very important to check for spelling and grammatical errors before publishing a page. A page that is published with errors will cause the user to immediately judge the site as unprofessional, and the accuracy of the information presented will be in question. It is a good idea to start a spell check at the top of the document because Dreamweaver searches from the insertion point down. If your insertion point is in the middle of the document, you will receive a message asking if you want to check the rest of the document, which wastes time. If a file you create in a word processor will be imported into Dreamweaver, make sure to run a spell check in the word processing program before you import it. 🔳🔳🔳🔳 You want to check the spelling on the spa page and correct any errors.

STEPS

QUICK TIP
You can also press [Ctrl][Home] to move the insertion point to the top of the document. (Mac users may not have a [home] key depending on their keyboard.)

1. **Place the insertion point in front of The Sea Spa Services heading**

2. **Click Commands on the Menu bar, then click Check Spelling**
   The Check Spelling dialog box opens, as shown in Figure D-26. The word *masage* is highlighted on the spa page, indicating a misspelled word.

3. **Click massage. in the Suggestions list if necessary, click Change, then click Ignore if it stops on any other words that you know are spelled correctly**
   The Check Spelling dialog box closes and a Dreamweaver dialog box opens stating that the Spell check is complete.

4. **Click OK**
   The Dreamweaver dialog box closes and the spa page redisplays with the word *massage* spelled correctly.

5. **Add the page title The Sea Spa to the Title text box on the Document toolbar**

6. **Click File on the Menu bar, click Save, click the Preview/Debug in browser icon 🌐 , then preview the spa page in your browser window**
   The spa page opens in your browser window as shown in Figure D-27.

7. **Close your browser, close all open pages, then exit Dreamweaver**

Using Find and Replace

Another useful editing command is Find and Replace, which is located on the Edit menu. You can use this command to make individual or global text edits in either Design or Code view. It is similar to Find and Replace commands in word processing programs, except that there is an added advantage in Dreamweaver. You can use Find and Replace to easily search through code if you are trying to locate and correct coding errors. For example, if you want to find a tag that formats a font with a specific color, you can search for that color number in the code. If you are searching for internal links that are incorrectly set as absolute links, you can enter the search term *src = "file"* to help you to locate them. You will learn more about absolute links in Unit F.

FIGURE D-26: Using the Check Spelling command

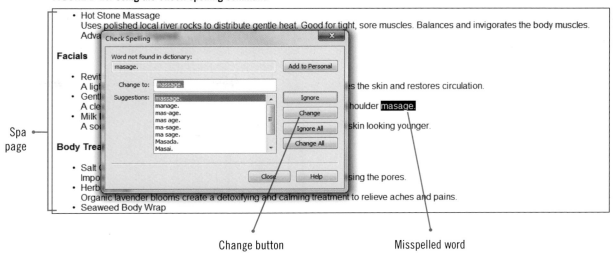

Spa page

Change button

Misspelled word

FIGURE D-27: The finished product

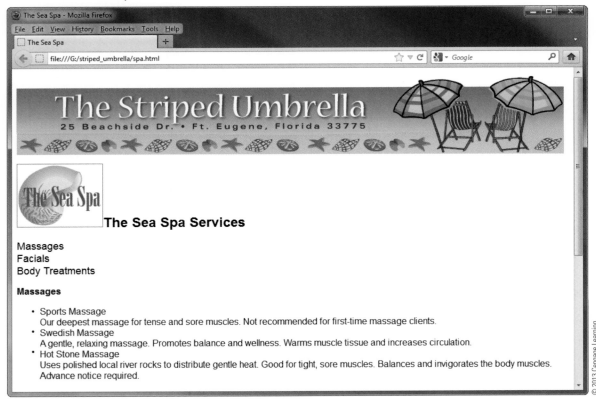

Practice

Concepts Review

Label each element in the Document window, as shown in Figure D-28.

FIGURE D-28

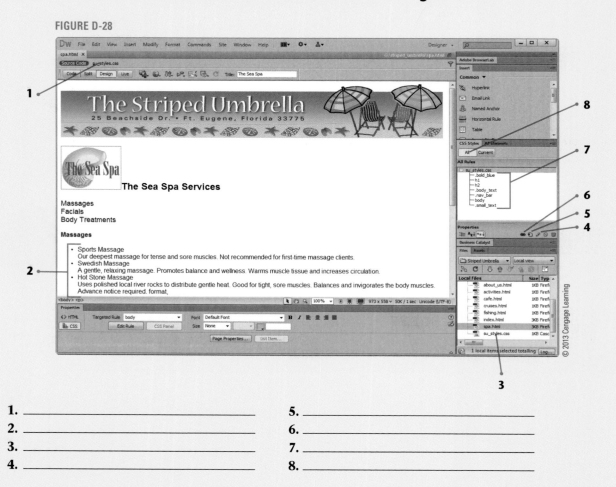

1. _____
2. _____
3. _____
4. _____

5. _____
6. _____
7. _____
8. _____

Match each of the following terms with the statement that best describes it.

9. **Sans-serif font**
10. **Property inspector**
11. **Ordered lists**
12. **Unordered lists**
13. **CSS styles**
14. **CSS Rule**
15. **External style sheet**
16. **Selector**
17. **Declaration**
18. **Serif font**

a. Numbered lists

b. Font without extra strokes at top and bottom

c. A set of formatting attributes that creates a style

d. A file attached or linked to a web page to format page elements

e. A style property and the value

f. Bulleted lists

g. A panel used for formatting page elements

h. The name or tag to which style declarations have been assigned

i. Font with extra strokes at the top and bottom

j. Sets of formatting attributes to format page elements

Select the best answer from the following list of choices.

19. The button used to select color is:
    a.
    b.
    c.
    d.

20. External CSS files are saved with the filename extension:
    a. .css
    b. .cas
    c. .stl
    d. .csf

21. A CSS Class Style name in the Styles panel is preceded by a:
    a. pound sign.
    b. period.
    c. dash.
    d. number.

22. Styles that are part of the head content of a web page are called:
    a. external styles.
    b. embedded styles.
    c. inline Styles.
    d. HTML styles.

23. The type of style used to redefine an HTML tag in the New CSS Rule dialog box is called:
    a. an Advanced style.
    b. a Class style.
    c. a Tag style.
    d. a Compound style.

Skills Review

Important: *If you did not create this website in Unit B and maintain it in Unit C, you will need to create a local site root folder for this website and define the website using files your instructor will provide. See the "Read This Before You Begin" section of this book for more detailed instructions.*

1. **Create a new page.**
   a. Start Dreamweaver.
   b. Open the Blooms & Bulbs website.
   c. Create a new HTML file and save it as **tips.html** in the Blooms & Bulbs website, overwriting the existing blank file.
   d. Add the page title **Blooms & Bulbs** in the title text box.
   e. Insert the banner from your website assets folder at the top of the page, add appropriate alternate text, then enter a paragraph break after the banner.
   f. Insert the file butterfly.jpg from the assets folder in the drive and folder where you store your Unit D Data Files, then add appropriate alternate text.

2. **Import text.**
   a. With the insertion point to the right of the butterfly image, import (Win) or copy and paste (Mac) the Word document gardening_tips.doc from the drive and folder where you store your Unit D Data Files.
   b. Use the Clean Up Word HTML command on the tips page, then save the tips page.

3. **Set text properties.**
   a. Select the Seasonal Gardening Checklist heading, then format the text with the Heading 1 format.
   b. Select the Basic Gardening Tips heading and format it with a Heading 1 format.
   c. Save your work.

4. **Create an unordered list.**
   a. Select the items under the Seasonal Gardening Checklist.
   b. Format the list of items as an unordered list. (*Hint*: Be sure *not* to select the return at the end of the last line or you will accidentally create a fifth item.)
   c. Select the items under Basic Gardening Tips, then format them as an ordered list. (*Hint*: If you have extra line breaks, you will need to delete them to have only six items in your list.)

5. **Understand Cascading Style Sheets.**
   a. Using a word processor or piece of paper, list the types of CSS categorized by their location in a website.
   b. Using a word processor or piece of paper, list the types of CSS categorized by their function in a website.

6. **Create a Style in a new Cascading Style Sheet.**
   a. Open the CSS Styles panel, if necessary.
   b. Create a new Class style named **bold_gray** in a new style sheet file.
   c. Save the new style sheet file with the name **blooms_styles.css** in the blooms folder.
   d. Set the Font-family for the bold_gray style as Arial, Helvetica, sans-serif.
   e. Set the Font-size as small, the Font-weight as bold, then the Color as #333.
   f. Save all files.

7. **Apply and edit a style.**
   a. Apply the bold_gray style to the words *Fall*, *Winter*, *Spring*, and *Summer*.
   b. Edit the style to increase the text size to medium.
   c. Save all files.

Skills Review (continued)

8. **Add styles to a Cascading Style Sheet.**
   a. Create a new Tag selector for the Heading 1 tag in the blooms_styles.css file.
   b. Set the Font-family as Arial, Helvetica, sans-serif.
   c. Set the Font-size as large, the Font-style as normal, then the Color as #000.
   d. Save all files.

9. **Attach a Cascading Style Sheet to a page.**
   a. Open the index page in the Blooms & Bulbs website.
   b. Attach the blooms_styles.css file to the index page.
   c. Move each of the internal styles to the external style sheet, delete the remaining <style> tag, then save all files and close the index page.
   d. On the tips page, apply the body_text rule to all of the text on the page that is not formatted with either a heading format or CSS rule, then save your work.

10. **Check for spelling errors.**
    a. Run a spell check on the tips page, correcting any misspelled words found, then save your work.
    b. Preview the page in your browser, then compare your screen to Figure D-29.
    c. Close your browser, then Exit (Win) or Quit (Mac) Dreamweaver.

FIGURE D-29

© 2013 Cengage Learning
Original photos courtesy of Sherry Bishop

Important: *If you did not create the following websites in Unit B and maintain them in Unit C, you will need to create a local site root folder for the websites in the following exercises and define the websites using files your instructor will provide. See the "Read This Before You Begin" section in this book for more detailed instructions.*

Independent Challenge 1

You have been hired to create a website for a river expedition company named Rapids Transit, located on the Buffalo River in Arkansas. In addition to renting canoes, kayaks, and rafts, they have several types of cabin rentals for overnight stays. River guides are available, if requested, to accompany clients on float trips. The clients range from beginners to experienced floaters. The owner's name is Mike Andrew. Mike has asked you to add a page to the site that will describe the lodge, cabins, and tents that are available to their customers.

a. Start Dreamweaver.

b. Open the Rapids Transit website.

c. Open the file dwd_1.html from the drive and folder where you store your Unit D Data Files, then save it as **lodging.html** in the Rapids Transit website, replacing the existing file, but not updating links.

d. Close dwd_1.html, then verify that the rapids banner path is set to the assets folder in the website.

e. Create an unordered list from the four types of lodging and their rates.

f. Create a new Tag Selector rule that modifies the Heading 1 tag, then save it in a new style sheet file named **rapids_transit.css** using the following settings: Font-family, Arial, Helvetica, sans-serif; Font-size, 16; Font-weight, bold; Color, #003.

g. Apply the Heading 1 format to the navigation bar text and the first sentence on the page.

h. Create a second Tag selector rule to modify the Heading 2 tag in the rapids_transit.css style sheet.

i. Format the <h2> rule with the following settings: Font-family Arial, Helvetica, sans-serif; Font-size 14; Font-style normal; Font-weight bold; and Color #003.

j. Open the index page, attach the rapids_transit.css file, move the internal body_text rule to the external style sheet, then delete the <style> tag in the CSS Styles panel.

k. Save all files, then on the lodging page, apply the Heading 2 format to the text "Rates are as follows:" and the body_text rule to the rest of the text on the page that is not formatted with a heading format.

l. Create a new class style in the rapids_transit.css style sheet named **contact_info** using Arial, Helvetica sans-serif; italic style; size 14, color #000; then apply it to the contact information on the index page.

m. Apply the Heading 1 format to the navigation bar text on the index page, then save your work using the Save All command on the File menu.

n. Preview the index page in your browser window, click the Lodging link, compare your screen to Figure D-30, close your browser window, close all files, then exit Dreamweaver. (*Hint*: Depending on whether you have clicked other links, your link colors may not match the links in the figure.)

FIGURE D-30

Independent Challenge 2

You are a marketing specialist for a travel outfitter named TripSmart. TripSmart specializes in travel products and services. In addition to selling luggage and accessories, they sponsor trips and offer travel advice. Your company is designing a new website and your job is to update the newsletter page on the current website with some timely travel tips.

a. Start Dreamweaver, then open the TripSmart website.

b. Open the file dwd_2.html and save it as **newsletter.html** in the TripSmart website, replacing the existing file, but not updating links, then close dwd_2.html.

c. Verify that the banner path is set to the assets folder of the website.

d. Create an ordered list from the 10 items on the page, starting with Be organized.

e. Create a new Tag Selector rule to modify the Heading 1 format, then save it in a new style sheet named **tripsmart_styles.css**.

f. Choose a font, size, style, color, and weight of your choice for the <h1> rule.

g. Apply the Heading 1 format to the Ten Tips for Stress-Free Travel paragraph heading.

h. Type **TripSmart - Serving all your travel needs** in the document title text box, then save your work.

i. Open the index page, delete the horizontal rule, attach the style sheet, then move the three internal rules to the external style sheet and delete the <style> tag left from the internal styles in the CSS Styles panel.

j. Create another class style in the tripsmart_styles.css style sheet named **contact_info** with settings of your choice, apply it to the contact information on the page, save your work, then close the page.

k. Apply the body_text rule to the two remaining paragraphs without styles applied, preview the newsletter page in your browser window, then compare it to Figure D-31 as an example for a possible solution.

l. Close your browser, close the file, then exit Dreamweaver.

FIGURE D-31

Our staff recently conducted a contest to determine ten top travel tips for stress-free travel. We compiled over forty great tips, but the following were selected as the winners. We hope you will find them useful for your next trip!

Ten Tips for Stress-Free Travel

1. Be organized.
   Make a list of what you want to pack in each bag and check it as you pack. Take this inventory with you in the event your bags are lost or delayed. Then use the list again when you repack, to make sure you haven't left anything behind.
2. Carry important information with you.
   Keep your important travel information in easy reach at all times. Include a list of your flight numbers, confirmation numbers for your travel and hotel reservations, and any car rentals. And don't forget printouts of your itinerary and electronic tickets. Remember to bring your passport, and keep a photocopy of it in another piece of baggage. Be sure to have copies of prescriptions, emergency phone numbers, telephone numbers and addresses of friends and relatives, complete lists of medications, and credit card information. It's not a bad idea to email this information to yourself as a backup if you will have email access.
3. Pack smartly.
   You know the old saying: lay out everything on your bed you plan to take with you, then remove half of it. Pack the remainder and carry your bags around the block once to make sure you can handle them yourself. If in doubt, leave it out! Use packing cubes or zip-top bags to organize your personal items, such as underwear and socks. Make distinctive-looking luggage tags with your name and address for easy identification, and be sure to include the same information inside your luggage.
4. Include basic medical necessities.
   Besides your prescription drugs, take a basic first aid kit with the basics: bandages, anti-nausea medications, anti-diarrhea medications, aspirin, antibiotics, and prescription drugs.
5. Wear comfortable shoes.
   Blisters can ruin a wonderful trip. Wear comfortable shoes and socks. Your priority should be comfortable, dry, warm feet — not fashion. Don't buy new shoes without breaking them in first.

Independent Challenge 3

Dr. Chappel is a government historian who is conducting research on the separation of church and state. He is using the Library of Congress website to find relevant information. Write your answers to the questions below on paper or using your word processor.

a. Connect to the Internet, then go to The Library of Congress website at www.loc.gov, shown in Figure D-32.

b. Is the content well organized?

c. What font or fonts are used on the pages for the main text? Are the same fonts used consistently on the other pages in the website?

d. Are there any ordered or unordered lists on the website? If so, how are they used?

e. View the source to see if CSS styles are used on the pages in the website.

f. Use a search engine to find another website of interest. Compare and contrast the use of text formatting on this site to that used on the Library of Congress website.

FIGURE D-32

Real Life Independent Challenge

This assignment will continue to build on the personal website that you created in Unit B and modified in Unit C. You have created and developed your index page. In this lesson, you will work with one of the other pages in your website.

    a. Consult your wireframe, then decide which page you would like to develop in this lesson.

    b. Create content for this page, then format the text attractively on the page using settings for font, size, text color, style, and alignment.

    c. Format some of the text on the page as either an ordered or unordered list.

    d. Create a style sheet with a minimum of two rules, then apply a rule to all text on the page.

    e. Attach the style sheet to any of the pages you have already developed, then apply rules to all text.

    f. Save the file, then preview the pages in your browser window.

After you are satisfied with your work, verify the following:

    a. Each completed page has a page title.

    b. All links work correctly.

    c. The completed pages appear correctly using at least two screen resolutions.

    d. All images are properly placed with a path to the assets folder of the website.

    e. A style sheet is used to format all text.

Visual Workshop

Your company has been selected to design a website for a catering business named Carolyne's Creations. Open the Carolyne's Creations website, open the file dwd_3.html, then save it as **recipes.html** in the Carolyne's Creations website, replacing the original file, and not updating the links. Close dwd_3.html, then format the page using styles so it looks similar to Figure D-33. (The text may wrap slightly different depending on the size of your browser window.) Save the file pie.jpg from the drive and folder where you store your Unit D Data Files to your website assets folder (*Hint*: Use the following styles and settings to match the figure, and save them in a CSS file named cc_styles.css. The small_text rule was not used on the recipes page, but for the copyright and last updated statements on the index page.)

.nav_bar	.body_text	.small_text
Font-family: Arial, Helvetica, sans-serif	Font-family: Arial, Helvetica, sans-serif	Font-family: Arial, Helvetica, sans-serif
Font-size: large	Font-size: medium	Font-size: small

h1	h2	.ingredients_list
Font-family: Verdana, Geneva, sans-serif	Font-family: Verdana, Geneva, sans-serif	Font-family: Arial, Helvetica, sans-serif
Font-size: 18px	Font-size: 16px	Font-size: medium
Font-weight: bold	Font-weight: bold	Text-indent: 30px
Color: #333	Color: #333	List style-type: none

If you have not maintained this website from the previous unit, then contact your instructor for assistance.

FIGURE D-33

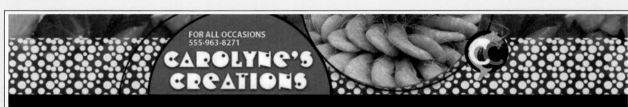

Home | Shop | Classes | Catering | Recipes

Caramel Coconut Pie

This is one of our most requested desserts. It is simple, elegant, and refreshing. It is easy to make in advance, because you keep it frozen until just before serving. It makes two pies — one to eat and one to give away!

Ingredients:

¼ cup butter
7 oz. dried coconut
½ cup chopped pecans
1 package (8 oz.) cream cheese, softened
1 can (14 oz.) sweetened condensed milk
1 container (16 oz.) whipped topping, thawed
1 jar (12 oz.) caramel ice cream topping
2 pie shells (9 in.), baked

Using and Managing Images

Files You Will Need:

To view a list of files needed for this unit, see the Data Files Grid in the back of the book.

Web pages with images are more interesting than pages with just text. You can position images on your web pages, then resize them, add borders, and customize the amount of space around them. You can also use images as a web page, table, or CSS layout block background. In this unit you learn how to incorporate images into a website and how to manage them effectively using the Assets panel. A photographer recently did a photo shoot of The Striped Umbrella property for some new brochures. You decide to incorporate several of the images on the about_us page so that the beauty of the resort comes across.

OBJECTIVES

Insert an image

Align an image

Enhance an image

Use alternate text and set Accessibility preferences

View the Assets panel

Insert a background image

Delete image files from a website

Create and find images for a website

Examine copyright rules

Inserting an Image

Images you import into a website are automatically added to the Assets panel. The **Assets panel**, located with the other panels on the right side of your workspace, lists the assets of the website, such as images and colors. As you add images to a web page, the page **download time** (the time it takes to transfer the file to a user's computer) increases. Pages that download slowly discourage users from staying on the site. To add an image to a page, you can either use the Insert, Image command on the Menu bar, use the Images button in the Common category on the Insert panel, or drag an image from the Assets panel onto the page. You want to place several photos of the resort on the about_us web page and check the file size of each in the Assets panel.

STEPS

TROUBLE

Your download time shown may vary according to the Connection Speed preferences set for your Status bar. To change your settings, click Edit (Win) or Dreamweaver (Mac) on the Menu bar, click Preferences, then click Status Bar.

1. **Start Dreamweaver, switch to Design view if necessary, open The Striped Umbrella website, open dwe_1.html from the drive and folder where you store your Unit E Data Files, save it as about_us.html in the striped_umbrella root folder, overwriting the existing file and not updating the links, then close dwe_1.html**

   The about_us page displays in Design view in your workspace. The Status bar displays the download time for the current web page, as shown Figure E-1.

2. **Click the Attach Style Sheet button in the CSS Styles panel, attach the su_styles.css style sheet, apply the nav_bar rule to the menu bar, the Heading 1 paragraph format to "Welcome guests!", and the body_text rule to all of the paragraph text on the page**

   The style sheet for the website is attached to the about_us page, and three rules are applied to the menu bar, heading, and two paragraphs.

3. **Click to the left of the word *When* in the first paragraph to place the insertion point, select the Common category on the Insert panel if necessary, scroll down and click the Images list arrow on the Insert panel, then click Image**

   The Select Image Source dialog box opens. This is the same dialog box you have been using to copy images from the Data Files folder to your site assets folder when you save new pages with images.

QUICK TIP

The Image Tag Accessibility Attributes dialog box contains Dreamweaver accessibility features, which you will learn about later in the unit.

4. **Navigate to the drive and folder where you store your Unit E Data Files, double-click club_house.jpg from the assets folder, type Club House as the Alternate text in the Image Tag Accessibility Attributes dialog box if prompted, then click OK**

5. **Expand the assets folder in the Files panel, if necessary, then click the Refresh Button on the Files panel toolbar if necessary**

   The club house image appears at the beginning of the first paragraph, as shown in Figure E-2. As indicated in the Files panel list, the club house image is located in the website assets folder. This is the location that will be used to load the image in the browser when the page is viewed.

QUICK TIP

You need to select club_house.jpg to see the thumbnail.

6. **Save the file, click the Assets panel tab, click the Images button on the Assets panel if necessary, then click at the bottom of the Assets panel, if necessary**

   The three images you added to The Striped Umbrella website—club_house.jpg, sea_spa_logo.jpg, and su_banner.gif—are listed in the Assets panel. When the Images button is selected, the Assets panel displays the images in the current website which, as shown in Figure E-3, is split into two panes. The lower window lists all of the images in the website, while the top window displays a thumbnail of the image currently selected in the list. The Dimensions column lists the height and width of each image.

TROUBLE

If the file names don't appear in the Files or Assets panels, click the Refresh button , or click while you hold down the [Ctrl] key.

7. **Repeat Steps 3 and 4 to insert the boardwalk.png image at the beginning of the second paragraph, if prompted use Boardwalk to the beach as alternate text, then save your work**

   The boardwalk image appears on the page at the beginning of the second paragraph and boardwalk.png is added to the list of images in the Assets panel. The Assets panel lists the four images shown in Figure E-4.

FIGURE E-1: Status bar displaying page download time

provides a safe route to the beach for both our guests and the native vegetation. The sea oats and other flora are tender. Please do not step on them or pick them. A lifeguard is on duty from 9:00 a.m. until sunset. Check the flag each time you head for the beach for the status of current swimming conditions and advisories. Jellyfish can be a problem at times, so be careful when you are walking along the beach, especially as the tide is retreating from high tide. We have beach chairs, umbrellas, and towels available to our guests. Check with the attendant on duty. Water, juices, and soft drinks are also available for purchase at the end of the boardwalk. Don't forget your sunglasses, hat, and sunscreen! A sunburn is sure way to ruin a nice vacation. The gift shop in The Club House is a

Your screen size might differ

Page download time (yours might differ, depending on connection speed)

FIGURE E-2: About_us page with image inserted

Images list arrow

Club house image

Correct path for image in the site assets folder

Image listed in assets folder

Original photo courtesy of Sherry Bishop

FIGURE E-3: Assets panel listing for The Striped Umbrella website

Images button

Thumbnail of selected image

List of images in The Striped Umbrella website

File dimensions

Your panel might be larger

FIGURE E-4: Assets panel with boardwalk.png image included

Four images now listed

Aligning an Image

Like text, images can be positioned on the page in relation to other page elements. Positioning an image is called **aligning** the image. Use CSS to align images. You can use a global rule to modify the <img> tag, or you can create separate rules for individual images. When you first place an image on a page, it has the **Default** alignment which aligns the bottom of the image with the text **baseline**—the bottom of a line of text, not including descending portions of characters such as y or g. You should experiment with CSS rule properties to find the best alignment for your images. After experimenting with several alignment options, you decide to stagger the alignment of the images on the page to make it appear more balanced.

STEPS

1. **Click the New CSS Rule button 🗗 in the CSS Styles panel**

   The New CSS Rule dialog box opens. You will create a new rule to align images to the left of other page content.

2. **Click Class in the Selector Type list box, type img_left_float for the Selector name, verify that it will be saved in the su_styles.css file, compare your screen to Figure E-5, then click OK**

   The CSS Rule Definition for .img_left_float in su_styles.css dialog box opens. Next, you add the Float property and value.

3. **Click the Box category, click the Float list arrow, click left, as shown in Figure E-6, then click OK**

   The Float property tells the browser to "float" the image to the left of other page content.

   QUICK TIP
   You can also right-click an image, point to CSS Styles, then click the rule you want to apply.

4. **Click the club house image if necessary, click the Class list arrow on the right side of the Property inspector, then click img_left_float**

   The text moves to the right side of the image, as shown in Figure E-7.

5. **Repeat Steps 1 through 3 to create another rule named img_right_float with a Float value of right**

6. **Apply the img_right_float rule to the boardwalk image**

   The boardwalk image floats to the right of the text. The images are now aligned on the page in staggered positions.

7. **Click File, Save All to save your work**

Design Matters

Using dynamic images

To make a page even more interesting, you can place images on the page that change frequently, such as a group of several images that are set to automatically cycle on and off the page, called **dynamic images**. You can use dynamic images to display multiple items with a similar layout. For example, a website for a retail store might display images of current sale items in one window on a web page, one item at a time. To insert dynamic images, you must first create a Spry Data Set to store the images using the [+] button in the Bindings panel. You then insert the images on the page using the Data sources option, rather than the File system option, in the Select Image Source dialog box.

FIGURE E-5: New CSS Rule dialog box

New Selector
Name is
img_left_float

The new rule will be saved in
the su_styles.css style sheet

Select the Class
Selector Type

FIGURE E-6: CSS Rule Definition for img_left_float in su_styles.css dialog box

Select the
Box category

Select the
left Float
value

FIGURE E-7: Club house image with img_left_float rule applied

Image floats
to the left
side of the
text

Original photos courtesy of Sherry Bishop

img_left_float
rule is applied

img_left_float
rule is listed in
the style sheet

Using and Managing Images

Enhancing an Image

After you select, place, and align an image on a web page, you can enhance its appearance. You can improve an image's appearance in Dreamweaver using borders, cropping, resizing, adjusting its brightness and contrast, and adjusting the horizontal and vertical space around an image. **Borders** are like frames that surround an image to make it stand out on the page. **Cropping** an image removes part of the image, both visually (on the page) and physically (the file size). A cropped image is smaller and takes less time to download. **Horizontal** and **vertical space** refers to blank space above, below, or on the sides of an image that separates the image from other elements on the page. ░░░░ You decide to enhance the images on the about_us page by using your image rules to add borders around the images, and adjust the horizontal and vertical space around each image.

STEPS

1. Click the img_left_float rule in the CSS Styles panel, click the Edit Rule button ✐, click the Border Category, enter the rule properties shown in Figure E-8, then click OK

2. Repeat Step 1 to add a border to the img_right_float rule
   Both images now have a thin border around them.

3. Edit the img_left_float rule again to add vertical and horizontal space by unchecking the "Same for all" check box under Margin in the Box category, then setting the Box Right Margin to 10 px as shown in Figure E-9, then click OK
   The text is more evenly wrapped around the image and is easier to read, because it is not so close to the edge of the image.

4. Using Step 3 as a guide, add a border and a 10 px left margin to the img_right_float rule, then compare your screen to Figure E-10

5. Save your work, open the spa page, then apply the img_left_float rule to the spa logo
   The headings wrap to the right side of the spa logo and look much better on the page.

6. Click File, Save All, to save all files, then close the spa page

Resizing an image using the Property inspector

To save space on a web page, you can crop an image. If you prefer to keep the entire image, you can resize it on the page instead. Simply select the image, then drag a selection handle toward the center of the image. Since dragging a selection handle can distort an image, press and hold [Shift] then drag a corner selection handle to retain the image's original proportions. (You can also enlarge an image using these methods.) After

you drag an image handle to resize it, the image dimensions in the Property inspector appear in bold and a black Refresh icon appears to the right of the dimensions. If you click the Refresh icon, the image reverts to its original size. Do not use this method to significantly resize an image. Instead resize it using an image editor and save a copy of it with the new settings.

FIGURE E-8: CSS Rule Definition for img_left_float dialog box

Same for all check boxes are checked

Border category

Style = solid

Color = #666

Width = thin

FIGURE E-9: CSS Rule Definition for img_left_float dialog box

Box category

Uncheck "Same for all"

Right margin = 10 px

FIGURE E-10: Viewing the images with borders and margins

When you arrive at The Striped Umbrella, check in at The Club House. Look for the signs that will direct you to registration. Our beautiful club house is the home base for our registration offices, The Sand Crab Cafe, and The Sea Spa. Registration is open from 8:00 a.m. until 6:00 p.m. Please call to make arrangements if you plan to arrive after 6:00 p.m. The cafe and spa hours are both posted and listed in the information packet that you will receive when you arrive. The main swimming pool is directly behind The Club House. A lifeguard is on duty from 8:00 a.m. until 9:00 p.m. The pool area includes a wading pool, a lap pool, and a large pool with a diving board. Showers are located in several areas for your use before and after swimming. We also provide poolside service from the cafe for snacks and lunch.

After you arrive, you will want to take a stroll down the boardwalk to the beach. The entrance to the boardwalk is just past the pool area. The boardwalk provides a safe route to the beach for both our guests and the native vegetation. The sea oats and other flora are tender. Please do not step on them or pick them. A lifeguard is on duty from 9:00 a.m. until sunset. Check the flag each time you head for the beach for the status of current swimming conditions and advisories. Jellyfish can be a problem at times, so be careful when you are walking along the beach, especially as the tide is retreating from high tide. We have beach chairs, umbrellas, and towels available to our guests. Check with the attendant on duty. Water, juices, and soft drinks are also available for purchase at the end of the boardwalk. Don't forget your sunglasses, hat, and sunscreen! A sunburn is sure way to ruin a nice vacation. The gift shop in The Club House is a convenient place to pick up any items that you may have forgotten to bring along, in addition to an extensive inventory of bathing suits, sandals, and other

Original photos courtesy of Sherry Bishop

Both images have borders and horizontal space separating them from the text

Design Matters

Resizing images using an external editor

Each image on a web page takes a certain amount of time to download, depending on the size of the file and the speed of the user's Internet connection. Larger files (in terms of kilobytes, not width and height) take longer to download than smaller files. Many designers feel that an ideal page should download in less than five or six seconds; to ensure that your page downloads quickly, your images should have the smallest file size possible while maintaining the necessary level of image quality. If you need to significantly resize an image, use an external image editor

instead of resizing it in Dreamweaver; resizing in Dreamweaver affects how an image appears onscreen, but does not alter the image file itself. Cropping an image in Dreamweaver, however, *will* modify the image file and decrease its overall size. As a general rule, it is better to crop your images using an external editor when you are making a significant change. Always save a copy of the original file before you crop it, then use the copy of the file to make your edits. This will always keep the original file intact in case you need it later.

Using Alternate Text and Setting Accessibility Preferences

One of the easiest ways to make your web page viewer-friendly and more accessible to individuals with disabilities is through the use of alternate text. **Alternate text** is descriptive text that can be set to appear in place of an image while the image is downloading. Some browsers can be set to display only text and to download images manually. In such instances, alternate text is used in place of images. Alternate text can be read by a **screen reader**, a device used by individuals with visual impairments to convert written text on a computer monitor to spoken words. Using a screen reader and alternate text, these users can have an image described to them in detail. You should also use alternate text when inserting form objects, text displayed as images, buttons, frames, and media files to enable screen reader usage. When loading a new installation of Dreamweaver, all the accessibility preferences are turned on by default. To make the alternate text more descriptive for screen readers, you want to edit the alternate text that describes each of the images on the about_us page. You also verify that the Images option in the Accessibility preferences is set so you will not forget to enter alternate text for each image.

STEPS

1. **Click the** club house image **to select it, select the text in the Alt text box in the Property inspector, type** The Striped Umbrella Club House, **press [Tab], then save the file**
   The alternate text is entered for the image, as shown in Figure E-11.

2. **Repeat Step 1 to edit the alternate text for the boardwalk image to read** Boardwalk to our private beach
   The alternate text is entered for the image, as shown in Figure E-12.

QUICK TIP
Once you set the Accessibility preferences, they will be in effect for all of your websites. You will not have to set each website separately.

3. **Click** Edit **on the Menu bar, (Win) or the Dreamweaver menu (Mac), click** Preferences, **click** Accessibility **in the Category list, click the** Show attributes when inserting check boxes **to select them if necessary, as shown in Figure E-13, then click** OK
   With these options selected, Dreamweaver will prompt you to enter alternate text for new objects you add to the website, including images.

QUICK TIP
If your Save option is not active, you do not need to save your file. However, you can use the Save All command in the File menu to make sure any changes you have made to an open page are saved.

4. **Save your work**

FIGURE E-11: Editing the alternate text for the club house image

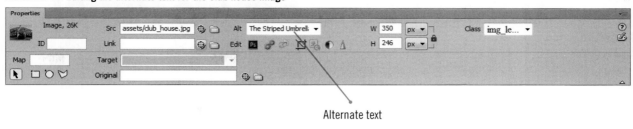

Alternate text

FIGURE E-12: Editing the alternate text for the boardwalk image

Alternate text

FIGURE E-13: Accessibility Preferences dialog box

Accessibility preferences category

Mac users may not see these options

Show attributes when inserting options

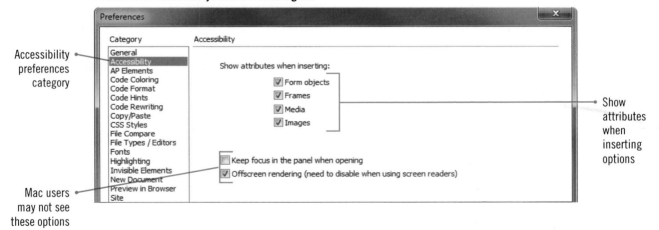

Design Matters

Providing for accessibility with alternate text

The use of alternate text is the first checkpoint listed in the web content Accessibility Guidelines (WCAG), Version 2.0, from the World Wide Web Consortium (W3C). It states that a website should "provide text alternatives for any non-text content so that it can be changed into other forms people need, such as large print, Braille, speech, symbols, or simpler language." The twelve WCAG guidelines are grouped together under four principles called the POUR principles: perceivable, operable, understandable, and robust. To view the complete set of accessibility guidelines, go to the Web Accessibility Initiative page (w3.org/WAI). A general rule is that if you need to enter more than 50 characters of alternate text, you should create a separate file with the information you want to convey. Enter the location of the file in the Long Description text box that appears under the Alternate Text text box in the Image Tag Accessibility Attributes dialog box that opens when you insert a new image.

Viewing the Assets Panel

As you have learned, the Assets panel displays all of the assets in a website. It is important to understand how the Assets panel organizes your assets so you can quickly identify and locate the various assets in your site. There are nine categories of assets, each represented by a button on the Assets panel: Images, Colors, URLs, SWF, Shockwave, Movies, Scripts, Templates, and Library. There are two options for viewing the assets in each category. You can click the Site option button to view all the assets in a website, or the Favorites option button to view those assets that you have designated as **favorites**—assets that you expect to use repeatedly while you work on the site. For more information about this topic see the *Using favorites in the Assets panel* Clues to Use box in this lesson. You can also use the Assets panel to insert images on your page by either dragging an asset to the page, or by selecting the image and clicking the Insert button. So far, your website includes several images and colors. You explore the Assets panel to understand how Dreamweaver organizes the image files and keeps track of the colors used in the site.

STEPS

QUICK TIP

Make sure that the page you have open is in the current website. If you open a page outside the current website, the Assets panel will not display the assets associated with the open page.

1. **Click the Assets tab in the Files Tab group, if necessary**

   The first time you use the Assets panel, it displays the Images category; after that, it displays the category that was selected during the last Dreamweaver session.

QUICK TIP

You can click the column headings in the Assets panel to sort the files by Name, Dimensions, Size, Type, and Full Path.

2. **Click the Images button on the Assets panel, if necessary**

   Each time you click a category button, the contents in the Assets panel window change. Figure E-14 displays the Images category, and lists the four images in the website. Remember to click the Refresh button [C] if you don't see all of your assets listed.

TROUBLE

If you see another color listed, click the Refresh button [C] to remove it. If you still see additional colors, you can either leave them or search for them in Code view and remove them.

3. **Click the Colors button ▦ to display the Colors category**

   Three colors are listed in the website, as shown in Figure E-15. They are gray, blue, and white. The gray and blue colors are used for formatting text and images and are located in the external style sheet. The white color formats the page background color. The Type column shows that each color is listed as Websafe. You learned about websafe colors in Unit C.

Using the terms *graphics* and *images*

In discussing design, people often use the terms **graphics** and **images**. This text uses the term *graphics* to refer to most non-text items on a web page, including photographs, logos, menu bars, Flash animations, graphs, background images, and illustrations. Any of these can be called a **graphic** or a **graphic file**. *Images* is a narrower term, referring to pictures or photographs. **Image files** are referred to by their file type, or file format, such as **JPEG** (Joint Photographic Experts Group), **GIF** (Graphics Interchange Format), or **PNG** (Portable Network Graphics). See Table E-1 on page 119 for descriptions for each of these formats. This text refers to the pictures that you see on the pages as images. But don't worry too much about which term to use; many people use one term or the other according to habit, region, or type of business, or use them interchangeably.

FIGURE E-14: **Assets panel showing Images category**

Images button selected

Favorites option button

Assets categories

Site option button

Four images in website

Original photo courtesy of Sherry Bishop

FIGURE E-15: **Assets panel showing Colors category**

Colors button

Type column

Colors used in site

Using Favorites in the Assets panel

For assets such as images that you plan to use repeatedly, you can place them in the Favorites list in the Assets panel to make them readily available. There are a few ways to add favorites to the Favorites list in the Assets panel. You can right-click an image in Design view, then click Add to Image Favorites. When you subsequently click the Favorites option button in the Assets panel, the image will display in the list. You can also right-click the name of an image in the Site list (when the Site option is selected in the Assets panel), then click Add to

Favorites. In addition, you can create a folder for storing assets by category by clicking the Favorites option in the Assets panel, clicking the Files panel options list arrow on the Files panel group, then clicking New Favorites Folder. You can give the folder a descriptive name, then drag assets from the Favorites list to move them to this folder. You can create nicknames for assets in the Favorites list by right-clicking (Win) or [ctrl]-clicking (Mac) the asset in the Favorites list, then clicking Edit Nickname.

Inserting a Background Image

Although you may consider them too plain, standard white backgrounds are many times the best choice for web pages. Some pages, however, look best when they utilize background colors or images. **Background images** are image files used in place of background colors to provide a depth and visual interest that a one-dimensional background color can't provide. Background images can create a dramatic effect; however, they may also be too distracting on an already full page. You can use background color for some areas of a page and background images on others. If you choose to use a background image, select one that is small in file size so the page will download quickly. Background colors and images are set using CSS. You can create a global rule to modify every page background or layout block or you can create individual rules that format individual sections or page elements. You are pleased with the current white background color of the about_us page, but want to see what a background image would look like.

STEPS

1. **Click Modify on the Menu bar, then click Page Properties**

   The Page Properties dialog box opens where you can add a background image to a web page by adding a link to the background image filename.

2. **Click the Appearance (CSS) category, if necessary**

3. **Click Browse next to the Background image text box, navigate to the assets folder in the unit_e folder in the drive and folder where you save your Data Files, double-click water.jpg, then click OK**

   The white background is replaced with a muted water image, as shown in Figure E-16. The color of the water is close to the blue in the banner, so the image fits in well with the other page colors. However, since it flows directly behind the text, it does not provide the good contrast that the white background did.

4. **Expand the CSS Styles panel if necessary, then compare your screen to Figure E-17**

   Since you used the Page Properties dialog box to insert the image background, Dreamweaver created an internal <body> rule to format the page background. Your external style sheet also has a <body> rule that sets a white page background. The internal rule takes precedence over the external rule, so for this page only, the white background is replaced with the water background.

   QUICK TIP
   Even when you remove an image from a web page, it remains in the assets folder in the local site root folder of the website.

5. **Click the <style> tag in the CSS Styles panel, then press the Delete button 🗑 on the CSS Styles panel**

   The about_us page background returns to white, since the external global body tag is again formatting the page background. The internal style is removed from the list in the CSS Styles panel, as shown in Figure E-18.

FIGURE E-16: about_us page with a background image

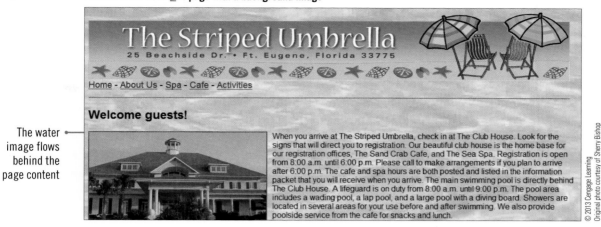

The water image flows behind the page content

© 2013 Cengage Learning
Original photo courtesy of Sherry Bishop

FIGURE E-17: The CSS Styles panel with the new embedded body rule added

Internal rule added to add background image

FIGURE E-18: The CSS Styles panel with the embedded body rule deleted

Internal rule is deleted

Integrating Photoshop and Fireworks with Dreamweaver CS6

Dreamweaver has many functions integrated with Photoshop CS6. For example, you can copy and paste images directly from Photoshop into Dreamweaver. Dreamweaver will prompt you to optimize the image by choosing a file format and settings for using the image in a web browser. Then it will paste the image on the page. If you want to edit the image later, select the image, then click the Edit button in the Property inspector to open the image in Photoshop. (The appearance of the Edit button will change according to the default image editor you have specified.) When you edit an image in Photoshop, you can export an updated Smart Object instantly. **Smart Objects** are layers with image source information that allow an image to be modified nondestructively without losing the original data. Photoshop users can set Photoshop as the default image editor in Dreamweaver for specific image file formats. Click Edit on the Menu bar, click Preferences (Win), or click Dreamweaver, click Preferences (Mac), click File Types/Editors, click the Extensions plus sign button, select a file format from the list, click the Editors plus sign button, use the Select External Editor dialog box to browse to Photoshop (if you don't see it listed already), then click Make Primary. Search the Adobe website (adobe.com) for a tutorial on Photoshop and Dreamweaver integration. Fireworks is another commonly used default image editor. Use the same steps to select it rather than Photoshop.

Deleting Image Files from a Website

As you work on a website, it is very common to accumulate files that end up never being used in the site. One way to avoid accumulating unnecessary files is to look at and evaluate an image first, before you copy it to the default images folder. If the file has already been copied to the default images folder, however, you should delete it (or at least move it to another location) to ensure that the Assets panel only lists the assets actually used in the site. This practice is considered good site management. To delete a file from the Assets panel, you can access the Locate in Site command, which is useful if you have a large number of images to search. If you just have a single file to delete, it's faster to just use the Delete command in the Files panel. Since you decided not to use the background image on the about_us page, you want to delete it from the assets folder.

STEPS

1. **Display the Assets panel if necessary, click the Images button ⊡ on the Assets panel, verify that the Site option is selected, then click the Refresh button ⟳ on the Assets panel**
   The background file remains in the Images list on the Assets panel. Even though you have deleted it from the body rule, you have not yet deleted them in the website assets folder.

2. **Right-click water.jpg in the Assets panel, then click Locate in Site, as shown in Figure E-19**
   The Files panel opens with the water.jpg file selected.

3. **Press [Delete] to delete the file, then click Yes in the confirmation dialog box**
   The water.jpg file is no longer listed in the Assets panel because it has been deleted from the site.

4. **Save your work, then preview your file in your browser**
   Your about_us page is completed and should resemble Figure E-20.

5. **Close the page, then Exit (Win) or Quit (Mac) Dreamweaver**

Inserting files with Adobe Bridge

You can manage project files, including video and Camera Raw files, with a file management tool called Adobe Bridge that is included with Dreamweaver. Bridge provides an easy way to view files outside the website before bringing them into the website. It is an integrated application, working with other Adobe programs, such as Photoshop and Illustrator. You can also use Bridge to add meta tags and search text in your files. To open Bridge, click the Browse in Bridge command on the File menu or click the Browse in Bridge button on the Standard toolbar.

FIGURE E-19: Using the Assets panel to locate a file in a site

water.jpg

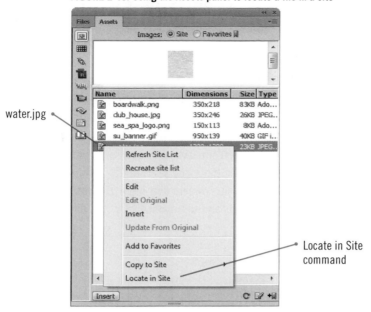

Locate in Site command

FIGURE E-20: The finished page

© 2013 Cengage Learning
Original photos courtesy of Sherry Bishop

Design Matters

Image file management

It is a good idea to have an additional storage location for your image files in addition to the website's assets folder. Keep all original image files outside the website and save them once with their original settings. As you edit them, save them using a different name. This way, you will always be able to find the original file before it is resized or edited. You may also have files you don't want to use now but may need later. Store them outside your website to keep them from cluttering up the assets folder.

Creating and Finding Images for a Website

There are several resources for locating high-quality images for a website. You can create original images using an image editing or drawing program, such as Fireworks, Illustrator, or Photoshop, or use original photographs for colorful, rich images. The Internet, of course, is a great source for finding images. Stock photos are photos on websites that are available to use by either paying a single fee per photo or a subscription fee for downloading multiple images. Table E-1 describes three image types that can be used on web pages. Now that you understand how to incorporate images into The Striped Umbrella website, you explore the advantages and disadvantages of the different ways to accumulate images.

DETAILS

- **Original images**

  Programs such as Fireworks and Photoshop give you the ability to create and modify original artwork. These image editing programs have numerous features for manipulating images. For example, you can adjust the color, brightness, or size of an image. You can also set a transparent background for an image. **Transparent backgrounds** contain transparent pixels, rather than pixels with color, resulting in images that blend easily on a page background. Only certain file types can be used to create transparent images, such as gifs and pngs. Illustrator is a drawing program that is used to create original vector graphics, which can then be converted to a usable format for the web, such as jpg, gif, or png files.

- **Original photography**

  High-quality photographs can greatly enhance a website. Fortunately, digital cameras and scanners have made this venture much easier than in the past. Once you scan a photograph or shoot it with a digital camera, you can further enhance it using an image editing software program, such as Photoshop or Fireworks. Photographs taken with digital cameras often have large file sizes, so be sure to create resized copies using an image editing program such as Photoshop before placing them on web pages. If you don't have Photoshop or another image editor, many digital cameras come with their own basic software that you can use to resize and enhance images.

- **The Internet**

  There are many websites from which you are able to find images, but look carefully for copyright statements regarding the legal use of images. Stock photos sites, such as iStockphoto, are excellent resources used by many professional designers. To use these sites, you first sign up to become a member, then you either purchase images as you need them, or purchase a subscription, which allows you to pay a set price for the number of files you expect to download each year. There are many collections of images online that are free, but some sites require that you credit them on your website with either a simple statement or a link to their website. Images that are labeled as public domain are free to use without restrictions. Figure E-21 is an example of a source for public domain images. If you are uncertain about whether you may use an image you find on a website, it's best to either contact the site's owner or find another image to use. *If you copy and paste images you find while accessing other websites and use them for your own purposes, you may be violating copyright laws.*

FIGURE E-21: Example of a website with public domain images

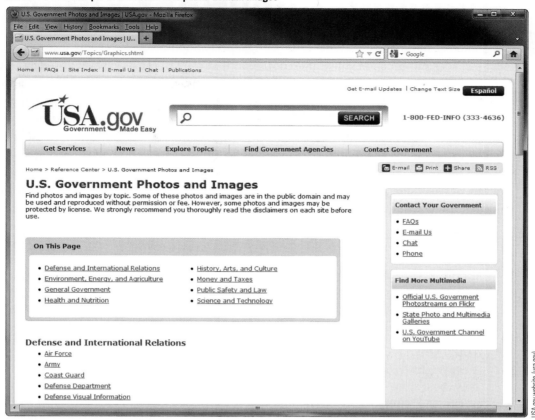

USA.gov website (usa.gov)

TABLE E-1: Common image file formats for images for web publication

format (file extension)	stands for	details
.jpg, .jpeg	Joint Photographic Experts Group	Pixel-based; a web standard. Can set image quality in pixels per inch (ppi), which affects file size. Supports millions of colors. Use for full-color images, such as photographs with large tonal range and those with lifelike artwork. This format is a good choice when targeting mobile devices.
.png	Portable Network Graphics	Can be compressed for storage and quicker download, without loss of picture quality. Supports variable levels of transparency and control of image brightness on different computers. Used for small graphics, such as bullets, as well as for complex photographic images. This format is also a good choice for targeting mobile devices. Not all browsers support the .png file format.
.gif	Graphics Interchange Format	Limited to 256 colors. Low color quality and limited detail are not suitable for printing. Small file size means faster transmission. Suitable for images with only a few colors, such as cartoons, simple illustrations, icons, buttons, and horizontal rules. This format is used for transparent images.

Examine Copyright Rules

The Internet has made it possible to locate compelling and media-rich content to use on websites. But just because you find content does not mean that you can use it however you want or under any circumstance. Learning about copyright law can help you decide whether and how to use content created and published by someone other than yourself. Before you decide whether to use media you find on a website, you must decide whether you can comply with its licensing agreement. A **licensing agreement** is the permission given by a copyright holder that conveys the right to use the copyright holder's work under certain conditions. Websites have rules that govern how a user may use its content, known as **terms of use**. Figures E-22 and E-23 are good examples of clear terms of use for the Library of Congress website. You decide to do some research on copyright law in relation to downloaded content from the Internet. There are several concepts to understand.

- **Intellectual property**

  Intellectual property is a product resulting from human creativity. It can include inventions, movies, songs, designs, clothing, and so on. The purpose of copyright law is to promote progress in society—not expressly to protect the rights of copyright owners. However, you should always assume that the majority of work you might want to download and use in a project is protected by either copyright or trademark law.

- **Copyright**

  A **copyright** protects the particular and tangible expression of an idea, not the idea itself. If you wrote a story about aliens crashing in Roswell, New Mexico, no one could copy or use your specific story without permission. However, anyone could write a story using a similar plot or characters—the actual idea is not copyright-protected. Generally, copyright protection in the United States lasts for the life of the author plus 70 years (most countries have similar regulations). A copyright attaches to a work as soon as it is created; you do not have to register it with the U.S. Copyright Office.

- **Trademark**

  A **trademark** protects an image, word, slogan, symbol, or design used to identify goods or services. For example, the Nike swoosh and the Google logo are images protected by trademark. Trademark protection lasts for 10 years, with 10-year renewal terms; it can last indefinitely provided the trademark is in active use.

- **Fair use**

  The law builds in limitations to copyright protection. One limitation to copyright is fair use. **Fair use** allows limited use of copyright-protected work. For example, you could excerpt short passages of a film or song for a class project. Determining if fair use applies to a work depends on the purpose of its use, the nature of the copyrighted work, how much you want to copy, and the effect on the market or value of the work. There is no clear formula on what constitutes fair use. It is always decided by the courts on a case-by-case basis. Except in cases of fair use, you must obtain permission from the copyright holder to use the work.

- **Derivative work**

  A **derivative work** is a work based on another pre-existing work, such as a movie adaptation of a book or a new musical arrangement of an existing song. Derivative works are included in the six rights of a copyright owner: reproduction (including downloading), creation of derivative works, distribution to the public, public performance, public display, and public performance by digital audio transmission of sound recordings. By default, only a copyright holder can create a derivative work of his or her original work.

- **Public domain**

  Work that is not protected by copyright is said to be in the public domain. Anyone can use it however they wish for any purpose, free of charge. In general, photos and other media on federal government websites are in the public domain, but some may have third-party ownership, so it's best to verify before you use them. For instance, there could be a photograph on the page that has a copyright restriction attached to it by the photographer. Websites will often state if their images or other content are in the public domain.

FIGURE E-22: Example of a website with a legal policy statement

Link to legal policy statement

Library of Congress website (loc.gov)

FIGURE E-23: Library of Congress legal policies

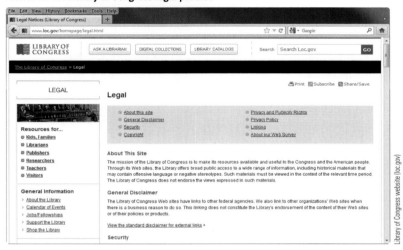

Library of Congress website (loc.gov)

Using proper methods to cite content

The familiar © symbol (or the word *Copyright*) is no longer required to indicate copyrighted materials, nor does it automatically register your work, but it does serve a useful purpose. When you post or publish the copyright term or symbol, you are stating clearly to those who may not know anything about copyright law that this work is claimed by you and is not in the public domain. If someone violates your copyright, your case is made even stronger if your notice is clearly visible. That way, violators can never claim ignorance of the law as an excuse for infringing. Common notification styles include using the word *Copyright* with the year, as in "Copyright 2013, Course Technology," or by using the copyright symbol ©, as in "© 2013 Course Technology."

You must provide proper citation for materials you incorporate into your own work. The following source was used for this lesson content and is referenced as follows:

- Waxer, Barbara M., and Baum, Marsha L. 2006. *Internet Surf and Turf – The Essential Guide to Copyright, Fair Use, and Finding Media.* Boston: Thomson Course Technology.

In addition to words that you quote verbatim, copyrights apply to ideas that you summarize or paraphrase. One prominent set of guidelines for how to cite material found in print or on the web (including text, images, sound, video, blogs, email and text messages, and so forth) is produced by the American Psychological Association (APA). To view these guidelines in detail, go to the APA website at apastyle.org. Other widely used guidelines are available from the Modern Language Association (mla.org) and the Chicago Manual of Style (chicagomanualofstyle.org).

Practice

Concepts Review

Label each element shown in Figure E-24.

FIGURE E-24

1. _____   5. _____
2. _____   6. _____
3. _____   7. _____
4. _____   8. _____

Match each of the following terms with the statement that best describes it.

9. **Assets panel**
10. **JPG**
11. **Aligning an image**
12. **Derivative work**
13. **Favorites list**
14. **Refresh button**
15. **Trademark**
16. **Copyright**
17. **Alternate text**
18. **Border**

a. Positioning an image on a page

b. Updates the current list of assets in the Assets panel

c. Includes only those assets designated as Favorites

d. Protects an image, word, slogan, symbol, or design used to identify goods or services

e. A work based on another pre-existing work

f. Used by screen readers to describe an image

g. A frame placed around an image

h. An image file format

i. Protects the particular and tangible expression of an idea, not the idea itself

j. Lists all the assets of the website, including favorites

Select the best answer from the list of choices.

19. The following category is not found on the Assets panel:

   a. URLs

   b. Colors

   c. Tables

   d. Movies

20. When you no longer need files in a website, you should:

   a. leave them in the Assets panel.

   b. drag them off the page to the Recycle bin.

   c. place them in the Site list.

   d. delete them from the site.

21. Background images:

   a. are never appropriate.

   b. are always appropriate.

   c. should be used carefully.

   d. cannot be added with a CSS rule.

22. The following image file format is not appropriate to use for web publication:

   a. jpg.

   b. gif.

   c. png.

   d. bmp.

Skills Review

Important: *If you did not create this website in Unit B and maintain it during the preceding units, you will need to create a local site root folder for this website and define the website using files your instructor will provide. See the "Read This Before You Begin" section in this book for more detailed instructions.*

1. **Insert an image.**
   a. Start Dreamweaver.
   b. Open the Blooms & Bulbs website.
   c. Open dwe_2.html from the drive and folder where you store your Unit E Data Files, then save it as **plants.html** in the Blooms & Bulbs website, overwriting the existing plants.html file but not updating the links.
   d. Close dwe_2.html.
   e. Insert the rose_bud.jpg file from the assets folder in the drive and folder where you store your Unit E Data Files, in front of the words *Who can resist....* (Enter alternate text, if prompted.)
   f. Insert the rose_bloom.jpg file in front of the words *For ease of growing....* (Enter alternate text, if prompted.)
   g. Insert the two_roses.jpg file in front of the words *The Candy Cane....* (Enter alternate text, if prompted.)
   h. Attach the blooms_styles.css file to the plants page.
   i. Apply the body_text style to all of the paragraph text on the page.
   j. Apply the HTML Heading 1 format to the text *Featured Spring Plant: Roses!*
   k. Save your work.

2. **Align an image.**
   a. Add a new class rule named img_left_float that adds a float property with a left value.
   b. Add another class rule named img_right_float that adds a float property with a right value.
   c. Apply the img_left_float rule to the rose_bud and two_roses images.
   d. Apply the img_right_float rule to the rose_bloom image, then save your work.

3. **Enhance an image.**
   a. Edit the img_left_float rule to add a border to all sides of an image with the following settings: Style=solid; Width=thin; Color=#333.
   b. Edit the Box Margin property to add a 10px margin to the right side only, then save your changes.
   c. Repeat Step a to add the same border to the img_right_float rule.
   d. Edit the Box Margin property of the img_right_float rule to add a 10px margin to the left side only, then save your changes.
   e. Save your work, preview it in the browser, then compare your screen to Figure E-25.

4. **Use alternate text.**
   a. If you did not add alternate text in Step 1 above, select the rose_bud.jpg image, then use the Property inspector to enter **Rose bud on bird bath** as alternate text.
   b. If necessary, add the alternate text **Rose bloom** for the rose_bloom.jpg image, and **Candy Cane Floribunda** for the two_roses.jpg image.
   c. If necessary, edit the website preferences to set the Accessibility prompt for images.
   d. Save your work.

Skills Review (continued)

5. View the Assets panel.

   a. Display the Assets panel, if necessary.

   b. View the Images list to verify that there are five images in the list. Refresh the Images list, if necessary.

   c. View the Colors list to verify that there are three websafe colors.

6. Insert a background image.

   a. Use Page Properties to insert the lady_in_red file as a background image and refresh the Assets panel. (This file is in the assets folder in the drive and folder where you store your Unit E Data Files.)

   b. Save the page, then view it in your browser.

   c. Close the browser window.

   d. Remove the lady_in_red.jpg image from the background by deleting the internal body rule it created, then save your work.

7. Delete image files from a website.

   a. Delete the lady_in_red.jpg file from the Files panel.

   b. Refresh the Files panel and verify that the lady_in_red.jpg file has been removed from the site. (You may have to re-create the site cache.)

   c. Preview the page in the browser, compare your screen with Figure E-25, and close the browser. (Your text may wrap differently.)

   d. Close the page, Exit (Win) or Quit (Mac) Dreamweaver.

FIGURE E-25

Featured Spring Plant: Roses!

Who can resist the romance of roses? Poets have waxed poetically over them throughout the years. Many persons consider the beauty and fragrance of roses to be unmatched in nature. The varieties are endless, ranging from floribunda to hybrid teas to shrub roses to climbing roses. Each variety has its own personality and preference in the garden setting. Pictured on the left is a Summer Breeze Hybrid Tea bud. This variety is fast growing and produces spectacular blooms that are beautiful as cut flowers in arrangements. The enchanting fragrance will fill your home with summer sweetness. They require full sun. Hybrid teas need regular spraying and pruning, but will reward you with classic blooms that will be a focal point in your landscaping and provide you with beautiful arrangements in your home. They are well worth the effort!

For ease of growing, Knock Out® roses are some of our all-time favorites. Even beginners will not fail with these garden delights. They are shrub roses and prefer full sun, but can take partial shade. They are disease resistant and drought tolerant. You do not have to be concerned with either black spot or dead-heading with roses such as the Knock out®, making them an extremely low-maintenance plant. They are also repeat bloomers, blooming into late fall. The shrub can grow quite large, but can be pruned to any size. The one you see on the right is Southern Belle. Check out all our varieties as you will not fail to have great color with these plants.

The Candy Cane Floribunda shown on the left is a beautiful rose with cream, pink, and red stripes and swirls. They have a heavy scent that will remind you of the roses you received on your most special occasions. These blooms are approximately four inches in diameter. They bloom continuously from early summer to early fall. The plants grow up to four feet tall and three feet wide. They are shipped bare root in February.

Important: *If you did not create the following websites in Unit B and maintain them during the preceding units, you will need to create a local site folder for the websites in the following exercises and define the sites using files your instructor will provide. See the "Read This Before You Begin" section for more detailed instructions.*

Independent Challenge 1

You have been hired to create a website for a river expedition company named Rapids Transit, located on the Buffalo River in Arkansas. In addition to renting canoes, kayaks, and rafts, they have lodging for overnight stays. River guides are available, if requested, to accompany clients on float trips. The clients range from experienced floaters to beginners. The owner's name is Mike Andrew. Mike has asked you to develop the page that introduces the Rapids Transit guides available for float trips. Refer to Figure E-26 as you work on this page.

a. Start Dreamweaver and open the Rapids Transit website.

b. Open dwe_3.html from the drive and folder where you store your Unit E Data Files and save it in the Rapids Transit website as **guides.html**, overwriting the existing file but not updating links.

c. Close dwe_3.html.

d. Check the path for the Rapids Transit banner and reset the path to the assets folder for the website, if necessary.

e. Attach the rapids_transit.css style sheet, then save your work.

f. Insert the image river_guide.jpg at an appropriate place on the page. (This file is in the assets folder in the drive and folder where you store your Unit E Data Files.)

g. Create alternate text for the river_guide.jpg image, then create a rule to add an image border, float, and margins with settings of your choice, then apply the new rule to the image.

h. Apply the Heading 1 format to the menu bar and the body_text style to the paragraph text.

i. Add a heading above the first paragraph and apply the Heading 2 rule to it.

j. Save your work, preview the page in the browser, then compare your workspace to Figure E-26. (Your image location, border size, and vertical and horizontal space settings may differ.)

k. Close the browser and Exit (Win) or Quit (Mac) Dreamweaver.

FIGURE E-26

Home — River Guides — Rates — Lodging — Before You Go

Our Guides

We have four of the best river guides you will ever find — Buster, Tucker, Max, and Scarlett. Buster has been with us for fourteen years and was born and raised here on the river. Tucker joined us two years ago "from off" (somewhere up north), but we've managed to make a country boy out of him! Max and Scarlett are actually distant cousins and joined us after they graduated from college last year. They're never happier than when they're out on the water floating and fishing. Each of our guides will show you a great time on the river.

Our guides will pack your supplies, shuttle you to the put-in point, maneuver the raging rapids for you, and then make sure someone is waiting at the take-out point to shuttle you back to the store. They haven't lost a customer yet! Give us a call and we'll set up a date with any of these good people. Here's a photo of Buster showing off his stuff. The river is always faster and higher in the spring. If you want to take it a little slower, come visit us in the summer or fall. Leave your good camera at home, though, no matter what the time of the year. You may get wet! Life jackets are provided and we require that you wear them while on the water. Safety is always our prime concern.

© 2013 Cengage Learning
Original photos courtesy of Sherry Bishop

Independent Challenge 2

Your company is designing a new website for TripSmart, a travel outfitter. TripSmart specializes in travel products and services. In addition to selling travel products, such as luggage and accessories, they sponsor trips and offer travel advice. Their clients range from college students to families and vacationing professionals. You are now ready to work on the destinations page. Refer to Figure E-27 as you work through the following steps.

a. Start Dreamweaver and open the TripSmart website.

b. Open dwe_4.html from the drive and folder where you store your Unit E Data Files and save it in the TripSmart website as **tours.html**, overwriting the existing tours file but not updating links.

c. Close dwe_4.html.

d. Check the path for the TripSmart banner and reset the path to the assets folder for the website, if necessary.

e. Attach the tripsmart_styles.css file to the page, then apply the HTML Heading 1 format to the Destination: The Galapagos heading and the body_text style to the rest of the text on the page. (*Hint*: You probably formatted your styles differently from the example, so your text may look different than Figure E-27.)

f. Change the site preferences to prompt you to add alternate text as you add new images to the website, if necessary.

g. Insert the images iguana_and_lizard.jpg and blue_footed_booby.jpg at the appropriate places on the page, adding alternate text for each image. (These files are in the assets folder in the drive and folder where you store your Unit E Data Files.)

h. Create a new CSS rule to format each image, then apply one to each image.

i. Save your work, preview the page in the browser, then compare your page to Figure E-27 for one possible design solution.

j. Close the browser and Exit (Win) or Quit (Mac) Dreamweaver.

FIGURE E-27

Destination: The Galápagos

We have a really special trip planned for next February. We have reserved ten cabins on the ship *The Wanderer* to explore the Galápagos Islands. The departure date is February 5 and the return date is February 21. This trip of a lifetime begins in Guayaquil, Ecuador. Guayaquil is a seaport on the southern coast of Ecuador. You will find it a vibrant center for business and tourism with lots of sites to explore. Stroll along the riverfront to enjoy colorful shops, lush parks, and street entertainment. After a night's rest, you will board your flight to Baltra Island in the Galápagos archipelago.

After arriving at Baltra's airport, you will board a bus for a short ride to the dock. Here you will find a welcoming committee of iguanas and sea lions. These natives love to sun on the docks and don't seem to mind sharing them with you as long as you don't come too close! *The Wanderer* is an exquisite touring ship licensed to explore the Galápagos by the Ecuadoran government. Tourism to the Galápagos is strictly regulated for the protection of the land, waters, and wildlife. You will use pangas for wet and dry landings to observe the wonderful variety of species of flora and fauna unique to the Galápagos, including the famous blue-footed booby. You will also have opportunities to swim, snorkel, and kayak with penguins. When your time on the ship ends, you will fly to Quito, the second-highest capital city in the world. Quito is a UNESCO World Heritage Site with beautiful colonial architecture. We recommend taking an extra day to explore its rich history and sample Ecuadoran cuisine.

To provide the finest in personal attention, this tour will be limited to no more than twenty people. The price schedule is as follows: Land Tour and Supplemental Group Air, $5,500.00; International Air, $1,350.00; and Single Supplement, $1,000.00. Entrance fees, hotel taxes, and services are included in the Land Tour price. Ship gratuities are also included for the Wanderer crew and guides. A deposit of $500.00 is required at the time the booking is made. Trip insurance and luggage insurance are optional and are also offered for an extra charge. A passport and visa will be required for entry into Ecuador. Call us at 555-555-0807 for further information and the complete itinerary from 8:00 a.m. to 6:00 p.m. (Central Standard Time).

Independent Challenge 3

Donna Stevens raises and shows horses professionally. She is learning how to use Dreamweaver to be able to create a website to showcase her horses. She would like to look at some other websites about horses to get a feel for the types of images she may want to use in her site. Use a word processor or paper to answer the questions below.

a. Connect to the Internet and go to USHorse.biz (ushorse.biz), as shown in Figure E-28.

b. How are background colors used? Would you have selected different ones? Why, or why not?

c. Evaluate the images used in the site. Do they add interest to the pages? Was alternate text used for any or all of the images?

d. How long did the home page take to download on your computer?

e. Are there too few images, too many, or just enough to add interest?

f. Go to Google (google.com) or Yahoo! (yahoo.com) to find another horse website.

g. Compare the site you found to the USHorse.biz site by answering questions b through e above.

FIGURE E-28

Website courtesy of USHorse.biz

Real Life Independent Challenge

This assignment will continue to build on the personal website that you created in Unit B. You have created and developed your index page. You have also added a page with either an ordered or an unordered list, and a CSS Style Sheet with a minimum of two rules. In this lesson, you work with one of the other pages of your site.

a. Consult your storyboard and decide which page you would like to develop in this lesson.

b. Create content for this page and format the text attractively on the page using CSS rules for all formatting.

c. Set the Accessibility option to prompt you for alternate text for new images added to the website, if necessary.

d. Add at least two images with appropriate alternate text. Resize the images in an image-editing program if they are too large to place on the page.

e. Use CSS rules to enhance the images to place them attractively on the page.

f. Document the source for the images and print some proof that they are in the public domain. Use your own photographs or drawings if you have difficulty obtaining public domain images.

g. Document the estimated download time for the page and the setting you used to estimate download time.

h. Save the file and preview the page in a browser.

After you are satisfied with your work, verify the following:

a. Each completed page has a page title.

b. All links work correctly.

c. The completed pages look good using a screen resolution of 1024 × 768.

d. All images are properly set showing a path to the assets folder of the website.

e. All images have alternate text and are legal to use.

Visual Workshop

Your company has been selected to design a website for Carolyne's Creations, a small catering business. Open your Carolyne's Creations website. Chef Carolyne has asked you to create a page that displays featured items in the kitchen shop. Open dwe_5.html from the drive and folder where your Unit E Data Files are stored. Save the file as **shop.html** in the Carolyne's Creations website, then add the peruvian_glass.jpg image from the drive and folder where you store your Unit E Data Files to create the page shown in Figure E-29. (*Hint*: You will need to attach the cc_styles.css style sheet to the page.) Apply the nav_bar rule to the menu bar, the body_text style to the paragraphs, and the Heading 1 HTML format to the heading "June Special: Peruvian Glasses". Use a CSS rule to add horizontal space and a border to the peruvian_glass image.

FIGURE E-29

Creating Links and Menu Bars

As you learned in Unit C, links are the real strength of a website, because they give users the freedom to open various web pages as they choose. You created a menu bar using a group of text links that helps users to navigate between pages of a website. In this unit, you will learn how to create a Spry menu bar and another type of link called an image map. A **Spry menu bar** is one of the preset widgets in Dreamweaver that creates a dynamic, user-friendly menu bar. A **widget** is a piece of code that allows users to interact with the program interface. An **image map** is an image with clickable areas defined on it that, when clicked, serve as links to take the user to another location. You begin working on the link structure for The Striped Umbrella website. You add links to area attractions on the activities page, create a menu bar that will be used on all pages in the website, create an image map, and run some site management reports.

OBJECTIVES

Understand links and paths

Create an external link

Create an internal link

Insert a named anchor

Create internal links to named anchors

Create a Spry menu bar

Add menu bar items

Format a menu bar

Copy a menu bar to other pages

Create an image map

Manage website links

Understanding Links and Paths

You can use two types of links (hyperlinks) on web pages. **Internal links** are links to web pages within the same website, and **external links** are links that connect to pages in other websites or to email addresses. Internal and external links both have two important parts that work together. The first part of a link is what the user actually sees and clicks, such as a word, an image, or a button. The second part of a link is the path, which is the name and physical location of the web page file that opens when the link is clicked. A link is classified as internal or external based on the information in its path. External paths reference links with a complete web address, while internal paths reference links with a partial address, based on the relation of the destination page to the page with the link. A link that returns an error message, or a broken link, occurs when files are renamed or deleted from a website, the filename is misspelled, or the website is experiencing technical problems. The majority of the time now you do not have to enter "http://" or "www" before a website URL when you are moving from site to site on the Internet. You spend some time studying the various types of paths used for internal and external links.

DETAILS

TROUBLE
The figures illustrating paths on page 133 are for illustrative purposes only. They are not intended to be working links.

- **Absolute paths**

  Absolute paths are used with external links. They reference links on web pages outside the current website, and include **"http"** (hypertext transfer protocol) and the **URL** (Uniform Resource Locator), or address, of the web page. When necessary, the web page filename and the folder hierarchy are also part of an absolute path. Figure F-1 shows an example of an absolute path.

- **Relative paths**

  Relative paths are used with internal links. They reference web pages and graphic files within one website and include the filename and the folder hierarchy where the file resides. Figure F-2 shows an example of a relative path. Relative paths are further classified as root-relative (relative to the local site root folder) and document-relative (relative to the current document).

- **Root-relative paths**

  Root-relative paths are referenced from a website's local site root folder. As shown in Figure F-3, a root-relative path begins with a forward slash, which represents the website's local site root folder. This method is used when several websites are published to one server, or when a website is so large that it uses more than one server.

- **Document-relative paths**

  Document-relative paths reference the path in relation to the web page that appears, and do not begin with a slash. A document-relative path includes only a filename if the referenced file resides in the same folder as the current web page. For example, index.html and spa.html both reside in the local site root folder for The Striped Umbrella. So you would simply type spa.html to link to the spa page from the index page. However, when an image is referenced in the assets folder, since the assets folder is a subfolder of the local site root folder, you must include the word assets/ (with the slash) in front of the filename, for example, assets/the_spa.jpg. See Figure F-4 for an example of a document-relative path.

  In the exercises in this book, you will use document-relative paths because it is assumed that you will not use more than one server to publish your websites. For this reason, it is very important to make sure that the Relative to text box in the Select File dialog box is set to Document, rather than Site Root, when creating links. This option can also be set in the Site Setup dialog box.

FIGURE F-1: **An example of an absolute path**

Protocol

Website URL

Path (folder name and filename)

© 2013 Cengage Learning

FIGURE F-2: **An example of a relative path**

Folder name

Filename

© 2013 Cengage Learning

FIGURE F-3: **An example of a root-relative path**

/downloads/lessons.html

© 2013 Cengage Learning

Begins with a forward slash

FIGURE F-4: **An example of a document-relative path**

downloads/lessons.html

© 2013 Cengage Learning

Begins with either a folder name or a filename

Design Matters

Ensuring error-free URLs

It is easy to make mistakes when you type long and complex URLs. One way to minimize errors is to copy and paste the URL of the web page that you would like to include as an external link in your website. To do this, open the web page then copy the link information in the Address text box (Internet Explorer) or the Location bar (Mozilla Firefox). Next, select the link text on your web page, then paste the link information in the Link text box in the HTML Property inspector. When you hear that text is "case sensitive," it means that the text will be treated differently when it is typed using uppercase letters rather than lowercase letters, or vice-versa. With some operating systems, such as Windows, it doesn't matter which case you use when you enter URLs. However, with other systems, such as UNIX, it does matter. To be sure that your links will work with all systems, use lowercase letters for all URLs. This is another good reason to select and copy a URL from the browser address bar, and then paste it in the Link text box or Dreamweaver code when creating an external link. You won't have to worry about missing a case change.

Creating an effective navigation structure

When you create a website, it's important to consider how your users will navigate from page to page within the site. A menu bar is a critical tool for moving around a site, so it's important that all text, buttons, and icons you use on a menu bar have a consistent look across all pages. If you use a complex menu bar, such as one that incorporates JavaScript or Flash, it's a good idea to include plain text links in another location on the page for accessibility. Otherwise, users might become confused or lost within the site.

A navigation structure can include more links than those included on a menu bar, however. For instance, it can contain other sets of links that relate to the content of specific pages. They can be placed at the bottom or sides of a page in a different format. No matter how you decide to design your navigation structure, make sure that every page includes a link back to the home page.

Other good navigation strategies that promote accessibility include adding keyboard equivalents for navigation elements, labeling all links, and incorporating jump menus to enable users to skip to links.

Creating an External Link

As you have learned, external links use absolute paths, which must include the complete name and path of the web address to link to the destination web page successfully. Because the World Wide Web is a constantly changing environment, you should check external links frequently. Websites may be up one day and down the next. If a website changes server locations or shuts down because of technical difficulties, the links to it may become broken. An external link can also become broken when an Internet connection is not working properly. Broken links, like misspelled words on a web page, indicate that the website is not being maintained diligently. Guests staying at The Striped Umbrella often ask for information about family activities in the surrounding area. Links to interesting attractions are helpful not only to currently registered guests, but to attract potential ones as well. You decide to create external links on the activities page that link to two websites for area attractions.

STEPS

1. **Open The Striped Umbrella website, open dwf_1.html from the drive and folder where you store your Unit F Data Files, then save it as activities.html in the striped_umbrella local site root folder, overwriting the existing file but not updating links**

   The new activities page opens in Design view. The activities page describes two popular area attractions of interest to resort guests. There are two broken image placeholders that represent images that must be copied to the website.

2. **Close dwf_1.html**

3. **Select the first broken image placeholder, click the Browse for File button 🗁 next to the Src text box in the Property inspector, select family_sunset.jpg from the assets folder in the location where you store your Unit F Data Files, click OK (Win) or Open (Mac) to save the image in your assets folder, then click to the right of the placeholder**

   The family_sunset image is copied to the website assets folder and now appears on the page.

4. **Select the second broken image placeholder, then repeat Step 3 to place the second image, two_dolphins.jpg on the page**

5. **Attach the su_styles.css file, then apply the body_text style to the paragraphs of text on the page (not to the menu bar)**

6. **Apply the img_left_float rule to the first image and the img_right_float rule to the second image**

7. **Scroll to the bottom of the page if necessary, then select the Blue Angels text in the second to the last paragraph on the page**

   You use the Blue Angels text to create an external link to the Blue Angels website.

8. **Click the Link text box in the HTML Property inspector, type http://www.blueangels.navy.mil, compare your screen to Figure F-5, then press [Tab]**

   The Blue Angels text is now a link to the Blue Angels website.

9. **Click File on the Menu bar, click Save, click the Preview/Debug in browser button ⚙., click Preview in [your browser], click Blue Angels on the web page, verify that the link works, then close your browser window**

10. **Scroll to the bottom of the page if necessary, select the USS Alabama text in the last paragraph on the page, then repeat Step 8 to create the link for the USS Alabama text, using the URL http://www.ussalabama.com**

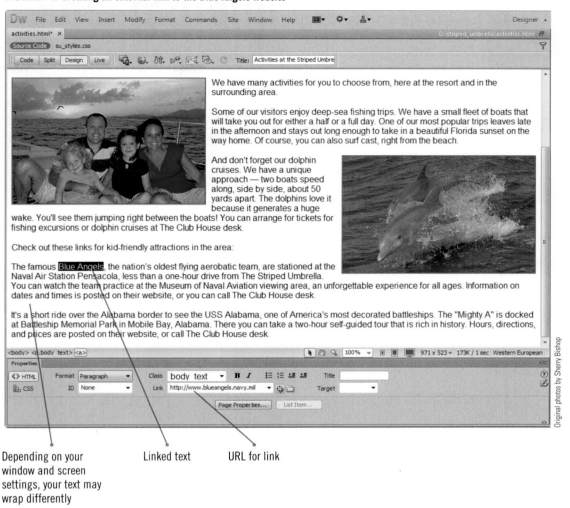

Depending on your
window and screen
settings, your text may
wrap differently

Linked text

URL for link

Design Matters

Understanding The Web Accessibility Initiative - Accessible Rich Internet Applications Suite

The Web Accessibility Initiative - Accessible Rich Internet Applications Suite (WAI-ARIA) is a resource for applying best practices when adding advanced user interface controls to a website. Functions such as drag-and-drop or browsing through a menu can be very difficult for users who rely on assistive devices to navigate a site. WAI-ARIA, at w3.org/WAI, provides guidelines and techniques for planning and implementing accessible content. It also provides presentations, handouts, and tutorials for developers who are interested in learning how to provide content that can be easily navigated by all users, such as providing alternative keyboard navigation for web objects primarily designed to function using mouse clicks. The information offered through WAI-ARIA is developed by the Protocols and Formats Working Group (PFWG), a part of the World Wide Web Consortium (W3C).

Creating an Internal Link

As you know, a website usually contains individual pages for each category or major topic covered in the site. Within those pages, internal links are used to provide a way to move quickly from page to page. The home page should provide intuitive navigation to individual pages for each category or major topic covered in a website. A good rule of thumb is to design your site so that users are never more than two or three clicks away from the page they are seeking. Refer to your wireframe frequently as you create pages to help manage your site's navigation structure. ⬛⬛⬛ You want to create an easy way for users to access the fishing and cruises pages from the activities page, so you create internal links on the activities page that will link to each of them.

STEPS

1. **Using Figure F-6 as a reference, select fishing excursions in the third paragraph**
   You use the fishing excursions text to create an internal link to the fishing page.

QUICK TIP
You can also select the file to which you want to link in the Files panel and drag it to the Link text box or use the Point to File button 🎯 in the Property inspector to create an internal link.

2. **Click the Browse for File button 🗀 next to the Link text box in the HTML Property inspector, make sure the Relative to text box is set to Document, then double-click fishing.html in The Striped Umbrella local site root folder in the Select File dialog box**
   Since you designated the fishing.html page as the target for the fishing excursions link, fishing.html is listed in the Link text box in the HTML Property inspector, as shown in Figure F-6.

3. **Select dolphin cruises in the same sentence**
   You use the dolphin cruises text to create an internal link to the cruises page.

4. **Click 🗀 in the Property inspector, double-click cruises.html in the Select File dialog box, then save your work**
   The dolphin cruises text is now an internal link to the cruises page in The Striped Umbrella website. There are now nine links on the activities page: seven internal links (five on the menu bar and two in the paragraph text linking to the fishing and cruises pages), and two external links (the Blue Angels and USS Alabama websites), as shown in Figure F-7.

5. **Close the activities page**

Design Matters

Linking to the home page

Every page in your website should include a link to the home page so a user who has become "lost" in your site can quickly go back to the starting point without relying on the Back button. Don't make users rely on the Back button on the browser toolbar to find their way back to the home page. It's possible that the user's current page might have opened as a result of a search and clicking the Back button will take the user out of the your website, which is not a good thing.

FIGURE F-6: Creating an internal link on the activities page

Selected text used for the link

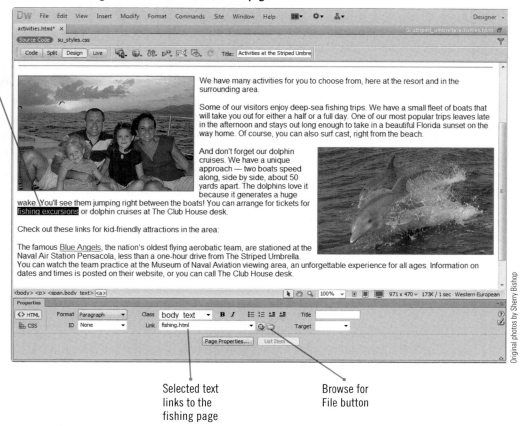

Selected text links to the fishing page

Browse for File button

FIGURE F-7: Viewing the internal and external links on the activities page

Internal links

External links

Inserting a Named Anchor

Some web pages have so much content that users must scroll repeatedly to get to information at the top and bottom of the page. To make it easier for users to navigate to specific areas of a page without scrolling, you can use a combination of internal links and named anchors. A **named anchor** is a specific location on a web page that is represented by a tag and an assigned descriptive name. You then create internal links on the page that the user clicks to browse to the named anchor location. For example, you can insert a named anchor called "top" at the top of a web page, then create a link at the bottom of the page that, when clicked, will display the anchor location (the top of the web page) when viewed in the browser. You can also insert named anchors at strategic places on a web page, such as before paragraph headings. The name chosen for a named anchor should be short and reflect its page location. Also, you should use only lowercase characters; do not use spaces or special characters, or begin an anchor name with a number. The logical order for creating and linking to named anchors is to create a named anchor before you create its link to avoid possible errors. The Spa Services categories on the spa page contain lists of the names and descriptions of the services offered for each category. To allow users to quickly find the services they are interested in without scrolling up and down the page, you insert four named anchors on the spa page: one for the top of the page and the other three for the Massages, Facials, and Body Treatments lists of services.

STEPS

1. **Open the spa.html page, click View on the Menu bar, point to Visual Aids, then click Invisible Elements to select it, if necessary**
    The Invisible Elements menu item must be selected in order for named anchor locations to be visible on the page in Design view.

2. **Click The Striped Umbrella banner, then press the left arrow key on your keyboard**
    The location for the first named anchor is positioned at the top of the page directly before the banner.

3. **Click the Common category on the Insert panel, if necessary**
    The command for inserting a named anchor object is located in the Common category on the Insert panel.

    > **TROUBLE**
    > If you don't see the Named Anchor icon on the page, make sure that Invisible Elements is selected in the Visual Aids menu.

4. **Click Named Anchor on the Insert panel, type top in the Anchor name text box in the Named Anchor dialog box, as shown in Figure F-8, then click OK**
    The Named Anchor icon appears before The Striped Umbrella banner. It may be above it or to the left of it depending on the size of your Document window in the workspace.

5. **Click to place the insertion point to the left of the Massages heading above the first unordered list, click Named Anchor on the Insert panel, type massages in the Anchor name text box, then click OK**
    The second named anchor appears before the Massages heading.

6. **Repeat Step 5 to insert named anchors to the left of the Facials and Body Treatments list headings, using the following names: facials and body_treatments, deselect the text, then click the body_treatments named anchor to select it**
    Named anchors appear blue when selected and yellow when not selected, as shown in Figure F-9. The name of the selected anchor appears in the Property inspector.

7. **Save your work**

FIGURE F-8: Named Anchor dialog box

Anchor name text box

Named Anchor command

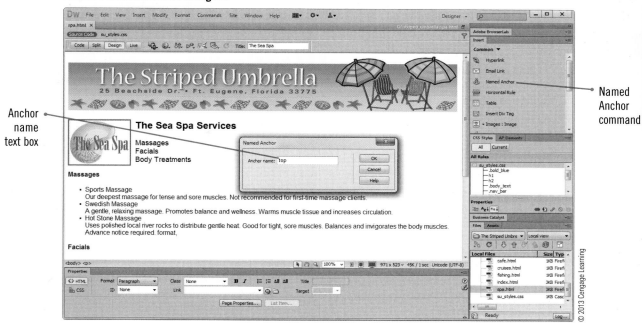

FIGURE F-9: Named anchor icons

Named anchors

Selected named anchor

Name of selected named anchor

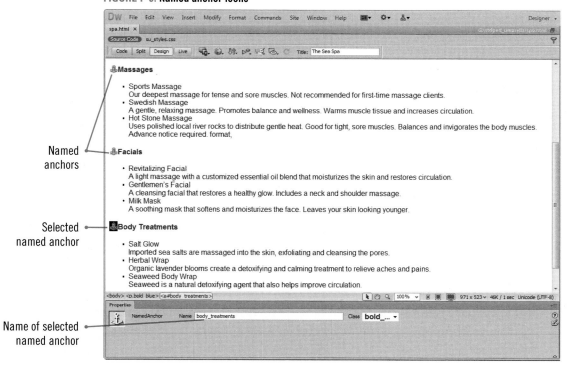

Using Visual Aids

The Visual Aids submenu on the View menu gives you several choices for displaying page elements in Design View, such as named anchor icons. Named anchor icons are considered invisible elements. When you check the Invisible Elements option, you will see the named anchor icons on the page. The icons do not appear when the page is viewed in a browser. Turning on visual aids makes it easier to edit the page. Other options in the Visual Aids menu are Fluid Grid Layout Guides, CSS Layout Backgrounds, CSS Layout Box Model, CSS Layout Outlines, AP Element Outlines, Table Widths, Table Borders, Frame Borders, and Image Maps. The Hide All option hides all of these page elements.

Creating Internal Links to Named Anchors

Named anchors act as targets for internal links. A **target** is the location on a web page that displays in the browser when a link is clicked. You can either drag a filename from the Files panel to selected text or use the Point to File button in the Property inspector to connect an internal link to a named anchor. Now that the named anchors are in place, you are ready to set up links for users to quickly access the information on the spa page. You want to create internal links for the four named anchors and link them to each named anchor on the page. You also decide to create a text link at the bottom of the page to make it easy for users to return to the top of the page.

TROUBLE

The line pointing from the Point to File button to the Massages heading may differ slightly in appearance depending on whether you are using a Mac or Windows.

1. **Using Figure F-10 as a guide, select the Massages heading to the right of The Sea Spa logo, then click and drag the Point to File button 🔘 in the HTML Property inspector on top of the massages named anchor in front of the Massages heading, as shown in Figure F-10**

   The named anchor, massages, is the target for the massages link. When viewing the spa page in the browser, the list of massages will display at the top of the window when Massages is clicked. The name of a named anchor is always preceded by a pound (#) sign in the Link text box in the HTML Property inspector, as shown in Figure F-10.

2. **Repeat Step 1 to create internal links for the Facials and Body Treatments headings by first selecting each heading next to the logo, then clicking and dragging 🔘 to the facials and body_treatments named anchors**

   The Facials and Body Treatments headings are now links to the Facials and Body Treatments unordered lists of services.

3. **Click at the end of the last line on the page, press [Enter] (Win) or [return] (Mac), then type Return to top of page**

   The Return to top of page text will be used to link to the named anchor at the top of the page. If the text you want to use for a link to a named anchor and the named anchor itself are far apart on the page, you can scroll up or down the page as much as you need to and still use 🔘 to create the link. As long as the text is still selected, it is not necessary to be able to see it when you point to the named anchor.

4. **Repeat Step 1 again to link the Return to top of page text to the named anchor in front of the banner**

   The top of page text is now a link to the top named anchor to the left of the banner at the top of the page.

QUICK TIP

To enable or disable the Code Navigator, click View on the Menu bar, click Code Navigator, then click the Disable check box. It takes a second or two for the Code Navigator to appear.

5. **Click anywhere in the Return to top of page text, wait for a few seconds until the Click indicator to bring up the Code Navigator icon 🕸 appears, then click 🕸**

   The Code Navigator, as shown in Figure F-11, indicates that the Return to top of page text has the body and body_text rules applied to it. When you placed the insertion point at the end of the paragraph and entered a paragraph break, the formatting was retained for the Return to top of page text.

6. **Save your work, preview the spa page in your browser, test each link, then close your browser**

   The page can only scroll as far as there is text on the page, so you may not see much change depending on your window size.

FIGURE F-10: Using the Point to File icon

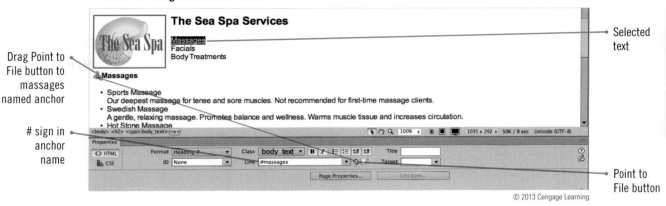

Selected text

Drag Point to File button to massages named anchor

sign in anchor name

Point to File button

© 2013 Cengage Learning

FIGURE F-11: Code Navigator displaying rule name

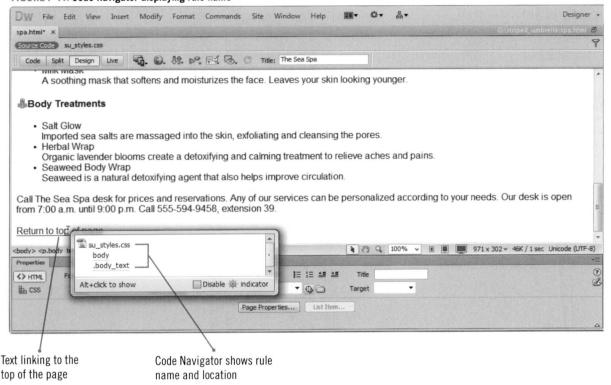

Text linking to the top of the page

Code Navigator shows rule name and location

Using the Code Navigator

When you click on a page element either in Code view or in Design view, wait a second or two; the Click indicator to bring up the Code Navigator icon will appear (you can also [Alt]-click (Win) or [Ctrl]-click (Mac) to display it instantly). Clicking will open a pop-up window called the Code Navigator. As you recall from Unit C, the Code Navigator lists the CSS rule name linked to the page element, along with the name of the style sheet that contains the rule. Pointing to the rule name will display the properties and values of the rule, as shown in Figure F-12. This is a quick way to view the rule definition. If you click the rule name, the code for the rule will open in Code and Design views, where you can then edit it.

FIGURE F-12: Code Navigator displaying rule properties

Pointing to the rule displays its properties and values

Mac users will see Cmd+Opt+click to show

Creating a Spry Menu Bar

Recall from Unit C that a menu bar is a set of text or image links that can be used to navigate between pages of a website. To make your site more visually appealing, you can use special effects to create a more professional look for your menu bars. One way to do this is to insert a Spry menu bar. A Spry menu bar is a type of menu bar that uses unordered lists, CSS, and Javascript to create an interactive menu bar with pull-down submenus. **Spry**, or **Spry framework**, is open source code developed by Adobe Systems to help designers quickly incorporate dynamic content on their web pages. Each link in a Spry menu bar is called an **item**. When you add a Spry menu bar, by default it first appears with placeholder text and generic settings for the menu bar properties, such as the width and background color for each item in the menu. The current menu bar for The Striped Umbrella site is a set of five text links. While they work perfectly well, you would like a more professionally designed look. You begin by creating a Spry menu bar that will contain five items: home, about us, cafe, spa, and activities.

STEPS

1. **Select the banner on the spa page, press the right arrow key, then press [Shift] [Enter] (Win) or [Shift] [return] (Mac)**

   The insertion point is positioned between the banner and the spa logo.

QUICK TIP
The Spry Menu Bar button is also in the Layout category on the Insert panel.

2. **Click the Insert panel list arrow on the Insert panel, click the Spry category, scroll down, if necessary, to click Spry Menu Bar, then click to select the Horizontal layout option button in the Spry Menu Bar dialog box, as shown in Figure F-13**

   The Horizontal layout option specifies that the menu bar will be placed horizontally on the page.

3. **Click OK**

   The Spry menu bar, which will be referred to from now on simply as the menu bar, displays selected under the banner. The menu bar contains four items by default and each item contains placeholder text, such as Item 1. Right above the upper left corner of the menu bar is the Spry menu bar label containing the default label name: MenuBar1. The Property inspector shows the menu bar properties. It lists the default items and submenu items, along with text boxes for linking each item and submenu item to the appropriate pages.

4. **Select MenuBar1 in the Menu Bar text box in the Property inspector, then type MenuBar**

   Item 1 is selected in the Item column (first column on the left) in the Property inspector.

5. **Select Item 1 in the Text text box in the right side of the Property inspector, type Home, select Item 1.1 in the first submenu column (second column) in the Property inspector, as shown in Figure F-14, then click the Remove menu Item button ▬ above the first submenu column**

   Item 1 is renamed Home and the default submenu item Item 1.1 is deleted.

QUICK TIP
You can add sub-menu items by click-ing the Add menu item button ➕.

6. **Click ▬ two more times**

   The remainder of the default submenu items—Item 1.2 and Item 1.3—for the Home item are deleted as well.

7. **Click the Browse for File button ▭ next to the Link text box in the Property inspector, double-click index.html in the local site root folder, then compare your Property inspector to Figure F-15**

   The Home item is linked to the home page.

QUICK TIP
If you have a gap between the banner and the menu bar, go to Code view to see if you have a <p> tag around the banner. If you do, delete the beginning and end-ing tag and the space will be removed.

8. **Click to place the insertion point to the right of the menu bar, enter a line break, compare your screen to Figure F-16, save your file, click OK to close the Copy Dependent Files dialog box, then refresh the Files panel if necessary**

   The menu bar displays with the first item named Home linked to the home page. The supporting files that are needed to format the Spry menu bar and make it function properly are added to the local site root folder. A new SpryAssets folder is added that contains a JavaScript file, a CSS file, and some images that are used in the Spry menu bar.

FIGURE F-13: **Spry Menu Bar dialog box**

Horizontal layout
option button

FIGURE F-14: **Property inspector with Menu Bar properties**

Menu Bar
text box

Home selected in
menu item column

Item 1.1 selected in
first submenu column

Remove menu
Item button

Text text box

FIGURE F-15: **Home item for the menu bar**

Browse for
File button

All submenu items
have been deleted

Link to index.html file

FIGURE F-16: **The Spry Menu bar on the spa page**

The named
anchor icon may
appear beside the
banner, depend-
ing on the width
of the window

Spry Menu
Bar label

Item 1 is
renamed
"Home"

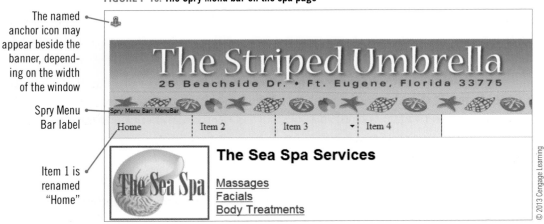

© 2013 Cengage Learning

Inserting a Fireworks menu bar

Another option for adding a menu bar to your page is to create a menu bar in Adobe Fireworks, open Dreamweaver, then import the menu bar onto the web page. Once you've created the Fireworks menu bar, you export the Fireworks file to a Dreamweaver local site root folder. This file contains the HTML code that defines the menu bar properties. Next, open the appropriate web page in Dreamweaver where you want to insert the menu bar, then use the Insert > Image Objects > Fireworks HTML command to add the HTML code to the page. You can also use Dreamweaver to import rollover images and buttons created in Fireworks.

Adding Menu Bar Items

After you create a menu bar, you can modify it by adding new menu items or submenu items or deleting those that you do not need. Submenus are also called **child menus**. Submenu items can also have submenus under them. The Property inspector is used to add, delete, rename, and link Spry menu items to pages in your website. You are ready to add the rest of the menu and submenu items to the menu bar so users will have access to each of the main pages from the menu bar. You want to rename the rest of the default menu items, add one additional menu item, then add two submenu items under the activities item for the cruises and fishing pages.

STEPS

1. **Click the Spry Menu Bar: MenuBar tab if necessary, then click Item 2 in the Item menu column (first column) in the Property inspector, select Item 2 in the Text text box, then type About Us**

   Item 2 is renamed About Us.

2. **Click the Browse button ☐ next to the Link text box, click about_us.html in the local site root folder, then click OK (Win) or Open (Mac) or double-click about_us.html**

   The About Us menu item is linked to the about_us page.

3. **Repeat Steps 1 and 2 to rename Item 3 Sand Crab Cafe and link it to the cafe.html page in the local site root folder**

4. **Delete each submenu item under the Sand Crab Cafe menu item, then click OK to close the warning box confirming the removal of each of the submenus**

   The submenu items under the Sand Crab Cafe menu item are deleted.

5. **Repeat Steps 1 and 2 to rename Item 4 The Sea Spa and link it to the spa.html page in the local site root folder**

   The Sea Spa menu item is linked to the spa page and remains selected in the Property inspector.

6. **Click the Add menu item button ➕ above the Item menu column (first column), select Untitled Item, in the Text text box type Activities, then link it to the activities.html page**

   The new menu item, Activities, is linked to the activities page and remains selected in the Property inspector.

7. **Click ➕ above the first submenu column (second column), select Untitled Item, type Cruises in the Text text box, then link it to the cruises.html page**

   A new submenu item, Cruises, is added under the Activities menu item that will link to the cruises page.

8. **Repeat Step 7 to add another submenu item named Fishing, link it to the fishing.html page, save your work, then compare your screen to Figure F-17**

   A second submenu item is added under the Activities menu item that will link to the fishing page.

9. **Create a new Tag rule in the su_styles.css file to modify the <img> tag, then set the Block Vertical-align to bottom**

   This rule will prevent a gap between the banner and menu bar.

TROUBLE
If a message appears that you need to install the Flash plug-in, go to adobe.com to download the plug-in or this feature will not work.

10. **Click the Switch Design View to Live View button ⬛ Live on the Document toolbar, view the menu bar, then compare your screen to Figure F-18**

    Live View shows you what the page will look like when opened in a browser. Not only is it a faster way to view your page than previewing it in a browser but it shows the interactive elements functioning. For more information about Live View read the Clues to Use box *Viewing your page in Live View*.

11. **Click ⬛ Live again**

    The spa page redisplays in your workspace in Design view without the interactive elements being functional.

FIGURE F-17: Adding menu items and submenu items to the menu bar

Menu item names   Submenu item names   Link to fishing page   Submenu items

FIGURE F-18: Viewing the spa page in Live View

Switch Design
View to Live
View button

Menu bar as
it will appear
in a browser

© 2013 Cengage Learning

Viewing your page in Live View

When you view your web pages in Dreamweaver, the page elements appear similar to the way they will look when viewed in a web browser. Live View gives you a more accurate picture of what the page will actually look like in a browser, with interactive elements active and functioning. You use the Switch Design View to Live View button on the Document toolbar to enable Live View. Next to this button is the Shows the Live View source in code view button, which displays the code. The code remains as read-only until you click the Shows the Live View source in code view

button again. When the Switch Design View to Live View button is active, the Shows the Live View source in code view button can be toggled on or off. If Live View is not active, selecting the Shows the Live View source in code view button will turn it on. When you first click the Live View button, you may see a message that you need to install the Flash plug-in from the Adobe website, adobe.com. Once you download the plug-in, your pages can then be viewed using Live View.

Formatting a Menu Bar

Once you create a Spry menu bar, you'll need to modify the default settings to adjust the appearance of the menu bar and its items. For example, you can adjust their height and width or specify the background color of each menu item. You can add special effects for menu bar items by changing the characteristics for each item's state. A **state** is the condition of the menu item relative to the mouse pointer. You can create a rollover effect by using different background and text colors for each state to represent how the menu item appears when users move their mouse over or away from it. The settings for the menu bar and menu items reside in CSS rules. To change them, you edit the default rules that were automatically created when the Spry menu bar was inserted on the page. 🔳🔳🔳 You format the Spry menu bar by editing the rules that control the appearance of the Spry menu bar items.

TROUBLE
If you don't see the rule listed, click the Switch to All (Document) Mode button [All] in the CSS Styles panel.

1. **Click the plus sign (Win) or right pointing arrow (Mac) next to SpryMenuBarHorizonal.css in the CSS Styles panel if necessary, select the rule ul.MenuBarHorizontal (the first rule listed in the style sheet), then click the Edit Rule button 🖉 on the CSS styles panel**
The CSS Rule Definition for ul.MenuBarHorizontal in SpryMenuBarHorizontal.css dialog box opens. This is where you define the global settings for all menu and submenu items.

2. **Click Type in the Category list, click the Font-family list arrow, click Arial, Helvetica, sans-serif, click the Font-size list arrow, click 14, click the Font-size unit of measure list arrow, click px, compare your screen to Figure F-19, then click OK**
The text size of the menu items becomes larger to reflect the new settings, which causes the text on the Sand Crab Cafe button to wrap to two lines. You want the menu bar to revert back to one line.

3. **Select the ul.MenuBarHorizontal li rule (the third rule listed) in the CSS Styles panel, click 🖉, click Box in the Category list, click the Width text box, type 190, click the Width unit of measure list arrow, click px, click in the Height text box, type 25, then compare your screen to Figure F-20**
The width of each menu item increases to 190 pixels wide and the height is set to 25 pixels.

4. **Click Block in the Category list, click the Text-align text box arrow, select center, then click OK**
The block settings include properties to change the spacing and alignment of the text in the menu bar. The Text-align setting adjusts the alignment of each text item on its "button." In this case, the menu items are set to appear centered within their button in the menu bar.

TROUBLE
If you don't see the u.MenuBarHorizontal a rule listed in the CSS Styles panel, click the Switch to (All) Document Mode button [All].

5. **Click ul.MenuBarHorizontal a (tenth rule) in the CSS Styles panel, click 🖉, click Type in the Category list, type #FFF in the Color text box replacing the current color, click Background in the Category list, type #09C in the Background-color text box, then click OK**
The menu items redisplay with white text on a blue background. This is how they appear in the menu bar when the mouse is *not* positioned over them.

QUICK TIP
To locate this rule, which is the longest rule, place your mouse over each rule name to see the extended names. You can also temporarily expand the CSS Styles panel width to see the entire name.

6. **Click ul.MenuBarHorizontal a.MenuBarItemHover, ul.MenuBarHorizontal a.MenuBarItemSubmenuHover, ul.MenuBarHorizontal a.MenuBarSubmenuVisible (twelfth rule) in the CSS Styles panel, then click 🖉**

7. **Click Type in the Category list, type #630 in the Color text box, click Background in the Category list, type #FC9 in the Background-color text box, then click OK**
The property values for the menu items and submenu items change to a sand background with brown text. This is how they appear when the mouse is positioned over them.

8. **Click File on the Menu bar, click Save All, preview your page in the browser, compare your screen to Figure F-21, test each link to ensure that each works correctly, then close the browser**
The button background colors are blue with white text when the pointer is not placed over them and sand-colored with brown text when the pointer is positioned over them.

FIGURE F-19: Adding properties for the .ulMenuBarHorizontal rule

Type category

Font-family list arrow

Font-size list arrow

Font-size unit of measure list arrow

FIGURE F-20: Modifying properties for the ul.MenuBarHorizontal li rule

Box category

Width text box

Height text box

Width unit of measure list arrow

FIGURE F-21: Spa page viewed in the browser with the updated menu bar

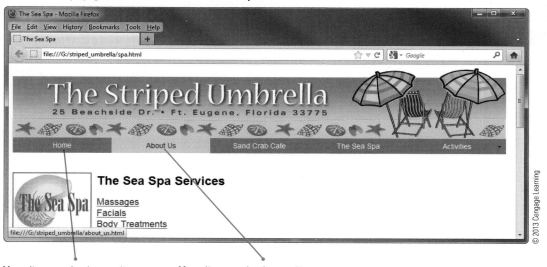

Menu items and submenu items are blue with white text when the pointer is not placed over them

Menu items and submenu items are sand colored with brown text when the pointer is placed over them

Creating Links and Menu Bars

Copying a Menu Bar to Other Pages

When you create a menu bar for one page in a website, you should copy it to all of the other pages in the site. This practice provides continuity in the navigation structure and makes it easy for users to navigate comfortably through pages in your site. ▨▨▨▨ The new Spry menu bar is an improvement over the menu bar with plain text links. You decide to replace all existing menu bars on the pages in the website with this menu bar to improve each page's design and promote consistency. You copy the menu bar to the about_us, index, and activities pages in The Striped Umbrella website.

STEPS

QUICK TIP

When you work on multiple open pages, use the file-name tabs at the top of the Document toolbar or press [Ctrl] [Tab] to move quickly between pages (Win).

1. **Click the Spry Menu Bar:MenuBar tab above the top left corner of the menu bar, as shown in Figure F-22, click Edit on the Menu bar, then click Copy**

   The menu bar is ready to be pasted on other pages in the website.

2. **Double-click activities.html on the Files panel**

   The activities page opens.

3. **Select the original menu bar on the page, click Edit on the Menu bar, click Paste, click to the right of the menu bar, add a line break, delete the horizontal rule, compare your screen to Figure F-23, then save the page**

   The new menu bar appears on the page in place of the previous one and the new styles are added to the page.

TROUBLE

If you have trouble with the alignment and spacing between the banner and the menu bar, look at the break tag after the banner. If it is on a separate line under the banner, move it to the end of the line of code for the banner.

4. **Open the index page, delete the current menu bar, delete any <p> tags around the banner, click the banner to select it, press the right arrow key, paste the Spry menu bar on the page, delete the horizontal rule, then insert a line break after the menu bar**

   The menu bar is pasted on the index page and the spacing after the menu bar is adjusted to match the other two pages.

5. **Open the about_us page, replace the current menu bar with the new menu bar, add a line break, delete the horizontal rule, then apply the body_text rule to the heading "Welcome guests!"**

   The menu bar is pasted on the about_us page, the horizontal rule is deleted, and the page heading is formatted to match the home, spa, and activities pages.

QUICK TIP

View the pages at a high resolution to ensure that the menu bars do not break into two lines.

6. **Click File on the Menu bar, click Save All, then preview each page in the browser**

   The menu bar appears consistently on the index, about_us, spa, and activities pages of The Striped Umbrella website. Although the cafe, fishing, and activities pages are not designed yet, you see that the links all work correctly. If the spacing between the menu bar and the rest of the page content is not consistent, add or remove <br> tags if necessary to adjust the spacing on each page.

7. **Hold the pointer over the Activities link, as shown in Figure F-24, close the browser, then close all open pages except the about_us page**

   When the pointer is placed over the Activities link, the submenu drops down with the two submenu links visible and active.

FIGURE F-22: Selecting the Spry menu bar on the spa page

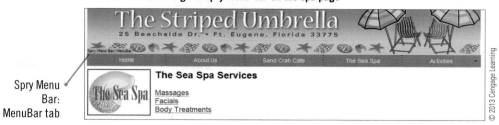

Spry Menu
Bar:
MenuBar tab

FIGURE F-23: Pasting the Spry menu bar on the activities page

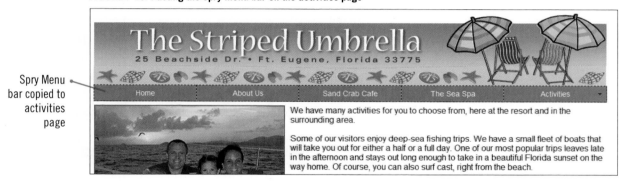

Spry Menu
bar copied to
activities
page

FIGURE F-24: Viewing the activities submenu items in the browser

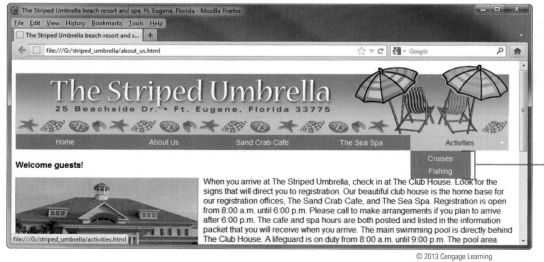

Submenu
items for
Cruises
and Fishing
pages

© 2013 Cengage Learning
Original photo courtesy of Sherry Bishop

Creating an Image Map

Another way to create navigation links for web pages is to create an image map. An image map is an image that has one or more hotspots placed on top of it. A **hotspot** is an active area on an image that, when clicked, links to a different location on the page or to another web page. For example, a map of the world could have a hotspot placed on each individual country so that users could click a country to link to more information. Hotspots are not visible in the browser window, but when users place their pointer over the hotspot, the pointer changes to a pointing finger, indicating the presence of a link. To create a hotspot, select the image on which you want to place the hotspot, draw the hotspot with one of the shape hotspot tools in the Property inspector, then add the link information, alternate text, and target information in the text boxes in the Property inspector. ⬛⬛⬛⬛ You want to create an image map on the activities page to provide another way for users to link to the index page.

STEPS

1. **Click The Striped Umbrella banner on the about_us page to select it, then double-click a blank area on the right side of the Property inspector to expand it, if necessary**

   The Property inspector displays the drawing tools for creating hotspots on an image in the lower-left corner.

TROUBLE
If you don't see the blue rectangle, click View, point to Visual Aids, then click Image Maps to select it.

2. **Click the Rectangle Hotspot Tool button ⬜ on the Property inspector, drag to create a rectangle that encompasses The Striped Umbrella name on the banner, release the mouse button, click OK to close the Dreamweaver dialog box, then compare your screen to Figure F-25**

   A shaded blue rectangle appears within the area that you outlined. This blue rectangle is the hotspot. The dialog box reminds you to add to the alternate text for the hotspot.

3. **Drag the Point to File button ⊚ next to the Link text box in the Property inspector to index.html in the Files panel**

   The hotspot is linked to the index.html file. If the hotspot is clicked, the index file opens.

TROUBLE
If you don't see the Map text box in the Property inspector, click the image map object on the banner to select it.

4. **Select Map in the Map text box in the Property inspector, then type home**

   The image map is named home. Each image map should have a unique name, especially if a page contains more than one image map.

5. **Click the Target list arrow in the Property inspector, then click _self**

   The _self target directs the browser to display the home page in the same browser window as the activities page, rather than opening a separate window. When the hotspot is clicked, the home page opens in the same browser window. See the Clues to Use box *Setting targets for links* to learn more about how the _self property, along with other property options, are used to set targets for links.

QUICK TIP
You should always assign a unique name for each image map to make them more accessible to users utilizing screen readers.

6. **Type Link to home page in the Alt text box in the Property inspector, as shown in Figure F-26**

   The descriptive information placed in the Alt text box provides a brief clue to the user about what further information awaits if the hotspot is clicked. The alternate text is also read by screen readers to tell users what will happen if they click the image map.

7. **Switch to Code view, locate the <br> tag that has been added below the ending </map> tag, then delete it**

8. **Place the insertion point right before the closing image tag for the banner, then type style="border:0"**

QUICK TIP
This additional code will prevent a border appearing around the banner in Internet Explorer.

9. **Return to Design view, save your work, preview the page in your browser window, test the link on the image map, then close the browser**

   The hotspot is not visible in the browser, but if you place the mouse over the hotspot, you will see the pointer change to 🖑 to indicate a link is present.

FIGURE F-25: Drawing a hotspot on The Striped Umbrella banner

Hotspot

Rectangle
Hotspot Tool

Pointer
Hotspot
Tool

Circle Hotspot Tool

Polygon Hotspot Tool

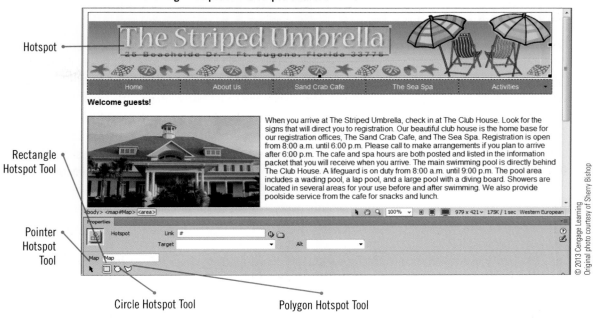

© 2013 Cengage Learning
Original photo courtesy of Sherry Bishop

FIGURE F-26: Adding a link, a target, and alternate text to a hotspot

Link text box

Target
text box

Alt
text box

Setting targets for links

You can set targets to determine how a new window will display in a browser when links on pages or in frames are clicked. A **frame** is a fixed region in a browser that can display a web page and act independently from other pages displayed in other frames within the browser. When you set a target for a link or frame, you have four options for how the new window will open after the link is clicked. These targets are set by clicking the Target list arrow in the HTML Property inspector and selecting the target you want. The _blank target displays the destination page in a separate browser window and leaves the original window open. The _parent target displays the destination page in the parent window or frameset, replacing the original window or frameset. The _self target displays the destination page in the same window or frame. The _top target displays the destination page in the whole browser window.

Design Matters

Creating and modifying hotspots

In addition to the Rectangle hotspot tool, ⬜ there are two other helpful shape tools: a Circle hotspot tool ⭕ and a Polygon hotspot tool ⬠. These tools can be used to create any shape hotspot that you need. For instance, the Polygon hotspot tool could be used to draw an outline around each state on a map of the United States. Hotspots can be easily changed and rearranged on an image using the Pointer hotspot tool ▸. First, select the hotspot you would like to edit, then drag one of the hotspot selector handles to change the size or shape of a hotspot. You can also move the hotspot by dragging it to a new position on the image. It is a good idea to limit the number of complex or irregularly shaped hotspots in an image because the code can become too lengthy for the page to download in a reasonable amount of time. You should also make the hotspot boundaries a little larger than they need to be to cover the area you want to set as a link. This allows a little leeway for users when they place their mouse over the hotspot by creating a larger target area for them.

Managing Website Links

As your website grows, so will the number of links on it. Checking links to make sure they work is a crucial and ongoing task that you should perform regularly. The Check Links Sitewide feature is a helpful tool for managing your links. It checks your entire website for the total number of links, categorizing them as OK, external, or broken, and then displays the information in the Link Checker panel. The Link Checker panel also provides a list of all the files used in a website, including those that are **orphaned files**, files that are not linked to any pages in the website. If you find broken internal links (links to files within the website), you should carefully check the code entered in the Link text box for errors. You can either use the Browse for File button in the Link Checker panel to correct the link, or type the correction in the Link text box in the Property inspector. You check broken external links (links to files outside the website) by testing the links in your browser. Due to the volatility of the web, it is important to check external links routinely as websites are often under construction or undergoing address changes. You have created three new external links in The Striped Umbrella website: two to external websites and one email link. You want to make sure you entered them correctly, so you run some reports to check the site for any broken links or orphaned files.

STEPS

TROUBLE
If any links are listed under the Broken Links category, click Site on the Menu bar, point to Advanced, click Recreate Site Cache, then run the report again.

1. **Click Site on the Menu bar, then click Check Links Sitewide**

   The Link Checker panel in the Results Tab group opens. By default, the Link Checker panel initially displays any broken internal links found in the website. The Striped Umbrella website has no broken links, as shown in Figure F-27.

QUICK TIP
To view all of the links without scrolling, you can float the Results Tab group.

2. **Click the Show list arrow in the Link Checker panel, click External Links, then compare your screen with Figure F-28**

   Two files are listed: the activities page and the index page. The activities page has two external links listed: one to the Blue Angels website and one to the U.S.S. Alabama website. The index page has an email link listed.

TROUBLE
If any orphaned files are listed under the Files category, click Site on the Menu bar, point to Advanced, click Recreate Site Cache, then run the report again.

3. **Click the Show list arrow, then click Orphaned Files**

   There are no orphaned files displayed in the Link Checker panel for the website, as shown in Figure F-29.

TROUBLE
If you don't see the links, click the Refresh button.

4. **Close the Results Tab Group, click the Assets tab on the Files Tab Group, then click the URLs button on the Assets panel**

   The list of external links in the Striped Umbrella website displays in the Assets panel. See Figure F-30.

5. **Close the about_us page, then Exit (Win) or Quit (Mac) Dreamweaver**

FIGURE F-27: Link Checker with Broken Links results displayed

Show list arrow

No broken links listed

FIGURE F-28: Link Checker with External Links results displayed

External links listed

FIGURE F-29: Link Checker with Orphaned Files results displayed

No orphaned files listed

FIGURE F-30: Assets panel with website external links displayed

URLs button

External links

Design Matters

Designing for easy navigation

As you work on the navigation structure for a website, you should try to limit the number of internal links on each page. You should also provide visual clues on each page to let users know where they are, much like a "You are here" marker on a store directory at the mall, or a bread crumbs trail. A **bread crumbs trail** is a list of links that provides a path from the initial page you opened in a website to the page that you are currently viewing. Many websites provide a list of all the site's pages, called a **site map**. A site map is similar to a table of contents; it lets users see how the information is divided between the pages and helps them to locate the information they need quickly.

Practice

Concepts Review

Label each element in the Dreamweaver window shown in Figure F-31.

FIGURE F-31

© 2013 Cengage Learning
Original photos courtesy of Sherry Bishop

1. _____   4. _____
2. _____   5. _____
3. _____   6. _____

Match each of the following terms with the statement that best describes its function.

7. **Internal links**

8. **External links**

9. **Broken links**

10. **Named anchor**

11. **Menu bar**

12. **Target**

13. **Image map**

14. **Hotspot**

15. **Orphaned file**

a. Links that do not work correctly

b. A set of text or image links used to navigate between pages of a website

c. An image with hotspots on it

d. Links to pages within the website

e. Active area on an image that serves as a link

f. A location on a web page that browsers will display when a link is clicked

g. A specific location on a web page, represented by a special icon, that will fully display in the browser window when a user clicks the link tagged to it

h. A file that is not linked to any pages on a website

i. Links to pages outside the website

Select the best answer from the following list of choices.

16. **Which type of path begins with a forward slash?**
    a. Document-relative
    b. Root-relative
    c. Absolute
    d. Image-relative

17. **Which button in the Property inspector do you use to connect an internal link to a named anchor?**
    a. Point to File
    b. Point to Anchor
    c. Anchor to File
    d. Point to Named Anchor

18. **The four target options for how a window will display in a browser when a link is clicked are:**
    a. _blank, _parent, _self, _top.
    b. _blank, _child, _self, _top.
    c. _blank, _parent, _child, _top.
    d. _blank, _parent, _self, _new.

19. **To see all links in a website, you click which button on the Assets panel?**
    a. Links
    b. Paths
    c. URLs
    d. Anchors

20. **Which dialog box shows you a list of orphaned files?**
    a. Orphaned Files
    b. Link Checker
    c. Check Links Sitewide
    d. Assets

Skills Review

Important: *If you did not create this website in Unit B and maintain it during the preceding units, you will need to create a local site root folder for this website and define the website using files your instructor will provide. See the "Read This Before You Begin" section for more detailed instructions.*

1. **Understand links and paths.**
    a. Write an example of an absolute path for a link.
    b. Write an example of a relative path for a link.
    c. Write a sentence explaining the difference between a document-relative path and a root-relative path.

2. **Create an external link.**
    a. Start Dreamweaver, then open the Blooms & Bulbs website.
    b. Open dwf_2.html from the drive and folder where you store your Unit F Data Files, save it as **newsletter.html** in the blooms local site root folder, replacing the existing file and not updating links, then close dwf_2.html.
    c. Click the first broken image placeholder for the ruby_grass.jpg file browse to the drive and folder where you store your Unit F Data Files to copy it to your assets folder, then apply the img_left_float rule to it.
    d. Repeat Step c to replace the next two broken image placeholders for the trees.jpg and plants.jpg files, apply the img_right_float rule to the trees image and the img_left_float rule to the plants image.
    e. Scroll to the bottom of the page, then link the National Gardening Association text to **http://www.garden.org**.
    f. Link the Organic Gardening text to **http://www.organicgardening.com**.
    g. Link the Southern Living text to **http://www.southernliving.com/southern**.
    h. Save the file, then preview it in your browser window.
    i. Test the links to make sure they all work correctly, then close the browser.

3. **Create an internal link.**
    a. Select the text "gardening tips" in the last sentence in the Gardening Issues paragraph.
    b. Use the Point to File button to link the text to the tips.html page.
    c. Change the page title to **Gardening Matters**.
    d. Create a new Tag rule in the blooms_styles.css style sheet that modifies the <h2> tag as follows: font-family: Arial, Helvetica, sans-serif font; font-size: medium; font-weight: bold; color: #000.

Skills Review (continued)

e. Create a new Tag rule in the blooms_styles.css style sheet that modifies the <h3> tag as follows: font-family: Arial, Helvetica, sans-serif; font-size: medium; font-weight: bold; color: #060.

f. Save all files, test the link in your browser, then close the browser.

g. Open the plants page, then add a new paragraph to the bottom of the page: **In addition to these marvelous roses, we have many annuals, perennials, and water plants that have just arrived.**

h. Apply the body_text rule to the paragraph if necessary.

i. Use the Files panel to create three new blank files in the local site root folder named: annuals.html, perennials.html, and water_plants.html.

j. Link the "annuals" text in the new paragraph to the annuals.html file, link the "perennials" text to the perennials.html file, then link the "water plants" text to the water_plants.html file.

k. Save your work, test the links in your browser, then close the browser. (*Hint*: These pages do not have content yet, but are serving as placeholders.)

4. **Insert a named anchor.**

   a. Switch to the newsletter page, then show the invisible elements if necessary.

   b. Insert a named anchor in front of the Grass subheading, then name it **grass**.

   c. Insert a named anchor in front of the Trees subheading, then name it **trees**.

   d. Insert a named anchor in front of the Plants subheading, then name it **plants**.

   e. Save the file.

5. **Create an internal link to a named anchor.**

   a. Using the Point to File button in the Property inspector, create a link from the word grass in the Gardening Issues paragraph to the grass named anchor.

   b. Create a link from the word trees in the Gardening Issues paragraph to the trees named anchor.

   c. Create a link from the word plants in the Gardening Issues paragraph to the plants named anchor.

   d. Save the file, then test the links in your browser window.

6. **Create a Spry menu bar.**

   a. Enter a line break after the banner on the newsletter page.

   b. Use the Spry category on the Insert panel to insert a Spry menu bar with a horizontal layout under the banner.

   c. Replace MenuBar1 in the Menu Bar text box in the Property inspector with the name **MenuBar**.

   d. Replace the name Item 1 in the Text text box with **Home**, then remove all submenu items from the Home item.

   e. Link the Home item to the index.html file.

   f. Switch to Code view, place your insertion point right after the ending tag for the unordered list, switch back to Design view, insert two line breaks, then save the file, copying the dependent files.

7. **Add menu bar items.**

   a. Rename the Item 2 menu item **Newsletter**, then link it to the newsletter page.

   b. Rename the Item 3 menu item **Plants**, then link it to the plants page.

   c. Rename the Item 4 menu item **Tips**, then link it to the tips page.

   d. With the Tips menu item selected, add a new menu item with the name **Workshops**, then link it to the workshops page.

   e. With the Plants menu item selected, rename submenu Item 3.1 **Annuals**, then link it to the annuals.html page.

   f. With the Plants menu item selected, rename submenu Item 3.2 **Perennials**, then link it to the perennials.html page.

   g. With the Plants menu item selected, rename submenu Item 3.3 **Water Plants**, then link it to the water_plants.html page.

   h. With the Annuals submenu item selected, delete its two submenu items, then save your work.

8. Format a menu bar.

   a. Expand the SpryMenuBarHorizonal.css style sheet in the CSS Styles panel, then edit the rule ul.MenuBarHorizontal with the following settings: Font-family: Arial, Helvetica, sans-serif; Font-size: 14 px.

   b. Edit the ul.MenuBarHorizontal li rule with the following settings: Box Width: 190 px; Box Height: 25 px; Block Text-align: center.

   c. Edit the following rule: ul.MenuBarHorizontal a with the following settings: Type Color: #030; Background-color: #99F.

   d. Edit the following rule: ul.MenuBarHorizontal a.MenuBarItemHover, ul.MenuBarHorizontal a.MenuBarItemSubmenuHover, ul.MenuBarHorizontal a.MenuBarSubmenuVisible with the following settings: Type Color: #FFC; Background-color: #030.

   e. Create a new Tag rule in the blooms_styles.css file to modify the <img> tag as follows: Block Vertical-align:bottom.

   f. Save your work, then test the menu bar on the page in the browser to make sure everything works correctly.

9. Copy a menu bar to other pages.

   a. Select and copy the menu bar, then open the index page.

   b. Select the banner, press the right arrow key, click the Format list arrow in the HTML Property inspector, then click None if necessary.

   c. Paste the menu bar at the insertion point, then delete the existing menu bar created with text links and the horizontal rule.

   d. Switch to Live View to view the placement of the menu bar on the page.

   e. Return to Design view; when you are satisfied with the page, save your work, then close the index page.

   f. Switch to the plants page, add a line break after the banner, paste the menu bar under the banner, then add another line break.

   g. Switch to Live view to check the placement of the menu bar, then return to Design view and save and close the page.

   h. Repeat Step f to add a menu bar on the tips page, apply the img_left_float to the butterfly image, then save the tips page. (*Hint*: If you see a space between the banner and the menu bar, go to Code view and look for <p> tags around the banner. If you see any, delete them.)

   i. Preview all pages in the browser window, checking the spacing for each page to ensure a uniform look, then close the browser. (*Hint*: The workshops, annuals, perennials, and water_plants pages are serving as placeholder pages and do not have content yet.)

10. Create an image map.

   a. On the newsletter page, create a rectangle hotspot over the words *Blooms & Bulbs* on the Blooms & Bulbs banner.

   b. Name the image map **home**, then link it to the index page.

   c. Set the target as _top.

   d. Enter the alternate text **Link to home page**.

   e. Switch to Code view, locate the <br> tag that has been added below the ending </map> tag, then delete it.

   f. Place the insertion point right before the closing image tag for the banner, then type this code: **style="border:0"**.

   g. Save all pages, then preview the newsletter page in the browser, testing all links. Refer to Figure F-32 to check your work.

FIGURE F-32

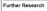

© 2013 Cengage Learning
Original photos courtesy of Sherry Bishop

Skills Review (continued)

11. Manage website links.

    a. Recreate the Site Cache, then use the Check Links Sitewide command to view broken links, external links, and orphaned files.

    b. Refresh the Site list in the Files panel if you see broken links or orphaned files. If any exist, locate them, analyze them, then correct any errors you find.

    c. View the external links in the Assets panel. Exit (Win) or Quit (Mac) Dreamweaver.

Important: *If you did not create the following websites in Unit B and maintain them during the preceding units, you must create a local site root folder for the websites in the following exercises and define the websites using files your instructor will provide. See the "Read This Before You Begin" section for more detailed instructions.*

Independent Challenge 1

You have been hired to create a website for a river expedition company named Rapids Transit, located on the Buffalo River in Gilbert, Arkansas. In addition to renting canoes, kayaks, and rafts, they have lodging available for overnight stays. River guides are available to accompany clients on float trips. The owner's name is Mike Andrew. Mike has asked you to create a new web page that lists helpful links for his customers. Refer to Figure F-33 as you work on this page.

    a. Start Dreamweaver, then open the Rapids Transit website.

    b. Open dwf_3.html in the drive and folder where you store your Unit F Data Files, then save it as **before.html**, replacing the existing file and without updating the links. You need to save the young_paddler.gif file (the photo) in the assets folder of the Rapids Transit website, then correct the path for the banner if necessary.

    c. Close the dwf_3.html file.

    d. Create the following links for the links listed on the page:

Buffalo National River	http://www.nps.gov/buff/
Arkansas, the Natural State	http://www.arkansas.com/
Buffalo River Floater's Guide	http://www.ozarkmtns.com/buffalo/index.asp

    e. Attach the rapids_transit.css style sheet, apply the body_text style to all text on the page, then apply the img_left_float rule to the young_paddler image.

Independent Challenge 1 (continued)

f. Design a Spry menu bar for the page using your choice of settings. The menu bar should include the following items: Home, Our Guides, Rates, Lodging, and Before You Go. Link the menu items to the appropriate files in your Rapids Transit site. Delete all submenus. (Remember to create a new Tag rule in the rapids_transit.css file to modify the `<img>` tag as follows: Block Vertical-align:bottom.)

g. Copy the completed menu bar to the guides, index, and lodging pages. Preview each page in the browser window to make sure the menu bar doesn't "jump," or shift position, when you move from page to page. (*Hint*: If you are having problems with spacing issues, look for stray `<p>`, `<br>`, or heading tags on your pages and remove them if necessary.)

h. Save your work, then test all links in your browser window.

i. Run reports for locate any broken links or orphaned files, then correct any that exist.

j. Exit your browser, then close all files and exit Dreamweaver.

FIGURE F-33

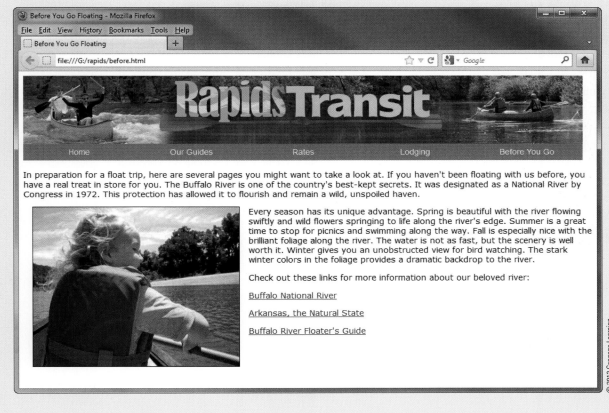

Independent Challenge 2

Your company is designing a new website for TripSmart, a travel outfitter. TripSmart specializes in travel products and services. In addition to selling travel products, such as luggage and accessories, they sponsor trips and offer travel advice. Their clients range from college students to families to vacationing professionals. You are now ready to work on the services page. This page will include several helpful links for clients to use when planning trips.

a. Start Dreamweaver, then open the TripSmart site.

b. Open the file dwf_4.html from the drive and folder where you store your Unit F Data Files, save it as **services.html** in the tripsmart local site root folder, replacing the existing file but not updating the links, then close dwf_4.html.

c. Apply the Heading 1 format from the attached style sheet to the four paragraph headings, then apply the body_text style to the rest of the text on the page.

d. Create the following links using the text in the unordered list at the bottom of the page:
CNN Travel Channel   http://www.cnn.com/TRAVEL
US Department of State   http://travel.state.gov
Yahoo! Currency Converter   http://finance.yahoo.com/currency-converter
The Weather Channel   http://www.weather.com

e. Create named anchors called **reservations**, **outfitters**, **tours**, and **links** in front of the respective headings on the page, then link each named anchor to "Reservations," "Travel Outfitters," "Escorted Tours," and "Helpful Links in Travel Planning" (respectively) in the first paragraph.

f. Create a Spry menu bar that links to the home, tours, newsletter, services, and catalog pages, replacing any existing menu bars. Delete all submenus.

g. Copy the menu bar to the other completed pages in the website: index, newsletter, and tours pages, replacing any existing menu bars. (*Hint*: If you are having problems with spacing issues, look for stray <p>, <br>, or heading tags on your pages and remove them if necessary.)

h. Add a new Tag rule in the tripsmart_styles.css file to set the Vertical-align for images to bottom.

i. Use the Link Checker to check for broken links and orphaned files.

J. Save any unsaved changes, preview the services page in the browser window, as shown in Figure F-34, then test all links.

k. Exit your browser, then close all files and exit Dreamweaver.

Independent Challenge 2 (continued)

FIGURE F-34

TripSmart has several divisions of customer service to assist you in planning and making reservations for your trip, shopping for your trip wardrobe and providing expert guide services. Give us a call and we will be happy to connect you with one of the following departments: Reservations, Travel Outfitters, or Escorted Tours. If you are not quite ready to talk with one of our departments and would prefer doing some of your own research first, may we suggest beginning with our Helpful Links in Travel Planning.

Reservations

Our Reservations Department is staffed with five Certified Travel Agents, each of whom is eager to assist you in making your travel plans. They have specialty areas in Africa, the Caribbean, South America, Western Europe, Eastern Europe, Asia, Antarctica, and Hawaii and the South Pacific. They also specialize in Senior Travel, Family Travel, Student Travel, and Special Needs Travel. Call us at *(555) 848-0807* extension 75 or e-mail us at *Reservations* to begin making your travel plans now. We will be happy to send you brochures and listings of Internet addresses to help you get started. We are open from 8:00 a.m. until 6:00 p.m. CST.

Travel Outfitters

Our travel outfitters are seasoned travelers that have accumulated a vast amount of knowledge in appropriate travel clothing and accessories for specific destinations. Climate and seasons, of course, are important factors in planning your wardrobe for a trip. Area customs should also be taken in consideration so as not to offend the local residents with inappropriate dress. When traveling abroad, we always hope that our customers will represent our country well as good ambassadors. If they can be comfortable and stylish at the same time, we have succeeded! Our clothing is all affordable and packs well on long trips. Most can be washed easily in a hotel sink and hung to drip-dry overnight. Browse through our on-line catalog, then give us a call at *(555) 433-7844* extension 85. We will also be happy to mail you a catalog of our extensive collection of travel clothing and accessories.

Escorted Tours

Our Escorted Tours department is always hard at work planning the next exciting destination to offer our TripSmart customers. We have seven professional tour guides that accompany our guests from the United States point of departure to their point of return.

Our current feature package tour is to Spain. Our local escort is Don Eugene. Don has traveled Spain extensively and enjoys sharing his love for this exciting country with others. He will be assisted after arrival in Spain with the services of archeologist JoAnne Rife, anthropologist Christina Elizabeth, and naturalist Iris Albert. Call us at *(555) 848-0807* extension 95 for information on the Spain trip or to learn about other destinations being currently scheduled.

Helpful Links in Travel Planning

The following links may be helpful in your travel research. Happy surfing!

- CNN Travel Channel - News affecting travel plans to various destinations
- US Department of State - Travel warnings, passport information, and more
- Yahoo! Currency Converter - Calculate the exchange rate between two currencies
- The Weather Channel - Weather, flight delays, and driving conditions

Dr. Joan Sullivent's patients often ask her questions about the current treatment protocol for Parkinson's disease, a debilitating neurological disease. She would like to post some helpful links in her clinic website to provide information for her patients. She begins her research at the National Institutes of Health website.

a. Connect to the Internet, then go to the National Institutes of Health website at nih.gov.

b. What do you like or dislike about the menu links?

c. Note the placement and appearance of the menu bar. Does it use text, images, or a combination of the two to form the links?

d. Using your favorite search engine, locate at least five helpful links that Dr. Sullivent should consider for her site, including the National Institutes of Health site pictured in Figure F-35.

FIGURE F-35

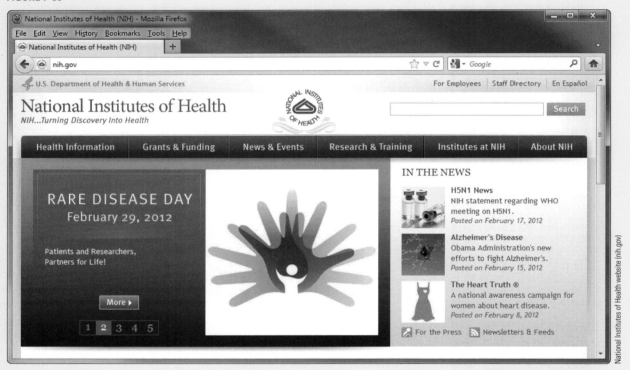

National Institutes of Health website (nih.gov)

Real Life Independent Challenge

This assignment will continue to build on the personal website that you created in Unit B. In Unit C you created and developed your index page. In Unit D you added a page with either an ordered or an unordered list, and a CSS style sheet with a minimum of two styles. In Unit E you added a page that included at least two images. In this lesson, you work with one of the other pages in your site.

a. Consult your wireframe and decide which page you would like to develop in this lesson.

b. Create content for this page and format the text attractively on the page using styles.

c. Add at least three external links to this page.

d. Think about a creative use for an image map, then add it to the page.

e. Add at least one named anchor and link to it.

f. Design a menu bar linking to the main pages of your site, then copy it to all of the main pages.

g. Save the file, then preview the page in the browser window.

After you are satisfied with your work, verify the following:

a. Each completed page has a page title.

b. All links work correctly.

c. The completed pages display correctly using a screen resolution of 1024 × 768.

d. All images are properly set showing a path to the website assets folder.

e. All images have alternate text and are legal for you to use.

f. The Link Checker shows no broken links or orphaned files. If there are orphaned files, note your plan to link them.

Visual Workshop

You are continuing your work on the Carolyne's Creations website that you started in Unit B and developed in subsequent units. Chef Carolyne has asked you to create pages describing her cooking classes offered every month. Use the following files for the tasks noted: dwf_5.html to replace the classes.html page; dwf_6.html to create a new children.html page; and dwf_7.html to create a new adults.html page. (Remember not to update the links when prompted.) Copy all new images, including the new banner, cc_banner_with_text.jpg, to the assets folder in the website. Next, create an image map at the bottom of the banner on the classes page with hotspots for each link, add the code **style="border:0"** to the image tag for the banner to prevent a blue outline appearing around the banner in Internet Explorer, and copy it to all pages in the website, replacing all existing menu bars. Create an email link on the classes page using the text "Sign me up!" and carolyne@carolynescreations.com for the link. Create links in the last sentence to the adults' and children's pages, as shown in Figure F-36. Refer to Figures F-36, F-37, and F-38 as you complete this project. Check that each completed page uses styles from the cc_styles.css file, and attach and apply these styles if you find pages without styles. The second image in Figure F-36 was aligned by creating a new rule based on the rule you created in Unit E, but with a different float property. (*Hint*: Remember to remove any formatting around the banners to prevent any pages from appearing to "jump.") Check for broken links and orphaned files. You will see that the former banner, cc_banner.jpg, is now an orphaned file.

FIGURE F-36

FIGURE F-37

© 2013 Cengage Learning
Original photo courtesy of Sherry Bishop

FIGURE F-38

© 2013 Cengage Learning
Original photo courtesy of Sherry Bishop

Using CSS and Tables to Position Content

You have learned how to position elements on a web page using alignment and paragraph settings. These settings let you create simple web pages, but they limit your design choices. The preferred method to position page elements is to use Cascading Style Sheets (CSS). You have already learned to use CSS to format individual page elements. Now you will learn to use CSS to place your content on pages using divs. With CSS layouts, you use blocks of content formatted with CSS rules to place information on web pages. Once you've completed this book, you will have the skills and understanding to efficiently design sites built entirely with CSS. You will also learn to use CSS to position data in tables. In this unit, you use a predesigned CSS layout with divs to create the cafe page for The Striped Umbrella website. You will add a table to the page to list the restaurant hours.

OBJECTIVES

Understand CSS layouts

Create a page using CSS layouts

Add content to CSS layout blocks

Edit content in CSS layout blocks

Edit CSS layout properties

Understand table modes

Insert a table and set table properties

Merge and split table cells

Insert and align images in table cells

Add text

Format and modify cell content

Format cells

Understanding CSS Layouts

Web pages built with Cascading Style Sheets use div tags to place and format page content. **Div tags** are HTML code segments that set the appearance and position of blocks of web page content. Think of div tags as building blocks. To build a web page with a layout based on CSS, you begin by placing div tags on the page to set up the framework to position the page content. Divs, the page elements created with div tags, can also be referred to as layout blocks, elements, or containers. Next, you add content and format the divs to position them on the page. For beginning designers, the predesigned CSS layouts that are available with Dreamweaver CS6 make creating pages based on CSS easy. You simply choose a predesigned CSS layout, and Dreamweaver places the div tags in the page code for you. ▓▓▓▓▓ You spend some time researching how style sheets are used for page layout.

DETAILS

Before using CSS layouts for page layout, you review the following concepts:

- **Using CSS vs. tables for page layout**

  Table were used previously by designers to position content on web pages. With CSS, designers have moved to positioning most page content with CSS layouts. Tables are still used for some layout purposes, such as placing tabular data on a page. Divs generate pages that are more compliant with current accessibility standards.

QUICK TIP
The Dreamweaver predesigned layouts have been tested using several different browsers.

- **Using Dreamweaver CSS page layouts**

  Dreamweaver offers 18 predesigned layouts in the New Document dialog box, as shown in Figure G-1. These layouts are a great way to learn how to create page layouts based on CSS. As you select each option, a preview of the layout appears on the right side of the New Document dialog box with a description below it. Once you select a layout, you can modify it to fit your needs. The two newest HTML5 page layouts use either a two column or three column layout. These layouts include new HTML tags to support semantic markup such as <section>, < header>, <footer>, <article>, and <aside>. Divs used for page layout are identified by an ID, or name. When the div tag is selected, the ID displays in both the HTML code for the div tag in the Property inspector, and in the CSS Styles panel. In Code view, the code for a div tag named header would be `<div id="header">`.

- **Using AP divs**

  One type of div is an AP div. AP stands for absolutely positioned, so an **AP div** has a specified position that doesn't change even when viewed in different-sized windows. An AP div creates a container called an **AP element**. You create an AP div by drawing the container with the Draw AP Div button, as shown in Figure G-2. When you create an AP div, a CSS rule is automatically created to apply the property values that determine its size and appearance on the page. You can stack AP divs on top of each other to create interesting effects such as animations. You can also use them to show or hide content on the page by using them with JavaScript behaviors. **JavaScript behaviors** are action scripts that allow you to add dynamic content to your web pages. **Dynamic content** is content that changes either in response to certain conditions or through interaction with the user. For example, the user might enter a zip code to display a local weather forecast. The code in the JavaScript behavior would direct the AP element with the correct forecast to appear after the user enters the corresponding zip code in a text box.

- **Using HTML5 and CSS**

  HTML has been in existence since the 1990s, but it wasn't until 1997 that the then current version, HTML4, became a W3C recommendation. HTML5 introduced new ways to add interactivity and tags that support semantic markup, such as the <nav> tag used for navigation links. Semantic markup refers to coding to convey meaning to other computer programs such as search engines. Semantics, or the meanings of words, when used with syntax, or the actual words and sentence structure, allows the computer to no longer just "read" words, but understand the meaning behind the words. HTML5 also introduces markup for Web applications (apps), an exploding sector of Web development. Other HTML5 tags include <header>, <footer>, <article>, <audio>, <section> and <video>. HTML5 is still a work in progress, but most modern browsers support it.

FIGURE G-1: New Document dialog box

FIGURE G-2: Inserting an AP div Tag using the Draw AP Div button

Using Dreamweaver sample pages

You can use either the Welcome Screen or the New Document dialog box, shown in Figure G-1, to create several different types of pages. The predesigned CSS page layouts make it easy for you to design accessible web pages using CSS without being an expert in HTML code. In the Page from Sample category, CSS Style Sheet and Mobile Starters are options that create pages you can use as starting points to develop pages for mobile devices and style sheets. Another choice in the New Document dialog box is the **Fluid Grid Layout**. This layout is used for designing adaptive websites based on a single fluid grid. It is worth the time to explore each category to understand what is available to you as a designer. Once you have selected a sample page, you can customize it to fit your needs and the site design. You can also find a variety of sample pages, or templates, on the Internet. Some sites offer templates free of charge, while others make templates available for purchase.

Creating a Page Using CSS Layouts

With the predesigned CSS layouts available in Dreamweaver, it is easy to create a page using CSS. After you choose a layout for a new page, the page opens with placeholder text displayed in the divs until you replace it with your content. Some divs not only have placeholder text, but also instructional text on how to modify the default settings, such as replacing a placeholder image with your image. Each div has preset styles applied. The properties and values of these styles are displayed in the CSS Styles panel, where you can modify them to fit your needs. Table G-1 lists some of the properties you can use to format divs. Dreamweaver's predesigned CSS layouts include one-, two-, and three-column layouts. Some layouts contain features such as sidebars, headers, and footers, and some are designed with a fixed width, while others are designed to stretch across a browser window. 🖌️ You decide to create the cafe page for the Striped Umbrella website based on a predesigned CSS HTML5 layout.

1. **Start Dreamweaver, open The Striped Umbrella website, then switch to Design view if necessary**

2. **Click File on the Menu bar, click New, verify that Blank Page is highlighted in the left section, click HTML in the Page Type column if necessary, then click HTML5: 2 column fixed, right sidebar, header and footer in the Layout column, as shown in Figure G-3**
   The layout description confirms that this is a fixed layout, measured in pixels. The preview of this page layout is displayed in the preview window. A **fixed layout** has columns expressed in pixels and will not change width when viewed in different window sizes. A **liquid layout** has columns expressed as percents based on the browser window width, so it will change width according to the dimensions of the browser window.

3. **If "Create New File" does not appear in the Layout CSS text box, click the Layout CSS list arrow, click Create New File, then if the su_styles.css file is shown in the Attach CSS file text box in the New Document dialog box, skip to Step 6. If not, click the Attach Style Sheet button 🔗 in the lower-right corner of the dialog box, then click Browse in the Attach External Style Sheet dialog box**
   The Select Style Sheet File dialog box opens.

4. **Click the su_styles.css file in the Select Style Sheet File dialog box, click OK (Win) or Open (Mac), then click OK to close the Dreamweaver confirmation box about the document-relative path**
   The links will not be document-relative until the page is saved in the website.

5. **Verify that the Add as: Link option button is selected in the Attach External Style Sheet dialog box, then click OK**
   The su_styles.css file is attached to the new page, as shown in Figure G-4.

6. **Click Create in the New Document dialog box, verify that the HTML5_twoColFixRtHdr.css file will be saved in the striped_umbrella local site folder in the Save Style Sheet File As dialog box, then click Save to close the Save Style Sheet File As dialog box. Open the CSS Styles panel if necessary, then expand the HTML5_twoColFixRtHdr.css and su_styles.css style sheets**
   A new page opens based on the predesigned CSS layout with blocks of placeholder content as shown in Figure G-5. It contains two columns, as well as a header and footer. Heading formats have been applied to the placeholder headings. There are two style sheets in the CSS Styles panel: the su_styles.css file you imported and the HTML5_twoColFixRtHdr.css style sheet file that was created to format the predesigned page layout.

7. **Save the file as cafe.html, overwriting the existing file**

Using CSS and Tables to Position Content

FIGURE G-3: Predefined layout selected for new page

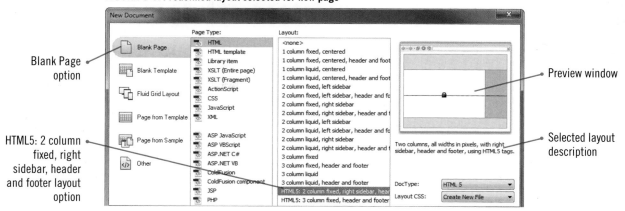

Blank Page option

HTML5: 2 column fixed, right sidebar, header and footer layout option

Preview window

Selected layout description

FIGURE G-4: The su_styles.css file attached to the new page

Choose Create New File

Layout CSS list arrow

Attach Style Sheet button

Attached su_styles.css file

FIGURE G-5: New page based on CSS HTML5 layout with placeholder content

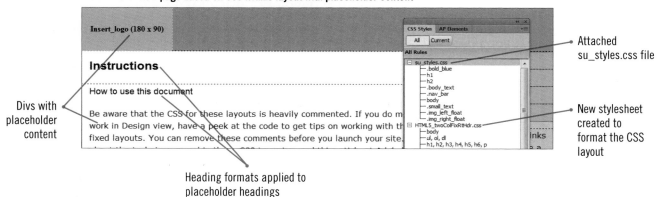

Divs with placeholder content

Heading formats applied to placeholder headings

Attached su_styles.css file

New stylesheet created to format the CSS layout

TABLE G-1: Div tag properties

property	function
ID	Displays the name used to identify the div in the code
Class	Displays the class style currently applied to the div
Float	Sets the float, or position, of the div in relation to adjacent elements as left, right, none, or inherit
Position	Sets the position of the div as absolute, fixed, relative, static, or inherit
Top	Sets the div position in relation to the top of the page or parent element
Right	Sets the right position of the div as either auto or inherit
Bottom	Sets the bottom position of the div as either auto or inherit
Left	Sets the div position in relation to the left side of the page or parent element
Width	Sets the width of the div, in pixels by default
Height	Sets the height of the div, in pixels by default
Overflow	Controls how the div will appear in the browser if the content is larger than the div

Adding Content to CSS Layout Blocks

A page built with all content placed inside divs makes it easy to apply formatting to all page elements. The div style properties and values set background and text colors, container widths, font settings, and alignment settings that are used to format all the images, links, tables, and text. Div styles also determine the content's position on the page. If you have developed your page content already, you can easily copy and paste it into the divs, replacing the placeholder content. You are ready to place the banner, menu bar, text, and images on the page, replacing the placeholder content.

STEPS

1. **Select all content between the Header and Footer in the main section, as shown in Figure G-6, then press [Delete]**

2. **Change to the HTML Property inspector, click the Format list arrow, then click Paragraph**
   Changing the format to paragraph removed the h1 tag that was left in the content div.

3. **Import the Word document cafe.doc from the drive and folder where you store your Unit G Data Files (Win) or copy and paste it (Mac) at the insertion point**
   The paragraph appears in a div on the new page, replacing the placeholder text. This div is named content.

QUICK TIP
Be careful not to delete the beginning and ending div tags.

4. **Switch to Code view, select the code between the beginning and end of the <div class="sidebar1"> tag, as shown in Figure G-7, then press [Delete]**

5. **Return to Design view, then type Reservations are recommended for Beach 25 (our main dining room) during the peak summer season. at the insertion point**

QUICK TIP
Press [Ctrl][Tab] to switch between two open pages.

6. **Delete all of the text in the footer block, type Copyright 2002 - 2015 The Striped Umbrella, as shown in Figure G-8, then save your work**

7. **Open the index page and copy both the banner and the menu bar, then close the index page**

QUICK TIP
If you struggle with the placement of the banner and menu bar, use Code view to copy the code from the index page then paste it into the code for the cafe page.

8. **Click the placeholder logo image on the cafe page, then paste the banner and menu bar in its place**

9. **Place the insertion point at the end of the paragraph ending with "poolside.", enter a paragraph break, insert cafe_photo.jpg from the assets folder in the drive and folder where you save your Unit G Data Files, then type Sand Crab Cafe photo for the alternate text**
   The content is placed on the page, replacing all placeholder content, as shown in Figure G-9.

Design Matters

Understanding selector types

When you have a mixture of style classifications—embedded styles, external styles, and styles-redefining HTML tags—there is an order of precedence that is followed. Styles are ranked in order of precedence as they are applied to page elements, thus the name "cascading style sheets." The first order of precedence is to find declarations that match the media type being used, such as a computer monitor. The second order of precedence is by importance and origin. The third order of preference is by specificity of the selector. **Pseudo class styles**, styles that determine the appearance of a page element when certain conditions are met, are considered as normal class styles. Sometimes styles with common formatting properties are grouped together to help reduce the size of style sheets. These styles are called **group selectors**.

Another type of selector is called a **descendant selector**. A descendant selector includes two or more selectors that form a relationship and are separated by white space.

FIGURE G-6: Selected placeholder text in the new cafe page

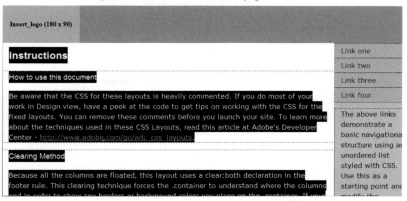

FIGURE G-7: Deleting the sidebar placeholder text

```
17    </header>
18    <div class="sidebar1">
19    <ul class="nav">
20        <li><a href="#">Link one</a></li>
21        <li><a href="#">Link two</a></li>
22        <li><a href="#">Link three</a></li>
23        <li><a href="#">Link four</a></li>
24    </ul>
25    <aside>
26        <p> The above links demonstrate a basic navigational structure using an unordered list styled with CSS. Use this as a
starting point and modify the properties to produce your own unique look. If you require flyout menus, create your own using
a Spry menu, a menu widget from Adobe's Exchange or a variety of other javascript or CSS solutions.</p>
27        <p>If you would like the navigation along the top, simply move the ul to the top of the page and recreate the styling.
</p>
28    </aside>
29    <!-- end .sidebar1 --></div>
30    <article class="content">
```

FIGURE G-8: New text for content, sidebar, and footer divs

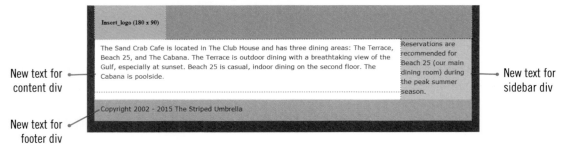

New text for content div

New text for footer div

New text for sidebar div

FIGURE G-9: Content added to cafe page

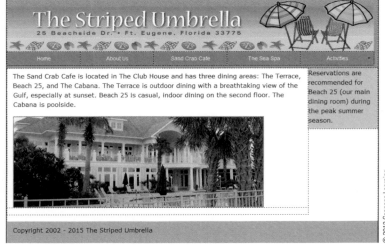

Editing Content in CSS Layout Blocks

After you replace placeholder content in divs with your website's content, you will probably want to adjust some of the formatting. Styles that you have previously applied might conflict with the div styles, so you may want to remove redundant style properties, such as font and alignment settings. It is generally better to use an external style sheet to format text, to provide consistency across the site. External style sheets use global styles. **Global styles** are styles used to apply common properties for certain page elements, such as text, links, or backgrounds. When you have styles that are defined in both the external style sheet that you created for your site and an external style sheet that was imported into your site after you created a new page based on a predesigned layout, you should evaluate which styles makes the most sense to use, based on the content each is intended to format. The styles for the div tags determine the placement and appearance of the divs, so analyze them carefully before you modify them. ███████ You continue to work on the new cafe page. You edit the rules for some of the divs to improve the appearance of the content within the divs.

STEPS

1. **Click the .sidebar1 rule in the HTML5_twoColFixRtHdr.css file in the CSS Styles panel, click the Edit Rule button** 🖉**, click the Block category, click the Text-align list arrow, then click center**

   You can also double-click a rule name to open the rule for editing.

QUICK TIP

You can enter either #FFFFFF or #FFF (the shorthand version).

2. **Click the Box category, change the Float from right to left, click the Background category, change the background color to #FFF, then click OK**

   The sidebar background changes to white, it moves to the left side of the page, and the text is centered inside the div, as shown in Figure G-10.

QUICK TIP

You can edit rule properties in either the CSS Styles Properties pane or by opening the CSS Rule definition dialog box.

3. **Click the header rule in the HTML5_twoColFixRtHdr.css file in the CSS Styles panel to select it, click the Edit Rule button** 🖉**, click the Background category, change the background color to #FFF, click the Box category, type 5 in the Top Margin text box, verify that the Same for all check box is checked, as shown in Figure G-11, then click OK**

   With the margins added, the banner and menu bar are centered in the header div and the div background is now white.

4. **Click the footer rule in the HTML5_twoColFixRtHdr.css file in the CSS Styles panel to select it, click the Edit Rule button** 🖉**, click the Background category, change the background color to #FFF, click the Block category, change the Text-align to center, then click OK**

   The footer text is now centered in the footer div with a white background, as shown in Figure G-12.

5. **Save your work**

Using CSS to organize web page layout

You can also use CSS3 to organize content by creating tabs, drop-down menus, and accordions. **Tabs** look similar to file folder tabs and are used for navigation above the top of the page content. You click a tab to display information. **Accordions**, also used for navigation, are buttons that, when clicked, open up like an accordion to display information that drops down below the button. Clicking the button again closes it. These features do not require images or JavaScript to work, but incorporate the animation capabilities of CSS3.

FIGURE G-10: Editing the properties of the .sidebar1 rule

© 2013 Cengage Learning

Sidebar moves to left side of the page, has a white background, and the content is centered

FIGURE G-11: Modifying the header rule

Same for all checkbox

Type 5 in the Top Margin text box

FIGURE G-12: Viewing the footer after editing the footer rule

Banner and menu bar are centered using margin settings for the header rule

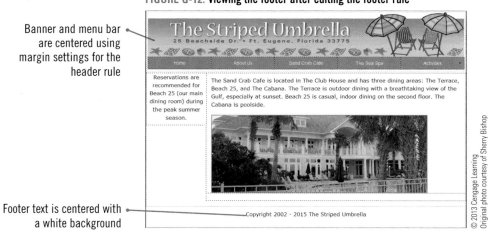

© 2013 Cengage Learning
Original photo courtesy of Sherry Bishop

Footer text is centered with a white background

Using Visual Aids to work with divs

There are several options for viewing your divs in Design view. You can choose to show or hide outlines, temporarily assign different background colors to each individual div, or view the **CSS Layout Box Model** (padding and margins included) of a selected layout. To change these options, use the View > Visual Aids menu, and then select or deselect the CSS Layout Backgrounds, CSS Layout Box Model, or CSS Layout Outlines menu choice. You can also use the Visual Aids button 👁 on the Document toolbar.

Editing CSS Layout Properties

It is unlikely that you will find a predesigned CSS page layout that is exactly what you have in mind for your website. However, once you have created a page with a predesigned CSS layout, it is easy to modify the properties for individual rules to better fit your needs. Ideally, every page element should be formatted using style sheets rather than by applying individual formatting properties with the Property inspector. You can apply the rules in attached external style sheets to format individual page elements with global styles, such as text or horizontal rules. The styles generated by the CSS page layout control the formatting of the divs, including the div width and background color, but, as you have seen, they can also include formatting for the page elements within the divs. ████ ████ You continue working on the new cafe page by changing more div properties and the page properties.

STEPS

1. **Select the body rule in the HTML5_twoColFixRtHdr.css file in the CSS Styles panel, click to select the existing background color in the Properties pane, type #FFF as shown in Figure G-13, then press [Enter] (Win) or [return] (Mac)**
   The body tag is used to format the page body—the area outside the divs. The body tag for the page is set to display a white background.

2. **Click .container in the HTML5_twoColFixRtHdr.css file in the CSS Styles panel, click the Edit rule button 🖉, then click the Border category**
   A border around the page sets it off from the extra space around it when it is viewed in a browser.

3. **Click the Top list arrow in the Style column, click solid, click the Top list arrow in the first text box in the Width column, click thin, click in the First color text box in the Color column, type #033, verify that the Same for all check box is selected in each of the three columns, compare your screen to Figure G-14, then click OK**
   The border properties for the container are set to include a thin solid line with a dark gray color.

4. **Type The Striped Umbrella Beach Resort and Spa, Ft. Eugene, Florida in the Title text box on the Document toolbar**

5. **Click to place the insertion point in front of the word "Reservations" in the sidebar, then enter a line break**

6. **Save your work, preview the page in the browser, compare your screen to Figure G-15, then close the browser**

FIGURE G-13: Editing the properties for the body rule

Select the body rule

Properties pane

Replace the existing color with #FFF

FIGURE G-14: Editing the properties for the container rule

Same for all checkboxes

Width category, Top list arrow

Style category, Top list arrow

Color category, Top text box

FIGURE G-15: Viewing the new cafe page in the browser

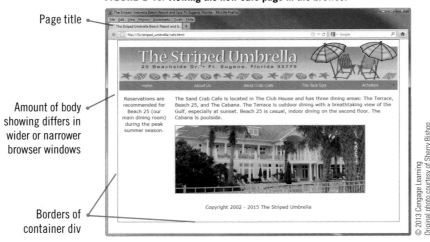

Page title

Amount of body showing differs in wider or narrower browser windows

Borders of container div

© 2013 Cengage Learning
Original photo courtesy of Sherry Bishop

Design Matters

Using the Adobe CSS Advisor and Adobe BrowserLab for cross-browser rendering issues

You can use the **Browser Compatibility Check (BCC)** feature to check for problematic CSS features that may render differently in multiple browsers. The BCC flags and rates code on three levels: an error that could cause a serious display problem; an error that probably won't cause a serious display problem; or a warning that unsupported code is present, but won't cause a serious display problem. Each bug is linked to the **CSS Advisor**, a part of the Adobe website that offers solutions for that particular bug and other helpful information for resolving any issues with your pages. To use the BCC feature, use the File > Check Page > Browser Compatibility command. Adobe also

has an online service called **Adobe BrowserLab** that is a useful tool for cross-browser and cross-platform compatibility testing. Since Adobe BrowserLab is an online service, you can access it from any computer with an Internet connection, but you must have an Adobe ID to use the service. There is no charge to create an Adobe ID. To connect to Adobe BrowserLab, open the Adobe BrowserLab panel, then click Preview. The Adobe BrowserLab panel is located above the Insert panel. The panel contains two buttons: one to connect to the service to preview your pages, and one to choose whether you want to preview the local or server version of your pages.

Understanding Table Modes

Tables are placeholders made up of small boxes called **cells**, which you can use to insert data. Cells are arranged horizontally in rows and vertically in columns. There are two ways to insert a table in Dreamweaver. You can use the Table button in either the Common or Layout category on the Insert panel or use the Menu bar to access the Table commands. When you insert, edit, or format a table, you have a choice of two ways to view the table: Standard mode and Expanded Tables mode. **Standard mode** displays the table with no extra space added between the table cells. **Expanded Tables mode** is similar to Standard mode but has expanded table borders and temporary space between the cells to make it easier to work with individual cells. You choose the mode that you want by clicking the Standard mode button or the Expanded Tables mode button in the Layout category on the Insert panel. It is common to switch between modes as you work with tables in Dreamweaver. Expanded Tables mode is used most often when you are doing precise work with small cells that are difficult to select or move between. You can also use the Import Tabular Data command on the Insert > Table Objects menu to place an existing table with its data on a web page. You review the two modes for inserting and viewing tables using the Standard and Expanded Tables modes.

- **Inserting a table in Standard mode**

    To insert a table in Standard mode, you click the Standard mode button in the Layout category on the Insert panel, then click the Table button. You then enter values for the number of rows and columns, the table width, border thickness, cell padding, and cell spacing in the Table dialog box. The **width** refers to the distance across the table, which is expressed either in pixels or as a percentage of page width. This difference is significant. When expressed as a percentage, the table width adjusts to the width of the page in the browser window. When expressed in pixels, the table width does not change, regardless of the size of the browser window. The **border** is the outline or frame around the table and the individual cells. It is expressed in pixels. **Cell padding** is the distance between the cell content and the **cell walls**, the lines inside the cell borders. **Cell spacing** is the distance between cells. Figure G-16 shows an example of a table viewed in Standard mode. You may see the table dimensions at the top, rather than at the bottom, of the table on the open page.

- **Viewing a table in Expanded Tables mode**

    Expanded Tables mode lets you view a table with expanded table borders and temporary cell padding and cell spacing. Since table rows and columns appear magnified when viewed on the page, this mode makes it easier to see how many rows and columns you actually have in your table. It is often difficult, especially after splitting empty cells, to place the insertion point precisely in a table cell, because empty cells can be such small targets. The Expanded Tables mode lets you see each cell clearly. After you select a table item or place the insertion point, it's best to return to Standard mode to maintain the WYSIWYG environment. WYSIWYG is the acronym for "What You See Is What You Get." This means that your web page should look the same in the browser as it does in the web editor. You can toggle between the Expanded Tables mode and Standard mode by pressing [Alt] [F6] (Win) or [option][F6] (Mac). Figure G-17 shows an example of a table in Expanded Tables mode. You can also use the View > Visual Aids > command to hide or show table borders.

Using HTML table tags

When formatting a table, you should understand the basic HTML tags used to define it. The tags that define a table are `<table>` and `</table>`. The tags that define table rows are `<tr>` and `</tr>`. The tags that define table data cells are `<td>` and `</td>`. Dreamweaver places the   code into each empty table cell at the time it is created. The   code inserts a **nonbreaking space**; this is a space that appears in a fixed location to keep a line break from separating text into two lines or, in the case of table cells, to keep an empty cell from collapsing. Some browsers collapse an empty cell, which can ruin the look of a table. The nonbreaking space appears in the cell by default until it is replaced with content.

FIGURE G-16: Table viewed in Standard mode

Selected table with no additional space between cells

Tag selector

Layout category

Standard mode button

Table button

Property inspector expanded to access cell properties

FIGURE G-17: Table viewed in Expanded Tables mode

Increased space between table cells

Expanded Tables mode button

Design Matters

Placing the most important information first

People on the Internet are notoriously hurried and will often read only information that is located on the first screen that they see on a web page, rather than scroll though the entire length of the page. Therefore, it is a good idea to put the most important information at the top of the page. In other words, the most important information should be on the part of the page that is visible before you have to scroll to see the rest. You can use guides to emulate a newspaper fold line, which represents the place where a newspaper is folded. The most important stories are usually printed "above the fold." You create guides by clicking and dragging from the horizontal or vertical ruler, down or across the page.

Inserting a Table and Setting Table Properties

Before you begin creating a table, it is important to decide what information you want to convey and how you want to achieve the desired look. Writing or sketching an overall plan before you begin saves a lot of development time. If you plan to insert images into a table, you should first determine where you want them to appear. You should also consider whether you want the table borders and the cell walls to appear in the browser. If you make a table "invisible" by setting the border value to zero, the user will not be aware that you used a table to arrange the text or images on the page. You format tables with CSS rules, so if you decide to add a table border, be sure to use a style tag rather than the Property inspector or the Table dialog box. ██████ After consulting with the restaurant manager, you have a plan for adding the dining room hours to the page. You begin the process by creating a table with three columns and five rows.

STEPS

QUICK TIP
The Table command is also located in the Layout category of the Insert panel.

1. **With the insertion point to the right of the cafe photo, enter a paragraph break, then click Table in the Common category of the Insert panel**

   The Table dialog box opens.

QUICK TIP
The Table dialog box will retain settings from the last table that was inserted, so be sure to delete any settings that remain in the dialog box that you do not want to use.

2. **Type 5 in the Rows text box, 3 in the Columns text box, click Top in the Header section if necessary, type The Sand Crab Cafe Hours in the Caption text box, compare your screen to Figure G-18, then click OK**

   A table with five rows and three columns displays on the page. The table appears very small because the width for the table has not yet been set. You will define a new Tag Selector rule to use to format the table.

3. **Click the New CSS Rule button 🗗 in the CSS Styles panel, choose Tag (redefines an HTML element) in the Selector Type text box, type table in the Selector Name text box, choose su_styles.css in the Rule Definition list box, then click OK**

   This rule will format the only table in the website. The table appears left-aligned and the table caption appears at the top of the table by default.

4. **Click the Box category, type 600 in the Width text box, verify that px is the unit of measure, change the Float to left, then click OK**

   The <table> rule modified the table by setting the width and alignment on the page, as shown in Figure G-19.

Selecting a table

There are several ways to select a table in Dreamweaver. You can click the insertion point in the table, click Modify on the Menu bar, point to Table, then click Select Table. You can also select a table by moving the pointer slowly to the top or bottom edge of the table, then clicking the table border when the pointer changes to ⬚. Finally, if the insertion point is inside the table, you can click <table> on the tag selector.

FIGURE G-18: Table dialog box

Rows text box

Columns text box

Table width list arrow

Table caption

FIGURE G-19: Table inserted and aligned in the div

Table caption

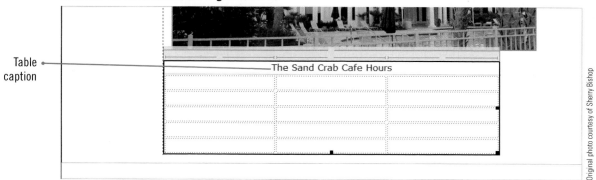

The Sand Crab Cafe Hours

Original photo courtesy of Sherry Bishop

Design Matters

Formatting Tables with HTML5 and CSS3

Many of the HTML codes used to format tables in HTML4 are now considered to be **deprecated,** or no longer within the current standard and in danger of becoming obsolete. Deprecated tags should be avoided. Deprecated HTML4 table tags include summary, cellpadding, cellspacing, align, width and bgcolor. Rather than format tables using the Table dialog box or the Property inspector, use CSS to format tables by creating a rules to modify table properties and table content. You can either add properties to the <table> tag itself or create new class rules

that can be assigned to specific tables. HTML5 tags you want to use are the <th> and <caption> tags. The table header <th> tag is a type of cell that contains header information. These are like column headings, and identify the content of the data cells below them. The caption <caption> tag is the caption, or title, of a table and describes the table content. These tags provide greater accessibility, as they are used by screen readers. They also add value as semantic markup because they help to label and describe table content.

Using CSS and Tables to Position Content

Dreamweaver CS6

Merging and Splitting Table Cells

In addition to resizing table columns and rows, you may need to adjust the table cells by splitting or merging them. **Splitting** a cell divides it into multiple rows or columns, while **merging** cells combines multiple adjacent cells into one cell. The ability to split and merge cells gives you more design flexibility for inserting images or text into your table. Merged cells are good placeholders for wide images or headings. For example, you could merge a row of cells to allot space for a heading. You can split merged cells and merge split cells. However, you can only merge cells that, when combined together, form the shape of a rectangle. When cells are merged, the HTML tag used to describe these cells changes from a width size tag to a column span or row span tag. You merge the top row of cells to make room for a heading across the table. You then split one cell to make room for a new image and its descriptive text in the first column. Finally, you merge four cells to create a larger area that will be used to describe room service availability.

STEPS

1. **Click to place the insertion point in the first cell in the top row, then drag the pointer to the right to select all three cells in the top row**

   A black border surrounds the cells, indicating that they are selected.

2. **Click the Merges selected cells using spans button ▣ in the Property inspector**

   The three cells are merged into one cell, as shown in Figure G-20. The heading will display nicely in this area.

3. **Place the insertion point in the first cell in the fifth row, then click the Splits cell into rows or columns button ⬚ in the Property inspector**

   The Split Cell dialog box opens. This is where you select the Rows or Columns option, then specify the number of rows or columns you want as a result of the split.

QUICK TIP
To create a new row identical to the one above it at the end of a table, place the insertion point in the last cell, then press [Tab].

4. **Click the Split cell into: Rows option button to select it if necessary, type 2 in the Number of rows text box if necessary, as shown in Figure G-21, then click OK**

   The dialog box closes, and the bottom-left cell is split into two rows. These rows will eventually contain the photograph of the featured dessert and its description.

5. **Click the Show Code view button ⬚ Code on the Document toolbar**

   The code for the split and merged cells displays, as shown in Figure G-22. Table row and table column tags denote the column span and the nonbreaking spaces ( ) inserted in the empty cells. The tag `<th colspan="3">` refers to the three top header cells that have been merged into one cell.

6. **Click the Show Design view button ⬚ Design on the Document toolbar, select and merge the first cells in rows 2, 3, 4, and 5 in the left column, deselect the cell, compare your screen to Figure G-23, then save your work**

   With the table framework completed, the table is now ready for content.

Using nested tables

Inserting another table inside a cell within another table creates what is called a **nested table**. Nested tables can be used effectively when you want parts of your table data to contain both visible and invisible borders. For example, you can nest a table with red borders inside a table with invisible borders. The process of creating a nested table is similar to the one used to add a new row or column to a table. Simply click to place the insertion point inside the cell where you want the nested table to appear, click Insert on the Menu bar, then click Table, or click the Table button on the Insert panel. A nested table is separate from the original table so you can format it however you wish. The more nested tables you add, however, the more complicated the coding becomes, making it challenging to select and edit each table. You may be able to achieve the same results by adding rows and columns or splitting cells instead of inserting a nested table.

FIGURE G-20: Merging selected cells into one cell

Resulting merged cells

Merges selected cells using spans button

FIGURE G-21: Split Cell dialog box

Rows option button

Number of rows text box

FIGURE G-22: Viewing the code for the merged and split cells

Opening table tag

Code for merged cells

Code for row with split cell

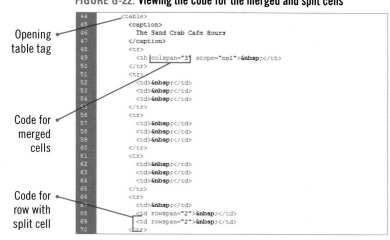

FIGURE G-23: Viewing the table after splitting and merging cells

Merged cells

Split cells

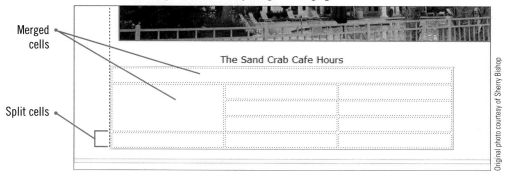

Adding and deleting rows and columns

As you add new content to your table, you may find that you have too many or not enough rows or columns. You can add or delete one row or column at a time or add several at once, using commands on the Modify menu. When you add a new column or row, you must first select an existing column or row to which the new column or row will be adjacent. The Insert Rows or Columns dialog box lets you choose how many rows or columns you want to insert and specify where you want them placed, relative to the selected row or column. To add a new row to the end of a table, simply press [Tab].

Using CSS and Tables to Position Content

Inserting and Aligning Images in Table Cells

You can type, import, or paste text into table cells. You insert images into cells just as you would insert them on a page. Use CSS rules to align the cell content by either creating a rule you apply to the table cell or by creating a rule that you then apply to cell content. Do not use the Property inspector to align cell content or your code will not be HTML5 compliant. As you add content to cells, the cells expand in height to make room for the content. ▄▄▄ You have a great photograph of a specialty chocolate cake that is featured in two of the dining areas. You insert the new image into the four merged cells in the first column of the table to add visual interest to the cafe page.

QUICK TIP

The last button that was selected on the Insert panel becomes the default button that's used until you select another one.

1. **Click to place the insertion point in the first cell in the second row of the table (below the merged cells in the top row), change to the Common category on the Insert panel, if necessary, click the Images button list arrow, click Image, navigate to the drive and folder where you store your Unit G Data Files, then double-click chocolate_cake.jpg from the assets folder**

   The Image Tag Accessibility Attributes dialog box opens. This is where you add the alternate text for screen readers.

TROUBLE

If you do not see an alternate text dialog box, type the text in the Alt text box in the Property inspector.

2. **Type Chocolate Grand Marnier Cake in the alternate text box, click OK, then refresh the Files panel**

   The image of the chocolate cake displays in the merged cells and is saved in the website assets folder.

3. **Click to the right of the chocolate_cake image in the same cell to place the insertion point**

   You will now add code to the table cell with the cake image to center-align the contents of the cell.

4. **Switch to Code view, then place the insertion point right after the code "<td rowspan="4"**

   This is the table cell that will be modified by adding a style to center-align the contents.

5. **Press the Spacebar to enter a space, then type style="text-align:center" as shown in Figure G-24**

   Notice how Dreamweaver helps you add code by providing **code hints**. Code hints is an auto-complete feature that displays lists of tags that appear as you type in Code view.

6. **Return to Design view, then save your work**

7. **Preview the page in your browser, view the table with the aligned image, as shown in Figure G-25, then close the browser**

   The image is still not in the exact position you intended. After you add more content to the table, the image will adjust to the correct position. You can also add rules to set the column widths in a table.

Using Live View to check pages

Live View is another option for previewing your pages. It is a quick way to see how your page will look without previewing the page in a browser window. Live View renders the page as though it were being viewed in a browser window with any active objects (such as a Spry menu bar) functioning. To use

Live View, open a page in Design view, then click the Switch Design View to Live View button ⟨ Live ⟩. Remember, a page cannot be edited in Live View. You must exit Live View to be able to make changes to the page content.

FIGURE G-24: **Aligning the contents of a single cell**

```
45          <caption>
46            The Sand Crab Cafe Hours
47          </caption>
48          <tr>
49            <th colspan="3" scope="col"> </th>
50          </tr>
51          <tr>
52            <td rowspan="4" style="text-align:center"> <img src=
       "assets/chocolate_cake.jpg" width="110" height="84" alt="Chocolate Grand Marnier
       Cake"></td>
53            <td> </td>
54            <td> </td>
55          </tr>
```

Code added to
align table cell

FIGURE G-25: **Viewing the table in a browser window**

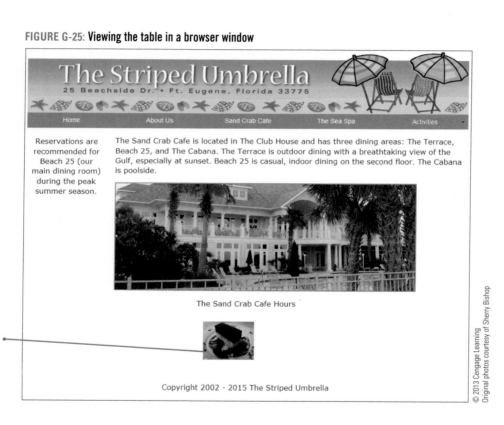

The table
borders are not
visible in the
browser

Design Matters

Recognizing and addressing printing issues

There are many factors that affect how a page will print compared to how it displays in a browser window. While a page background color will display in a browser window, it will not print unless the print option to print background colors is selected by the user. Although the width of the page in the browser window may fit on the screen, it could actually be too wide to print on a standard printer in portrait orientation.

Also, table borders, horizontal rules, and CSS divs may not print exactly how they look in a browser. Printing your pages to see how they actually appear will allow you to address most of these issues. You can also go to a site, such as the World Wide web Consortium (W3C) at w3.org, to find the best solutions to any problems you identify.

Using CSS and Tables to Position Content

Adding Text

You can enter text in table cells by typing it in the cell, copying it from another source and pasting it into the cell, or importing it into the cell from another program. You can then format the text for readability and appearance with CSS. If you import text from another program, you should use the Clean Up HTML or Clean Up Word HTML command to remove unnecessary code. ▰▰▰▰ You add a heading to the table and a caption for the chocolate cake image. You also add the hours of operation for the three dining areas in the second column. Finally, you include a short description of room service options as well.

STEPS

TROUBLE
If you can't see the last lines you typed, click the `<div.container>` tag on the Tag selector to refresh the container size on the screen, resize the Dreamweaver application window, or close and reopen the page.

1. **Click in the first cell in the last row (below the chocolate cake image), type Chocolate, press [Shift] [Enter] (Win) or [shift] [return] (Mac) to add a line break, type Grand Marnier, add another line break, then type Cake**

   The text appears in the first cell in the last row below the chocolate cake image. The cell widths will change as you fill them with content. Don't be concerned about matching the figures exactly until you have completed inserting all content and set the table width.

2. **Click in the top row of the table, then type Our individual dining areas are listed below:**

   The header text appears centered and boldfaced in the table. Note that a header row in a table appears boldfaced and centered by default. Recall that the top row header was selected when the table was created. The caption appears above the table.

QUICK TIP
You can press [Tab] to move your insertion point to the next cell in a row, and press [Shift] [Tab] to move your insertion point to the previous cell.

3. **Enter the names for each dining area and its hours in rows 1 through 3, as shown in Figure G-26**

   The dining room areas and respective hours are listed in the table with the font properties from the body tag applied to them through the rules of inheritance. This means that if formatting is not specified for a child tag inside a parent tag, the parent tag properties and values will format the child tag content.

4. **Merge the second and third cells in the last row, then type the room service information from Figure G-26 with a line break after 12:00 a.m.**

   The room service hours are displayed at the bottom of the table.

TROUBLE
As you add content to the table, the data may not display correctly on the page. Clicking the `<table>` tag or resizing the screen refreshes the display and corrects this.

5. **Click the `<table>` tag on the Tag selector**

   The Room service information wraps to a second line, which looks a bit awkward. The width of the table could be extended to the right where there is more room.

6. **Click the table rule in the CSS Styles panel, click the Edit rule button 🖉, click the Box category, change the Box width to 635 px, click OK, then compare your screen to Figure G-27**

   The table is resized to 635 pixels wide, allowing room for the lengthy sentence to remain on one line.

7. **Save your work**

FIGURE G-26: Table with data entered

Top row header

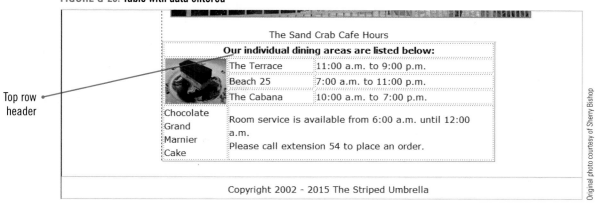

Original photo courtesy of Sherry Bishop

FIGURE G-27: Increasing the width of the table to accommodate data

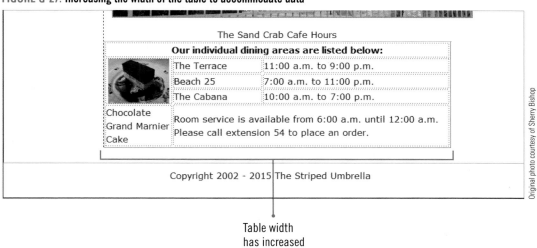

Table width
has increased

Original photo courtesy of Sherry Bishop

Importing and exporting tabular data

You can import and export tabular data into and out of Dreamweaver. **Tabular data** is data that is arranged in columns and rows and separated by a **delimiter,** such as a comma, tab, colon, semicolon, or similar character, that tells Dreamweaver where to break the data into table cells. **Importing** means to bring data created in another software program into Dreamweaver, and **exporting** means to save data that was created in Dreamweaver in a different file format so that other programs can read it. Files containing tabular data that are imported into Dreamweaver must first be saved as delimited text files. Programs such as Microsoft Word and Excel offer many file formats for saving files, including saving as delimited text. To import a delimited file, click File on the Menu bar, point to Import, then click Tabular Data. The Import Tabular Data dialog box opens, offering you choices for the resulting table that will appear on the web page. To export a table that you created in Dreamweaver, click File on the Menu bar, point to Export, then click Table. The Export Table dialog box opens, letting you choose the type of delimiter and line breaks you want for the delimited file when you save it.

Formatting and Modifying Cell Content

You format cell content by changing the font, size, or color of the text by applying styles. You can also resize images placed in cells. If you have a simple table that can share the same formatting between all of the table elements, you can add all formatting rules to the table by adding properties and values to the `<table>` tag. ▓▓▓▓ Now that you have your text in place, you are ready to format it using CSS. You modify the table tag to set text properties for all table content, then you create a new rule to use for the image caption.

STEPS

1. **Expand the CSS Styles panel group if necessary**
   Formatting the text in the table cells will make the cafe page look more professional.

2. **Click the table rule in the CSS Styles panel, click the Edit Rule button 🖉, click the Type category, click the Font-family list arrow, click Arial, Helvetica, sans-serif, click the Font-size list arrow, click medium, as shown in Figure G-28, then click OK**
   The type in the table changes to assume the properties of the modified table rule. You want the name of the featured dessert, Chocolate Grand Marnier Cake, to stand out on the page but there isn't an existing rule that suits your needs.

3. **Click the New CSS Rule button 🖅, then create a new class selector type rule called featured_item in the su_styles.css style sheet file**
   Creating a new style for this specific text will give it a unique look.

4. **In the Type category, set the Font-size to 14, the Font-weight to bold, the Font-style to italic, the Color to #003, as shown in Figure G-29, then click OK**
   Since you did not specify a Font-family in the CSS Rule Definition dialog box, the font will remain the same, as it is inherited from the body rule in the HTML5_twoColFixRtHdr.css file.

5. **Select the Chocolate Grand Marnier Cake text under the chocolate cake image, click the CSS button 🔳 css in the Property inspector, then apply the featured_item rule to the text**
   All text on the page now has a rule applied.

6. **Click after the word Cake in the bottom-left cell, then press [Tab]**
   A new row is added. Pressing the Tab key while the insertion point is in the last cell of the table creates a new row. Even though it appears as if the cell with the room service information is the last cell, it is not because of the merged cells.

7. **Merge the cells in the new row, click in the merged cells, click Insert on the Menu bar, point to HTML, then click Horizontal Rule**
   A horizontal rule is displayed in the merged cells in the last row. Horizontal rules are used frequently to set off or divide sections on a page.

8. **Save your work, preview the cafe page in your browser, compare your screen to Figure G-30, then close your browser**
   The page looks much better with the formatted text.

FIGURE G-28: Modifying the table rule

FIGURE G-29: Creating the .featured_item rule

FIGURE G-30: Rules applied to text and horizontal rule added

body_text
rule applied

featured_items
rule applied

Horizontal rule
added in new row

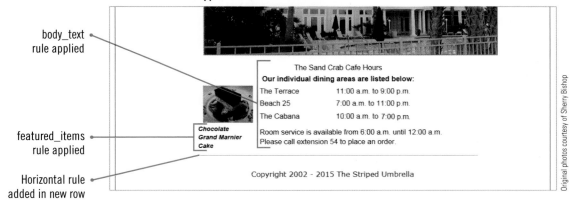

Original photos courtesy of Sherry Bishop

Using CSS and Tables to Position Content

Formatting Cells

Formatting a cell can include setting properties that visually enhance the cell's appearance, such as setting a cell width, assigning a background color, or setting global alignment properties for the cell content. To format a cell, with code that is HTML5 compliant, you can use tags to define a column group style <colgroup>, which will format all cells in a particular column. You can also use the column tag <col> to apply formatting styles to singular cells in a column. Once you have created your rules, you add them to the code for the appropriate columns or cells you wish to format. You can also add code to the tag for an individual cell. Formatting cells is different from formatting cell contents. When you format cell contents, you must select the contents and then apply a rule. See the Clues to Use *Using inherited properties to format cells and cell content* at the bottom of this page for more information. ▓▓▓ You decide to experiment with the placement and alignment of the current page content. You change the horizontal and vertical alignment settings for some of the table cells to improve the appearance of the cell contents on the page.

STEPS

1. **Click to place the insertion point in the cell with the chocolate cake caption**

   Notice that the .featured_item rule is applied to the text. You will modify the .featured_item rule to add an alignment value.

2. **Click the .featured_item rule in the CSS Styles panel, then click the Edit Rule button** 🖉

   The CSS Rule Definition for .featured_item in su_styles.css dialog box opens.

3. **Click the Block Category, click the Text-align list arrow, click center, then click OK**

   The cake text is now centered in the cell, as shown in Figure G-31. Next you will align the contents of the cell describing room service. Since there is not a separate rule applied to this text, you modify the cell tag code to align the cell contents.

4. **Place the insertion point in the cell with the room service information, then switch to Code view**

5. **Place the insertion point at the end of the opening td tag, type** `style="text-align: center"`**, as shown in Figure G-32**

   The page displays as it will appear in your browser. The table looks more organized and professional with the new alignment settings.

6. **Save all files, switch to Design View, click the Switch Design View to Live View button** [Live]**, then compare your screen to Figure G-33**

   The room service text is centered in the cell.

7. **Return to Design view, close all open pages, then exit Dreamweaver**

Using inherited properties to format cells and cell content

If a table is inside a CSS layout, you can simply let the properties from the existing CSS rules format the content, rather than applying additional rules. This is called inheritance. When a tag is placed, or nested, inside another tag (the parent tag), the properties from the parent tag are inherited by any tags nested within that tag. For example, if you set the Font-family property in the body tag, all content on the page inherits and displays that same font family unless you specify otherwise.

FIGURE G-31: Setting horizontal cell alignment

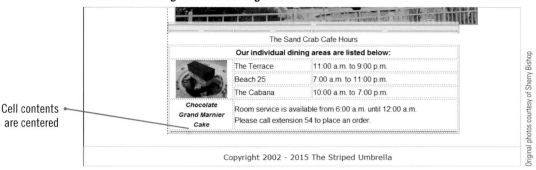

Cell contents
are centered

Original photos courtesy of Sherry Bishop

FIGURE G-32: Adding an align property to a cell tag

Add to the code
for the cell tag
to set the cell
alignment to
center

```
59        </tr>
60        <tr>
61          <td>The Cabana</td>
62          <td>10:00 a.m. to 7: 00 p.m.</td>
63        </tr>
64        <tr>
65          <td colspan="2" rowspan="2" style="text-align:center">Room service is available from 6:00 a.m. until 12:00 a.m.<br>
66          Please call extension 54 to place an order.</td>
67        </tr>
68        <tr>
69          <td class="featured_item">Chocolate<br>
70          Grand Marnier<br>
71          Cake</td>
72        </tr>
```

FIGURE G-33: The finished product

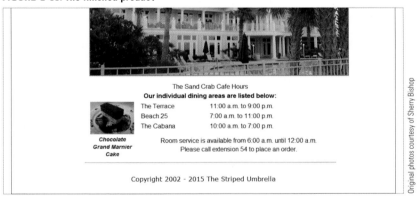

Original photos courtesy of Sherry Bishop

Using grids and guides for positioning page content

The View menu offers a number of options to help you position your page content more precisely. **Grids** consist of horizontal and vertical lines resembling graph paper that fill the page. You can edit the colors of the lines, the distance between them, whether they are displayed using lines or dots, and whether or not objects "snap" (automatically align) to them. **Guides** are horizontal or vertical lines that you place on the page yourself, by clicking and dragging onto the page from the vertical and horizontal rulers. Unlike grids, which fill the page, you can have as many or as few guides as you need. Both grids and guides are used to position page elements using exact measurements.

You can edit both the color of the guides and the color of the **distance,** a screen tip that shows you the distance between two guides when you hold down the control key (Win) or command key (Mac) and place the mouse pointer between the guides. You can lock the guides so you don't accidentally move them, and you can set them either to snap to page elements or have page elements snap to them. To display grids or guides, click View on the Menu bar, point to either Grid or Guides, then select an option from the displayed menu. Grids and guides only appear in Dreamweaver—they do not display when viewed in the browser.

Practice

Concepts Review

Label each element shown in Figure G-34.

FIGURE G-34

1. _____   5. _____
2. _____   6. _____
3. _____   7. _____
4. _____   8. _____

Match each of the following terms with the statement that best describes its function.

9. **Cells**

10. **Standard mode**

11. **div tags**

12. **Import**

13. **Fixed layout**

14. **CSS page layouts**

15. **Deprecated tags**

16. **CSS Layout box model**

17. **Export**

18. **Dynamic content**

a. Small boxes arranged in columns and rows

b. Pages built using div tags and CSS

c. Save data that was created in Dreamweaver with a different file format

d. Tags that are no longer considered to be the current standard

e. Page content that changes either in response to certain conditions or through interaction with the user

f. A layout with the width of content blocks based on pixels

g. The mode that does not include temporary cell padding and spacing

h. Bring data into Dreamweaver from another program

i. A view that displays padding and margins for divs

j. HTML tags that determine the appearance and position of containers of content

Skills Review

(If you did not create this website in Unit B and maintain it during the preceding units, you will need to create a local site root folder for this website and define the website using files your instructor will provide. See the "Read This Before You Begin" section for more detailed instructions.)

1. Create a page using CSS layouts.

   a. Start Dreamweaver, then open the Blooms & Bulbs website.

   b. Create a new blank HTML5 page with the 2 column fixed, right sidebar, header and footer layout, then attach the blooms_styles.css file to the page and save the new stylesheet file, HTML5_twoColFixRtHdr.css, in the blooms local site folder.

   c. Add the page title **Blooms & Bulbs – Your complete garden center** in the Title text box.

   d. Save the file as **workshops.html**, overwriting the existing workshops page.

2. Add content to CSS layout blocks.

   a. Open the index page, then copy the banner and menu bar. (Hint: Select the banner, hold down your Shift key, then click directly under the menu bar to select both.)

   b. Close the index page, then on the workshops page, delete the logo placeholder in the header and paste the banner and menu bar in the header block.

   c. Delete the footer placeholder text, then type **Copyright 2001 – 2015 Blooms & Bulbs** in the footer block.

   d. Delete the placeholder content from the content block.

   e. Type **New Composting Workshop!**, enter a paragraph break, then import the composting.doc file from the drive and folder where you store your Unit G Data Files.

   f. Enter a paragraph break after the last paragraph, then insert the chives.jpg file from the drive and folder where you store your Unit G Data Files. Add the alternate text **Even chives can be beautiful** to the image when prompted.

   g. Save your work.

3. Edit content in CSS layout blocks.

   a. Select the footer rule in the CSS Styles panel, then change the Text-align property in the Block category to center.

   b. Select the heading "New Composting Workshop!" and format it using the Heading 1 paragraph format if necessary.

4. Edit CSS layout properties.

   a. Select the header rule in the CSS Styles panel and change its background color to #FFF.

   b. Repeat Step a to change the background color of the sidebar1 rule to #FFF and the footer rule to #AFA19E.

   c. Edit the header rule so that the header has a 5-pixel margin on all sides.

   d. Edit the body rule in the HTML5_twoColFixRtHdr.css file to change the Font-size to 14 pixels.

   e. Edit the sidebar1 rule Float to left.

   f. Save your work.

5. Insert a table and set table properties.

   a. Delete the placeholder text in the sidebar, including the links, then insert a table with a header at the top of the table, eight rows, and two columns.

   b. Edit the sidebar1 rule to center-align the contents.

   c. Create a new Tag selector in the blooms_styles.css file to modify the table tag by setting the table Box width property to 180 pixels.

   d. Save your work.

Skills Review (continued)

6. **Merge and split cells.**
   a. Merge the two cells in the first row.
   b. Merge the two cells in the last row.
   c. Save your work.

7. **Insert and align images in table cells.**
   a. Use the Insert panel to insert gardening_gloves.gif from the drive and folder where you store your Unit G Data Files in the last row of the table. Add the alternate text **Gardening gloves** to the image when prompted.
   b. Save your work.

8. **Add text.**
   a. Type **Currently Scheduled Workshops** in the merged cells in the first row, using a line break after "Scheduled".
   b. Type the names and dates for the workshops from Figure G-35 in each row of the table.
   c. Save your work.

9. **Format and modify cell content.**
   a. Edit the table rule to center-align the contents.
   b. Save your work.

10. **Format cells.**
   a. Edit the table rule to add a left padding of 5 pixels.
   b. Place the insertion point in the top cell, switch to Code view, and add the following code to the end of the opening table data tag: **style="background-color:#C8DBB5"**. (Hint: When you finish editing the code it will read: <th colspan="2" scope="col" style="background-color:#C8DBB5">)
   c. Save your work, preview the workshops page in the browser, then compare your screen to Figure G-35.
   d. Close the browser and close all open pages.

Skills Review (continued)

FIGURE G-35

Important: *If you did not create the websites used in the following exercises in Unit B, you need to create a local site root folder for each website and define the websites using files your instructor provides. See the "Read This Before You Begin" section for more detailed instructions.*

Independent Challenge 1

You continue your work on the Rapids Transit website. After studying Cascading Style Sheets, you decide to experiment with predesigned CSS layouts. You create a new rates page based on a CSS HTML5 layout and add a table to list the equipment rental rates.

a. Open Dreamweaver, then open the Rapids Transit website.

b. Create a new HTML5 page based on the 2 column fixed, right sidebar, header and footer layout, and attach the rapids_transit.css file to the page. Verify that the new HTML5_twoColFixRtHdr.css file will be copied to the local site folder, then save it as rates.html, replacing the blank placeholder page.

c. Add the page title **Rapids Transit – Buffalo River Outfitters**.

d. Copy the banner and menu bar from the index page to the new, untitled page, replacing the logo placeholder, then close the index page.

e. Delete the placeholder text in the main content div, then import the file rentals.doc to take its place.

f. Replace the footer placeholder text with **Copyright 2001 - 2015 Rapids Transit. All rights reserved**.

g. Switch to Code view, delete all the placeholder content in the sidebar1 div, switch back to Design view, then insert girl_floating.jpg from the drive and folder where you store you Unit G Data Files. Add alternate text when prompted.

h. Edit the sidebar1 rule to change the box width to 240 pixels and the background to #FFF.

i. Edit the content rule to change the box width to 720 pixels.

j. Edit the header div to change the background color to #FFF, the text align to center, and add a box margin of 5 pixels on all sides.

k. Save your work.

l. Edit the footer rule to change the text-align to center and the font-style to italic.

m. Place the insertion point at the end of the last paragraph after the word "float" and insert a table with a top header, six rows, and four columns.

n. Create a new Tag Selector rule to modify the table tag with the following settings: Box width: 600 pixels, Box left margin: 60 pixels, Block text-align: left.

o. Merge the cells in the top row and type **Rental Rates per Day**.

p. Enter the rental information listed in Figure G-36 in the next three rows.

q. Merge the third and fourth cells in the fifth row, then insert the image rt_logo.gif. Add alternate text when prompted.

r. Merge the cells in the last row, then insert a horizontal rule.

s. Switch to Code view, then edit the header cell tag by adding following code: `style="text-align:center"`.

t. Edit each of the four cells under the header tag by adding the following code: `style="width:25%"`. (*Hint*: you will not see the column widths change to 25 percent unless you view the page in Live view or in a browser.

u. Save your work, preview the page in Live view or the browser, compare your screen to Figure G-36, make any spacing adjustments to improve the appearance if necessary, then close all pages and exit Dreamweaver.

Independent Challenge 1 (continued)

FIGURE G-36

Home	Our Guides	Rates	Lodging	Before You Go

You may be wondering why we charge to use our equipment when we are already charging a fee for the float. We do this because we have many repeat customers who have invested in their own gear. We want to be able to charge them a lower price than we charge those who don't own equipment. Therefore, the more you bring along with you, the less your float will cost! Our basic float price is $20.00 without equipment. Add the amounts on the table for the equipment you will need to the basic price, and you will have the total price of the float. We also take an action shot of you on the water that is included in the price of the float.

Rental Rates per Day

Canoe	$15.00	Life jacket	$3.00
Kayak	$19.00	Helmet	$2.00
Two-man raft	$22.00	Dry Packs	$1.00

Copyright 2001 - 2015 Rapids Transit. All rights reserved.

Independent Challenge 2

You continue your work on the TripSmart website. You are ready to begin work now on a page featuring a catalog item. You plan to use a CSS HTML5 layout with a table to place the data about the item.

a. Open Dreamweaver, open the TripSmart website, then create a new page based on the HTML5: three column fixed, header and footer CSS layout. Attach the tripsmart_styles.css file, verify that the new style sheet file that formats the page layout will be saved in the tripsmart local site root folder, then save the file as catalog.html, replacing the placeholder catalog page in the website.

b. Open the index page, copy the banner and menu bar, then close the index page.

c. Delete the logo image placeholder in the header, then paste the banner and menu bar in the header block.

d. Replace the placeholder text in the footer rule with **Copyright 2002 – 2015**, then edit the footer rule in the HTML5_thrColFixHdr.css style sheet to center align the content and set the background color to #FFF.

e. Edit the header rule to change the background to #FFF and add margins of 5 pixels to each side.

f. Edit the body rule in the HTML5_thrColFixHdr.css style sheet to change the Font-family to Arial, Helvetica, sans-serif, the Font-size to 14 pixels, and the background color to #FFF.

g. Save your work.

h. Delete the placeholder content in the content block, then type **This Week's Featured Catalog Item**.

i. Delete the placeholder text in the sidebar1 div (first column) and type **These are the lengths available for order:**. (Hint: Remember it is much easier to select all of the placeholder content in Code view.)

j. Delete the placeholder text in the aside div (third column) then type **Special Shipping Offer**, enter a paragraph break, type **Order two or more walking sticks this week and your shipping is free. Enter the code twosticks when you check out to receive free shipping.** then apply the Heading 2 format to the Special Shipping Offer text.

k. Create a new Tag rule in the tripsmart_styles.css style sheet that modifies the Heading 2 tag as follows: Font-family: Arial, Helvetica, sans-serif; Font-size: 16 pixels; Type Color: #54572C, then create a new Tag rule in the tripsmart_styles.css file to modify the Heading 1 tag with settings of your choice.

l. Create a new Class rule called centered_text in the tripsmart_styles.css style sheet and set the Text-align property to center. Select the Special Shipping Offer heading and apply the centered_text rule.

m. Enter a paragraph break after the heading in the second column, then insert the image walking_stick.jpg from the drive and folder where you store your Unit G Data Files, adding appropriate alternate text.

n. Create a new class rule named catalog_images in the tripsmart_styles.css file that will add a border of your choice around the image, set the float to left, and add a margin to all sides with settings of your choice. Apply the catalog_images rule to the walking stick image.

o. Edit the sidebar1 rule and the aside rule to set the background color for each rule to #FFF.

p. Edit the footer rule to add a top border of your choice.

q. Edit the container rule to add a border with your choice of settings around all sides.

r. Edit the content rule to change the width to 580 pixels, 10-pixel padding for all sides, and the file tripsmart_gradient.jpg for a background image.

s. Place the insertion point to the right of the walking stick image, then import the file walking sticks.doc from the drive and folder where you store your Unit G Data Files.

t. Insert a table under the text "These are the lengths available for order." with the following settings: rows: 8, columns: 2, Header: top.

u. Create a rule in the tripsmart_styles.css file to modify the table tag as follows: Box width: 175 px; border: solid; border width: thin; border color: #BABD9F, text-align: center.

v. Insert the data for the table using the information in the table in Figure G-37.

w. Add the page title **TripSmart - Serving all your travel needs.**

x. Save your work, preview the page in the browser, and compare your screen to Figure G-37.

y. Close the browser, close all open pages, then exit Dreamweaver.

Independent Challenge 2 (continued)

FIGURE G-37

Independent Challenge 3

Dell Patterson has opened a new shop called CollegeFandz, an online source for college students' clothing and collectibles. She is considering creating a website to promote her products and would like to gather some ideas before she hires a web designer. She decides to visit websites to look for design ideas, and asks you for your help.

- **a.** Connect to the Internet, then go to sfbags.com, as shown in Figure G-38.
- **b.** View the source code for the index page and locate the HTML tags that control the CSS on the page.
- **c.** How is CSS used on this site?
- **d.** List at least five div IDs that you find on the index page.
- **e.** Use the Reference panel in Dreamweaver to look up two sets of code used in this site for page layout that you don't understand.

FIGURE G-38

Waterfield Designs website (sfbags.com) © 2012 Waterfield Designs, Inc.

Real Life Independent Challenge

For this assignment, you will continue to work on the website that you have been developing since Unit A. You are building this website from unit to unit, so you must do each Real Life Independent Challenge to complete your website. There are no Data Files supplied. You will continue building your website by designing and completing a page that uses CSS for page layout.

a. Consult your wireframes to decide which page to create and develop for this unit. Draw a sketch of the page to show how you will use CSS to lay out the content.

b. Create the new page for the site using one of the predesigned CSS layouts. Add or edit the divs on your page, making sure to name each one.

c. Add text, images, or background colors to each div.

d. Copy the menu bar from an existing page to the new page.

e. Update the menu bar, if necessary, to include a link to the new page.

f. Consider using the new page as an example to redesign the existing pages with CSS.

g. Save your work, preview each page in your browser, then make any necessary modifications to achieve a clean, consistent, attractive design for each page.

h. Consult your wireframe to see if you have a need to incorporate a table into one of the pages.

i. If you decide to add a table, create rules to format the table elements.

j. Add the data in your plan to the table cells, modifying the appearance as necessary.

k. View your table in a browser, close your browser, close all open pages, then exit Dreamweaver.

Visual Workshop

Use Figure G-39 as a guide to continue your work on the Carolyne's Creations website. Create a new catering page based on the HTML5: 2 column fixed, right sidebar, header and footer page layout. Remember to attach the website style sheet to the page and save the HTML5_thrColFixHdr.css file in the local site root folder. The image, marshmallows.jpg, is found in the assets folder in the drive and folder where you store your Unit G Data Files. Experiment with your CSS settings to create your unique design for the page.

FIGURE G-39

Adding Media and Interactivity

Files You Will Need:

To view a list of files needed for this unit, see the Data Files Grid in the back of the book.

There are many ways to make a website more compelling for users. Most users would rather feel that they are interacting with a site, rather than passively reading information. Adding media objects, such as rollover images, behaviors, Flash video, Flash movies, and sound, provides more interest than static text and images. You decide to add more interactivity to The Striped Umbrella website. You begin by exploring the various options available to you as a designer.

OBJECTIVES

Understand media objects

Add Flash objects

Add behaviors

Edit behaviors

Add rollover images

Add video

Add sound

Update files

Incorporate Web 2.0 technology

Understanding Media Objects

While a website with text and static images is adequate for presenting information, you can create a much richer user experience by adding movement and interactive elements. You can use Dreamweaver to add media objects created in other programs to the pages of your website. The term *media object* can have different meanings, depending on the industry it is applied to. For our purposes, **media objects** are combinations of visual and audio effects and text used to create an interactive experience within a website. You want to add interest to The Striped Umbrella site by including media objects. You begin by learning about media objects and how they can help you achieve your remaining website goals.

- **Role of media objects**

  The role of a media object is to enhance the user's experience while visiting a website. Thus, each media object that you add should provide a specific purpose that could not be achieved as well without it. As with the use of images, there is a fine balance between providing a rich experience for users, cluttering your page, and not adding enough interesting detail. Too many media objects on a page can slow the time it takes the page to load and be a problem for users with slow connection speeds. Strive to use the smallest possible file size for your media objects to keep download time at a minimum. Also, provide accessibility by using alt or title tags when you insert media objects. Figure H-1 shows an example of the NASA website, which uses video, rollovers, and audio files.

- **Types of media objects**

  You can use Dreamweaver to insert a variety of media effects into your web pages, including Flash movies, video, and a series of built-in JavaScript behaviors, such as sounds, rollover images, drop-down menus, Go to URLs, and menus. **Go to URLs** direct the browser to use a link to open a different window. Some of the external media file types include Adobe Fireworks menu bars, rollover images, and buttons; video, sound, and animation; Flash Paper; Director and Shockwave movies and presentations; Java applets; ActiveX controls; server-side controls; and a variety of plug-ins. A **plug-in** (also called an **add-on**) is a small computer program that works with a host application, such as a web browser, to enable it to perform certain functions. In order to play a Flash SWF file in a web browser, you would need to install the Flash Player plug-in. In order to read Adobe PDF files, you would need to install the Adobe Reader plug-in. Plug-ins allow you to extend the capabilities of the browser to display content, letting you create complex, interactive websites with media effects that can be viewed within the pages themselves. Another advantage of plug-ins is that they eliminate the need to load an external document player, such as Windows Media Player. The future of Flash technology has been a topic of discussion recently. Some devices, such as the iPhone and iPad, do not support the Flash Player plug-in. With the development of HTML5, CSS3, Adobe Edge, Adobe Air, and Adobe Flex, we will probably be seeing some shifting in the methods we have used in the past to create animation and motion.

- **Adding media objects with HTML5**

  Although Adobe Flash is still the premier tool used for creating animation, with the development of HTML5 and CSS3, we have new ways available now for incorporating motion and animation. HTML5 includes new tags for animation and video such as the <audio> tag and the <video> tag with attributes such as autoplay, controls, loop, and src. With CSS3, there are new styles for enhancing appearance of page objects such as rounded corners and gradients. Adobe Edge, a new program introduced by Adobe, combines the new capabilities of HTML5, CSS3, and JavaScript but uses a program interface similar to Flash. Like Flash, a stage, timeline, playhead, symbols, frames, and layers are used to manipulate text, shapes, and images. Unlike Flash, Edge codes in JSON (JavaScript Object Notation), a subset of JavaScript rather than ActionScript. This means that Edge creates animation that is coded entirely with HTML and JavaScript, so browsers that support HTML5 will not need a plug-in to play the animations. Edge also integrates with font services such as Typekit or FontSquirrel.

NASA website (nasa.gov)

Dreamweaver CS6

Using Adobe Flash Player to view Flash content

To view Flash movies, you need to install Adobe Flash Player. This program is included in the latest versions of Internet Explorer, Mozilla Firefox, Safari, and Opera. If you are using an older browser that does not support the version of Flash used to create your movie, you can download the latest Flash Player from the Adobe website, located at adobe.com. Almost all browsers use Adobe Flash Player. However, the mobile and touch markets are not as supportive. Internet Explorer 10 Metro and Apple iOS devices do not support the Flash plug-in. When you use the Insert panel to add Flash content to a web page, the code that links and runs the content (such as detecting the presence of Flash Player and directing the user to download it if necessary) is embedded into the page code.

Adding Flash Objects

Flash is a program that allows you to create low-bandwidth, high-quality animations and interactive elements called Flash movies that you can place on your web pages. **Low-bandwidth** animations are animations that don't require a fast connection to work properly. These animations use a series of vector-based graphics to create short movies that download quickly. **Vector-based graphics** are scalable graphics that are built using mathematical formulas, rather than pixels. When you use the Insert panel to add Flash content to a web page, the code that links and runs the content is embedded into the page code. Thus, the presence of a Flash player can be identified by the computer, which will then provide a prompt to the user to download the player if it is not detected. The original Flash file is stored as a separate file in the local site root folder. Flash movies have the .swf file extension. The cafe logo displayed at the top of the cafe page is an attractive image. However, an animated logo would add movement and more interest to the page. You decide to replace the current logo image with a Flash movie.

STEPS

1. **Start Dreamweaver, switch to Design view if necessary, open the cafe page in The Striped Umbrella website, then place the insertion point in the sidebar to the left of the word "Reservations"**

   You will insert a Flash movie above the reservations sentence.

2. **Click the Media button list arrow in the Common category on the Insert panel, then click SWF**

   The Select SWF dialog box opens. You use this dialog box to locate the Flash movie.

   > **QUICK TIP**
   > If you already have a Flash .swf file in your local site root folder, you can drag and drop it from the Assets panel or Files panel instead of using the Insert panel or Insert menu.

3. **Navigate to the drive and folder where you store your Unit H Data Files, click crabdance.swf, click OK (Win) or Open (Mac), click Yes in the Dreamweaver dialog box, then click Save**

   The movie is copied and saved in the local site root folder of The Striped Umbrella website. An Object Tag Accessibility Attributes dialog box opens. This is where you add a title for screen readers.

4. **Type Cafe logo animation in the Title text box, click OK, select FlashID in the ID text box in the Property inspector, type crabdance, then press [Enter] Win or [return] Mac**

   A Flash movie placeholder appears on the page, as shown in Figure H-2. The title and ID provide accessibility for the Flash movie. The Loop check box in the Property inspector is currently selected, which means that the Flash movie will play continuously (loop) by default while the page is viewed.

   > **QUICK TIP**
   > Mac users do not have a Play button on the Property inspector.

5. **With the placeholder selected, click the Play button in the Property inspector, then click Stop (Win), or skip to Step 6 (Mac)**

   The movie plays in a continuous loop until you stop it.

   > **QUICK TIP**
   > You may have to refresh your Files panel to see the new Scripts folder.

6. **Click the Loop check box to deselect it, save your work, then click OK to close the Copy Dependent Files dialog box**

   Two supporting files, expressInstall.swf and swfobject_modified.js, are copied to a new Scripts folder. These files are necessary for the movie to play in the browser correctly. Deselecting the Loop check box stops the Flash movie from playing continuously.

   > **QUICK TIP**
   > If your Flash movie is too close to the menu bar, insert a line break between them.

7. **Click the Switch Design View to Live View button (Live), then compare your screen to Figure H-3**

   The page is displayed in Live View, with all active content functioning. As it will do when viewed in a browser, the Flash movie plays one time and then stops.

8. **Click (Live), then close the cafe page**

FIGURE H-2: The Flash movie inserted on the cafe page

Flash movie placeholder

Loop check box

ID text box | Name of Flash file | Play button (Mac users do not have a Play button) | Media button list arrow

© 2013 Cengage Learning
Original photo courtesy of Sherry Bishop

FIGURE H-3: Viewing the Flash movie with Live View

Switch Design View to Live View button

Flash movie

© 2013 Cengage Learning
Original photo courtesy of Sherry Bishop

Using Flash movies

Using Flash, you can create Flash movies that include multimedia elements, such as audio files (both music and voice-overs), animated objects, scripted objects, and clickable links. You can use Flash movies to add content to your existing website or to create an entire website. To add a Flash movie to a web page, click SWF from the Media menu in the Common category on the Insert panel to open the Select SWF dialog box, and then choose the Flash movie you want to insert. As with images, always add a title tag when inserting Flash content to provide accessibility. You also need to include code that will instruct the browser to check for and load a Flash player so the user can view the Flash content on the page. To preview your Flash movies, you can either use Live view or preview them in a browser window. See "Using Adobe Flash Player to view Flash content" at the bottom of page 203 for an additional way to add Flash content without using the Flash player.

Adding Behaviors

You can make your web pages come alive by adding interactive elements, such as special effects, to them. These special effects are called **actions**. For example, you could attach an action to an image that would result in a descriptive drop-down message when the mouse is rolled over it. You add actions to elements by attaching behaviors to them. **Behaviors** are sets of instructions that tell the page element to respond in a specific way when an event occurs, such as when the mouse pointer is positioned over the element. When you attach a behavior to an element, Dreamweaver generates the JavaScript code for the behavior and inserts it into your page code. ▒▒▒▒▒ The Striped Umbrella staff would like guests to know ahead of time that feeding the birds and other wildlife around the property is prohibited. You decide to add an action to the activities page that will automatically open a new browser window with a related message.

STEPS

1. **Open the file dwh_1.html from the drive and folder where you store your Unit H Data Files, save it in the local site root folder as wildlife_message.html without updating links, then close dwh_1.html and wildlife_message.html**

    The wildlife_message page is already linked to the su_styles.css style sheet and coded with the body_text style. (The connection became active when the file was saved to the website.)

2. **Open the activities page, select the family_sunset image on the activities page, click Window on the Menu bar, then click Behaviors**

    The Tag Inspector panel opens with the Behaviors tab selected. With the family_sunset image selected, any action that is selected will apply to the image.

> **QUICK TIP**
> An event can be changed by clicking it and choosing a different event.

3. **Click the Add behavior button ✚▾ on the Behaviors panel toolbar, as shown in Figure H-4, then click Open Browser Window**

    The Open Browser Window dialog box opens. This is where you select the file to be opened, the window size, and other options. The name of the event is onClick. Once an action is selected, the name of the event will appear by default in the left column of the Behaviors.

4. **Click Browse next to the URL to display text box to open the Select File dialog box, navigate to the local site root folder if necessary, then double-click wildlife_message.html**

    You identify the location where the message resides. The message will display when the family_sunset image is clicked.

5. **Type 300 in the Window width text box, type 300 in the Window height text box, type message in the Window name text box, compare your screen to Figure H-5, then click OK**

    The new dimensions will be applied to the page when it opens in a browser window.

> **QUICK TIP**
> The information bar at the top of the window will display specific instructions for your browser type.

6. **Save your work, preview the page in your browser, then click the family_sunset image, as shown in Figure H-6**

    The wildlife_message page opens in a new browser window that is 300 pixels wide and 300 pixels high.

7. **Close both browser windows**

Using the Behaviors panel to add Actions

You can use the Behaviors panel to insert a variety of JavaScript-based behaviors on a page. For instance, you can automate tasks, respond to user selections and mouse movements with drop-down menus, create games, go to a different URL, or add automatic dynamic effects to a web page. To insert a behavior, click the Add behavior button on the Behaviors panel to open the Actions menu, then click an action from the menu. Actions are triggered by events. For instance, if you want the user to see a page element slide across the page when the element is clicked, you would attach the Slide action using the **onClick** event to trigger the action. Other examples of events are onMouseOver and onLoad. The **onMouseOver** event will trigger an action when the mouse is placed over an object. The **onLoad** event will trigger an action when the page is first loaded in the browser window.

FIGURE H-4: **Behaviors panel with the Actions menu displayed**

Add behavior button

Actions menu

Open Browser Window action

FIGURE H-5: **Setting Open Browser Window options**

URL to display text box

Window width text box

Window name text box

Window height text box

FIGURE H-6: **Viewing the wildlife message in a browser**

Wildlife message displayed in new browser window

Clicking the family_sunset image triggers the event

© 2013 Cengage Learning
Original photos courtesy of Sherry Bishop

Using the Spry framework

Some of the behaviors that you can add to web pages use a JavaScript library called the **Spry framework for AJAX. Asynchronous JavaScript and XML (AJAX)** is a method for developing interactive web pages that respond quickly to user input, such as clicking a map. The JavaScript library contains **spry widgets**, which are prebuilt components for adding interactivity to pages, and **spry effects**, which are screen effects, such as fading and enlarging page elements. When you add a spry effect to a page element, Dreamweaver automatically adds a **SpryAssets folder** to the local site root folder with the supporting files located inside the folder.

Adding Media and Interactivity

Editing Behaviors

Once a behavior has been added to a web page or web page object, it is easy to modify the action or event by using the Behaviors panel. To change an event, click the left column in the Behaviors panel to display the list of events, then choose the event you would like to use. To change the action, click the right column to display the list of actions, then choose the action you would like to use. You can edit an existing behavior by clicking the right column of the existing behavior, then clicking Edit Behavior. ▄▄▟▟▟ The current browser window that displays the wildlife message is a little too large. You want to resize the window so it will fit the message better. You would also prefer that the event for this behavior opens a new window when the mouse is simply placed over the image rather than clicked. You decide to use the Behaviors panel to make the necessary adjustments to the page.

STEPS

1. **Click the** family_sunset image **if necessary, right-click (Win) the** Open Browser Window **action in the right column of the Behaviors panel, then click** Edit Behavior

   The Open Browser Window dialog box opens. This is where you adjust the window properties and settings, such as establishing window dimensions, including a status bar, or adding scrollbars as needed.

QUICK TIP

Your window may appear slightly different depending on the browser you are using to view the page.

2. **Change the window height to** 245, **click** OK, **save your changes, preview the page in your browser, then click the** family_sunset image

   The browser window with the wildlife message is not as tall as it was, as shown in Figure H-7.

3. **Close both browser windows**

4. **Click the** left column **of the Open Browser Window action in the Behaviors panel, click the** events list arrow, **then click** onMouseOver, **as shown in Figure H-8**

   The onMouseOver selection specifies that the event of placing the mouse over an image triggers an action. The Open Browser Window action remains the same.

TROUBLE

If you see a message that pop-ups are disabled in your browser, click the prompt to temporarily allow popups.

5. **Save your work, preview the page in the browser, then move the mouse over the family_sunset image**

   Simply placing the mouse over the image, rather than clicking it, triggers the Open Browser Window action.

6. **Close the browser windows, then close the Behaviors panel**

Using the Server Behaviors panel

In addition to the Behaviors panel, Dreamweaver also has a Server Behaviors panel, which is located in the Dynamic Content Tab group with the Databases, Bindings, and Components panels. The **Server Behaviors** panel is used to add server behaviors. Server behaviors are tools that write server-side code, such as ASP, PHP, or ColdFusion. For example, you can add code to create a login page or create a page that is password protected. You can also build search pages that will enable users to search a website for specific content. After you have created a server behavior and enabled Dreamweaver to display live data, you can add, edit, or delete the server behavior while you are in Design view, but viewing the page in Live View.

FIGURE H-7: Viewing the edited window size

Reduced
window
size with
wildlife
message
displayed

© 2013 Cengage Learning
Original photos courtesy of Sherry Bishop

FIGURE H-8: Editing the event for the Open Browser Window action

© 2013 Cengage Learning
Original photos courtesy of Sherry Bishop

onMouseOver event

Adding Rollover Images

A **rollover image** is an image that changes its appearance when the mouse pointer is placed over it in a browser. A rollover image actually consists of two images. The first image is the one that displays when the mouse pointer is not positioned over it, and the second image is the one that displays when the mouse pointer is positioned over it. Rollover images are often used to help create a feeling of action and interest on a web page. When a rollover image is inserted into a page, Dreamweaver automatically adds two behaviors: a Swap Image behavior and a Swap Image Restore behavior. A **Swap Image behavior** is JavaScript code that directs the browser to display a different image when the mouse is rolled over an image on the page. A **Swap Image Restore behavior** restores the swapped image back to the original image when the mouse is moved away from the image. ▟▟▟▟▟ You have a photograph of a dolphin that would be perfect on the activities page. To add some interactivity to the page, you decide to include the photograph as a rollover image for the current image of two dolphins.

STEPS

1. **Select the image of the two dolphins, then delete it**

   The rollover image will be placed in the same position on the page as the deleted two_dolphins image.

2. **Click the Images list arrow in the Common group on the Insert panel, then click Rollover Image**

   The Insert Rollover Image dialog box opens. This is where you specify the name of the image and link to the images you will use for both the original image and the rollover image.

3. **Type dolphins in the Image name text box, click Browse next to the Original image text box, browse to the drive and folder where you store your Unit H Data Files, open the assets folder, then double-click one_dolphin.jpg**

   You specify the image name for the rollover and identify the name and location for the original image. The original image is the one that initially displays in the browser window.

QUICK TIP
To prevent one of the images from being resized during the rollover, both images should be the same height and width.

4. **Click Browse next to the Rollover image text box, browse to the drive and folder where you store your Unit H Data Files if necessary, double-click two_dolphins.jpg, then overwrite the two_dolphins.jpg file in your website assets folder**

   You specify the name and location for the rollover image. The rollover image is the image that displays in the browser window when the mouse rolls over the original image. This version of the two_dolphins image is a different size from your original file.

QUICK TIP
The Preload rollover image option ensures that the rollover image displays without a delay.

5. **Type Dolphins riding the surf in the Alternate text text box, verify that the Preload rollover image check box is selected, compare your screen to Figure H-9, then click OK**

   The single dolphin image displays on the page. The two_dolphins image will only appear in the browser window when the mouse rolls over it.

TROUBLE
If you don't see the rollover image, temporarily direct your browser to allow blocked content.

6. **Select the image, apply the img_right_float rule to it, save your work, preview the page in your browser, move your mouse pointer over the single dolphin image, then compare your screen to Figure H-10**

   The image is aligned to the right of the paragraph with a left margin of 10px. When you point to the image, the single dolphin image is swapped with the two-dolphin image. When you move the mouse away from the image, it is swapped again.

7. **Close the browser, then click the Show Code view button** `Code`

   The code for the swap image behavior displays, as shown in Figure H-11. The code directs the browser to display the image with one dolphin "onmouseout"—when the mouse is not over the image. It directs the browser to display the image with two dolphins "onmouseover"—when the mouse is over the image.

8. **Click the Show Design view button** `Design`

Dreamweaver CS6

FIGURE H-9: Setting rollover image properties

Image name text box

Original image text box

Rollover image text box

Preload rollover
image check box

Alternate text
text box

FIGURE H-10: Viewing the rollover image in a browser

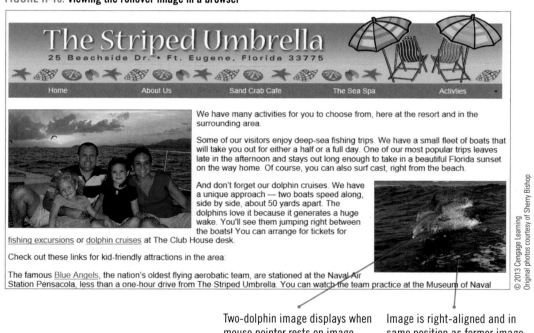

© 2013 Cengage Learning
Original photos courtesy of Sherry Bishop

Two-dolphin image displays when
mouse pointer rests on image

Image is right-aligned and in
same position as former image

FIGURE H-11: Viewing the code for the rollover image

onmouseout
command

onmouseover
command

Adding Video

Another way to add rich media content to your web pages is to insert video files. Of the several available video formats, one of the most popular is the MP4 format. You can insert a video in Dreamweaver with the Insert > Media > Plugin command. HTML5 introduced a way to add video with the <video> tag. The advantages of this method are numerous: it supports video in native formats, is compatible in all browsers, and the video controls can be accessed with a keyboard. You can also include code to link multiple video formats to provide access for all browsers and make your videos searchable by search engines. To add video with the <video> tag, you add the tags in Code view. Used sparingly, video can be an effective way to add interest and depth to your web pages. The **skin** is the bar at the bottom of the video with the control buttons. Every guest is given a small beach umbrella anchor as a welcome gift, which then can be used to secure a beach umbrella in the sand. Since guests sometimes have trouble figuring out this procedure, you decide to add a short Flash video to the about_us page that demonstrates the process.

STEPS

1. **Using Windows Explorer (Win) or Finder (Mac), copy the file umbrella_anchor_video.mp4 from the drive and folder where you store your Unit H Data Files, paste it into the assets folder in The Striped Umbrella local site root folder, close Windows Explorer (Win) or Finder (Mac), then return to Dreamweaver**

   The file is copied to the local site assets folder and ready to insert in the page.

2. **Open the about_us page, click to place the insertion point at the end of the last paragraph on the page, enter a paragraph return, click the Media list arrow in the Common category on the Insert panel, then click Plugin**

   The Select File dialog box opens. This is where you enter the name of the video.

3. **Browse to your local site assets folder if necessary, double-click umbrella_anchor_video.mp4, then enter four paragraph breaks after the plug-in placeholder**

   The video plug-in placeholder is inserted on the page, as shown in Figure H-12.

4. **Select the plug-in placeholder, change the W value in the Property inspector to 220, and the H value to 200, click the Parameters button, click the Add button, enter autostart for a Parameter and false for the Value, as shown in Figure H-13, then click OK**

   The placeholder for the plug-in now fits the size of the video plus a little extra for the controls. The video will not start until the user clicks the play button.

5. **Place the insertion point to the right of the video placeholder image, type Visit us at the front desk to pick up your complimentary Umbrella Anchor! using line breaks as shown in Figure H-14, then apply the img_left_float rule to the plug-in placeholder.**

   The explanatory text helps guests understand the purpose of the video.

6. **Apply the H3 format and the body_text rule to the sentence, switch to Code view, then delete the ending < /embed> tag from the code that embeds the video on the page**

   The code will work just fine without the < /embed> tag, but leaving it in the code will keep the page from passing HTML5 validation.

7. **Save your work, preview the page in the browser, compare your screen to Figure H-14, click the Play button ▶, close the browser, return to Design view, then close the about_us page**

FIGURE H-12: Inserting a video on the activities page

After you arrive, you will want to take a stroll down the boardwalk to the beach. The entrance to the boardwalk is just past the pool area. The boardwalk provides a safe route to the beach for both our guests and the native vegetation. The sea oats and other flora are tender. Please do not step on them or pick them. A lifeguard is on duty from 9:00 a.m. until sunset. Check the flag each time you head for the beach for the status of current swimming conditions and advisories. Jellyfish can be a problem at times, so be careful when you are walking along the beach, especially as the tide is retreating from high tide. We have beach chairs, umbrellas, and towels available to our guests. Check with the attendant on duty. Water, juices, and soft drinks are also available for purchase at the end of the boardwalk. Don't forget your sunglasses, hat, and sunscreen! A sunburn is sure way to ruin a nice vacation. The gift shop in The Club House is a convenient place to pick up any items that you may have forgotten to bring along, in addition to an extensive inventory of bathing suits, sandals, and other beachwear.

Video placeholder inserted on page

Original photos courtesy of Sherry Bishop

FIGURE H-13: Editing the settings for the video

Value = false

New parameter = autostart

H = 200   W = 220   Parameters button

FIGURE H-14: Viewing the video in a browser

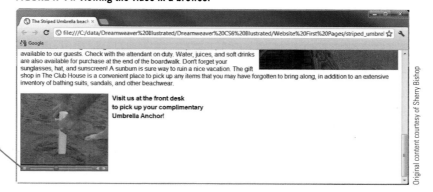

Play button becomes pause button while video is playing

Original content courtesy of Sherry Bishop

Comparing video file formats

There are several file format choices for publishing video files. Among them are **AVI** (Audio Visual Interleave), a Microsoft format; **MOV** (Apple QuickTime); **MP4** (a digital video compression standard); **FLV** (Adobe Flash Video); **WebM** (Google developed open-source format); and **Ogg** (Ogg Theora), an open-source format developed by Xiph.org. Of these file formats, MP4, WebM, and Ogg are the three HTML5 supported video formats.

Adding Sound

There are several ways to incorporate sound into a website. Sound files are relatively small in file size and easy to add to a page. You can embed them as a background sound, embed them on a page with visible sound controls, link them to a page, or add them to a page with the new <audio> tags introduced in HTML5. A few audio file formats do not require a plug-in to play, such as the wav (Waveform Extension) and aif or aiff (Audio Interchange File Format) file formats. Files that do require a plug-in are mp3 or MPEG (Motion Picture Experts Group) files, which can be played using QuickTime, Windows Media Player, or RealPlayer plug-ins. As with incorporating video, when you incorporate sound files, you should provide more than one audio format if possible to make sure all browsers will have a format they can play. Before you decide to add a sound to a page, think about the purpose you have in mind. Will the sound add to a rich media experience for your users? What devices will your users use to play the sound? Have you tested the audio file to make sure the sound quality is excellent? You decide to add a few guest comments to the activities page. It will be much more interesting to insert an audio file on the page rather than printed comments.

STEPS

1. **Use Windows Explorer (Win) or Finder (Mac) to copy the file** interviews.mp3 **from the drive and folder where you store your Unit H Data Files to your website assets folder**
   This is the audio file with the recorded guest comments.

2. **On the activities page, add a paragraph break after the last paragraph, then type Here are some comments from recent guests describing their favorite activities at The Striped Umbrella.**

3. **Add another paragraph break, click** Insert **on the Menu bar, point to** Media, **click** Plugin, **browse to find the interviews.mp3 file in your website assets folder, then double-click interviews.mp3**
   A plug-in icon placeholder appears on the page, as shown in Figure H-15. You create a rule to modify the placeholder appearance.

4. **Select the plug-in placeholder, then use the Property inspector to change the W value to 200 and the H value to 20**
   The plug-in placeholder image is longer.

5. **Click** Parameters **in the Property inspector, click the** Add **button, enter** autostart **for a Parameter and** false **for the Value, as shown in Figure H-16, then click** OK

QUICK TIP
If the file won't play in your browser, it's possible that you are missing a plug-in. Contact your technical support for instructions.

6. **Save the activities page, preview the page in a browser, then play the file, as shown in Figure H-17**

7. **Close the browser, then switch to Code view**

8. **Scroll to locate the** <embed> **tag for the audio file, delete the ending** < /embed> **tag at the end of the line, then save your work, switch back to Design view, and close the page**
   The code will work just fine without the < /embed> tag, but leaving it will keep the page from passing HTML5 validation.

FIGURE H-15: Inserting a sound file on the activities page

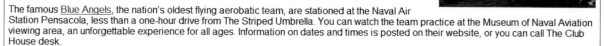

Check out these links for kid-friendly attractions in the area:

The famous Blue Angels, the nation's oldest flying aerobatic team, are stationed at the Naval Air Station Pensacola, less than a one-hour drive from The Striped Umbrella. You can watch the team practice at the Museum of Naval Aviation viewing area, an unforgettable experience for all ages. Information on dates and times is posted on their website, or you can call The Club House desk.

It's a short ride over the Alabama border to see the USS Alabama, one of America's most decorated battleships. The "Mighty A" is docked at Battleship Memorial Park in Mobile Bay, Alabama. There you can take a two-hour self-guided tour that is rich in history. Hours, directions, and prices are posted on their website, or call The Club House desk.

Here are some comments from recent guests describing their favorite activites at the Striped Umbrella:

Plug-in placeholder image

FIGURE H-16: Adding a parameter to the sound object

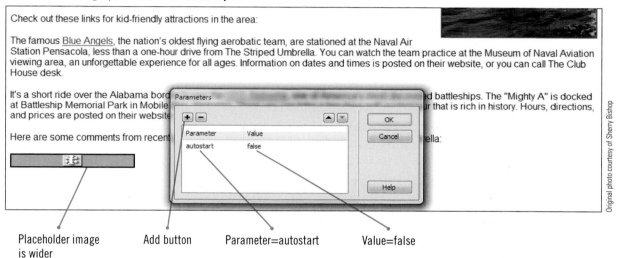

Placeholder image is wider   Add button   Parameter=autostart   Value=false

---

FIGURE H-17: Viewing the sound file on the activities page

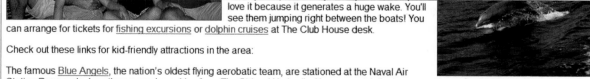

love it because it generates a huge wake. You'll see them jumping right between the boats! You can arrange for tickets for fishing excursions or dolphin cruises at The Club House desk.

Check out these links for kid-friendly attractions in the area:

The famous Blue Angels, the nation's oldest flying aerobatic team, are stationed at the Naval Air Station Pensacola, less than a one-hour drive from The Striped Umbrella. You can watch the team practice at the Museum of Naval Aviation viewing area, an unforgettable experience for all ages. Information on dates and times is posted on their website, or you can call The Club House desk.

It's a short ride over the Alabama border to see the USS Alabama, one of America's most decorated battleships. The "Mighty A" is docked at Battleship Memorial Park in Mobile Bay, Alabama. There you can take a two-hour self-guided tour that is rich in history. Hours, directions, and prices are posted on their website, or call The Club House desk.

Here are some comments from recent guests describing their favorite activites at the Striped Umbrella:

The skin will vary in appearance depending on the browser used

Updating Files

As your website grows and you have additional folders and files to keep track of, it is imperative to keep your files in good order. Deleting files that are no longer needed and keeping your other files updated are important to insure quality websites. In Unit F, you learned to run reports to identify broken links and orphaned files. When you are using incomplete pages as placeholder pages, they will not show up as orphaned files if they contain links from other pages. Before publishing your site to a web server, however, be sure to complete all pages; publishing incomplete pages is considered unprofessional. You are ready to finalize the fishing and cruises pages. You replace the placeholder pages with completed pages so that all of the pages are up to date.

STEPS

1. **Open the file dwh_2.html from the folder where you store your Unit H Data Files, then save it as fishing.html in the striped_umbrella local site root folder, overwriting the existing fishing page but not updating links**

   Although the page is saved, the image will continue to display as a broken link on the fishing page until the image is saved in the website.

2. **Click the broken graphic placeholder, click the Browse for File button 🗀 next to the Src text box in the Property inspector, browse to where you store your Unit H Data Files, open the assets folder, then double-click the file fisherman.jpg to copy the file to the striped_umbrella assets folder**

   The file is copied to the site assets folder.

3. **Deselect the image placeholder**

   The page displays with fisherman's image, as shown in Figure H-18. Since the code was already in place on the page linking the su_styles.css to the file, the text is automatically updated with the body_text style. The Spry Menu bar is also formatted correctly.

4. **Close the file dwh_2.html, close the fishing page, then switch back to Design view**

5. **Open the file dwh_3.html from where you store your Unit H Data Files, then save it as cruises.html in the striped_umbrella local site root folder, overwriting the existing cruises page but not updating links**

   The page is saved, but the image link remains broken because the image has not been saved in the website.

6. **Close the dwh_3.html page, click the broken graphic placeholder, click 🗀 next to the Src text box in the Property inspector, browse to where you store your Unit H Data Files, open the assets folder, double-click the file boats.jpg, click Yes to copy the file to the striped_umbrella assets folder, then click Save**

   The file is copied to the site assets folder.

7. **Deselect the image placeholder**

   The image displays on the page, as shown in Figure H-19. Since the code was already in place on the page linking to the su_styles.css style sheet, the text is automatically updated with the body_text style.

8. **Save and close the page, then exit Dreamweaver**

FIGURE H-18: Fishing page updated

We have several boats available for fishing trips that can be rented by the hour, half day, or full day. You may choose to go out to sea several miles for deep-sea fishing, or fish in one of several bays not far from the resort. Call the front desk to schedule your trip and let them know the fishing gear you will need us to provide. Bring your catch back and our chefs will be happy to prepare it to your specifications for dinner!

Be sure to apply sunscreen liberally before you arrive at the dock. A large hat with a tie is highly recommended to protect your head and neck while you are on the open water. We will provide a cooler with bottles of water, but you will need to provide your own snacks or lunch. The Sand Crab Cafe will be happy to prepare these for you if you call several hours in advance.

© 2013 Cengage Learning
Original photo courtesy of Sherry Bishop

FIGURE H-19: Cruises page updated

This is the Dolphin Racer at dock. We leave daily at 4:00 p.m.and 6:30 p.m. for 1-1/2 hour cruises. There are snacks and restrooms available on board. We welcome children of all ages. Our ship is a U.S. Coast Guard approved vessel and our captain is a former member of the Coast Guard. Call The Club desk for reservations.

If you plan to join us, please apply sunscreen liberally before you leave. A hat that can be securely tied to your head is a must. Be sure to bring your video camera because you will not want to miss the opportunity to take some great footage of the dolphins at play.

© 2013 Cengage Learning
Original photo courtesy of Sherry Bishop

Using HTML5 compliant media tags

As HTML5 gains support across all browsers, you will want to use HTML5 tags to insert and format your media content. For example, to insert a Flash SWF file, while the code you used in this unit works fine in all browsers that support the Flash plug-in, you will want to use code that will be supported by those browsers that support HTML5 media tags rather than plug-ins like Flash. As you learned, you can use this code to insert the crabdance.swf file: `<object width="140" height="114" data="crabdance.swf"></object>`. To insert video files, use `<video>` tags, to insert audio, use `<audio>` tags.

Incorporating Web 2.0 Technology

The term **Web 2.0** describes the recent evolution of web applications that facilitate and promote information sharing among Internet users. These applications not only reside on computers, but on cell phones, in cars, on portable GPS devices, and in game devices. **GPS (Global Positioning System)** devices are used to track your position through a global satellite navigation system. They are regularly used for assistance with driving directions, hiking locations, and map making. Web 2.0 applications do not simply display information; they enable users to actively direct or contribute to the web page content. Web 2.0 technology could potentially transform The Striped Umbrella website from a strictly informative site to one that is interactive and fully engaging. You decide to research Web 2.0 technology and analyze which web applications could be incorporated into the current site.

DETAILS

- ### RSS feeds and podcasts

  RSS feeds are an easy way to share information with users. **RSS (Really Simple Syndication)** feeds are regularly scheduled information downloads used by websites to distribute news stories, information about upcoming events, or announcements. Web users can subscribe to RSS feeds to receive regular releases of information from a site. Users can also download and play the digitally broadcasted files called **podcasts** (which stands for **Programming On Demand**) using devices such as computers or MP3 players. Many news organizations and educational institutions publish both audio and video podcasts. Video podcasts are also sometimes referred to as **vodcasts** or **vidcasts**.

- ### Social networking

  Web 2.0 also includes the ever-increasing use of social networking. **Social networking** refers to any web-based service that facilitates social interaction among users. One example of a social networking site is **Facebook**, which allows users to set up profile pages and post information for others to view. Facebook pages often contain lots of text, images, and videos. To fully view and post to an individual's page, you must be accepted by that person as a "friend," which lets them control who has access to page content.

- ### Wikis

  The term **wiki** (named for the Hawaiian word for "quick") refers to a site where a user can use simple editing tools to contribute and edit the page content in a site. A good example is **Wikipedia**, an online encyclopedia. Wikipedia allows users to post new information and edit existing information on any topic. Although people have different opinions about the reliability of the information on Wikipedia, it is generally viewed as a rich source of information. Proponents argue that its many active and vigilant users maintain its accuracy.

- ### Blogs

  Blogs are websites where the website owner regularly posts commentaries and opinions on various topics. Content can consist of text, video, or images. Users can respond to the postings and read postings by other users as well. **Twitter** is a website where users post short messages, called tweets. Twitter is considered a **micro blog**, because you cannot enter more than 140 characters in each post. To use Twitter, you must first join by creating a free account. Then you can post messages about yourself, "follow" other people's tweets, and invite others to follow you. It is a quick and easy way to exchange short bits of information.

- ### Video sharing applications

  There are many video sharing applications, such as Skype, Google Video Chat, and YouTube. **Skype** and **Google Video Chat** are free applications that you use to communicate live through video conferencing, using a high-speed Internet connection and a digital video camera connected to your computer, called a **webcam**. You can also use Skype or Google Chat to make regular telephone calls over the Internet. **YouTube** is a website where you can view or upload videos. To upload videos, you need to register with the site.

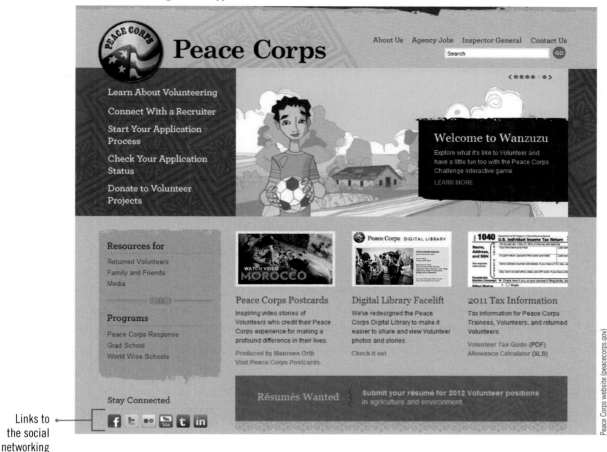

Links to the social networking pages

Peace Corps website (peacecorps.gov)

Design Matters

How to incorporate Web 2.0 components

Most websites today engage their users with one or more Web 2.0 component applications. The Peace Corps website, shown in Figure H-20, has links to Facebook, Twitter, flickr, YouTube, Tumblr, and LinkedIn. When you are designing a site, one of the decisions you must make is not if but how you will incorporate technology to fully engage users. To incorporate one of these applications into your website, first register to set up an account on the social networking site, then place a link on one of your site's pages (usually the home page) that links to the social networking site and opens your page. For example, if your Twitter account is located at twitter.com/your_name, add this link to your home page using the Twitter logo as a graphic link. You can download social networking sites' logos from their websites. You can also enter plain text links if you prefer, but most people are familiar with the logos and used to seeing them used for links.

Practice

Concepts Review

Label each element in the Dreamweaver window shown in Figure H-21.

FIGURE H-21: Concepts review

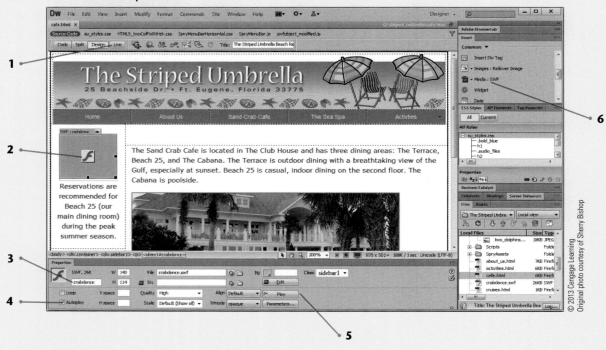

1. _____   4. _____
2. _____   5. _____
3. _____   6. _____

Match each of the following terms with the statement that best describes it.

7. **Skin**
8. **Low-bandwidth animation**
9. **Media objects**
10. **Plug-in**
11. **Vector graphic**
12. **Rollover image**
13. **Behavior**

a. Combinations of visual and audio effects and text used to create a fully engaging experience with a website

b. A scalable graphic that is built using mathematical formulas rather than pixels

c. A set of instructions that is attached to page elements and tells the page element to respond in a specific way when an event occurs

d. The bar at the bottom of a video with the control buttons

e. An image that changes its appearance when the mouse pointer is placed over it in a browser

f. A small computer program that works with a host application to enable certain functions

g. Does not require a fast connection to work properly

Select the best answer from the following list of choices.

14. **The file extension for a Flash video file is:**
    - **a.** .vid.
    - **b.** .fla.
    - **c.** .swf.
    - **d.** .flv.

15. **The panel that is used to add JavaScript functions to page elements is:**
    - **a.** the Behaviors panel.
    - **b.** the Server Behaviors panel.
    - **c.** the JavaScript panel.
    - **d.** the Functions panel.

16. **Which event will trigger an action when a mouse is placed over a page element?**
    - **a.** onMouseOut
    - **b.** onMouseOver
    - **c.** onLoad
    - **d.** onClick

17. **Web 2.0 technology includes:**
    - **a.** wikis.
    - **b.** blogs.
    - **c.** podcasts.
    - **d.** all of the above

18. **When you add a Spry effect to a page element, which folder is automatically created?**
    - **a.** SpryAssets folder
    - **b.** Spry folder
    - **c.** SpryEffects folder
    - **d.** Effects folder

Skills Review

Important: *If you did not create this website in Unit B and maintain it during the preceding units, you will need to create a local site root folder for this website and define the site using files your instructor will provide. See the "Read This Before You Begin" section for more detailed instructions.*

1. **Understand Media objects.**
   - **a.** List three different types of media objects that you can add to a web page.
   - **b.** Write a short paragraph that explains how to make media objects accessible and HTML5 compliant.
   - **c.** Write a few sentences that explain what a plug-in does. Give two examples.

2. **Add Flash objects.**
   - **a.** Start Dreamweaver, switch to Design view if necessary, open the Blooms & Bulbs website, then open the workshops page.
   - **b.** Add a paragraph break after the last paragraph, then insert the garden_quote.swf Flash movie from the drive and folder where you store your Unit H Data Files at the insertion point.
   - **c.** Type **Garden quote** in the Object Tag Accessibility Attributes dialog box, then add eight block quotes in front of the Flash object.
   - **d.** Play the garden_quote.swf movie in Dreamweaver (Win), save your work, click OK to close the Copy Dependent Files dialog box, preview the page in your browser, compare your screen to Figure H-22, then close your browser.
   - **e.** Close the workshops page.

FIGURE H-22

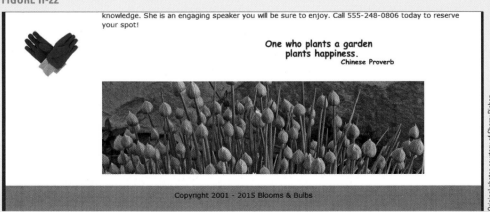

Skills Review (continued)

3. Add Behaviors.

a. Open the file dwh_4.html from the drive and folder where you store you Unit H Data Files, save it in the blooms root folder as **annuals.html**, overwriting the existing annuals page, but not updating links, then close the dwh_4.html file.

b. Select the broken image placeholder, then browse to select the coleus.jpg file in the Unit H Data Files assets folder and save it in the website assets folder.

c. Select the coleus image, then use the Behaviors panel to add the Appear/Fade effect so that the image will fade from 100% to 50% when clicked, select the Toggle effect check box, click OK, then save the page. (*Hint:* Dreamweaver will add the SpryEffects.js supporting file to the SpryAssets folder.)

d. Preview the page in the browser, then close the browser. (*Hint:* Click the image to test the behavior. The image will alternate between 100% and 50% opacity each time you click the mouse.)

4. Edit Behaviors.

a. Edit the behavior to onMouseOver, then save your work.

b. Preview the page in the browser. (*Hint:* Place the mouse over the image twice to test the behavior.)

c. Close the browser, then close the annuals page.

5. Add Rollover images.

a. Open the tips page, then delete the butterfly image at the top of the page.

b. Verify that your insertion point is still positioned at the deleted butterfly graphic location.

c. Insert a rollover image from the drive and folder where you store your Unit H Data Files (*Hint:* Click Insert on the Menu bar, point to Image Objects, then click Rollover Image.) Type **butterfly_rollover** as the image name, insert butterfly1.jpg from where you store your Data Files as the original image, insert butterfly2.jpg from where you store your Data Files as the rollover image, type **Butterflies** as the alternate text, then click OK. Save each image in the site's assets folder.

d. Apply the img_left_float rule to the rollover image.

e. Save your work, preview the page in the browser to test the rollover, close the browser, then close the tips page.

6. Add video.

a. Open the plants page, click at the end of the last sentence on the page, then insert two paragraph breaks.

b. Insert the hanging_baskets.mp4 file from drive and folder where you store your Unit H Data Files folder and save it in your local site assets folder.

c. Type **Join us Saturday at 9:00 for a class on hanging baskets.** after the last sentence on the page.

d. Use the Property inspector to set the width of the video placeholder to **250**, the height to **200**, and add a new parameter to set autostart to false.

e. Place the insertion point to the left of the placeholder, switch to Code view, click to the left of > at the end of the opening embed tag, then enter **style="margin-left:400px"** after the opening < /embed> tag, then delete the ending < /embed> tag.

f. Save your work, preview the page and play the movie in the browser, then compare your screen to Figure H-23.

g. Close the plants page.

FIGURE H-23

pruned to any size. The one you see on the right is Southern Belle. Check out all our varieties as you will not fail to have great color with these plants.

The Candy Cane Floribunda shown on the left is a beautiful rose with cream, pink, and red stripes and swirls. They have a heavy scent that will remind you of the roses you received on your most special occasions. These blooms are approximately four inches in diameter. They bloom continuously from early summer to early fall. The plants grow up to four feet tall and three feet wide. They are shipped bare root in February.

In addition to these marvelous roses, we have many annuals, perennials, and water plants that have just arrived. Join us Saturday at 9:00 for a class on hanging baskets.

Original content courtesy of Sherry Bishop

Skills Review (continued)

7. Add sound.

   a. Copy the file seeds_audio.mp3 from the drive and folder where you save your Unit H Data Files to your website assets folder.

   b. Open the tips page, place the insertion point after the last tip listed, enter two paragraph breaks to end the list, then type **Tip of the Week: Starting seeds for your vegetable garden**, then apply the H1 tag.

   c. Enter a paragraph break, then click Insert on the Menu bar, point to Media, click Plugin, browse to and select the file seeds_audio.mp3, then copy it to the site assets folder.

   d. Select the plug-in placeholder, then use the Property inspector to change the W value to **200** and the H value to **20**.

   e. Add a parameter to set autostart to false.

   f. Delete the ending < /embed> tag from the code for the audio file.

   g. Save the tips page and test the audio file in the browser, comparing your screen to Figure H-24.

   h. Close the browser and close the tips page.

FIGURE H-24

- **Winter** – The time to prune fruit trees and finish planting your bulbs. Don't forget to water young trees when the ground is dry.
- **Spring** – The time to prepare your beds, plant annuals, and apply fertilizer to established plants. Remember to mulch to maintain moisture and prevent weed growth.
- **Summer** – The time to supplement rainfall so that plants get one inch of water per week. Plant your vegetable garden and enjoy bountiful harvests until late fall.

Basic Gardening Tips

1. Select plants according to your climate.
2. In planning your garden, consider the composition, texture, structure, depth, and drainage of your soil.
3. Use compost to improve the structure of your soil.
4. Choose plant foods based on your garden objectives.
5. Generally, plants should receive one inch of water per week.
6. Use mulch to conserve moisture, keep plants cool, and cut down on weeding.

Tip of the Week: Starting seeds for your vegetable garden

8. Update files.

   a. Open the file dwh_5.html from the drive and folder where you store your Unit H Data Files, then save it as **perennials.html**, overwriting the blank placeholder page in the blooms local site root folder, but do not update links. Close dwh_5.html.

   b. Save the file fiber_optic_grass.jpg from the unit_h/assets folder in the blooms assets folder, then save and close the perennials page.

   c. Repeat Steps a and b to replace the blank placeholder water_plants page with the file dwh_6.html and save the file water_lily.jpg in the blooms assets folder.

   d. Save your work, then close all open files and exit Dreamweaver.

Important: *If you did not create this website in Unit B and maintain it during the preceding units, you will need to create a local site root folder for this website and define the website using files your instructor will provide. See the "Read This Before You Begin" section for more detailed instructions.*

Independent Challenge 1

You have been hired to create a website for a river expedition company named Rapids Transit, located on the Buffalo River in Northwest Arkansas. You have completed the main pages in the site, but would like to add a slideshow of some river photographs to the guides page. You have selected seven photographs to use and plan to place them on the page, replacing the existing image, as shown in Figure H-25.

a. Start Dreamweaver, then open the Rapids Transit website.

b. Open the before page, then select and delete the young_paddler image on the page.

c. Insert the file river_scenes.swf from the drive and folder where your Unit H Data Files are stored at the insertion point, adding **River Scenes** as the title.

d. Assign the rule img_left_float to the swf placeholder.

e. Use the Property inspector to uncheck the Loop check box so the file will only play through one time when it's viewed in a browser.

f. Enter the ID **river_photos** in the ID text box.

g. Save your work, then use Live View to preview the slideshow.

h. Return to Design view, preview the page in the browser, then compare your screen to Figure H-25.

i. Close the browser, close the before page, then exit Dreamweaver.

FIGURE H-25

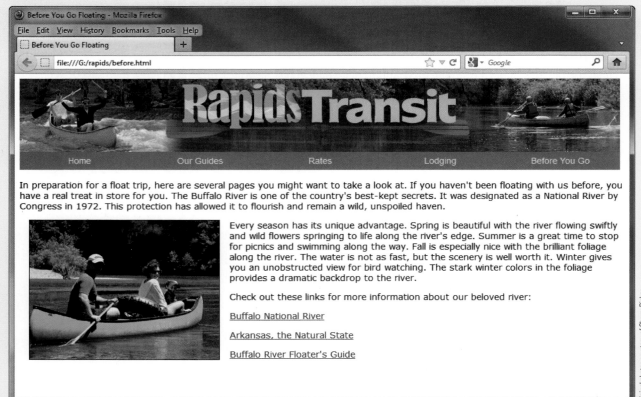

Independent Challenge 2

In this exercise, you will continue your work on the TripSmart website. You are ready to work on the tours, Peru, and Galapagos pages. You add content to the tours, Peru and Galapagos pages, and update all pages with a revised menu bar that includes links to the Peru and Galapagos pages. You also add a video to the Galapagos page.

a. Start Dreamweaver, open the TripSmart website, then open the file dwh_7.html from the drive and folder where you store your Unit H Data Files, then save it as **peru.html** in the tripsmart local site root folder. Do not update links.

b. Click the broken image placeholder, browse to the drive and folder where you store your Unit H Data Files, select the machu_picchu_from_high.jpg file in the assets folder, and then copy it to the local site's assets folder without updating the links.

c. Repeat Step b to replace the next broken image placeholder with the file llama.jpg.

d. Close the file dwh_7.html.

e. Use your existing styles or create new ones to format and position the text and images on the page, then save the Peru page.

f. Open the tours.html page from your local site root folder, then save it as **galapagos.html**.

g. Close the tours page, then create a page to replace your current tours page using the file dwh_8.html from the drive and folder where you store you Unit H Data Files. Save the files sea_lions_in_surf.jpg and machu_picchu_ruins.jpg in your local site assets folder.

h. Notice that the menu bar on the new tours page includes submenus for the Peru and Galapagos pages. Use this menu bar to replace the menu bars on all other pages.

i. Save your work, then use the navigation links to preview each page in the browser. Make any spacing adjustments you feel would improve the appearance of each page.

j. Close all pages except the Galapagos page.

k. Insert the file sealions_video.mp4 from the drive and folder where you store your Unit H Data Files after the last paragraph on the page, then delete the ending < /embed> tag.

l. Type a short introduction to the video similar to Figure H-26.

m. Use the Property inspector to set the Width and Height of the video to 400 × 240, then add a parameter to keep the movie from playing automatically.

n. Add any additional settings to improve the appearance of the page, save your work, preview the page in the browser, close the browser, then close all open pages.

FIGURE H-26

Galápagos, including the famous blue-footed booby. You will also have opportunities to swim, snorkel, and kayak with penguins. When your time on the ship ends, you will fly to Quito, the second-highest capital city in the world. Quito is a UNESCO World Heritage Site with beautiful colonial architecture. We recommend taking an extra day to explore its rich history and sample Ecuadoran cuisine.

To provide the finest in personal attention, this tour will be limited to no more than twenty people. The price schedule is as follows: Land Tour and Supplemental Group Air, $5,500.00; International Air, $1,350.00; and Single Supplement, $1,000.00. Entrance fees, hotel taxes, and services are included in the Land Tour price. Ship gratuities are also included for the Wanderer crew and guides. A deposit of $500.00 is required at the time the booking is made. Trip insurance and luggage insurance are optional and are also offered for an extra charge. A passport and visa will be required for entry into Ecuador. Call us at 555-555-0807 for further information and the complete itinerary from 8:00 a.m. to 6:00 p.m. (Central Standard Time).

This is a sea lion family out for the day. It's amazing how close you can come to the wildlife. They have very little fear of people, as they have been protected so well by the government regulations for visiting them.

Independent Challenge 3

Angie Wolf is an amateur astronomer. She would like to design a website about planets. She would like to use Dreamweaver to build her site and incorporate Flash elements, rollovers, and video to the site.

a. Connect to the Internet then go to the United States Navy website at www.navy.mil, as shown in Figure H-27.

b. Search for ".swf" and ".mp4" in the code for several pages to locate media objects.

c. Do you see any objects in the site that are made with rollover images?

d. How has adding Flash effects improved the appearance of this site?

e. Do you see any links to Web 2.0 applications that are being used? If so, list them.

f. Create a sketch of Angie's site that contains at least five pages. Indicate in your sketch what media elements you would insert in the site, including where you would add Flash objects, rollover images, and video.

FIGURE H-27

United States Navy website (navy.mil)

Real Life Independent Challenge

This assignment will continue to build on the personal website that you created in Unit B. In Unit C, you created and developed your index page. In Unit D, you added a page with either an ordered or an unordered list, using CSS with a minimum of two styles. In Unit E, you added a page that included at least two images. In Unit F, you added a page that included several links and an image map. In Unit G, you redesigned the index page based on CSS. In this lesson, you will continue building your site by designing and completing a page that contains rich media content or by adding media content to existing pages. After completing your site, be sure to run appropriate reports to test the site.

a. Evaluate your wireframes, then choose a page or series of pages to develop in which you will include Flash objects as well as other media content, such as rollover images, video, and behaviors.

b. Plan the content for your new page so that the layout works well with both the new and old pages in your site. Sketch a plan for your wireframes for the media content you wish to add, showing which media elements you will use and where you will place them.

c. Create or find the media you identified in your sketch, choosing appropriate formatting.

d. Add the rollover images to the page.

e. Add a video to the page.

f. Add a behavior to a page element, then specify the action you would like to use with it.

g. Run a report on your new page(s) to ensure that all links work correctly.

h. Preview the new page or pages in your browser and test all links. Evaluate your pages for content and layout.

i. Make any modifications that are necessary to improve the page.

After you are satisfied with your work, verify the following:

a. Each completed page has a page title.

b. All links work correctly and styles are used consistently for all content.

c. The completed pages are attractive using screen resolutions of 1024 × 768.

d. All images are properly linked to the assets folder of the website.

e. All images have alternate text and are legal to use.

f. All media content works as you intended and downloads quickly.

g. The link checker shows no broken links or orphaned files. If there are orphaned files, note your plan to link them.

h. Run reports for untitled documents and missing alternate text. Make any corrections necessary.

Visual Workshop

Use Figure H-28 as a guide to continue your work on Carolyne's Creations. You thought it might be fun to add an effect to the photo of the two young boys cooking on the children page. After you have added your choice of effects, preview the page in the browser and test the effect.

FIGURE H-28

Collecting Data with Forms

Forms are a way to add interactivity and collect information on a web page, by presenting users with a series of options for collecting and entering information. Dreamweaver lets you easily create forms by adding form objects to the page, such as check boxes and option buttons. The form then sends information that users enter to the host web server to be collected and processed. Forms are useful for such things as ordering merchandise, responding to requests for customer feedback, and requesting information. The Striped Umbrella Marketing Department wants interested guests to be able to request information about the fishing and dolphin cruises online. You decide to design and add this type of form to the activities page to collect the name and address of guests who make inquiries, along with their response to an offer to send them a quarterly newsletter.

OBJECTIVES

Understand forms and form objects

Create and insert a form on a page

Add a text form field

Add a radio group

Add a check box group

Insert a submit and a reset button

Format and test a form

Understanding Forms and Form Objects

Forms are a convenient and efficient way to obtain information from website users. A form can either be a page by itself, collecting several pieces of information from a user with numerous form objects, or it can take up only a small part of a page. **Form objects** are the individual form components that accept individual pieces of information. They include check boxes, radio buttons, text fields, and buttons. Many web pages include a form with only two form objects, such as a text box and a submit button. See Figures I-1 and I-2 for examples of long and short types of forms. You can insert tables in more complex forms to help organize the objects into rows and columns. Pages can have more than one form. However, you cannot place a form inside a form. Before you begin work on the form, you review the various form objects you might use to collect information from guests.

DETAILS

As you create forms, you can choose from the following objects:

- **Form fields**

  A **field** is a form area into which users can insert a specific piece of data, such as their last name or address. Form fields include text fields, hidden fields, and file fields. **Text fields** can accept both numbers and letters, known as **alphanumeric** data. A text field can contain single or multiple lines of data. **Hidden fields** store information about the user and can be used by the company originating the form at a later time, such as the next time the user visits its website. **File fields** allow users to browse to a file on their computer and **upload** it to the form host web server. To upload a file means to transfer a copy of the file to a server.

- **Radio buttons**

  Radio buttons are option buttons that appear as small empty circles on a form that users click to select a choice. A selected radio button has a black fill. Radio buttons in a group are mutually exclusive, meaning that the user can select only one choice at a time.

- **Check boxes**

  Check boxes are small squares on a form. To select a choice, users click to place a check mark inside the box. In contrast to a group of radio buttons, with a series of check boxes it is possible to select more than one check box.

- **Lists and menus**

  Lists and menus provide the user with a list or menu of choices to select. Lists display the choices in a scrolling format while menus display the choices in a pop-up set of choices. Lists and menus provide a fast method of entering information that may be tedious for the user to type.

- **Buttons**

  Buttons (not to be confused with radio buttons) are usually small rectangular objects containing a text label. When a user clicks a button, a task is performed, such as submitting or clearing a form. To **submit** a form means to send the information on the form to the host web server for processing. Clearing or **resetting** the form means to erase all form entries and set the values back to the default settings.

Design Matters

Planning form layout

Before you begin creating your form, you should take the time to write down the information you want to collect and the order in which you want it to appear on the form. It's also a good idea to make a sketch of the form to make sure that all of the form objects are placed in a logical order that will make sense to the user. Position the most important information at the top of the form to make it more likely that users will complete it.

FIGURE I-1: Example of a long form

Menu

Text boxes

Radio buttons

Menu

Social Security Administration website (ssa.gov)

FIGURE I-2: Example of a short form

Text box

Search button is the Submit button

Federal Bureau of Investigation website (fbi.gov)

Design Matters

Accessible forms

To ensure that your forms are accessible, you should use the Accessibility preference for Form Objects. To select it, click Edit on the Menu bar, click Preferences, click the Accessibility category, then select the Form objects check box. With this option selected, each time you insert a new form object, Dreamweaver will prompt you to enter a label tag and attach it to that object. These labels are read by screen readers.

Creating and Inserting a Form on a Page

Before you can begin adding form objects to a page, you must create the form that will contain them. You create a form by using the Form command on the Insert menu, or by using the Form button on the Insert panel. When you create a form, Dreamweaver adds beginning and ending form tags to the HTML code. Once it is created, you replace the default form name with a descriptive name that the program will use when it processes the data from the form. ████ The form on the activities page will include form objects to collect information from guests who are seeking information about fishing and dolphin cruises excursions. You create the form and then insert it at the bottom of the activities page.

STEPS

1. **Start Dreamweaver, open The Striped Umbrella website, then open the activities.html page**

2. **Place the insertion point after the audio placeholder image on the page, then insert a paragraph break**

   The insertion point is positioned where you want the form to reside, at the bottom of the page.

> **TROUBLE**
>
> If a message appears about needing to view invisible elements to see the form outline on the page, click View on the Menu bar, point to Visual Aids, then click Invisible Elements.

3. **Click the Form button in the Forms category on the Insert panel**

   The form displays as a red dotted outline (Win) or red solid outline (Mac), on the page. Although the Property inspector displays the form properties, the form objects won't display until you insert them.

4. **Click to place the insertion point in the Form ID text box in the Property inspector, type feedback, press [Tab], then compare your screen to Figure I-3**

   The form ID text box now contains the name *feedback* and the Tag selector shows the form tag with the name of the form `<form#feedback>`. The rest of the form properties identify how the information users enter will be processed on the host server. The Action and Target fields, for example, should remain blank unless your instructor provides you with the appropriate information. (The programming involved in processing a form is beyond the scope of this book.)

5. **Click the Show Code view button** `Code`

   The form code appears, as shown in Figure I-4. The form is surrounded by beginning and ending form tags as well as the attributes for the form ID, form name, form method, and form action. The form method information directs the way that the data will be sent to the server.

6. **Click the Show Design view button** `Design`

   Your page redisplays in Design view.

Design Matters

Creating user-friendly forms

When a form contains several required fields—fields that must be filled out before the form can be processed—it is a good idea to provide visual clues to alert the user. Adding asterisks in different font colors with an accompanying note is an easy way to increase the visibility of required fields. An asterisk is often placed right next to a required field with a corresponding note at either the top or the bottom of the form explaining that all fields marked with asterisks are required. This encourages users to complete these fields initially, rather than submitting the form and then receiving an error message asking them to complete required fields that were left blank.

FIGURE I-3: **Form on the activities page**

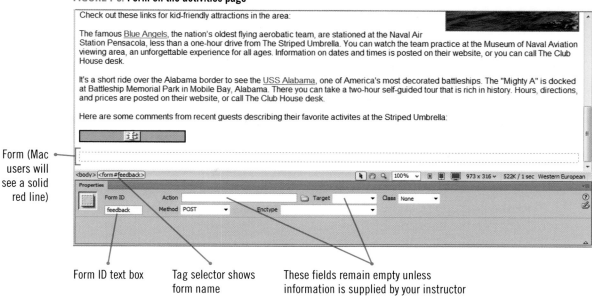

Form (Mac users will see a solid red line)

Form ID text box

Tag selector shows form name

These fields remain empty unless information is supplied by your instructor

FIGURE I-4: **HTML code for the form on the activities page**

Form tags

Form action

Form method

Form name

Form id

Processing forms

An attractive, user-friendly form serves no purpose without a way to process and store the information. Sending emails with form information is not a time efficient or effective process. It is more practical to send form information directly to a server to read, store, and process the data. The data collection stage of form processing is called **front-end processing**, which denotes the beginning of the processing cycle. The data processing stage is accordingly called **back-end processing**, as it references the end of the processing cycle. Forms are processed according to the properties specified in the form action attribute. The **form action attribute** is the part of the form tag that specifies how the data in

the form will be processed. If you do not need to save the data that a user enters on a form, it is better to use **client-side scripting**. This means that the form is processed on the user's computer. An example of this is a mortgage calculator that allows you to estimate mortgage payments. **Server-side scripting** is used if data entered on a form needs to be stored and processed on the form's host web server. An example of this is ordering books on a bookstore website. Client-side scripting is written with programming languages such as JavaScript or VBScript. Server-side scripting is written with programming languages, such as Common Gateway Interface (CGI).

Adding a Text Form Field

One of the most common form fields is a text field. Dreamweaver has three types of text fields: single-line text fields, multi-line text fields, and password fields. For more information, see the Clues to Use *Understanding text fields*. Each field should have a descriptive label so users have a visual clue as to the type of information required. Form field names should not include spaces, punctuation, or uppercase letters, to ensure that they can be read properly by the program that will process the form data. ▚▚▞▞▞ You want to make sure that the form objects display in an organized manner so you place a table inside the form. You then add single-line text fields for the name and address information.

STEPS

1. **Place the insertion point inside the form if necessary, then click Table in the Common category on the Insert panel**

   The Table dialog box opens. This is where you set the table properties such as the table width, the number of rows and columns, and the accessibility tags.

2. **Set the table rows to 8, the table columns to 3, select the Top header option if necessary, then click OK**

   The Table dialog box closes and the table is inserted inside the form, ready for placement of the form fields. The table is formatted with the table rule in the su_styles.css file that you defined earlier. This rule specifies the font, font size, table width, and left float.

> **QUICK TIP**
> If you try to insert a form object before you create the form, Dreamweaver will ask if you want to add form tags before inserting the form object.

3. **Using Figure I-5 as a guide, enter the labels for your text fields into the table beginning in the first cell in the second row (press [down arrow] to move the insertion point to each position)**

   The labels for the text fields are entered in the first column. The second column remains empty until you insert the next set of text fields. The top row is left blank, as the table header will be placed there. Don't be concerned with the width of the table cells. They will adjust as more content is entered.

4. **Place the insertion point in the second cell in the second row, then click the Text Field button in the Forms category on the Insert panel**

   The Input Tag Accessibility Attributes dialog box opens. This dialog box is used to enter the accessibility attributes for the form field.

> **QUICK TIP**
> Characters beyond those allotted in the width setting field will be submitted with the form data even if they are not visible.

5. **Type first_name in the ID text box, click the No label tag option button in the Style section to select it, click OK, type 30 in the Char width text box in the Property inspector, then type 60 in the Max chars text box**

   The text field for the First Name label is placed on the form with a black dotted outline. The Property inspector displays the text field ID first_name. The Char width and Max chars settings set the size of the text field and limit the number of characters that can be input in the field.

> **QUICK TIP**
> If you have to create many fields of the same size, you can copy the first field, paste it in the new locations, then change the name and properties for each one.

6. **Repeat Steps 4 and 5 to enter additional single-line text fields, using the information in Table I-1**

   All text fields are placed in the form with labels, IDs, settings for the character width that will display in the text field and the maximum characters the user can enter in each field.

7. **Click the first_name field to select it, save your work, then compare your screen to Figure I-6 (You are only selecting this field to be able to compare your field properties with the figure.)**

   The form field properties for the first_name field are displayed in the Property inspector.

FIGURE I-5: Adding form labels for text fields

It's a short ride over the Alabama border to see the USS Alabama, one of America's most decorated battleships. The "Mighty A" is docked at Battleship Memorial Park in Mobile Bay, Alabama. There you can take a two-hour self-guided tour that is rich in history. Hours, directions, and prices are posted on their website, or call The Club House desk.

Here are some comments from recent guests describing their favorite activites at the Striped Umbrella:

First Name
Last Name
Street
City
State
Zip Code

FIGURE I-6: Text form fields added to the feedback form

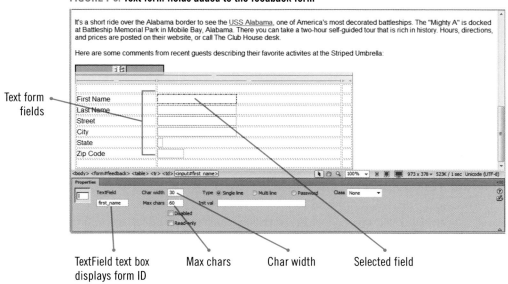

Text form fields

TextField text box displays form ID   Max chars   Char width   Selected field

TABLE I-1: Form field attributes for the feedback form

label	ID	char width	max chars
First Name	first_name	30	60
Last Name	last_name	30	60
Street	street	30	60
City	city	30	60
State	state	2	2
Zip Code	zip_code	10	10

Understanding text fields

Single-line text fields are useful for small pieces of data, such as a name or telephone number. **Multi-line text fields**, also called **Text area fields**, are useful for entering comments that may take several sentences to complete. **Password fields** are unique fields that display asterisks or bullets in place of text on the screen, to prevent others from viewing the data as it is entered. There are three ways to create a Multi-line text field. You can click the Text Field button in the Forms category on the Insert panel, select the field, then click the Multi line option on the Property inspector. Or you can create a Text area field by clicking the Text area button in the Forms category on the Insert panel. You can also use the Insert, Form submenu on the Menu bar. To create a Password field, create a text field, select the field, then select the Password option in the Property inspector.

Adding a Radio Group

Radio buttons let users select options. Two or more radio buttons together are called a **radio group**. When used in a group, radio buttons are mutually exclusive; if a user tries to select two radio buttons in the same group, the first one becomes deselected when the second one is selected. Radio buttons are useful in situations where you want users to select only one choice from a group of possible choices. For example, on a shoe order form, radio buttons could represent the different shoe sizes. To order one pair of shoes, users would select only one size. It is important to include labels to help users understand how to complete each item in the form. It is also important to set an appropriate default value to form objects. A default value will prevent users from unintentionally skipping over items or mistakenly sending unintentional information when they submit the form. You continue working on the form by adding a group of two radio buttons for users to indicate whether they would like to receive newsletters.

STEPS

1. **Select the third cells in the second, third, and fourth rows, expand the Property inspector if necessary, then click the** Merges selected cells using spans button ▣ **in the Property inspector**

   Merging these cells provides a good-sized location to position the radio group.

2. **Place the insertion point in the newly merged cell, then type** Would you like to receive our quarterly newsletters?

   This text will appear above the radio button group so the user will understand the significance of this group.

3. **Press [Shift][Enter] (Win) or [shift][return] (Mac), then click the** Radio Group button **in the Forms category on the Insert panel**

   The Radio Group dialog box opens, as shown in Figure I-7. This is where you specify the name of the radio group and the label and value for each button. You can choose whether to use line breaks or a table to position the buttons.

4. **Type** newsletters **in the Name text box**

   The radio group is assigned the name *newsletters*.

5. **Click** Radio **in the first row of the Label column to select it, type** Yes, **then press [Tab]**

   "Yes" will display as the label for the first radio button. The default value for the first radio button is selected.

6. **Type** positive

   "positive" is set as the value that, after users select the "Yes" option, will be sent to your script or program when the form is processed.

7. **Repeat Steps 5 and 6 for the second row of the Label and Value columns and enter the label** No **with a value of** negative **to create the second radio button**

8. **If necessary, click the** Lay out using: Line breaks (
 tags) **option button to select it, compare your screen to Figure I-8, then click** OK

   The radio group appears on the form.

9. **Save your work, click to the right of the form, then compare your screen to Figure I-9**

> **TROUBLE**
> If you see empty space displayed at the bottom of the table, click the Table tag in the Tag selector to close it up.

Design Matters

Creating good form field labels

Because labels are so important in identifying the information that the form collects, you must use form field labels that make sense to your users. For example, First Name and Last Name are good form field labels because users understand clearly what information they should enter. A generic label, such as Name, isn't as specific. If creating a simple and obvious label is impossible, include a brief preceding paragraph that describes the information that should be entered into the form field. You can add labels to a form using one of three methods: type a label in the appropriate table cell of your form; use the Label button in the Forms category on the Insert panel to link the label to the form object; or use the Input Tag Accessibility Attributes dialog box. The Input Tag Accessibility Attributes dialog box will prompt you to add a label if you have set your preferences to provide accessibility attributes for form objects.

FIGURE I-7: Radio Group dialog box properties

Radio Group name text box

Delete Radio button

Add Radio button

Label column

Click to change the button order

Value column

Lay out using option buttons

FIGURE I-8: Radio Group properties for newsletters radio group

Name of radio group

Radio button labels

Lay out using Line breaks (
 tags) option button

Radio button values

FIGURE I-9: The radio group added to the form

It's a short ride over the Alabama border to see the USS Alabama, one of America's most decorated battleships. The "Mighty A" is docked at Battleship Memorial Park in Mobile Bay, Alabama. There you can take a two-hour self-guided tour that is rich in history. Hours, directions, and prices are posted on their website, or call The Club House desk.

Here are some comments from recent guests describing their favorite activites at the Striped Umbrella:

First Name		Would you like to receive our quarterly newsletters?
Last Name		○ Yes
Street		○ No
City		
State		
Zip Code		

Radio group buttons and labels

Adding a Check Box Group

Check box groups are very much like radio button groups, in that a user can simply click one to select it. However, with check boxes, the user can select more than one choice when appropriate. For example, a form with hobby check box options would allow users multiple selections since many people have more than one hobby. Using check boxes rather than radio buttons gives users the opportunity to select both options. You decide to insert a check box group in the form so users can request more information about both the fishing trips and dolphin cruises.

STEPS

1. **Select the next two cells in the third column under the radio group, then click the Merges selected cells using spans button 🖳 in the Property inspector**

   Merging these cells provides a good location to position the check boxes.

2. **Place the insertion point in the newly merged cell, type Please select the materials you would like to receive:, then press [Shift][Enter] (Win) or [shift][return] (Mac)**

   This text will display above the check boxes. It serves as a user prompt to direct the response for the check boxes on the form.

3. **Click Checkbox Group in the Forms category on the Insert panel**

   The Checkbox Group dialog box opens, as shown in Figure I-10. This is where you enter the name, labels, and values. These attributes are essential for creating an accessible form.

4. **Type brochures in the Name text box, click Checkbox in the first row of the Label column to select it, type Fishing, press [Tab], then type fishing in the value column**

5. **Click Checkbox in the second row of the Label column to select it, type Cruises, press [Tab], type cruises in the Value column, click the Lay out using: Line breaks (
 tags) option button if necessary, compare your screen to Figure I-11, then click OK**

   The check box group is assigned a name and each check box is assigned a label and a value, as shown in Figure I-11.

6. **Click to deselect the text if necessary, compare your screen to Figure I-12, then save your work**

   The check boxes are placed in the form.

Design Matters

Creating accessible HTML form objects

When users enter information in form fields, they use [Tab] to move the insertion point from field to field. By default, the insertion point moves through fields from left to right across the page and screen readers read from left to right. However, you can set your own tab order to override the default. For example, regardless of where the fields for First Name and Last Name are placed on the form, you can direct the insertion point to move directly from the First Name field to the Last Name field, even if there are other fields between them. To change an existing form object's tab order, right-click the form object (Win), or [Ctrl] + click the form object (Mac). Click Edit Tag <input>, click the Style Sheet/Accessibility category in the Tag Editor – input dialog box, then change the Tab index number. To assign the subsequent fields to move to after the user presses [Tab], type the number 2 in the Tab index box to denote the second field; type 3 to assign the third field, and so forth. You can also assign Tab Index values in the Input Tag Accessibility Attributes dialog box when you create the tag. Tab orders will only work if each tab is assigned an index number.

FIGURE I-10: Checkbox Group dialog box properties

Name text box •

Label column •

Value column

Lay out using option buttons •

FIGURE I-11: Checkbox Group properties for brochures checkbox group

Name of Checkbox Group •

Check box labels •

Check box values

Lay out using Line breaks (
 tags) option button

FIGURE I-12: Viewing the check boxes

User prompt text

Check boxes

Inserting a Submit and a Reset Button

Buttons are small rectangular objects that have actions assigned to them. An **action** is a response to an event trigger that causes a change, such as text changing color or a form being processed. Actions trigger **events** that take place after a user clicks a button. Button properties include a name, a label, and an action. As with all selected objects, you assign button properties using the Property inspector. There are two reserved button names that have assigned meanings: Submit and Reset. These should only be used for buttons that are used to submit or reset a form; no other buttons should use these names. Submit means to send the form data to the processing program or script for processing. **Reset** means to clear the form fields to the original values. ⬛⬛ You want to add two buttons to the form: one that will submit the form for processing and another to clear the form in case the user needs to erase the information and start over.

STEPS

1. **Place the insertion point in the third column of the next to last row**

2. **Click Button in the Forms category on the Insert panel, click the No label tag option button in the Style section of the Input Tag Accessibility Attributes dialog box, then click OK**

   A Submit button appears on the form, without a label next to it, and the Property inspector displays its properties.

3. **If necessary, click the Submit form option button next to Action in the Property inspector, then type Submit in the Button name text box, as shown in Figure I-13**

   When a user clicks this Submit button, the information in the form is sent to the server for processing.

4. **Click to place the insertion point to the right of the Submit button, click Button on the Insert panel, click the No label tag option in the Input Tag Accessibility Attributes dialog box if necessary, click OK, select the newly placed Submit button if necessary, then click the Reset form option button next to Action in the Property inspector**

   The second Submit button changes to a Reset button. When a user clicks this Reset button, the form will clear any information he or she has typed.

5. **Verify that the Button name text box and the Value text box contain Reset, compare your screen to Figure I-14, then save your work**

Design Matters

Using the Adobe Exchange

To obtain form controls designed for creating specific types of forms, such as online tests and surveys, you can visit the Adobe Marketplace & Exchange (adobe.com/cfusion/exchange/). This is a central storage location on the Adobe website for program extensions, also known as **add-ons**. You can search the site by entering keywords in a standard Search text box, similar to using the Dreamweaver Help Search text box.

FIGURE I-13: Inserting a Submit button

Button name   Button value   Button action   Submit button   Button button

FIGURE I-14: Inserting a Reset button

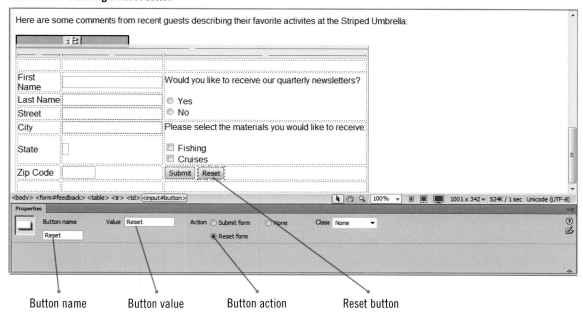

Button name   Button value   Button action   Reset button

Setting the Form Properties

Once you've inserted a form, you can then assign the properties for the application that you want to process the form information and the method you want it transmitted to the processing application. The **Action property** in the Property inspector specifies the application or script that will process the form data. The **Method property** specifies the protocol used to send the form data to the web server.

The **Get method** specifies that the data collected in the form be sent to the server as appended to the URL of the web page in the Action property. The **Post method** specifies that the data be sent to the processing script as a binary or encrypted file, allowing you to send the data securely. This information must be obtained from your instructor in order to be able to process the form.

Formatting and Testing a Form

In addition to adding descriptive labels to each form object, there are several ways you can format a form to make it easier to use. You can add brief instructions to the top of the form that will guide the user in filling it out correctly. Simple formatting such as adding a horizontal rule above and below the form can set it off from the rest of the page content. ▰▰▰▰ You decide to add a short instructional sentence to serve as the form header at the top of the form, right-align some of the labels, then accentuate the form with a horizontal rule.

STEPS

1. **Merge the top three cells in the first row of the table, then type** To request further information, please complete this form. **in the merged cell**

   Because it is a table header, this text is automatically centered across the table and appears bold. The table rule is applied as well.

2. **Click the** New Rule button 🗐 **in the CSS Styles panel, then create a new Class rule named** right_aligned_cells **in the su_styles.css style sheet with the following properties: Block Text-align: right; Box Width: 120px; Box Padding: Right: 10px, apply the right_aligned_cells rule to the cells in the first column, then deselect the text**

   The labels are now a set width and right-aligned in the table cells with spacing to separate them from the text boxes to the right of them, as shown in Figure I-15.

3. **Place the insertion point in the last cell in the first column of the table, select all the cells in the row, then merge them**

   The new row is merged.

4. **Place the insertion point in the newly merged cell, click** Insert **on the Menu bar, point to** HTML, **then click** Horizontal Rule

   A horizontal line displays selected at the end the form.

QUICK TIP
Recall that you can click the table tag in the tag selector to select a table.

5. **Select the table, press** [left arrow key], **then click the** Blockquote button 🗐 **on the Property inspector four times**

   The form is indented to center it on the page.

6. **Save your work, click the** Preview/Debug in Browser button 🗐, **then select** Preview in [your browser name], **enter some dummy data in the form, then click the** Reset button

   The Reset button works correctly, but the Submit button will not. Recall from the second lesson that you have not set the form properties to send the data to a web server. You need additional information from your instructor to do this.

7. **Compare your finished project to Figure I-16, then close your browser window**

8. **Run reports on the Entire Current Local Site to check for Missing Alt Text and Untitled Documents**

   There are no pages with missing alternate text or missing page titles.

9. **Recreate the site cache, then run reports for broken links and orphaned files**

   There are no broken links or orphaned files.

10. **Close the page, then exit Dreamweaver**

FIGURE I-15: Formatting text field labels with CSS

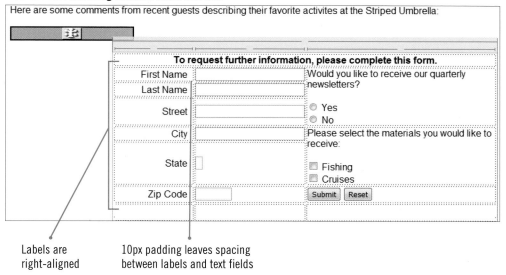

Labels are right-aligned

10px padding leaves spacing between labels and text fields

FIGURE I-16: The finished project

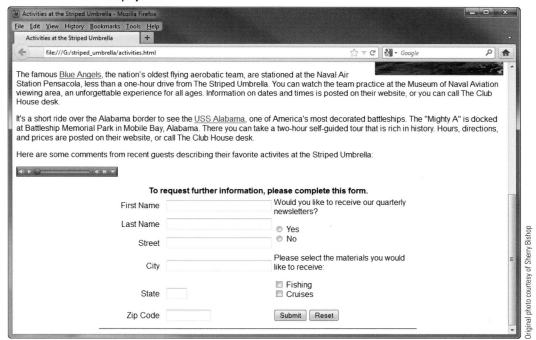

Original photo courtesy of Sherry Bishop

Adding a site search form

There are many ways to add an HTML5 compliant site search feature with a simple search form. This is a convenient feature to provide your users with a quick way to find content on your site. Most site search forms appear at the top right corner of a page, so that's a good place to put them since people are used to looking for them there. One example of a set of HTML5 tags to create a basic search text box for a site search form is as follows:

```
<form method="get" action="http://www.
google.com/search">
<input type="text"   name="q" size="25"
maxlength="255" value="" />
<input type="submit" value="search" />
<input type="hidden"   name="sitesearch"
value="sitename.com" />
</form >
```

You test a search form after you've published the site.

Practice

Concepts Review

Label each element in the Dreamweaver window shown in Figure I-17.

FIGURE I-17

1. _____   5. _____
2. _____   6. _____
3. _____   7. _____
4. _____   8. _____

Match each of the following terms with the statement that best describes it.

9. **Check boxes**	**a.** Set(s) the form object values to the default settings
10. **Radio buttons**	**b.** Are mutually exclusive; only one in each group can be selected
11. **Submit button**	**c.** What happens after a button is clicked
12. **Reset button**	**d.** Display(s) data as asterisks or bullets
13. **Event**	**e.** Send(s) the data to be processed
14. **Password fields**	**f.** Contain(s) space for more than one line of data
15. **Multi-line text fields**	**g.** More than one can be selected

Select the best answer from the following list of choices.

16. Which of the following is not classified as a form field?
- **a.** text field
- **b.** hidden field
- **c.** default field
- **d.** file field

17. Button properties include:
- **a.** a name, a field, and an action.
- **b.** a name, a label, and an action.
- **c.** a name, a label, and a value.
- **d.** a name, a value, and an action.

18. Server-side scripting means that:
- **a.** the form is processed on the user's computer.
- **b.** the form is processed by a JavaScript program.
- **c.** the form is processed on the form's host server.
- **d.** b and c.

Skills Review

Important: *If you did not create this website in Unit B and maintain it during the preceding units, you will need to create a local site root folder for this website and define the website using files your instructor will provide. See the "Read This Before You Begin" section for more detailed instructions.*

1. Understand forms and form objects.
- **a.** Refer to Figure I-18 to locate a text field, a check box, a radio button, and a Submit button.

2. Create and Insert a form on a page.
- **a.** Start Dreamweaver and open the tips.html page in the Blooms & Bulbs website.
- **b.** Place the insertion point after the audio file placeholder image on the page and a paragraph break.
- **c.** Insert a form.
- **d.** Name the form **tips**.
- **e.** View the HTML code for the form.
- **f.** Return to Design view.
- **g.** Save your work.

3. Add a text form field.
- **a.** Place the insertion point inside the form and insert a table with 10 rows, 3 columns, and a Top header.
- **b.** Using Figure I-18 as a guide, enter labels that will be used for Single line text fields in the first column, beginning in row 2.

FIGURE I-18

Skills Review (continued)

    c. Use the information in Table I-2 to add text fields with no label tags in the column next to the labels, beginning in row 2.

    d. Save your work.

    e. Merge the second through fifth rows in the third column.

    f. Type **My favorite gardening tip:** in the resulting merged cell.

    g. Create a line break after the text and insert a Multi-line text field (or a Textarea field) with no label.

    h. Name the new Textarea field **my_tips**, then set the Char width to **40** and the Num lines to **4**.

    i. Click the table tag to remove any empty space displayed in the table, then save your work.

TABLE I-2: Form field attributes for the tips form

label	form field ID	char width	max chars
First Name	first_name	40	40
Last Name	last_name	40	40
Street	street	40	40
City	city	40	40
State	state	2	2
Zip Code	zip_code	10	10
Email Address	email	40	40

4. Add a radio group.

    a. In the third column in the third-to-the-last row, insert a radio group.

    b. Name the radio group **contact**.

    c. Enter the label **Please contact me with special offers** for the first radio button, then enter a value of **yes**.

    d. Enter the label **Don't contact me** for the second radio button, then enter a value of **no**.

    e. Use line breaks to lay out the radio group.

    f. Save your work.

5. Add a check box group.

    a. In the cell below the My favorite gardening tip text area, type **I would be interested in reading Gardening Tips:**.

    b. In the same cell, below the text, insert a check box group with the name **tips**.

    c. Enter the label **On the Web** for the first check box, then enter a value of **web**.

    d. Enter the label **By Email** for the second check box, then enter a value of **email**.

    e. Add another check box, enter the label **By mail**, then add the value **mail**.

    f. Save your work.

6. Insert a Submit and a Reset button.

    a. Insert a Submit button with no label tag in the first column of the last row.

    b. Change the button name to **Submit**.

    c. Insert a Reset button in the second column of the last row.

    d. Verify that **Reset** is the button name, **Reset** is the value, and the action is set to **Reset form**.

    e. Save your work.

7. Format a form.

    a. Merge the cells in the top row of the table, type **Do you have a gardening tip you would like to share with us?**.

    b. Merge the cells in the row above the Submit and Reset buttons.

    c. Place a horizontal rule in the new row and another one above the header in the top row.

Skills Review (continued)

d. Create a new Class rule in the blooms_styles.css file named **form_table** using the following properties: Type: Font-family: Arial, Helvetica, sans-serif; Font-size: medium; Block: Text-align: left; Box: Width: 750px.

e. Select the table, then apply the form_table rule.

f. Enter three Blockquotes in front of the table to space the table more to the center of the page.

g. Switch to Code view, then add the following code to the <th> tag for the table header:
style="text-align:center" to center the table header. (The form_table rule left-aligned the header.)

h. Save your work, preview the page in the browser, compare your screen to Figure I-18, test all fields, then test the Reset button.

i. Close the browser, close all open files, then exit Dreamweaver.

Important: *If you did not create these websites in Unit B and maintain them during the preceding units, you will need to create a local site root folder for these websites and define the websites using files your instructor will provide. See the "Read This Before You Begin" section for more detailed instructions.*

Independent Challenge 1

You have been hired to create a website for a river expedition company named Rapids Transit, located on the Buffalo River in Northwest Arkansas. Mike Andrew, the owner of Rapids Transit, has asked you to add a form to the page that describes the three categories of lodging available. The purpose of this form will be to allow clients to request brochures for each lodging category.

    a. Start Dreamweaver, then open the Rapids Transit website.

    b. Open the page lodging.html.

    c. Place a paragraph break after the last sentence on the page and insert a form called **lodging**.

    d. Insert a table inside the form with 7 rows and 3 columns, and a Top header.

    e. Enter text labels in the first column beginning with the second row, using Figure I-19 as a guide.

FIGURE I-19

© 2013 Cengage Learning
Original photos courtesy of Sherry Bishop

Independent Challenge 1 (continued)

f. Add Single line text fields with no label tags in the column next to the text labels using 40 characters for both the character width and maximum characters for all text fields except for the state and zip code; use a width of 2 for the state and 10 for the zip code. Name the fields appropriately.

g. Merge the third cells in the second, third, fourth, fifth, and sixth rows.

h. In the merged cells, type **Please check the brochures you would like to receive.**

i. Enter a line break after the sentence, then insert a check box group named **brochures**.

j. Enter the label **The Lodge** for the first check box, then enter a value of **lodge**.

k. Enter the label **Jenny's Cabins** for the second check box, then enter a value of **jenny**.

l. Enter the label **Jon's Camp** for the third check box, then enter a value of **jon**.

m. Insert a Submit button in the third column of the last row.

n. Insert a Reset button to the right of the Submit button in the same cell, and change the Action to **Reset form**, the button value to **Reset**, and the Button name to **Reset**.

o. Create a new class rule in the rapids_styles.css style sheet named form_table with the following properties: Font-family: Arial, Helvetica, sans-serif; Font-size: medium; Box Width: 800px. Apply the new form_table rule to the table, then indent the table using three block quotes.

p. Merge the cells in the top row, then type **If you would like to receive a brochure describing our lodging choices, please complete the form below.**

q. Insert a new row at the end of the table and merge the cells in the new row. (*Hint:* Place the insertion point in the last cell in a table, then press the [Tab] key to insert a new row at the end of the table.)

r. Insert a horizontal rule.

s. Insert another horizontal rule in the cell with the header, but under the header.

t. Preview the page in the browser, compare it to Figure I-19, then test the text fields and the Reset button.

u. Make any adjustments to improve the page, then save your work.

v. Run reports for broken links, orphaned files, untitled documents, and missing alternate text, correcting any errors that you find.

w. Close the page, then exit Dreamweaver.

Independent Challenge 2

In this exercise you will continue your work on the TripSmart website. The owner, Thomas Howard, wants you to create a form to collect data from users who are interested in receiving more information about one or more of the featured trips.

a. Start Dreamweaver, open the TripSmart website, then open the tours page.

b. Insert a paragraph break after the last sentence on the page, then insert a form named **tours**.

c. Insert a table in the form that contains 11 rows, 2 columns, and a Top header.

d. Merge the cells in the top row, type **Please complete this form for additional information on these tours.**

e. Beginning in the second row, type the following labels in the cells in the first column: **First Name**, **Last Name**, **Street**, **City**, **State**, **Zip Code**, **Phone**, **Email**, and **I am interested in:**.

f. Insert single-line text fields in the first eight cells in the second column beginning with row 2 and assign the following names: **first_name**, **last_name**, **street**, **city**, **state**, **zip_code**, **phone**, and **email**; setting the Char width to **40** and the Max Chars to **100** for each of these text fields. (*Hint*: To save time create the first_name field, then use copy and paste to create the other fields, changing the name of each pasted field in the Property inspector.)

g. In the second cell of the tenth row, insert a check box group with the name of **tours**.

h. Enter the label **Peru** for the first check box, then enter a value of **peru**.

i. Enter the label **The Galapagos** for the second check box, then enter a value of **galapagos**.

j. Create a new class rule in the tripsmart_styles.css style sheet named form_table with the following properties: Font-family: Verdana, Geneva, sans-serif; Font-size: medium; Block Text-align: left; Box Width: 650px. (Add the inline rule to modify the table header tag to center it if you wish.)

k. Apply the form_table rule to the table.

l. Insert a Submit button and a Reset button in the second cell of the eleventh row with appropriate names, values, and actions.

m. Insert a new merged row at the bottom of the table, then insert a horizontal rule, then use Blockquotes to indent the table to a position of your choice.

Independent Challenge 2 (continued)

n. Run reports for untitled documents, missing alternate text, broken links, and orphaned files.

o. Save your work, preview the page in your browser, test the form, compare your screen to Figure I-20, close your browser, then close the tours page. (*Note:* the table border in the example is inherited from the table rule in the style sheet.)

FIGURE I-20

Destinations: The Galápagos and Peru

We are featuring two new trips for the coming year. The first is to the Galápagos. We will depart on February 5 and arrive in Lima, Peru. After arriving, we will stay at the Miraflores Park Hotel and enjoy the sights for two days in Lima. Next, we will fly to Guayaquil, Ecuador and stay overnight at the Hilton Colón before continuing on to Baltra Island in the Galápagos archipelago. After landing in Baltra, we will take a van to the dock and board the ship to begin our wonderful adventure. Our course will take us to several islands. The Galápagos archipelago consists of thirteen large islands and six small ones, along with over forty islets. The Galápagos is where Charles Darwin visited in 1835 and wrote his book "The Origin of Species." It is home to a variety of wildlife unlike anywhere else in the world. The expert local guides and naturalists will introduce you to the incredible Galápagos wildlife as you explore the islands and attend informative lectures each day.

The second trip we are featuring is to Peru. Our Peru trip will depart on May 5 and last for ten days. We will arrive in Lima, where we will check into the Miraflores Park Hotel. After two days in Lima we will depart for Cusco, where we will stay at the Hotel Monasterio for three days. The hotel's amenities include an option to have fresh oxygen pumped into your room, due to the high altitude of Cusco! While in Cusco we will visit the Cathedral, the ruins of Sacsayhuaman, and the Sacred Valley of the Incas. Machu Picchu is our next destination. We will travel by train from Ollanta, enjoying the scenery as we follow the Urubamba River to Machu Picchu. Our time at Machu Picchu will be simply magical. The meticulous preservation of the site helps you to envision the lives of those who lived here centuries ago.

Please complete this form for additional information on these tours.

First Name	
Last Name	
Street	
City	
State	
Zip Code	
Phone	
Email	
I am interested in:	☐ Peru ☐ The Gálapagos

Submit Reset

Independent Challenge 3

Paul Patrick and his partner Donnie Honeycutt have a construction business in Southern California. They have recently published a website for their business and would like to add a search form to help their customers quickly find the data they are looking for. They begin this task by researching other website search pages on the Internet.

a. Connect to the Internet, then go to the Internal Revenue Service site at irs.gov.

b. Click the Advanced Search link to search the IRS site, as shown in Figure I-21.

c. How is the search form organized?

d. What form objects were used?

e. Click the Search Tips link. What information did you find to help users search the website?

f. Find one more example of a site that uses a search page and explain which of the two sites you prefer and why.

FIGURE I-21

Real Life Independent Challenge

This assignment will continue to build on the personal website that you created in Unit B. In Unit C, you created and developed your index page. In Unit D, you added a page with either an ordered or an unordered list, using CSS with a minimum of two styles. In Unit E, you added a page that included at least two images. In Unit F, you added a page that included several links and an image map. In Unit G, you redesigned the index page based on CSS. In Unit H, you added some media elements. In this lesson, you will add a form to one of the pages in your website.

    a. Consult your wireframe and decide which page you would like to develop in this lesson.

    b. Sketch a layout for your page to place the form objects you would like to use.

    c. Create the form using at least three different form objects. Include clear instructions that will help users fill out the form correctly.

    d. Add text labels to each form object.

    e. Add a Submit and Reset button and format them appropriately.

    f. Format the form with CSS to help it stand out on the page.

    g. Save the file and preview the page in the browser, testing the Reset button to make sure it works correctly.

    h. Make any adjustments that are necessary to improve the appearance of your form.

After you are satisfied with your work, verify the following:

    1. Each completed page has a page title.

    2. All links work correctly.

    3. The completed pages look good using a screen resolution of 1024 × 768.

    4. All images are properly linked to the assets folder of the website.

    5. All images have alternate text and are legal to use.

    6. The link checker shows no broken links or orphaned files. If there are orphaned files, note your plan to link them.

    7. All main pages have a consistent navigation system.

    8. The form is attractive and easy to understand and use.

Visual Workshop

Use Figure I-22 as a guide to continue your work on the Carolyne's Creations website. You are adding a form to the classes page that will allow customers to sign up for a class. Since the customers are faxing their forms, there is no need for a Submit button. You can add a Reset button if you wish. Use form properties and settings of your choice. Use a table to lay out the form and create a new class rule to format the table. Run reports for missing alt text, untitled documents, broken links, and orphaned files. If cc_banner.jpg is listed as an orphaned file, delete it, as you no longer need it. (*Hint*: To match the figure, edit the text in the last paragraph before inserting the form.)

FIGURE I-22

Cooking Classes are fun!

Chef Carolyne loves to offer a fun and relaxing cooking school each month in her newly refurbished kitchen. She teaches an adults' class on the fourth Saturday of each month from 6:00 to 8:00 pm. Each class will learn to cook a complete dinner and then enjoy the meal at the end of the class with a wonderful wine pairing. This is a great chance to get together with friends for a fun evening.

Chef Carolyne also teaches a children's class on the second Tuesday of each month from 4:00 to 5:30 pm. Our young chefs will learn to cook two dishes that will accompany a full meal served at 5:30 pm. Children aged 5–8 years accompanied by an adult are welcome. We also host small birthday parties where we put the guests to work baking and decorating the cake! Call for times and prices.

We offer several special adults' classes throughout the year. The **Valentine Chocolate Extravaganza** is a particular favorite. You will learn to dip strawberries, make truffles, and bake a sinful Triple Chocolate Dare You Torte. We also host the **Not So Traditional Thanksgiving** class and the **Super Bowl Snacks** class each year with rave reviews. Watch the website for details!

Prices are $40.00 for each adults' class and $15.00 for each children's class. Sign up for classes by calling 555-963-8271, by emailing us, or by faxing the form below to 555-963-8272.

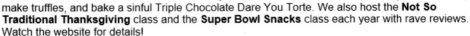

March Class Registration	
Please check which class you are signing up for:	
Adult: Peruvian Cuisine	☐
Child: Oven chicken fingers, chocolate chip cookies	☐
First Name	
Last Name	
Contact number or Email address	

UNIT J
Dreamweaver CS6

Presenting and Publishing a Website

There are many items to verify and tests to run before a website is ready to be finalized, presented to a client for approval, and published on the web. For instance, you need to confirm that all issues that could be affected by end-user technical factors have been resolved so that all page elements will work well under most operating environments. As recommended, testing your website should be an ongoing process that happens throughout the development cycle. It is much easier to make incremental corrections rather than last minute corrections. You review the many factors that contribute to successful project completion.

OBJECTIVES

Collect feedback

Run site reports

Validate HTML and CSS markup

Test for browser compatibility

Use media queries

Evaluate and present a website to a client

Set up remote access

Publish a site

Collecting Feedback

Although you may be satisfied with the website that you have designed and developed, it is important to ask for and receive constructive feedback before you present it to the client and publish. Feedback is most helpful when it is solicited from a variety of sources, such as other content contributors, clients, and objective participants who are not connected to the project. Feedback should be solicited both during the project cycle and after the website is published. You decide to identify some of the methods you can use to collect final feedback on your website.

DETAILS

- ### Site usability tests
  Once you have at least a prototype of the website ready to evaluate, it is a good idea to conduct a **site usability test**. This process involves obtaining website feedback from users who are not connected to the project. Usability test participants, often selected from external marketing sources, are instructed to objectively evaluate the site based on a standard set of directions. A comprehensive usability test will include pretest questions, participant tasks, a posttest interview, and a posttest survey. The goal of this test is to obtain much-needed information as to how usable the site is to those unfamiliar with it. Typical questions include: "What are your overall impressions?", "What do you like the best and the least about the site?", and "How easy is it to navigate around the site?". It is helpful to have a test monitor observe the testers as they navigate the site to record the time it takes for them to locate information. For more detailed information about this topic, go to w3.org and search for "site usability test."

- ### Surveys
  Once the website is published, surveys are a great way to collect user feedback. A well-designed survey with articulate and pertinent questions can provide you with valuable feedback regarding issues about the website itself or regarding the company's products or services. You can request feedback with email solicitations sent to the company's clients or request feedback from the users while they are using a website. Users who complete surveys are often interested in supplying helpful information to a company. However, incentives such as discounts or promotional gifts are also used to increase levels of participation. The US Navy website, shown in Figure J-1, solicits user feedback on their website with a survey that the user is asked to complete and submit.

- ### Points of contact
  All websites should have several points of contact. A physical address, a mailing address, a telephone number, and an email address are all good points of contact. By providing your clients' users with multiple points of contact, you give them a choice as to how they would like to contact your client when they have problems or questions.

- ### Web 2.0 Technology
  As you learned in Unit H, many websites today are incorporating some form of Web 2.0 technology to interact with their users. Blogs and other social networking sites function as valuable communication tools between companies and their target audiences. For example, posts on such applications as Twitter or Facebook provide instant information as well as allow users the opportunity to post feedback directly back to the website. The White House website, shown in Figure J-2, has links to several Web 2.0 applications to encourage sharing information and gathering feedback.

FIGURE J-1: The US Navy website with form for feedback

Paragraph requesting feedback from users

Form for user feedback

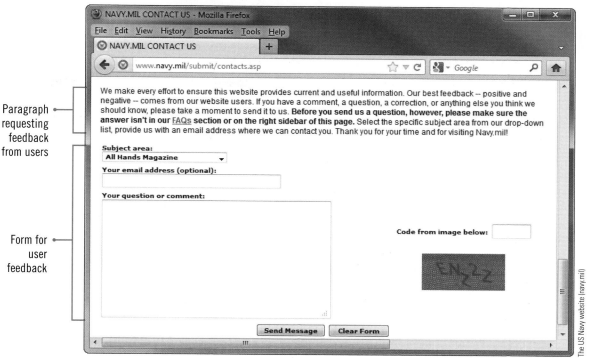

The US Navy website (navy.mil)

FIGURE J-2: The White House website with social networking links

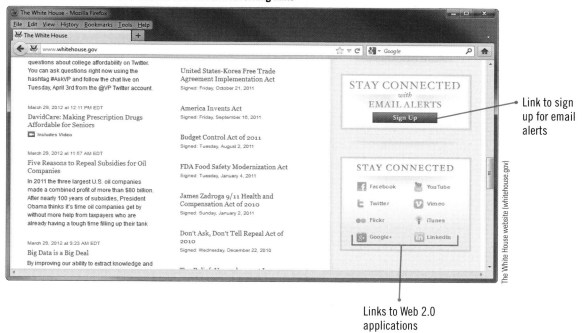

Link to sign up for email alerts

Links to Web 2.0 applications

The White House website (whitehouse.gov)

Running Site Reports

Dreamweaver has several helpful reports you can run to identify problems in your website. The more frequently you run these reports, the easier it will be to correct any errors. If you allow errors to build up, it will be more difficult to find and correct them. You should also check your completed pages against your wireframes to make sure that you have followed the design plan and included all required components. You want to review and run some of the site reports available in Dreamweaver.

DETAILS

- **Run site reports**

  Dreamweaver is capable of running any type of report as frequently as you want, as required by your project needs. The Reports command on the Site menu provides a list of reports that you can generate for your website. You can generate reports for the current document, the entire local site, selected files in the site, or a selected folder. These reports are grouped by type. The first type of report includes three categories of workflow reports. **Workflow reports** are useful when working in a team environment. For instance, you can run a workflow report that enables you to see files that other designers are using or produce a report that will list all files that have been modified recently. You can also generate a report that lists **Design Notes**—notes directed to other content creators who are working on different parts of your site. In addition to workflow reports, there are five categories of **HTML reports**: Combinable Nested Font Tags, Missing Alt Text, Redundant Nested Tags, Removable Empty Tags, and Untitled Documents. The Missing Alt Text and the Untitled Documents reports are especially important for website accessibility. After you run a report, you can save it as an XML file in a database, spreadsheet, or template for subsequent use.

- **Check links**

  The Link Checker in the Results panel provides you with a way to check external and internal links in your website. Link Checker alerts you to any broken internal links and helps you repair them; although it does list external links, it does not verify their validity. You can either check the links on a single page, the entire site, or selected files or folders. In addition, the Link Checker alerts you to orphaned files. Even if you are not ready to link these files, routinely running a list of orphaned files will remind you of the work you must complete in preparation for linking them to the website. You can fix a broken link in the Link Checker panel, or by using the Property inspector. To correct a broken link, use the Browse for File button to browse to the file that is the correct destination.

STEPS

QUICK TIP

It is a good idea to recreate the site cache before running reports to refresh the file listing.

1. **Start Dreamweaver, open The Striped Umbrella website in the Files panel, click Site on the Menu bar, click Reports, click the Report on list arrow, click Entire Current Local Site, click the Untitled Documents check box, as shown in Figure J-3, then click Run**

   There are no untitled documents listed in the Site Reports panel, as shown in Figure J-4.

2. **Repeat Step 1 to run a Missing Alt Text report**

   No files are listed with missing alt text, as shown in Figure J-5.

3. **Click Site on the Menu bar, then click Check Links Sitewide**

   No broken links are listed in the Link Checker panel, as shown in Figure J-6.

4. **On the Link Checker panel, click the Show list arrow as shown in Figure J-7, click Orphaned Files, then close the Results Tab Group**

   No orphaned files are listed.

FIGURE J-3: Reports dialog box

Specify the scope of the report to run from this list

Report on list arrow

Select check box to run a workflow report

Select check box to run an HTML report

FIGURE J-4: Site Reports panel displaying no pages without titles

No untitled documents are listed

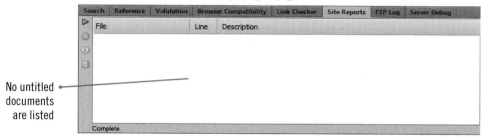

FIGURE J-5: Site Reports panel displaying no pages with missing alt text

No files are listed with missing alt text

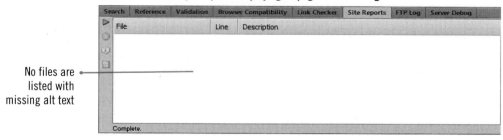

FIGURE J-6: Link Checker displaying no files with broken links

No broken links are listed

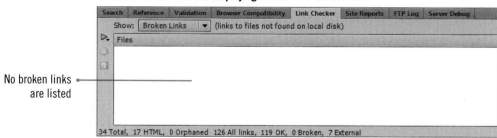

FIGURE J-7: Link Checker displaying no orphaned files

No orphaned files are listed

Show list arrow

Validating HTML and CSS markup

Because you can use several different markup languages to create web pages, it's important to make sure that the code is compatible with the document type you are using. Dreamweaver can validate your markup (code) by submitting it to the W3C validation service. **Validating markup** means comparing code against the current standards and identifying code that is not compliant. To validate HTML code, use the W3C Validation button ▷ᵥ on the Document toolbar or use the Window > Results > Validation command. The code will then be sent live to the W3C site to be validated. To validate CSS code, go to jigsaw.w3.org/css-validator and upload the style sheet you want to validate. ▰▰▰▰ You submit the pages in The Striped Umbrella site to the W3C validation service to identify any coding errors that may need correcting. You then submit the style sheets to the CSS Validation Service using the CSS Validation Service website.

STEPS

1. **Open the index page**

2. **Click the W3C Validation button ▷ᵥ on the Document toolbar, click Validate Current Document (W3C), as shown in Figure J-8, then click OK to close the W3C Validator Notification dialog box**

   No errors are found, as shown in Figure J-9.

3. **Repeat Steps 1 and 2 to check each page in the site. If you find errors, evaluate and correct them**

   You will find one error on the activities page because you probably have not added an action to your form on the page. It is flagging this code to remind you to add one when you have the information available. You will find three errors on the about us page because the swf file is not inserted according to HTML5 standards. After the Flash technology issues are all settled, this can be corrected, but meanwhile, the existing code will work in most desktop browsers with no problems.

   TROUBLE
   Depending on the browser you are using, you may see a Choose button instead of a Browse button.

4. **Open your browser, go to jigsaw.w3.org/css-validator, click the By file upload tab, click the Browse button, browse to The Striped Umbrella local site root folder, then double-click su_styles.css**

5. **Click More Options, click the Profile list arrow, click CSS level 3 if necessary, then click the Check button, as shown in Figure J-10**

   The W3C CSS Validator results for su_styles.css (CSS level 3) opens showing no errors were found, as shown in Figure J-11.

6. **Close the browser**

The Evolution of HTML5

HTML has been in existence since the early 1990s, but it wasn't until 1997 that the then current version, HTML4, became a W3C recommendation. Many HTML4 attributes such as body background, align, cellpadding, and hspace are now added using CSS3. HTML5 introduced new ways to add interactivity and tags that support semantic markup, such as the <nav> tag used for navigation links. In Unit D you learned about using semantic markup to incorporate meaning with your HTML markup. Other semantic HTML5 tags include <header>, <footer>, <article>, <audio>, <hgroup>, <figure>, <embed>, <wbr>, <canvas>, <section> and <video>. HTML5 is still a work in progress, but most modern browsers support it. HTML5 also introduces markup for web applications (apps), an exploding sector of web development.

FIGURE J-8: Validating the index page

W3C
Validation
button

Validate
Current
Document
(W3C)

© 2013 Cengage Learning

FIGURE J-9: The index page with no errors found

No errors
are found

FIGURE J-10: The W3C Validation Service website

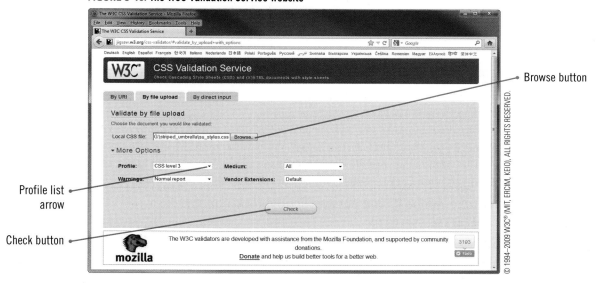

Browse button

Profile list
arrow

Check button

© 1994–2009 W3C® (MIT, ERCIM, KEIO), ALL RIGHTS RESERVED.

FIGURE J-11: The su_styles.css file with no errors found

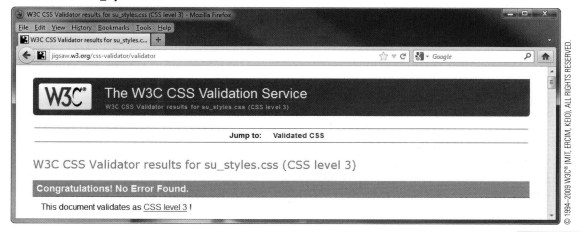

© 1994–2009 W3C® (MIT, ERCIM, KEIO), ALL RIGHTS RESERVED.

Testing for Browser Compatibility

Before finalizing a website, each web page should be retested for design layout, using several types and versions of browsers, various screen resolutions, and different platforms. Some page elements such as fonts, colors, horizontal rules, and CSS div properties do not look the same in all browsers and operating systems. Notice how long it takes each page to download, and consider trimming pages that download slowly. You learned in Unit G about Adobe BrowserLab, the Adobe online service is that can be used to test your CSS layouts across several of the major browsers. This means you do not have to have multiple browsers installed on your computer to be able to test them with your pages. You can also use Dreamweaver's Live view for CSS inspection and debugging and the Browser Compatibility check feature. It is a good idea to view your pages in several different live browsers. Factors such as download speeds, screen resolutions, operating systems, and browser types that will vary by user should have been included in the development process. See Table J-1 on page 267 for a checklist of factors that should be considered. ▓▓▓ You use Adobe BrowserLab to view the index page in several different browsers.

STEPS

QUICK TIP

To see which browsers are being checked, click the Check Browser Compatibility button ▷ in the Browser Compatibility panel, then click Settings.

1. **With the index page open, click File, point to Check Page, then click Browser Compatibility**

   The Browser Compatibility panel opens and shows no issues were detected, as shown in Figure J-12.

2. **Close the Results Tab Group, then click the Adobe BrowserLab panel tab to expand the panel**

3. **Click the Preview button**

   Adobe BrowserLab opens and asks for your Adobe ID and password. You must have an Adobe ID to use BrowserLab, but an Adobe ID is free. If you don't have an Adobe ID, click Create an Adobe ID to create one. (If you are opening BrowserLab for the first time, a dialog box will open asking you to allow BrowserLab to transfer your files. Click the Allow button, then click OK to allow BrowserLab to work.)

4. **Type your Adobe ID and password, then click Sign In**

   After the last browser that was accessed is loaded, the index page appears, as shown in Figure J-13.

QUICK TIP

You can also view two browsers simultaneously, either side by side or one on top of the other (Onion Skin) by clicking the View list arrow, then making a selection.

5. **Click the Browser list arrow, as shown in Figure J-14, point to All Browsers, then choose another browser**

6. **Close the browser to close Adobe BrowserLab**

Using the Browser Compatibility check to manage styles

There are several tools available to assist you in defining, modifying, and checking CSS rules, such as the Code Navigator and Live view. Another is the Browser Compatibility check feature. This feature flags issues on a page that may present a problem when viewed in a particular browser. To use the Browser Compatibility check feature, open a web page, the use the File > Check Page > Browser Compatibility command to locate issues that may be a problem. Any issues Dreamweaver finds are listed in the Browser Compatibility panel in the Results panel group with the line number and issue listed for each item. To modify the settings to add additional versions of browsers, click the arrow menu in the top left corner of the panel, then click Settings.

FIGURE J-12: The Browser Compatibility panel with no browser compatibility errors found

Check browser compatibility button

No errors detected

FIGURE J-13: Viewing the index page in Adobe BrowserLab

Internet Explorer 9.0 is the current browser shown (yours may differ)

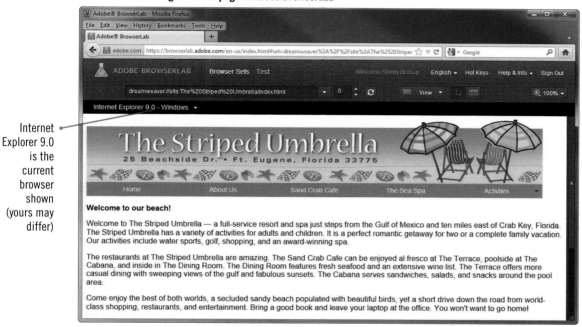

© 2013 Cengage Learning
Courtesy of Adobe Systems, Inc.

FIGURE J-14: Choosing another browser in Adobe BrowserLab

Browser list arrow

Point to All Browsers

Select a browser from the list

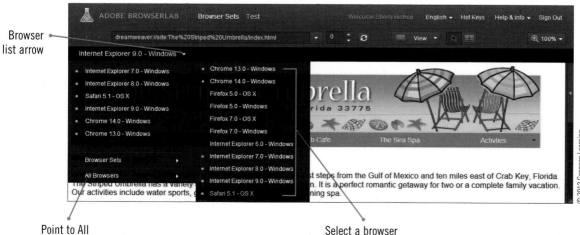

© 2013 Cengage Learning
Courtesy of Adobe Systems, Inc.

Using Media Queries

Today it is no longer enough to design a web page that that looks and functions well on a desktop monitor alone. Users will expect to be able to access your site using multiple mobile devices, such as tablets and smart phones, so you'll have to design your pages so they display correctly on all of them. To do this, you'll find media queries to be a great tool. **Media queries**, a new feature introduced in Dreamweaver 5.5, are style sheet files that specify set parameters for displaying pages on separate devices, such as tablets or smart phones. Media queries, combined with the new features of CSS3, enable you to create pages with content that can be modified to fit different sized devices. You decide to learn more about media queries and how they might be used to modify the content in The Striped Umbrella website.

DETAILS

- **Using Media Queries**
  - Media queries specify a different style sheet for each device: a style sheet for a desktop monitor, a style sheet for a tablet, and a style sheet for a smart phone. Dreamweaver has a function named Media Queries that, like a traffic policeman, directs each device to the correct style sheet so the page will display correctly on that device. You can find the Media Queries command on the Multiscreen Preview menu or the Modify menu. When you click the Multiscreen Preview command, you see the page content rendered on three different simulated screens such as a laptop, a cell phone, and a tablet, sometimes referred to as a 3-up preview.
  - Figure J-15 shows the index page that has not been designed for multiple devices. Notice how you have to scroll horizontally to see the content. Figure J-16 shows the index page after media queries were used. No horizontal scroll bars are required to view the content, since the page has been correctly sized for each device. For more information on how to use media queries, visit the Adobe website and search for "media queries." The Adobe TV website, tv.adobe.com, has free instructional videos about media queries that are very helpful.
  - Another option for designing for multiple screen sizes is to use the Dreamweaver File > New > Fluid Grid Layout command to create a page layout with preset code for designing adaptive websites. **Adaptive websites** are websites that adjust or modify the page content to fit the user's needs and device type used to view the site. This grid contains three CSS layouts and typography presets based on a single fluid grid. You can save the styles Dreamweaver creates automatically in your existing style sheet.

FIGURE J-15: Multiscreen Preview before using media queries

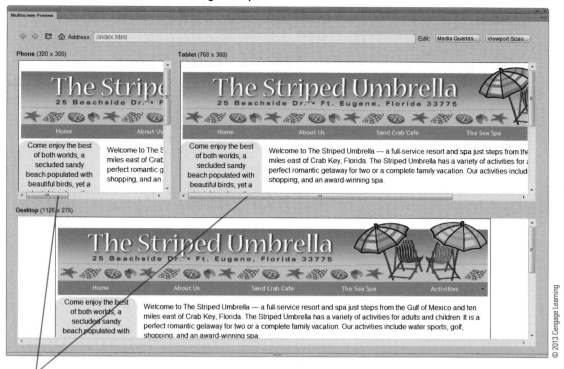

Horizontal scroll
bars are needed to
read content

FIGURE J-16: Multiscreen Preview after using media queries

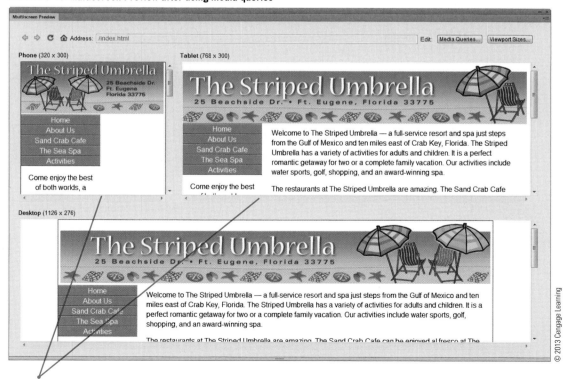

Horizontal scroll
bars are not needed
to read content

Evaluating and Presenting a Website to a Client

Even if you create a great website, poor communication can put the project at risk. Ideally, a prototype of the website was approved at the beginning of the process. Before you present a website to a client as a finished product, you should answer a few key questions. If you are satisfied with your answers, it is time to present the project to your client. The method you choose will depend on the project, your client, and your preferred method of communication. **▓▓▓▓** You review a checklist of questions and when you are satisfied with the answers, you want to evaluate the options for presenting the work to your client.

DETAILS

- **Are you ready to present your work?**

  After running the battery of technical tests, you should answer the following questions:
  - Do all of your final design and development decisions reflect your client's goals and requirements and meet the needs of the intended audience?
  - Did you follow good web development practices and current accessibility standards?
  - Did you check your pages against your wireframes as you developed them?
  - Did your final delivery date and budget meet the goals?

  If your answer to the final question is "no," then you need to determine the reason why before your presentation. If you find that you did spend more time on the site than you expected, determine if it was because you underestimated the amount of work it would take, ran into unforeseen technical problems, or because the client changed the requirements or increased the scope of the project as it went along. If you underestimated the project or ran into unexpected difficulties, you usually cannot expect the client to make up the difference without a prior agreement. Any time there are budget and time considerations, it is best to communicate frequently with status updates during the project.

- **Did you follow your wireframe?**

  Compare each completed page against its corresponding wireframe to make sure that all page elements have been placed in their proper locations on the page. Verify that all specified links have been included and test them to make sure that they work correctly. You might also consider hiring site-usability testers to test your site navigation. A site-usability test provides impartial feedback on how intuitive and user-friendly your site is to use.

- **How should you present your work?**

  The best option for presenting the final project is to invite the client to your office and perform a full walkthrough of the site, if at all feasible. This offers your client a chance to ask questions. Alternately, consider publishing the site to a server and sending the client a link to view the completed site. Creating PDFs of the site and sending them to the client for approval is another possible method.

Design Matters

Using wireframes for planning, development, and presentation

You may have chosen to use low-fidelity wireframes, such as those created in Microsoft PowerPoint or Adobe Photoshop, or you may have used high-fidelity wireframes that are interactive and multi-dimensional, such as those created in OverSight, Protoshare, or Adobe Proto, shown in Figure J-17. Another popular method is BaseCamp, a professional web-based project collaboration tool that focuses on collaboration and communication between you and your client. You should select your tool based on the size and complexity of the website, the budget, and your personal preferences. Used correctly, wireframes provide the basic framework of the site, the placement of the main page elements, and serve as a guide for all phases of development. They should be presented to the client for the initial project approval and used at the end of the project to document that the plan was executed as planned.

FIGURE J-17: Adobe Proto

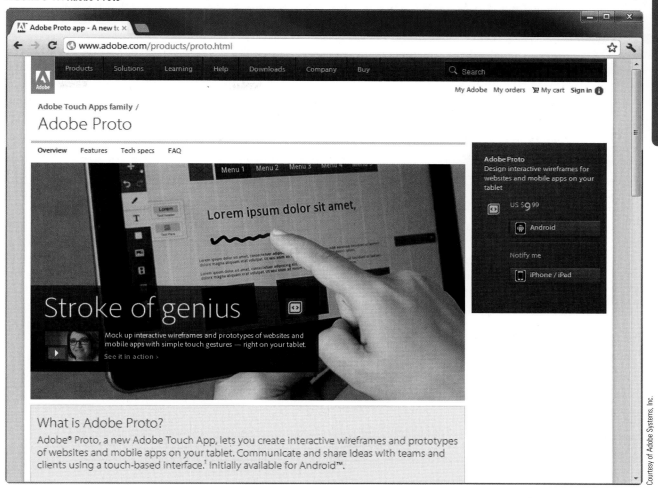

TABLE J-1: End-User Considerations for Development and Design

page element	design considerations
Tables	Are table widths sized for viewing in various screen resolutions? Are they sized to print correctly? Do they include summaries or headings?
Colors	Will users be able to successfully navigate the website in case the colors do not render exactly as intended? Do any page elements rely on the use of color alone?
Text	Are the font sizes large enough for users to read? Is the contrast between the text and the page background strong?
Media Objects	Has the embedded code been provided that searches for the appropriate plug-ins and prompts missing plug-ins to download? Are there too many media objects that will slow the download time appreciably? Do all media objects have a purpose in presenting the page content?
Images	Are all images as small in file size as possible? Do they all include alternate text?
Accessibility	Will the site pass the W3C Priority 1 Checkpoints and the W3C Priority 2 POUR principles for making a website accessible?

Setting up Remote Access

Once your files are ready to publish, you must specify where Dreamweaver should place the files. Most Dreamweaver users begin first by creating a local site root folder to store all of their website files, called the **local site**. Next, they gain access to a remote site. A **remote site** is a folder on a web server that is connected to the Internet with software for hosting websites, and is not directly connected to the computer housing the local site. Often the **ISP (Internet Service Provider)** will furnish users with space for publishing web pages. You can also use other host providers such as EarthLink. This space then becomes the remote site. ░░░░░ You want to review the processes available in Dreamweaver for setting up a remote site.

DETAILS

- **Using the Site Setup dialog box**

  When your pages are ready to publish, the files must be transferred from the local site to the remote site. In Dreamweaver, you use the Site Setup dialog box to enter the information about the remote server, such as the FTP address, root directory, username, and password. **FTP (File Transfer Protocol)** is the process of uploading and downloading files to and from a remote site. To open the Site Setup dialog box, use the Site > New Site; or Site > Manage Sites > Edit commands on the Menu bar. To enter the server information, click Servers, then click the Add new Server button. The choices for remote access appear when you click the Connect using list arrow, as shown in Figure J-18. After the remote site information is entered, you click the Put button in the Files panel to transfer the files.

- **Setting up FTP**

  Most users transfer files using FTP. If you select this file-transfer method, additional options will appear, as shown in Figure J-19. Some of the specific information, such as Username and Password, can be obtained from your host provider. The FTP Address is the address on the Internet where you will send your files. The Root Directory is your folder on the remote server where you will place your files.

STEPS

To set up remote access on an FTP site:

1. Click Site on the Menu bar, then click Manage Sites

2. Click the website name in the Manage Sites dialog box, then click the Edit the currently selected site button ✏

3. Click Servers in the Site Setup dialog box, click the Add new Server button ➕, type your server name in the Server Name text box, click the Connect using list arrow, then click FTP if necessary

4. Enter the FTP Address, Username, Password, Root Directory, and Web URL information in the dialog box

5. Click Test

   The test button tests the connection between your computer and the server.

6. Click Save, click Save again, click OK to recreate the cache, then click Done

   The dialog boxes close.

To view a website on a remote server:

1. Click the View list arrow in the Files panel, then click Remote server

2. Click the Expand to show local and remote sites button ▣

   The Remote site and the Local files panes display an expanded Files panel, as shown in Figure J-20.

3. Click the Collapse to show only local or remote site button ▣, click the View list arrow, then click Local view

   Your window returns to Local view.

FIGURE J-18: Site Setup dialog box

Servers category

Connect using options

FIGURE J-19: Site Setup dialog box server settings

Server name

Your host provider will furnish this information

Root Directory name furnished by host provider

Test button

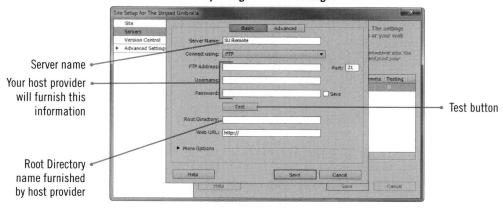

FIGURE J-20: Viewing the Remote Server and Local Files

Collapse to show only local or remote site button

Choosing remote access options

Remote access choices include FTP, Local/Network, WebDAV, RDS, and Microsoft Visual SourceSafe. **Local/Network** refers to publishing a website on either the local drive (that is, your own hard drive) or a local network drive. **WebDAV (Web-based Distributed Authoring and Versioning)** is used with servers such as the Microsoft Internet Information Server (IIS) and Apache Web server.

RDS (Remote Development Services) is used with a remote folder running ColdFusion. Finally, **Microsoft Visual SourceSafe** is available under the Windows platform using Microsoft Visual SourceSafe Client. **Secure FTP (SFTP)** is an FTP option which lets you encrypt file transfers to protect your files, user names, and passwords.

Publishing a Site

After setting up remote access and completing your website, you click the Put button on the Files panel to transfer a copy of your files to a remote server. This is a similar process to the one used by FTP client programs. Transferring your files from your computer to a remote computer is called **uploading** or **publishing**. Transferring files from a remote computer to your computer is called **downloading**. To download a copy of your files click the Get button on the Files panel. To see both the remote and local versions of a site, you can expand the Files panel by clicking the Expand to show local and remote sites button 🗖. To collapse the Files panel, click the Collapse to show only local or remote site button 🗖. You want to review the processes available in Dreamweaver for publishing a website.

DETAILS

- **Using Put and Get**

  When you transfer dependent files; this transfers associated files, such as image files, in the local site to the server. The following buttons, shown in Figure J-21, are used for transferring files:

button		task
Put File(s) to (remote site name) button	⬆	Transfers files from the Local site to the Remote site; will connect to a remote server automatically once you've selected the files you want to transfer and clicked the Put File(s) button
Connect to Remote Server button	🔌	Connects to the remote server
Get File(s) from (remote site name) button	⬇	Transfers the files from the Remote site to the Local site.

- **Synchronizing files**

  The Synchronize command allows you to **synchronize** your files, transferring only the latest versions rather than all the website files. To synchronize your site, click Synchronize with (remote site name) button 🔄 on the Files panel or click Site on the Menu bar, then click Synchronize Sitewide. The Synchronize Files dialog box, shown in Figure J-22, is used to specify which files to synchronize and the direction in which to synchronize them. If the files have not changed since the last transfer, Dreamweaver notifies you that you do not need to synchronize. You can also use a remote SVN (Apache Subversion) repository to save and maintain current and previous versions of your files.

STEPS

To upload files for publication:

1. Click the name of the file, folder, or site you want to publish, then click the Put Files(s) to (remote site name) button ⬆ in the Files panel
2. Click Yes to include the dependent files if necessary

To synchronize files:

1. Click Site on the Menu bar, then click Synchronize Sitewide
2. Click the Synchronize list arrow, then click Entire '(Site name)' Site
3. Click the Direction list arrow, then click Put newer files to remote
4. Click Preview, then click OK

QUICK TIP

If your files do not need synchronizing, you will see a message asking if you want to view the list of files to synchronize manually. Click No if you do not want to synchronize manually.

FIGURE J-21: **Files panel**

Connect to
Remote Server
button

Get (file)s from
(remote site
name) button

Expand to
show local
and remote
sites

Put file(s) to
(remote site
name) button

FIGURE J-22: **The Synchronize with Remote Server dialog box**

Synchronize list arrow

Direction list arrow

Cloaking files to exclude them from being uploaded to a server

There may be times when you want to exclude a particular file from being uploaded to a server. For instance, suppose you are not quite finished working on a particular web page. You can exclude a file by cloaking it. **Cloaking** is the process of marking a file or files for exclusion when the commands Put, Get, Synchronize, Check In, and Check Out are used. Cloaked files can also be excluded from site-wide operations such as checking for links or updating a template or library item. You can also cloak a folder or specify a type of file to cloak throughout the site. The cloaking feature is enabled by default. To cloak a file, select the file, click the Files panel Options button, point to Site, point to Cloaking, and then click Cloak.

Managing a website with a team

When you work on a large website, chances are that many people will be involved in developing and keeping the site up to date. Different individuals will need to make changes or additions to different pages of the site by adding, changing, or deleting content. If everyone had access to the same pages at the same time, problems could arise. Fortunately, Dreamweaver's collaboration tools eliminate such problems. For example, the **Check Out** feature enables only one person at a time to work on a file. This ensures that content contributors cannot overwrite each other's pages. To access the Check Out feature, you must first enable it in the Remote Info settings of the Site Setup dialog box. To check out a file, select the file name in the Files panel, then click the Check Out File(s) button 🔽 on the Files panel. Another file management tool is Subversion control. A remote SVN (Apache Subversion) repository is used to maintain current and historical versions of your website files. It is used in a team environment to move, copy, and delete shared files. You can protect files from being accessed using the svn:ignore property to create a list of files that are to be ignored in a directory.

Practice

Concepts Review

Label each element in the Dreamweaver window shown in Figure J-23.

FIGURE J-23

1. _____   5. _____
2. _____   6. _____
3. _____   7. _____
4. _____   8. _____

Match each of the following terms with the statement that best describes it.

9. **Check out feature**   a. To transfer files from your computer to a remote server
10. **Link Checker**   b. To transfer files from a remote server to your computer
11. **Upload**   c. A command that allows you to transfer only the latest versions of files
12. **Cloak files**   d Allows a file to be used by only one user at a time
13. **Synchronize**   e. Used to check for orphaned files and broken links
14. **Download**   f. To mark files for exclusion from several Commands, including Put, Get,
                               Synchronize, check In, and check Out

Select the best answer from the following list of choices.

15. The process that involves requesting unbiased users who are not connected to the project to use to evaluate a site is called:

   a. a trial run.

   b. a test drive.

   c. a clinical trial.

   d. a site usability test.

16. What technology describes the recent evolution of Web applications that facilitate and promote information sharing among Internet users?

   a. Web 1.0 technology

   b. Web 2.0 technology

   c. Web 3.0 technology

   d. Virtual technology

17. A point of contact can include:

   a. A telephone number.

   b. An email address.

   c. A physical address.

   d. All of the above.

18. Which of the following is not an Html report?

   a. Untitled Documents

   b. Missing Alt Tag

   c. Design Notes

   d. Combinable Nested Font Tags

19. Which button is used to validate HTML code?

   a.

   b.

   c.

   d.

20. Media queries are used to:

   a. Identify the device that is being used to view a page.

   b. Direct which style sheet a page should use for a specific device.

   c. Prevent users from needing horizontal scroll bars to view page content.

   d. All of the above.

Skills Review

Important: *If you did not create this website in Unit B and maintain it during the preceding units, you will need to create a local site root folder for this website and define the website using files your instructor will provide. See the "Read This Before You Begin" section for more detailed instructions.*

1. **Collect feedback.**
   a. Start Dreamweaver, then open the Blooms & Bulbs website.
   b. Write a paragraph describing how a usability test would be conducted for a website.
   c. List three different methods for collecting feedback from website users.
   d. List four good points of contact that could be included on a website for website users to use to contact the company.
   e. Describe three social networking sites that you would consider using for a website to add interaction with users.

2. **Run site reports.**
   a. Run a site report for untitled documents.
   b. Add page titles to any pages you find without a title.
   c. Run a site report for missing alt text.
   d. Add alternate text to any page elements that are listed with missing alt text.
   e. Run a site report for orphaned files.
   f. If you see any orphaned files listed, evaluate whether they should be deleted or linked to a page.
   g. Run a site report for broken links, and repair any broken links that you find.

3. **Validate HTML and CSS markup.**
   a. Open the index page.
   b. Use the W3C Validation button to validate the HTML markup.
   c. Repeat Step b to validate each page in the site and note any errors that you find.
   d. Go to the W3C Validator at jigsaw.w3c.org/css-validator, then validate the blooms_styles.css file against CSS level 3 standards.

4. **Test for browser compatibility.**
   a. With the index page open, use the Browser Compatibility panel to check for browser compatibility.
   b. Connect to Adobe BrowserLab, then preview the index page using three different browsers.
   c. Close Adobe BrowserLab.

5. **Use media queries.**
   a. With the index page open, use the Multiscreen preview to preview the page with the default settings.
   b. Write a plan to improve the appearance of the page so you can eliminate the need for horizontal scroll bars when the page is viewed on a tablet or smart phone.

6. **Evaluate and present a website to a client.**
   a. Check your pages against your wireframes to see if you developed each page according to plan.
   b. Write a plan to present the website to a client, including the software you will use.

7. **Set up remote access.**
   a. Open the Manage Sites dialog box, then add a new server using either FTP or Local/Network for the connection.
   b. If you don't have the information to use FTP, create a folder named **blooms_yourlastname** on your local computer to set up the Local/Network connection.
   c. Test the connection with the Test button. When you are successful, close the Manage Sites dialog box and view the Remote server in the Files panel.
   d. Return to Local view.

Skills Review (continued)

8. Publish a site.

   a. Use the Put File(s) button to upload the local site root folder to the remote server.

   b. Expand the Files panel to view both the remote site and the local site files, then compare your screen to Figure J-24.

   c. Collapse the Files panel, close all open files, then close Dreamweaver.

FIGURE J-24

Important: *If you did not create the following websites in Unit B and maintain them during the preceding units, you must create a local site root folder for the websites in the following exercises and define the websites using files your instructor will provide. See the "Read This Before You Begin" section for more detailed instructions.*

Independent Challenge 1

You have been hired to create a website for a river expedition company named Rapids Transit. The owner's name is Mike Andrew. The website is almost complete and you are ready to run reports and conduct tests to make sure the site is ready to publish.

    a. Start Dreamweaver, then open the Rapids Transit website.

    b. Run a site report for untitled documents and add page titles to any pages you find without a title.

    c. Run a site report for missing alt text and add alternate text to any page elements that are listed with missing alt text.

    d. Run a site report for orphaned files. If you see any orphaned files listed, evaluate whether they should be deleted or linked to a page.

    e. Run a site report for broken links, and repair any broken links that you find.

    f. Open the index page, then use the W3C Validation button to validate the HTML markup.

    g. Open and validate the rest of the pages in the site and note any errors that you find.

    h. Go to the W3C Validator at jigsaw.w3c.org/css-validator, then validate the rapids_transit.css file against CSS level 3 standards.

    i. With the index page open, use the Browser Compatibility panel to check for browser compatibility.

    j. Connect to Adobe BrowserLab, preview the index page using three different browsers, then close Adobe BrowserLab.

    k. Open the Manage Sites dialog box, then add a new server using either FTP or Local/Network for the connection. If you don't have the information to use FTP, create a folder named **rapids_yourlastname** on your local computer to set up a Local/Network connection.

    l. Test the connection with the Test button. When you are successful, close the Manage Sites dialog box, view the Remote server in the Files panel, then return to Local view.

    m. Use the Put File(s) button to upload the local site root folder to the remote server.

    n. Expand the Files panel to view both the remote site and the local site files, then compare your screen to Figure J-25.

    o. Collapse the Files panel, close all open files, then close Dreamweaver.

FIGURE J-25

Independent Challenge 2

You are ready to do the final check on the TripSmart website before you present it to the owner, Thomas Howard, for his approval. You also set up the remote server information to upload the files after you receive the authorization.

a. Start Dreamweaver, then open the TripSmart website.

b. Run a site report for untitled documents and add page titles to any pages you find without a title.

c. Run a site report for missing alt text and add alternate text to any page elements that are listed with missing alt text.

d. Run a site report for orphaned files. If you see any orphaned files listed, evaluate whether they should be deleted or linked to a page.

e. Run a site report for broken links, and repair any broken links that you find.

f. Open the index page, then use the W3C Validation button to validate the HTML markup.

g. Open and validate the rest of the pages in the site and note any errors that you find.

h. Go to the W3C Validator at jigsaw.w3c.org/css-validator, then validate the tripsmart_styles.css file against CSS level 3 standards.

i. With the index page open, use the Browser Compatibility panel to check for browser compatibility.

j. Connect to Adobe BrowserLab, preview the index page using three different browsers, then close Adobe BrowserLab.

k. Open the Manage Sites dialog box, then add a new server using either FTP or Local/Network for the connection. If you don't have the information to use FTP, create a folder named **tripsmart_yourlastname** on your local computer to set up a Local/Network connection.

l. Test the connection with the Test button. When you are successful, close the Manage Sites dialog box, view the Remote server in the Files panel, then return to Local view.

m. Use the Put File(s) button to upload the local site root folder to the remote server.

n. Expand the Files panel to view both the remote site and the local site files, then compare your screen to Figure J-26.

o. Collapse the Files panel, close all open files, then close Dreamweaver.

FIGURE J-26

Independent Challenge 3

You are interested in learning more about designing websites for multiple devices. You would like to understand how media queries work and what other options besides media queries are available to you as a designer. You decide to visit several websites and view them on your desktop, a tablet, and a smart phone.

a. Connect to the Internet, then go to Table 22 at table22branson.com.

b. View the website on a desktop, then open it on a tablet or smart phone.

c. Figure 27 shows the website viewed on a desktop. Figure 28 shows the website viewed on an iPad. Notice how the pages are different in content and appearance.

d. View the page source to see if you can find any clues as to how this site adapts itself to the device being used to view it.

FIGURE J-27

Table 22 website used with permission from Table 22 (table22branson.com)

FIGURE J-28

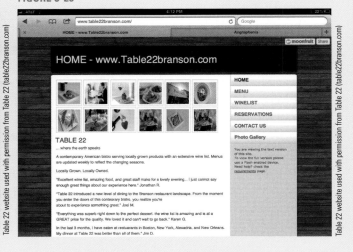

Table 22 website used with permission from Table 22 (table22branson.com)

Real Life Independent Challenge

This assignment will continue to build on your personal website that you created in Unit B. In Unit C, you created and developed your index page. In Unit D, you added a page with either an ordered or an unordered list, and a style sheet with at least two rules. In Unit E, you added a page that included at least two images. In Unit F, you added a page that included several inks and an image map. In Unit G, you created a page based on a CSS layout with a small table for tabular data. In Unit H, you added a media file. In Unit I, you added a form to a page. In this unit, you will be checking your site for broken links, orphaned files, untitled documents, and missing alt text. You will check the files against HTML and CSS standards and use Adobe BrowserLab to view the pages using several different browsers.

a. Run the following site reports: Untitled Documents and Missing Alt Text.

b. Check for broken links and orphaned files.

c. Use the W3C Validation button to validate the code for each page.

d. Go to jigsaw.w3.org/css-validator/ and validate your style sheets.

e. Set up your remote server and upload the website files.

After you are satisfied with your work, verify the following:

a. The site does not have any pages without titles or media files without alternate text.

b. The site does not have any broken links or orphaned files.

c. The style sheets meet CSS3 compliance.

d. Each page passes HTML validation.

e. Each pages displays appropriately in at least three different browsers.

Visual Workshop

You are ready to do the final check on, and publish, the files in the Carolyne's Creations website. Run the appropriate site reports and verify that your links all work correctly. Validate your page code and your style sheets. View the pages on several browsers to verify that the content displays correctly. When you are finished, set up a remote server and upload all files. Compare your remote and local files lists to Figure J-29.

FIGURE J-29

Using Templates

When designing a new website, it is important to include best practices that promote consistency across the site, with each page a part of the overall design plan. The use of CSS, consistent navigation links, standard fonts, reusable assets, and library objects are some of the ways you can accomplish this design goal. Another way to promote consistency as well as save development time is to use templates. Templates are web pages that contain the basic layout for related pages in a website. Template-based pages enable you to update your site information quickly and easily. As your organization grows, you consider the advantages of incorporating templates in your increasingly complex website.

OBJECTIVES

Understand templates

Create a template

Create a template based on an existing page

Create and edit editable regions

Build pages from templates

Understanding Templates

When you create a website, it's important to make sure that each page has a unified look so that users know they are in your site no matter what page they are viewing. Common elements, such as the menu bar and company banner, should appear in the same place on every page, and every page should have the same background color scheme. If you are the only site developer, you can easily copy elements from one page to another. As your organization grows and your website becomes more complex, one way to update your site and maintain a consistent appearance on every page is through the use of templates. ▓▓▓▓▓ You begin by looking at the advantages that templates offer for creating and updating websites. You want to learn how to use templates to streamline the work flow and create consistent page layouts.

DETAILS

- **Templates save development time, especially when different people will be creating pages for your site**

  The ideal process for using templates is for one person to create a page and save it as a template. This person is referred to as the **template author**. Other team members or content contributors can then use this template when creating additional pages for the site. A template usually consists of two types of regions: those that can be changed by others and those that cannot. **Locked regions** are areas of the page that only the template author has access to. These regions contain design elements common to every page in the site that is based on that template. The content of a locked region usually contains information that does not need to be changed on a regular basis, such as a website banner. **Editable regions**, in contrast, are areas in which content can be added or changed by other designers. Figure AP 1-1 shows an example of a template with an editable region.

- **Templates ensure both continuity and flexibility throughout a website**

  Each page that a team creates from a template is connected to the original template file, so if the template author changes the template, all pages to which the template is attached are automatically updated. **Nested templates** are templates that are based on other templates. Templates also allow for design flexibility; an **optional region** is an area in the template that other content contributors can choose to show or hide, such as time-sensitive content that you do not want displayed except on specific dates or as a result of certain conditions.

- **Templates simplify the updating process**

  Website pages based on a template, or a group of nested templates, can be quickly and easily updated. Figure AP 1-2 shows the New Document dialog box with the Blank HTML template option selected. This is the dialog box that you use to create a new template. When updates to the website are necessary, the template is distributed to content contributors, who, in turn, can add the appropriate content to the editable regions of each page.

FIGURE AP 1-1: Template with editable region

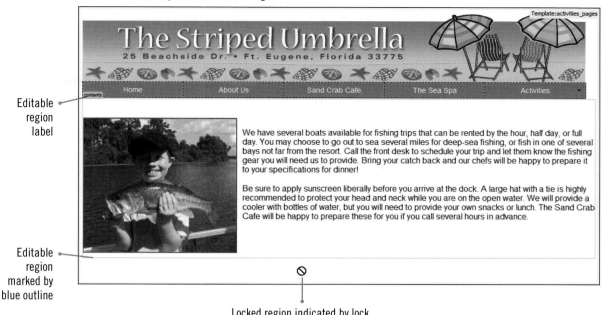

Editable region label

Editable region marked by blue outline

Locked region indicated by lock icon when pointer is over it

© 2013 Cengage Learning
Original photo courtesy of Sherry Bishop

FIGURE AP 1-2: Template Type and Layout options

Blank Template options

Using InContext Editing

Another way to allow users to modify web pages is through InContext Editing (ICE). **InContext Editing** is an online service that enables users to make changes to designated editable regions on a page while viewing it in a browser. This service requires little knowledge of HTML or Dreamweaver. The commands to create editable regions are found in the InContext Editing category on the Insert panel. For more information, search either the Adobe Help files or the Adobe website at adobe.com.

Creating Templates

You can create a new template using the New Document dialog box or, if you have already created and designed a page you want for the layout and design for other pages in your site, you can save that page as a template using the Save as Template command. Templates are saved with a .dwt extension and are stored in the Templates folder in the local site root folder for your website. If your site does not have a Templates folder, one will automatically be created for you the first time you save a template. To view a list of templates in your site, open the Templates folder in the Files panel. To preview a template before opening it, open the Assets panels, click the Templates button on the Assets panel toolbar, then click a template in the list. The template appears in the preview window, as shown in Figure AP 1-3. See Table AP 1-1 for a description of the available regions. You want to review the steps to create a new template to use for each of the activities pages.

STEPS

To create a new template:

1. **Open Dreamweaver, select the website you wish to edit, click File on the Menu bar, click New, click Blank Template, click HTML template in the Template Type column, choose a layout from the Layout column, choose the location to save the CSS file, then click Create**
   In this example, as the web page author, you select the HTML template option.

2. **Replace any existing placeholder text with your page content**
   The template placeholder text includes many helpful hints for working with the template. It's a good idea to read through the text before you delete it if it is the first time you are using the template.

3. **Select the content that you would like to use to create a template region, click the Templates list arrow in the Common category on the Insert panel, as shown in Figure AP 1-4, click one of the template region options, type a name for the region in the dialog box, click OK, then add your content to the region**
   By default, all template content is locked except for editable regions, which allows content contributors to add their own content. You will learn more about editable regions in the next lesson.

4. **Click File on the Menu bar, click Save As Template, type a template name in the File name text box, click Save, then refresh the Files panel if you don't see the template listed**
   A Templates folder under the local site root folder is created with the new template listed inside the folder, as shown in Figure AP 1-5. This Templates folder was automatically created since your site did not have an existing one.

TABLE AP 1-1

region type	definition
Editable	A region that allows users to edit the content
Optional	A region that allows users to choose to either show or hide content
Repeating	A region that contains content that is used multiple times
Editable Optional Region	A region that allows users to both edit the content and choose to show or hide the content
Repeating Table	A table that has a predefined structure and allows users to add content

FIGURE AP 1-3: Viewing a template in the Assets panel

Preview of activities_pages template

Templates button

activities_pages template

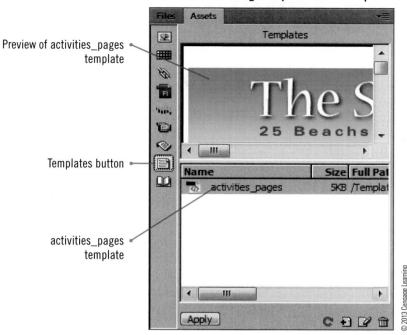

FIGURE AP 1-4: Using the Insert panel to create template regions

Templates list arrow

Make Template options

Template region options

FIGURE AP 1-5: Viewing the Templates folder

Templates folder

Template file

Using Templates

Creating Templates Based on an Existing Page

If you have already created and designed a page that you like, you can use the layout and design for other pages in your site using the Save as Template command. When you save the page as a template, all of the content on the page will be locked. In order for other users to add content to your page, you will need to create at least one editable region. This is the same procedure you follow when you create a new template that is not based on an existing page. ▨▨▨ You review the steps to create a new template based on one of the existing activities pages.

STEPS

To create a new template based on an existing page:

1. **Open an existing page**

2. **Click File on the Menu bar, then click Save as Template**

   The Save As Template dialog box opens, as shown in Figure AP 1-6. This is where you assign a name for the template.

TROUBLE

If you don't see the website listed that you want to save the template in, click the Site list arrow, then select the correct website.

3. **Verify that the website name is displayed in the Site text box, type a file name for the new template in the Save as text box, click Save, then click Yes to update links**

   If this is the first template created, a Templates folder is created under the local site root folder with the new template inside the folder.

FIGURE AP 1-6: **Saving an existing page as a template**

Website name displayed in Site text box: your name might differ

Existing template name: your name might differ; you may also see more than one template listed

File name for the new template: your name might differ

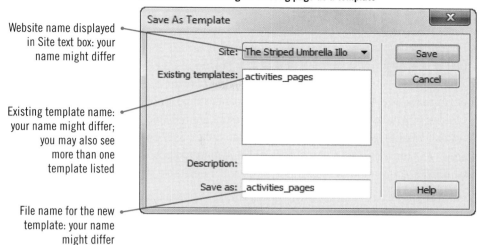

Finding downloadable templates

It is not necessary to create all of your templates from scratch or from existing pages. You can also use templates from outside sources, such as the Internet. A wide range of templates is available for web page components, such as introductions and logos, as well as entire websites. These can include sites for businesses, charities, events, and many other venues. Go to your favorite search engine and type "website templates" in the Search text box. For example, templatemonster.com offers many types of templates, both free and for sale.

Creating and Editing Editable Regions

By default, when you save a template, all content on the page will be locked. You must insert at least one editable region for a template to be functional. Editable regions are outlined in blue on the template page, and the names of the editable regions appear in blue shaded boxes, as shown in Figure AP 1-7. In addition to editable regions, you can also add optional regions, repeating regions, editable optional regions, and repeating tables. ░░░░░ You want to review the steps to add an editable region to a template.

STEPS

QUICK TIP
You can also press [Ctrl][Alt][V] (Win) or [command][option] [V] (Mac) to open the New Editable Region dialog box.

1. **Select the existing content on the page where you want to create the editable region**

2. **Select the Common category on the Insert panel, if necessary**

3. **Click the Templates list arrow in the Common category, then click Editable Region**
   The New Editable Region dialog box opens. This is where you specify a name for region.

TROUBLE
If the blue shaded box does not display, click View on the Menu bar, point to Visual Aids, then click Invisible Elements.

4. **Type a name for the editable region in the Name text box, as shown in Figure AP 1-8, then click OK**
   The editable region appears selected on the page. A blue shaded box containing the name of the editable region displays above the top left corner of the region. To remove an editable region from a template, select the editable region in the document window, click Modify on the Menu bar, point to Templates, then click Remove Template Markup. (This does not remove the actual content from that region.)

Understanding optional regions

In addition to editable regions, you can also add optional regions to a template. An **optional region** is an area in a template that users can choose to either show or hide. An optional region's visibility is controlled by the conditional statement *if*. You can specify a page element as an optional region using the New Optional Region dialog box. You can name the region and specify whether to show or hide it by default. The Editable and Optional Region dialog boxes are both accessed by clicking the Templates list arrow in the Common category of the Insert panel.

FIGURE AP 1-7: **Viewing an editable region in a template**

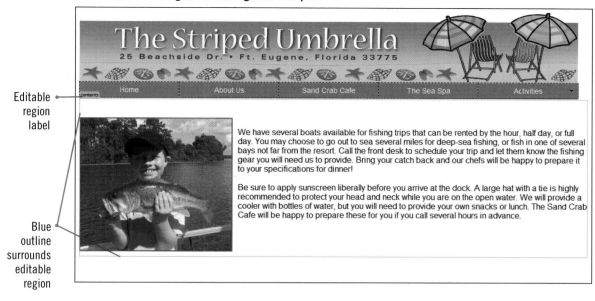

Editable
region
label

Blue
outline
surrounds
editable
region

FIGURE AP 1-8: **New Editable Region dialog box**

Name of new Editable Region:
your name might differ

Building Pages From Templates

There are many advantages to using a template to create a page. First, it saves time since some or all of the content and format are already set. Second, it ensures that the page you create is consistent with the look and format of other pages in the site. It is important to use document-relative links for links on pages based on templates; otherwise, the links will not work. The path to a link actually goes from the template file (not from the template-based page) to the linked page. To ensure that all of your links are document-relative, select the page element to which you want to add a link, and then drag the Point to File button from the Property inspector to the page you want to link to in the Files panel. You want to review the steps to create a page from a template.

STEPS

QUICK TIP

Another method is to right-click (Win) or [control]-click (Mac) a template in the Assets panel, and then click New from Template.

1. **Click File on the Menu bar, then click New**

   The New Document dialog box opens. This is where you select the template you want to use to create the new page.

2. **Click Page from Template, as shown in Figure AP 1-9**

3. **Verify that the correct site name is selected in the Site column, click the name of the template in the Template for Site column, then click Create**

   A new Dreamweaver document opens, as shown in Figure AP 1-10, based on the template you selected. This is where you add content to the editable regions.

4. **Save the page**

Attaching a template to an existing page

Sometimes you might need to apply a template to a page that you have already created. For example, suppose you create a page for your department in your company's website, and then your manager tells you that it must be based on the template created by the marketing department. Before you attach a template to an existing page, you should delete any elements from your page that also appear in the template. For instance, if both your page and the template have a company logo, you should delete the logo on your page so that it doesn't appear twice. Once you delete the duplicate content on your page, attach the template by opening your page, selecting the template in the Assets panel, then clicking the Apply button in the Assets panel. The resulting Inconsistent Region Names dialog box enables you to specify in which regions of the template to place the document head and body content from your page. To detach a template from a page, open the page, click Modify on the Menu bar, point to Templates, then click Detach from Template. You can also attach a template to an open page by dragging the template from the Assets panel to the Document window.

FIGURE AP 1-9: New Document dialog box

Template name:
your name
might differ

Page from
Template

Website name:
your name
might differ

© 2013 Cengage Learning
Original photo by Sherry Bishop

FIGURE AP 1-10: Viewing a new page based on a template

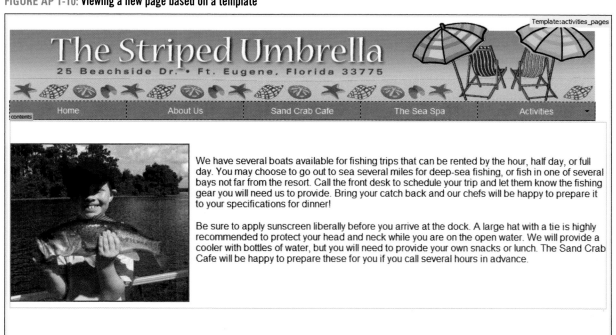

© 2013 Cengage Learning
Original photo by Sherry Bishop

Practice

Concepts Review

Match each of the following terms with the statement that best describes it.

1. **Locked region**
2. **Editable region**
3. **Optional region**
4. **Nested template**
5. **ICE**
6. **Template**

a. Area in a template that users can choose to either show or hide.
b. A template based on another template.
c. Area of a template that users cannot modify.
d. An online hosted service for editing pages while viewing them in a browser.
e. Area of a template where users can add or edit content.
f. Pages that can be used as a basis for creating other pages.

Select the best answer from the following list of choices.

7. **An area in a template where users can add or change content is called:**
   a. a locked region.
   b. an editable region.
   c. an optional region.
   d. a hidden region.

8. **The name of the folder that is created when a template is first saved is called:**
   a. Templates.
   b. TemplateAssets.
   c. TemplatePages.
   d. Temp.

9. **Which of the following appears when the mouse pointer is placed over a locked region in a template?**
   a. ▷
   b. 👆
   c. ➡
   d. None of the above

10. **Which type of region must every template contain?**
    a. Repeating region
    b. Editable region
    c. Optional region
    d. Repeating table

Working with AP Divs

Div tags, as you have learned, are used to place content on web pages. One particular type of div tag is an AP div. An AP (absolutely positioned) div is a div you use to place content on a web page in a fixed position that will not shift when the page is displayed at different size resolutions. By contrast, **relative positioning** places divs relative to other page content. AP divs can also be used to create interest on a page by combining them with special effects. As you gain experience using div tags, you decide to explore the possibilities AP divs might have to add interest to The Striped Umbrella site.

OBJECTIVES
Edit CSS layout properties
Insert an AP div
Position and size an AP div
Add content to an AP div
Use the AP Elements panel

Inserting an AP Div

An AP (absolutely positioned) div is a div you use to place content on a web page in a fixed position. AP divs are also referred to as AP elements. You can specify a selected AP div's exact position using either the Left or Top settings on the Property inspector or by editing the rule in the CSS Styles panel. You can stack AP divs on top of each other as if they were transparency sheets and specify that only certain divs be visible at certain times or in specified conditions. To insert an AP div, you click the Draw AP Div button in the Layout category on the Insert panel, then drag a rectangular shape anywhere on a page. AP divs are useful for placing time-sensitive information on a page that might be used for only a set period of time. Since it won't affect the page layout when it is added or removed, it is a useful design tool for showing temporary content, such as advertising space. Guides are lines you can drag onto your pages to help you place objects more precisely. Guides are not visible in the browser. Once you place a guide on the page, you can reposition it by dragging it to a different location. ████ You have been asked to place a temporary advertisement for parasailing on the index page. An AP div would be a good way to display the ad. You review the steps for inserting an AP div on the page. (The instructions below were used with a new index page based on a CSS layout. If you want to follow the steps exactly, rather than with a generic page, create a new index page based on the activities_pages template before you begin with Step 1.)

STEPS

1. **Place your insertion point on a page based on a CSS layout where you want to insert an AP div, click the Insert panel list arrow, click Layout if necessary, then click Draw AP Div**

   The pointer changes to a plus sign when placed over the page, indicating that it is ready to draw an AP div.

2. **Drag a rectangle on the page, as shown in Figure AP 2-1**

   As you drag you can see the height and width values change in the Property inspector. A new AP div appears on the page, but it is not selected. An AP Div icon ▣ appears in the upper-left corner of the div.

3. **Click the AP Div icon ▣ above the AP div to select it**

   Sizing handles appear around the AP div, indicating that it is selected. The Property inspector options change to show properties for an AP div.

4. **With the AP div selected, select apDiv1 in the CSS-P Element text box in the Property inspector, then type a name for the AP div**

   Giving an AP div a unique name helps you to identify the div quickly as you view the code.

5. **Select the AP div name in the Tag selector if necessary, click the Overflow list arrow in the Property inspector, then click auto**

   The Overflow property controls how the content in an AP div will appear in a browser if there is insufficient space to fit the content in the AP div. The Auto setting enables the overflow content to display, and will add scroll bars, if necessary, at the side or bottom of the AP div when it is viewed in the browser window.

6. **Click the Vis list arrow, then click visible, as shown in Figure AP 2-2**

   The Vis property specifies whether the AP div is visible or not when the page loads in the browser.

Positioning Elements with CSS

When you place a div on a page, you have several choices for specifying how the div will be positioned on the page when it is viewed in a browser. The default position is **static**, which means that the div will follow the natural document flow of the other page elements. Other positions include absolute, fixed, relative, and inherit. **Absolute** means the div will be positioned relative to its parent, or ancestor element. **Fixed** means the div will be positioned relative to the browser window. **Relative** means the div will be positioned relative to its default or previously specified position. **Inherit** means the div will be positioned with the same position property as its parent element (inherited).

FIGURE AP 2-1: New AP div added to a page

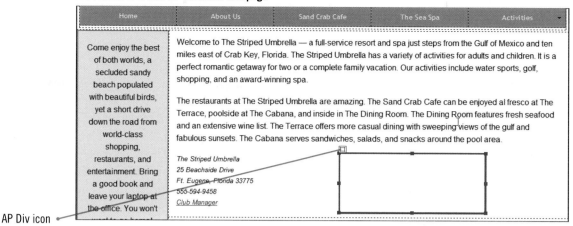

AP Div icon

FIGURE AP 2-2: Property inspector showing properties of selected AP div

AP Div icon

Selected AP div

CSS-P Element text box

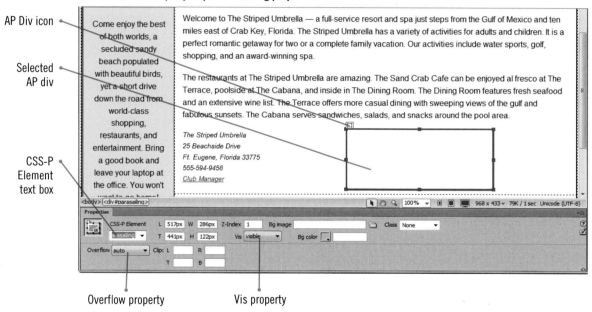

Overflow property

Vis property

Design Matters

Creating special effects with AP divs

Advanced designers use AP divs to create special effects on web pages. They might create a rollover effect so that when the user places the mouse pointer over an AP div, another AP div appears. Or they might make an AP div appear to move along a path, or change size, visibility, or position using a JavaScript feature called a **timeline**. Another effect allows users to drag AP divs across the page; this feature might be used to create a puzzle where users can move puzzle pieces into the correct position. Some interactive games allow you to drag and drop objects to target areas,

such as dragging chess pieces on a virtual chessboard. In Dreamweaver, a designer would use the Behaviors panel to assign behaviors to AP divs. A behavior is a preset piece of JavaScript code that can be attached to divs. A behavior tells the div to respond in a specific way when an action occurs, such as when the mouse pointer is positioned over the div, or when a user clicks the mouse over a div. The action triggers an event that causes a behavior to start, such as the AP div changing size or disappearing.

Positioning and Sizing an AP Div

To use AP divs, you must understand absolute positioning. An AP div is positioned absolutely by specifying the distance between the top-left corner of the AP div and the top-left corner of the page or parent container. The default reference point is the top-left corner of the page. You control the placement of AP divs by setting attributes in the Property inspector. The **Left property (L)** specifies the distance between the left edge of an AP div and the left edge of the page or parent container, such as another div. The **Top property (T)** specifies the distance between the top edge of the AP div and the top edge of the page or div that contains it. The **Width (W)** and **Height (H) properties** specify the dimensions of the AP div in either pixels or as a percentage of the page. If your pages are based on a CSS layout that is centered on the page, you must change the default reference point from the top-left corner of the page to the top-left corner of the parent container, such as a CSS layout block. First, move the code for the AP div after the opening tag for the CSS layout block serving as the parent container. Second, edit the code for the parent container by changing the Positioning property value to relative. The AP div will then align itself in a fixed position relative to the parent container despite browser window size. The top and left properties of the AP div use the top-left corner of the parent div, rather than the top-left corner of the browser window to determine where to place the AP div. The parent div must then be set to align relatively. ▓▓▓▓▓ With the AP div in position on a page, the following steps can be used to determine the size and position of the content on the page.

STEPS

QUICK TIP
Your div id and class may differ.

1. **Switch to Code view, select the code `<div id="parasailing"></div>` if necessary, then press [Ctrl][X] (Win) or [command][X] (Mac) to cut it**
   The code is removed from the page and placed on the Clipboard.

2. **Locate the code `<div class="container">`, enter a line break at the end of this code, press [Ctrl][V] (Win) or [command][V] (Mac) to paste `<div id="parasailing"> </div>`, then compare your screen to Figure AP 2-3**
   The placement of the AP div code is repositioned inside the opening and closing tags for the div named *container*.

QUICK TIP
If the CSS layout was based on a left align-ment rather than a center alignment, these steps would not be necessary.

3. **Switch back to Design view, double-click the container rule in the CSS Styles panel, click Positioning in the Category list, click the Position list arrow, click relative, then click OK**
   The position property for the container rule is set to relative. The combination of changing the container rule position to relative and moving the AP div code after the container opening tag works together to ensure that the AP div remains in a constant position in the browser window, regardless of the width of the window.

QUICK TIP
Your values for the next three steps may differ.

4. **Click the AP div border to select the AP div if necessary, select the current text in the L text box in the Property inspector, type 560px, then press [Enter] (Win) or [return] (Mac)**
   The left side of the AP div automatically moves to 560 pixels from the left side of the container.

5. **Select the current text in the T text box, type 410px, then press [Enter] (Win) or [return] (Mac)**
   In the browser window, the AP div will not appear as close to the last line of text.

QUICK TIP
You can press [Enter] or [Tab] to enter options in the Property inspector, but [Tab] will also move the insertion point to the next text box.

6. **Select the current text in the W text box, type 350px, press [Tab], type 206px in the H text box, press [Tab], save your work, then compare your screen to Figure AP 2-4**
   The AP div automatically adjusts to the updated width and height specifications and the upper-left corner remains in its original position.

FIGURE AP 2-3: AP div code repositioned after container div code

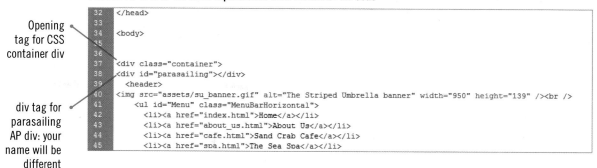

Opening tag for CSS container div

div tag for parasailing AP div: your name will be different

```
32    </head>
33
34    <body>
35
36
37    <div class="container">
38    <div id="parasailing"></div>
39      <header>
40    <img src="assets/su_banner.gif" alt="The Striped Umbrella banner" width="950" height="139" /><br />
41        <ul id="Menu" class="MenuBarHorizontal">
42          <li><a href="index.html">Home</a></li>
43          <li><a href="about_us.html">About Us</a></li>
44          <li><a href="cafe.html">Sand Crab Cafe</a></li>
45          <li><a href="spa.html">The Sea Spa</a></li>
```

FIGURE AP 2-4: Resized AP div

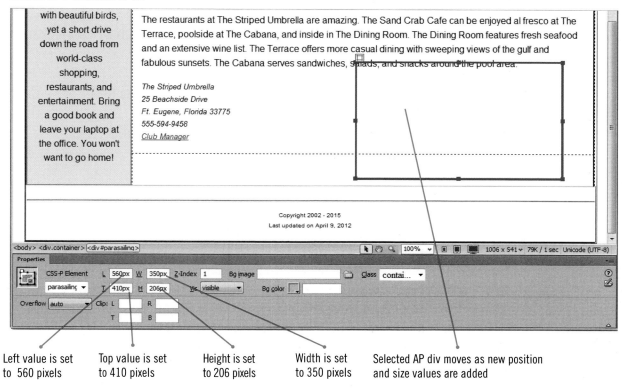

Left value is set to 560 pixels

Top value is set to 410 pixels

Height is set to 206 pixels

Width is set to 350 pixels

Selected AP div moves as new position and size values are added

Understanding the z-index property

The **z-index property** in the Property inspector is used to specify the vertical stacking order of multiple AP divs on a page. If you think of the page as being AP div 0, then any number higher than that will appear on top of the page. For instance, if you have three AP divs with z-index values of 1, 2, and 3, then 1 will appear underneath 2 and 3, while 3 will always appear on top of 1 and 2. AP divs are assigned default z-index values as they are created beginning with the number 1, but you can easily change the stacking order by reassigning the z-index values in either the CSS Styles panel or in the AP Elements panel.

Working with AP Divs

Adding Content to an AP Div

Because an AP div is like a separate document within a web page, it can contain the same types of elements that a page contains, such as background colors, images, links, tables, and text. If you add more content than will fit in the present size, the AP div will enlarge to display the content on your page in Dreamweaver. However, when you preview the page in a browser, the amount displayed will depend on how you set your Overflow settings. As with formatting text on web pages, you should use CSS to format text on an AP div. ▦▦▦▦ You review the following steps to add a background image and text to an AP div.

STEPS

1. **Select the AP div if necessary, then click the Browse for File button 🗀 next to the Bg image text box in the Property inspector**
   The Select Image Source dialog box opens.

2. **Navigate to the drive and folder where you store your images, double-click an image to place it in the div, then compare your screen to Figure AP 2-5**
   The image fills the background of the AP div.

   > **QUICK TIP**
   > Your image filename will differ.

3. **Refresh the Files panel to verify that image was copied to the assets folder of the website**

   > **TROUBLE**
   > If you are having trouble setting the insertion point, click or double-click directly in the middle of the AP div.

4. **Click inside the AP div**
   The insertion pointer displays as a blinking line on the left side of the div.

5. **Type appropriate text using line breaks between lines**
   The text displays on top of the image since the image was used as a background image rather than just inserted onto the div.

   > **TROUBLE**
   > If you don't see the div rule listed in the CSS Styles panel, click the plus sign next to <style> to expand it.

6. **Select the parasailing rule (or the name of the AP div rule you created) in the CSS Styles panel, then click the Edit Rule button 🖉**
   The parasailing rule was created when the AP div name "parasailing" was assigned to replace the default AP div name.

7. **Edit the rule properties to format and place the text in the AP div**

   > **QUICK TIP**
   > When you type text on an AP div, you should always format the text using styles in the CSS Styles panel, rather than using manual formatting.

8. **Save your work, preview the page in your browser, compare your screen with Figure AP 2-6, close your browser, make any line adjustments if necessary, save the page, then Exit (Win) or Quit (Mac) Dreamweaver**

FIGURE AP 2-5: AP div with a background image

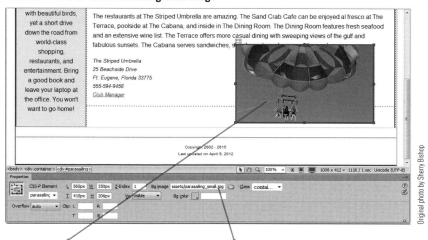

Image serves as AP div background (your image will differ)

Path to background image is set to the site assets folder

FIGURE AP 2-6: Index page with the formatted AP div

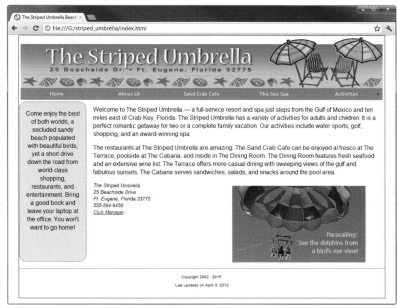

Understanding the Overflow property

Sometimes there is more content than will fit in the dimensions of an AP div. To account for this possibility, you can set the Overflow property to direct the browser to display the extra content or to hide it, by assigning one of four possible values. The visible value means that the AP div will stretch to display any extra content. The hidden value means that extra content will not be displayed. The scroll value means that the browser will display scroll bars in the AP div whether they are needed or not. The auto value means that extra content will be displayed, and scroll bars will be added if needed.

Using the AP Elements Panel

The easiest way to manage AP divs is with the AP Elements panel, which is in the CSS tab group next to the CSS Styles panel. The **AP Elements panel,** opened through the Window menu, is used to control the properties of all AP divs on a web page. The AP Elements panel provides a quick way to scan the number of AP divs on a page, their names, their z-indexes, and to control their visibility settings. ▰▰▰ You study the uses of the AP Elements panel to better understand how to manage your AP divs. As you add more AP divs to the website pages, the need for good organization practices becomes even more important.

DETAILS

- **Change AP div order and names**

  The AP Elements panel lists all AP divs on the open page in order of their z-index. The first AP div you create appears by default at the bottom of the stack, with the most recent at the top. You can reorder them by changing the z-index settings. Assigning an AP div a logical name that represents its content helps you quickly identify each page div. To rename an AP div, double-click its default name in the Property inspector, then enter a new name.

- **Select AP divs**

  When you select the AP div name from the list in the AP Elements panel, the AP div will be selected on the page. This feature is helpful when you are trying to select an AP div from the bottom of a stack.

- **Control visibility**

  The first column in the AP Elements panel contains icons that show the visibility setting for each AP div, with eye icons representing the visibility settings. An open eye icon 👁 means that the AP div is visible on the page. A closed eye icon 👁 means the AP div is not visible on the page. If neither icon appears in the column, the AP div will inherit the visibility status of its parent object; see Figure AP 2-7. If an AP div is not part of a group, the parent object is the web page or CSS container. Clicking the column next to a div will toggle between the icons, thus changing the visibility settings for that div.

- **Control the visible stacking order and overlaps**

  You can change the stacking order of an AP div by dragging the AP div name up or down in the AP Elements panel. As you drag past other names in the list, a placement line appears to let you know where the AP div would move if you released the mouse button. After you drag an element in the list, its z-index changes automatically to reflect its new position in the stacking order. See Figures AP 2-8 and 2-9.

- **Use nested AP divs**

  Besides stacking, another option for placing AP divs is nesting. **Nested AP divs** are AP divs whose HTML code resides inside other AP divs. In the AP Elements panel, nested AP divs are indented under the parent AP div. Nesting AP divs ties them together for such purposes as visibility. Nested AP divs move with their parent AP divs. If you want to nest AP divs, be sure that the Prevent overlaps check box is deselected in the AP Elements panel. You must also select the Nest when created within an AP div check box in the Dreamweaver Preferences dialog box, as shown in Figure AP 2-10. To create a nested AP div, click to place the insertion point inside an existing AP div, then use the Insert > Layout Objects > AP Div command to insert a new AP div.

> **QUICK TIP**
>
> If you want to show or hide all AP divs on a page, click the header eye icon at the top of the column to toggle between all visible or all hidden.

> **QUICK TIP**
>
> You can also change the z-index by entering a new value in the Z-Index text box in the Property inspector.

Understanding AP div code

As you examine the HTML code for AP divs, you will see that the code is actually split between the head section and the body section of the code. The head section contains the code that sets the position, size, overflow, and formatting. Comments are also included that provide explanation for each style. The body section contains the code for the div ID and div content. This is similar to the way CSS styles are written: the code for the CSS style, properties, and values resides in the head section for internal style sheets. For external style sheets, the code linking the style sheet to the page resides in the head section. The code where each CSS style is applied to a page element resides in the body section.

FIGURE AP 2-7: **The AP Elements panel visibility settings**

Eye header icon

Open eye icon

Closed eye icon

No eye icon displayed

FIGURE AP 2-8: **The border AP div with a z-index of 2**

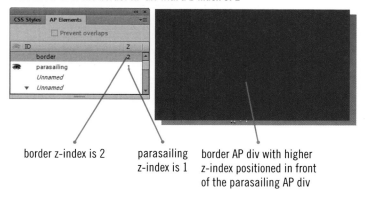

border z-index is 2

parasailing z-index is 1

border AP div with higher z-index positioned in front of the parasailing AP div

FIGURE AP 2-9: **The border AP div with a z-index of 1**

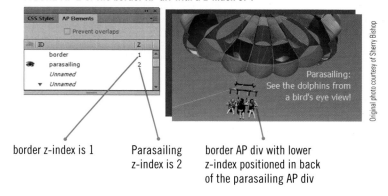

Original photo courtesy of Sherry Bishop

border z-index is 1

Parasailing z-index is 2

border AP div with lower z-index positioned in back of the parasailing AP div

FIGURE AP 2-10: **Viewing AP Elements preferences**

Nest when created within an AP div option checkbox currently unselected

Practice

Concepts Review

Label each element shown in Figure AP 2-11.

FIGURE AP 2-11

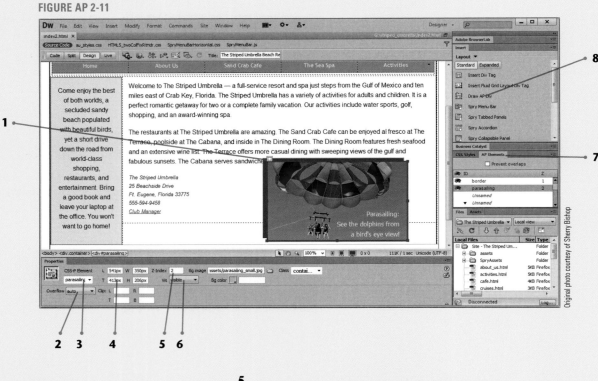

1. _____   5. _____
2. _____   6. _____
3. _____   7. _____
4. _____   8. _____

Match each of the following terms with the statement that best describes its function.

9. **AP Elements panel**   a. A div with a specified, fixed position on a page

10. **z-index property**   b. A preset piece of JavaScript code that can be attached to divs

11. **Behaviors**   c. Lines you can drag onto a page to help place objects

12. **AP div**   d. The location used to control the properties of AP divs

13. **Relative positioning**   e. Page content that changes either in response to certain conditions or through interaction with the user

14. **Absolute positioning**

15. **JavaScript behaviors**   f. Divs are placed on a page relative to other page content

16. **Guides**   g. An AP div whose code is inside another AP div's (parent) code

17. **Nested AP div**   h. The property that determines the stacking order of multiple AP divs

18. **Dynamic content**   i. Action scripts that allow you to create dynamic page content

j. Divs placed on a page in a fixed position

Data Files for Dreamweaver CS6 Illustrated

To complete the lessons and practice exercises in this book, students need to use Data Files that are supplied by Cengage Learning. Below is a list of the Data Files that are supplied and the unit and practice exercise to which the files correspond. For information on how to obtain Data Files, please refer to the inside front cover of this book. The following list includes only Data Files that are supplied; it does not include the website files students create from scratch or the files students create by revising supplied files.

Unit	Location file is used in unit	Folder location for files	Files supplied
BRIDGE	Lessons (The Striped Umbrella site)	Bridge folder	blooms_banner.jpg
			blue_footed_booby.jpg
			boardwalk.png
			boats.jpg
			butterfly.jpg
			butterfly1.jpg
			butterfly2.jpg
			cafe_photo.jpg
			cc_banner.jpg
			cc_banner_with_text.jpg
			children_cooking.jpg
			chives.jpg
			chocolate_cake.jpg
			club_house.jpg
			coleus.jpg
			cookies_oven.jpg
			crabdance.swf
			family_sunset.jpg
			fiber_optic_grass.jpg
			fish.jpg
			fisherman.jpg
			garden_quote.swf
			gardening_gloves.gif

Unit	Location file is used in unit	Folder location for files	Files supplied
			girl_floating.jpg
			hanging_baskets.mp4
			iguana_and_lizard.jpg
			interviews.mp3
			lady_in_red.jpg
			llama.jpg
			machu_picchu_from_high.jpg
			machu_picchu_ruins.jpg
			marshmallows.jpg
			one_dolphin.jpg
			peruvian_appetizers.jpg
			peruvian_glass.jpg
			pie.jpg
			plants.jpg
			pool.jpg
			river_guide.jpg
			river_scenes.swf
			rose_bloom.jpg
			rose_bud.jpg
			rt_banner.jpg
			rt_logo_gif
			ruby_grass.jpg
			sea_lions_in_surf.jpg
			sea_spa_logo.png
			sealions_video.mp4
			seeds_audio.mp3
			su_banner.gif
			trees.jpg
			tripsmart_banner.jpg
			tripsmart_gradient.jpg
			tulips.jpg
			two_dolphins.jpg
			two_roses.jpg
			umbrella_anchor_video.mp4
			walking_stick.jpg
			water.jpg
			water_lily.jpg
			young_paddler.jpg

Unit	Location file is used in unit	Folder location for files	Files supplied
UNIT A	Lessons (The Striped Umbrella site)	Unit A folder	dwa_1.html
		Unit A assets folder	pool.jpg
			su_banner.gif
	Skills Review (Blooms & Bulbs site)	Unit A folder	dwa_2.html
		Unit A assets folder	blooms_banner.jpg
			tulips.jpg
	Independent Challenge 1 (TripSmart site)	Unit A folder	dwa_3.html
		Unit A assets folder	tripsmart_banner.jpg
UNIT B	Lessons (The Striped Umbrella site)	Unit B folder	dwb_1.html
		Unit B assets folder	su_banner.gif
	Skills Review (Blooms & Bulbs site)	Unit B folder	dwb_2.html
		Unit B assets folder	blooms_banner.jpg
	Independent Challenge 1 (Rapids Transit site)	Unit B folder	dwb_3.html
		Unit B assets folder	rt_banner.jpg
	Independent Challenge 2 (TripSmart site)	Unit B folder	dwb_4.html
		Unit B assets folder	tripsmart_banner.jpg
	Visual Workshop (Carolyne's Creations site)	Unit B folder	dwb_5.html
		Unit B assets folder	cc_banner.jpg
UNIT C			No Data Files supplied
UNIT D	Lessons (The Striped Umbrella site)	Unit D folder	spa.doc
		Unit D assets folder	sea_spa_logo.png
	Skills Review (Blooms & Bulbs site)	Unit D folder	gardening_tips.doc
		Unit D assets folder	butterfly.jpg
	Independent Challenge 1 (Rapids Transit site)	Unit D folder	dwd_1.html
		Unit D assets folder	rt_banner.jpg
	Independent Challenge 2 (TripSmart site)	Unit D folder	dwd_2.html
		Unit D assets folder	tripsmart_banner.jpg
	Visual Workshop (Carolyne's Creations site)	Unit D folder	dwd_3.html
		Unit D assets folder	cc_banner.jpg
			pie.jpg

Unit	Location file is used in unit	Folder location for files	Files supplied
UNIT E	Lessons (The Striped Umbrella site)	Unit E folder	dwe_1.html
		Unit E assets folder	boardwalk.png
			club_house.jpg
			su_banner.gif
			water.jpg
	Skills Review (Blooms & Bulbs site)	Unit E folder	dwe_2.html
		Unit E assets folder	blooms_banner.jpg
			lady_in_red.jpg
			rose_bloom.jpg
			rose_bud.jpg
			two_roses.jpg
	Independent Challenge 1 (Rapids Transit site)	Unit E folder	dwe_3.html
		Unit E assets folder	river_guide.jpg
			rt_banner.jpg
	Independent Challenge 2 (TripSmart site)	Unit E folder	dwe_4.html
		Unit E assets folder	blue_footed_booby.jpg
			iguana_and_lizard.jpg
			tripsmart_banner.jpg
	Visual Workshop (Carolyne's Creations site)	Unit E folder	dwe_5.html
		Unit E assets folder	cc_banner.jpg
			peruvian_glass.jpg
UNIT F	Lessons (The Striped Umbrella site)	Unit F folder	dwf_1.html
		Unit F assets folder	family_sunset.jpg
			su_banner.gif
			su_banner.gif
			two_dolphins.jpg
	Skills Review (Blooms & Bulbs site)	Unit F folder	dwf_2.html
		Unit F assets folder	blooms_banner.jpg
			plants.jpg
			ruby_grass.jpg
			trees.jpg
	Independent Challenge 1 (Rapids Transit site)	Unit F folder	dwf_3.html

Unit	Location file is used in unit	Folder location for files	Files supplied
		Unit F assets folder	rt_banner.jpg
			young_paddler.jpg
	Independent Challenge 2 (TripSmart site)	Unit F folder	dwf_4.html
		Unit F assets folder	tripsmart_banner.jpg
	Visual Workshop (Carolyne's Creations site)	Unit F folder	dwf_5.html
			dwf_6.html
			dwf_7.html
		Unit F assets folder	cc_banner_with_text.jpg
			children_cooking.jpg
			cookies_oven.jpg
			fish.jpg
			peruvian_appetizers.jpg
UNIT G	Lessons (The Striped Umbrella site)	Unit G folder	café.doc
		Unit G assets folder	cafe_photo.jpg
			chocolate_cake.jpg
	Skills Review (Blooms & Bulbs site)	Unit G assets folder	chives.jpg
			composting.doc
			gardening_gloves.gif
	Independent Challenge 1 (Rapids Transit site)	Unit G folder	rentals.doc
		Unit G assets folder	girl_floating.jpg
			rt_logo.gif
	Independent Challenge 2 (TripSmart site)	Unit G folder	walking sticks.doc
		Unit G assets folder	tripsmart_gradient.jpg
			walking_stick.jpg
	Visual Workshop (Carolyne's Creations site)	Unit G assets folder	marshmallows.jpg
UNIT H	Lessons (The Striped Umbrella site)	Unit H folder	crabdance.swf
			dwh_1.html
			dwh_2.html
			dwh_3.html
			interviews.mp3
			umbrella_anchor_video.mp4

Unit	Location file is used in unit	Folder location for files	Files supplied
		Unit H assets folder	boats.jpg
			fisherman.jpg
			one_dolphin.jpg
			two_dolphins.jpg
	Skills Review (Blooms & Bulbs site)	Unit H folder	dwh_4.html
			dwh_5.html
			dwh_6.html
			garden_quote.swf
			hanging_baskets.mp4
			seeds_audio.mp3
		Unit H assets folder	butterfly1.jpg
			butterfly2.jpg
			coleus.jpg
			fiber_optic_grass.jpg
			water_lily.jpg
	Independent Challenge 1 (Rapids Transit site)	Unit H folder	river_scenes.swf
	Independent Challenge 2 (TripSmart site)	Unit H folder	dwh_7.html
			dwh_8.html
			sealions_video.mp4
		Unit H assets folder	llama.jpg
			machu_picchu_from_high.jpg
			machu_picchu_ruins.jpg
			sea_lions_in_surf.jpg
	Visual Workshop (Carolyne's Creations site)		
UNIT I			No Data Files supplied
UNIT J			No Data Files supplied

Glossary

Absolute path A path containing an external link that references a web page outside the current website, and includes the prefix http:// and the URL of the web page; *see also* URL.

Accordion A CSS style that creates a method of organizing data on a page with buttons that, when clicked, open up like an accordion with information that drops down below the button.

Action A response to an event trigger that causes a change, such as text changing color or a form being processed.

Action property Specifies the application or script that will process form data.

Active panel A panel displayed as the front panel in an expanded panel group with the panel options displayed.

Adaptive website A website that can adjust or modify the page content to fit the user's needs and device type used to view the site.

Add-on *See* plug-in.

Adobe Air An Adobe product used for developing content that can be delivered with a browser or as a desktop application.

Adobe BrowserLab An Adobe online service for cross-browser and cross-platform compatibility testing.

Adobe Community Help A collection of materials that includes tutorials, published articles, and blogs, in addition to the regular Help content. All content is monitored and approved by the Adobe Community Expert program.

Adobe Flash Player A free program included with most browsers that allows you to view content created with Adobe Flash.

Advanced style A style used to format combinations of page elements; *also called* compound style.

Alias An icon that represents a program, folder, or file stored on your computer.

Align an image Position an image on a web page in relation to other elements on the page.

Alphanumeric field A type of form field that will accept both numbers and letters or a combination of the two.

Alternate text Descriptive text that can be set to display in place of an image or while the image is downloading.

AP div A div that is assigned a fixed position on a page (absolute position); *also called* AP element.

AP element *See* AP div.

AP Elements panel The panel used to control the properties of all AP elements on a web page.

Application bar (Win) A toolbar located above the Document window that includes menu names, a Workspace switcher, and other application commands. In Bridge, the toolbar that contains the navigation buttons, the Workspace buttons, and the Search text box.

Assets panel A panel that contains nine categories of assets, such as images, used in a website; clicking a category button will display a list of those assets.

AVI (Audio Visual Interleave) A digital video format.

Back-end processing The end of the form processing cycle when the data is processed.

Background image An image used in place of a background color to provide depth and visual interest.

Banner An image that generally appears across the top of a web page and can incorporate information such as a company's logo and contact information.

Baseline The bottom of a line of text, not including descending portions of characters such as in y or g.

Behavior An action script that allows you to add dynamic content to your web pages by allowing an object to respond to user input or as a result of a defined condition.

Blog A website containing regularly posted commentaries and opinions on various topics written and maintained by the website owner.

Body The part of a web page that contains all of the page content users see in their browser window, such as text, graphics, and links.

Border An outline that surrounds an image, cell, table, or div.

Bread crumb trail A list of links that provides a path from the initial page you opened in a website to the page that you are currently viewing.

Broken link A link that cannot find the intended destination file.

Browser Compatibility Check (BCC) A feature on the Adobe website that is used to check for problematic CSS features that may render differently in multiple browsers.

Browser Navigation toolbar A toolbar that contains navigation buttons you use when following links on your web pages in Live view.

Buffer A temporary storage area that acts as a holding area for Flash content as it is being played.

Bullet A small image used to call attention to items in an unordered list.

Bulleted list An unordered list that uses bullets. *See also* bullet.

Button On a form, a small rectangular object with a text label that usually has an action attached to it.

Cascading Style Sheets (CSS) Sets of formatting rules used to format web pages to provide a consistent presentation for content across a website.

Cell A small box within a table that is used to hold text or images; cells are arranged horizontally in rows and vertically in columns.

Cell padding In a table, the distance between the cell content and the cell walls.

Cell spacing In a table, the distance between cells.

Cell wall In a table, the edge surrounding a cell.

Check box A classification of a form object that appears as a box that, when clicked by the user, has a check mark placed in it to indicate that it is selected.

Check Out A feature that enables only one person at a time on a team to work on a file.

Child keyword In Bridge, a keyword that is a sub-category of a parent keyword; *also known as* a sub keyword.

Child menu A submenu.

Class style A style that can be used to format any page element.

Client-side scripting A script that is processed on the user's computer.

Clip art collection A group of image files collected on CDs, DVDs, or downloaded from the Internet and sold with an index or directory of the files.

Cloak The process of marking a file or files for exclusion.

Code and Design views A combination of Code view and Design view; each layout displays in a separate window within the Document window.

Code hint An auto-complete feature that displays lists of tags that appear as you type in Code view.

Code Navigator A small window that opens with code for a selected page element.

Coder layout A layout in the Dreamweaver workspace in which the panels are docked on the left side of the screen and Code view is the default view.

Code view The view that fills the Document window with the HTML code for the page and is primarily used when reading or directly editing the code.

Coding toolbar A toolbar used when you are working with code.

Collections panel In Bridge, a panel used to group assets located in different locations into a single collection.

Compact mode A Bridge mode with a smaller, simplified workspace.

Compound style *See* advanced style.

Content panel In Bridge, the center pane where thumbnails of the files from the selected drive and folder in the Folders panel appear.

Copyright Protects the particular and tangible expression of an idea, but not the idea itself.

Crop To remove a part of an image, both visually (on the page) and physically (the file size).

CSS Advisor A part of the Adobe website that offers solutions for problems with CSS.

CSS Layout Box Model A view option in Dreamweaver that displays CSS divs with the margins and padding applied.

Debug To correct errors in code.

Declaration Part of a Cascading Style Sheet rule; consists of a property and a value.

Default alignment For images, the automatic alignment with the text baseline.

Default text color The color the browser uses to display text when another color is not specified.

Definition lists A list composed of terms that are displayed with a hanging indent and is often used with terms and definitions.

Delimiter A comma, tab, colon, semicolon, or similar character that separates tabular data in a text file.

Deliverables Products that will be provided to a client upon project completion, such as the creation of new pages or graphic elements.

Deprecated A feature that is being phased out and will soon be invalid or obsolete, such as directory or menu lists.

Derivative work An adaptation of another work, such as a movie version of a book; a new, original product that includes content from a previously existing work.

Descendant selector A selector that includes two or more selectors that form a relationship and are separated by white space.

Description A short summary of website content; resides in the head section.

Designer layout A layout in the Dreamweaver workspace, in which panels are docked on the right side of the screen and Design view is the default view.

Design note A note directed to other content creators who are working on a website with a team.

Design view The view that shows a page in the entire Document window and is primarily used when designing and creating a web page.

Diagonal symmetry Web page elements are balanced along the invisible diagonal line across the page.

Distance A feature that shows you the distance between two guides.

Divs A page element created with a div tag that is used to position and style content.

Div tag An HTML tag that is used to format and position divs.

Document-relative path A path referenced in relation to the web page that is currently displayed.

Document toolbar A toolbar that contains buttons for changing the current web page view, previewing and debugging web pages, and managing files.

Document window The large area under the document toolbar that encompasses most of the Dreamweaver workspace; open web pages appear in this area.

Domain name An IP address expressed in letters instead of numbers, usually reflecting the name of the business, individual, or other organization represented by the website.

Download To transfer files from a remote computer to your computer.

Download time The amount of time it takes to download a file.

Drop zone The position on the screen where a panel that is being moved will be docked when you release the mouse button.

Dual Screen layout A layout that utilizes two monitors: one for the document window and Property inspector and one for the panels.

Dynamic content Content that changes either in response to certain conditions or through interaction with the user.

Dynamic image An image that is replaced with another image.

Edit To insert, delete, or change page content, such as inserting a new image, adding a link, or correcting spelling errors.

Editable region In a template, an area the template author creates that allows content contributors to insert text or images.

Embedded style A style whose code is stored in the head content of a web page, rather than in a separate external file. *See also* internal style.

Essentials workspace The default workspace in Bridge that includes all of the menus, panels, buttons, and panes that are used to organize media files.

Event A reaction to an action that causes a behavior to start.

Expanded Tables mode Displays a table with expanded table borders and temporary space between the cells to simplify working with individual cells.

Export data To save data that was created in Dreamweaver in a different file format so that other programs can read it.

Export panel In Bridge, a panel used to optimize images by saving them as JPEGs for use on the web.

Extensible Metadata Platform (XMP) standard The standard Adobe uses to save metadata.

External link A link that connects to a web page in another website.

External style sheet A single file, separate from the web page, that contains formatting code and can be attached to a web page to quickly apply formatting to page content.

Facebook A social networking site that enables a user to set up a profile page in order to post and exchange information with others.

Fair use An exemption to copyright that allows limited reproduction of copyright-protected work for certain permissible purposes such as research and reporting.

Favorite An asset that you expect to use repeatedly while you work on a site and that is categorized separately in the Assets panel; also, the Dreamweaver Help feature that allows you to add topics to the Favorites window that you might want to view later without having to search again.

Favorites panel In Bridge, a panel used to quickly access folders that are designated as folders used frequently.

Field A form area into which users can insert a specific piece of data, such as their last names or addresses.

File field In a form, a field that lets users browse to and upload a file.

Files panel A file management tool similar to Windows Explorer or Finder, where Dreamweaver stores and manages your website files and folders.

Filter panel In Bridge, a panel used to filter files to view in the Content panel.

Fixed layout A CSS layout that uses columns expressed in pixels that will not change sizes when viewed in different window sizes.

Fixed position A CSS property that places an element relative to the browser window.

Flash movie Low-bandwidth animation and interactive element created with the Adobe Flash program.

Flash player *See* Adobe Flash Player.

Flash video A video that has been converted from a digital file format to a .flv file using Adobe Flash.

Fluid Grid Layout A layout used for designing adaptive websites based on a single fluid grid.

FLV Adobe Flash video format.

Focus group A marketing tool that gathers feedback from a specific group of people about a product, such as the impact of a television ad or the effectiveness of a website design.

Folders panel In Bridge, a panel used to navigate through your folders to select a folder and view the folder contents.

Font-combination A set of font choices that specifies which fonts a browser should use to display text, such as Arial, Helvetica, sans serif. *Also known as* a font stack. Font-combinations that a user creates are called custom font stacks.

Font stack *See* font-combination.

Form A collection of input fields that allows one to obtain information from website users.

Form action attribute Part of a form tag that specifies how the form will be processed.

Form object An individual component of a form that accepts an individual piece of information.

Frame A fixed region in a browser that can display a web page and act independently from other pages displayed in other frames within the browser.

Front-end processing The beginning of the processing cycle when the data is collected.

FTP (File Transfer Protocol) The technology used to upload and download files to and from a remote site.

Gestures Interactions with a touch screen, usually with a combination of fingers and a thumb.

Get method Specifies that the data collected in a form be sent to the server encoded into the URL of the web page in the form action property.

GIF (Graphics Interchange Format) A type of file format used for images placed on web pages, is used for images with transparent backgrounds.

Global style A style used to apply common properties for certain page elements, such as text, links, or backgrounds.

Google Video Chat A video and audio sharing application.

Go to URL Directs the browser to use a link to open a different window.

GPS (Global Positioning System) A device used to track your position through a global satellite navigation system.

Graphic A picture or design element that adds visual interest to a page.

Graphic design elements Elements that combine to promote a pleasing page design such as the way lines, shapes, forms, textures, and colors are used to create and place elements on a page.

Graphic design principles The use of emphasis, movement, balance, unity, symmetry, color, white space, alignment, line, contrast, rule of thirds, proximity, and repetition to create an attractive and effective page design.

Graphic file A graphic in digital format.

Grid A set of horizontal and vertical lines resembling graph paper that fills the page.

Group selector A group of rules with common formatting properties that are grouped together to help reduce the size of style sheets.

Guide A horizontal or vertical line that you drag onto a page from a ruler, used to position objects; guides are not visible in the browser.

Head content Items such as the page title, keywords, and description that are contained in the head section; *see also* description, head section, keyword, meta tag, and page title.

Heading One of six different text styles that can be applied to text: Heading 1 (the largest size) through Heading 6 (the smallest size).

Head section The part of a web page that is not visible in the browser window; *see also* head content.

Height property (H) The height of an AP element expressed either in pixels or as a percentage of the page.

Hexadecimal value A numerical value that represents the amount of red, green, and blue in a color.

Hidden field On a form, an invisible field that stores user information.

History panel A Dreamweaver panel that lists the steps that have been performed while editing and formatting a document.

Home page The first web page that appears when you access a website.

Horizontal space Blank space above and below an image that separates the image from the text or other elements on the page.

Horizontal symmetry Web page elements are balanced across the page.

Hotspot A clickable area on an image that, when clicked, links to a different location on the page or to another web page.

HTML (Hypertext Markup Language) The acronym for Hypertext Markup Language; the language web developers use to create web pages.

HTML5 The current version of HTML that added new ways to incorporate interactivity with tags that support semantic markup. Examples of added tags are <header>, <footer>, <article>, <section>, <video>, <hgroup>, <figure>, <embed>, <wbr>, and <canvas>.

HTML reports Five reports that check files in a website: Combinable Nested Font Tags, Missing Alt Text, Redundant Nested Tags, Removable Empty Tags, and Untitled Documents.

HTML style A style used to redefine an HTML tag.

http (Hypertext transfer protocol) The hypertext protocol that precedes absolute paths to external links.

Hyperlink *See* link.

Hypertext Markup Language *See* HTML.

Image A graphic such as a photograph or a piece of artwork; images in a website are known as assets or dependent files.

Image map An image that has clickable areas defined on it that, when clicked, serve as a link that takes the user to another location.

Import data To bring data created in another software program into Dreamweaver.

InContext Editing An online service that enables users to make changes to designated editable regions on a page while viewing it in a browser.

Index A directory, or list of files.

Inline style A style that uses code stored in the body content of a web page. *See also* embedded style and internal style.

Insert bar *See* Insert panel.

Insert panel A panel with buttons for creating or inserting objects.

Intellectual property A product resulting from human creativity.

Internal link A link to a web page within the same website.

Internal style A style whose code is stored within the code of a web page, rather than in an external style sheet file.

Internal style sheet A style sheet whose code is saved within the code of a web page, rather than in an external file. *See also* embedded style and inline style.

Intranet An internal website without public access; companies often have intranets that only their employees can access.

IP (Internet Protocol) address An assigned series of four numbers separated by periods, that indicates the address of a specific computer or other piece of hardware on the Internet or an internal computer network.

ISP (Internet Service Provider) A company that supplies Internet access.

Item Each link in a Spry menu bar.

JavaScript Code that adds interaction between the user and a web page, such as rollovers or interactive forms.

JavaScript behavior An action script that allows you to add dynamic content to your web pages.

JPEG (Joint Photographic Exports Group) A file format used for images that appear on web pages; many photographs are saved in JPEG format.

Keyword A word that provides information about the content of a website.

Keyword (Bridge) In Bridge, a word that is added to a file to identify, group, and sort files.

Keywords panel In Bridge, a panel that lists the keywords assigned to a file.

Left property (L) The distance between the left edge of an AP element and the left edge of the page or parent container, such as another div.

Licensing agreement Permission given by a copyright holder that conveys the right to use the copyright holder's work under certain conditions.

Line break Code that places text on a separate line without creating a new paragraph. You create a line break by pressing [Shift][Enter] (Win) or [shift][return] (Mac).

Line number Provide a point of reference when locating specific sections of code.

Link An image or text element on a web page that users click to display another location on the page, another web page on the same website, or a web page on a different website; *also called* hyperlink.

Liquid layout A CSS layout that uses columns expressed as percents based on the browser window width, so they will change width according to the dimensions of the browser window.

List A form object that provides the user with a list or menu of choices to select. Lists display the choices in a scrolling menu.

Live view The view that displays an open document with its interactive elements active and functioning, as if you were viewing the document in a browser.

Local/Network The setting used in Dreamweaver to publish a website on either the local drive (that is, your own hard drive) or a local network drive.

Local site The folder that contains all the files for a website.

Local site root folder A folder on your hard drive or other storage device that will hold all the files and folders for a website.

Locked region An area on a page that only the template author has access to change.

Low-bandwidth animation Animation that doesn't require a fast connection to work properly.

Mailto: link A link to an email address on a web page for users to contact the website's point of contact.

Media object A combination of visual and audio effects and text used to create an interactive experience with a website.

Media queries Style sheets that specify set parameters for displaying pages such as tablets or smartphones.

Menu A form object displayed in a shortcut menu that provides the user with a list of options to select.

Menu bar A bar located at the top of the Dreamweaver workspace that includes menu names, a workspace switcher, and other program commands; *see also* Application bar (Win).

Menu bar (Bridge) A bar at the top of the Bridge workspace with the program commands.

Merge cells To combine multiple adjacent cells into one cell.

Metadata (Bridge) File information you add to a file with tags (words) that are used to identify and describe the file.

Metadata panel In Bridge, a panel that lists the metadata for a selected file.

Meta tag HTML code that includes information about the page such as keywords and descriptions.

Method property Specifies the protocol used to send form data to a web server.

Micro blog A blog that only allows users to post short posts, such as Twitter.

Microsoft Visual SourceSafe A remote access option used on the Windows platform using Microsoft Visual SourceSafe Client.

Mini Bridge A panel that opens directly within the Photoshop and InDesign programs; a simplified version of Bridge.

MOV Apple QuickTime video format.

MP4 The digital video compression standard.

MPEG (Motion Picture Experts) A video file format.

Multi-line text field In forms, a data entry area that is useful for entering text that may take several sentences to complete; *also called* text area field.

Multiple Document Interface (MDI) All the document windows and panels are positioned within one large application window.

Multiscreen preview Dreamweaver feature that allows you to see what a page would look like if it were viewed on a mobile hand-held device, such as a smartphone or tablet. *Also known as* a 3-up preview.

Named anchor A specific location on a web page that is represented by an icon and an assigned descriptive name.

Nested AP div An AP div whose HTML code resides inside another AP div.

Nested table A table that is placed inside the cell of another table.

Nested template A template that is based on another template.

Nonbreaking space A space that appears in a fixed location to keep a line break from separating text into two lines or, in the case of table cells, to keep an empty cell from collapsing.

Ogg (Ogg Theora) Open-source video format developed by Xiph.org.

onClick An event when a mouse is clicked on a page element that triggers an action.

onLoad An event when a page is loaded in a browser window that triggers an action.

onMouseOver An event that occurs when a mouse is placed over a page element that triggers an action.

Optional region In a template, an area that content contributors can choose to show or hide.

Ordered list A list of items that are placed in a specific order and is preceded by numbers or letters.

Orphaned file A file that is not linked to any page in the website.

Page title The title of a page that appears in the title bar in a browser when a web page is viewed in a browser.

Panel A tabbed window in Dreamweaver that displays information on a particular topic or contains related commands.

Panel group A set of related panels that are grouped together and displayed through the Window menu; *also called* a tab group.

Panel group title bar The dark colored bar at the top of each panel group.

Parent keyword In Bridge, the top level for a keyword with child keywords under it.

Password field In a form, a field that displays asterisks or bullets when a user types in a password.

Path The name and physical location of a web page file that opens when a link is clicked.

Path bar In Bridge, the bar where the path of the selected folder in the Folders panel appears.

Plug-in A small computer program that works with a host application such as a web browser to enable it to perform certain functions; *also called* add-on.

PNG (Portable Network Graphics) A file format used for web page images; capable of showing millions of colors, but is small in file size.

Podcast (Programming on Demand) Digital media files that are downloaded from web pages.

Point of contact A place on a web page that provides users a means of contacting a company if they have questions or problems.

Post method Specifies that the data be sent to the processing script as a binary or encrypted file.

Preview panel In Bridge, a panel where a preview of a selected file appears.

Programming on Demand *See* podcast.

Progressive download video A type of video which can be played while it is downloading to the user's computer. If the playback rate exceeds the download rate, a delay is experienced.

Properties panel *See* Property inspector.

Property inspector A panel that displays the properties of a selected object.

Pseudo class style A style that determines the appearance of a page element when certain conditions are met.

Publish a website To make a website available for viewing on the Internet or on an intranet.

Radial symmetry Balance that runs from the center of the page outward, like the petals of a flower.

Radio button An option button on a form that appears as a small empty circle that users click to select a choice.

Radio group Two or more radio buttons grouped together on a form.

RDS (Remote Development Services) A remote access option used with a remote folder running ColdFusion.

Reference panel A panel that is used to find answers to coding questions, covering topics such as HTML, JavaScript, and accessibility.

Related Files toolbar A toolbar located below an open document's filename tab that displays the names of any related files.

Relative path A path used with an internal link to reference a web page or a file within a website.

Relative positioning The placement of div tags in relation to other web page elements.

Remote site The folder location on a web server that is connected to the Internet with software for hosting websites, not directly connected to the computer housing the local site.

Reset a form To erase the entries that have been previously entered in a form and set the values back to the default settings.

Rollover A screen element that changes in appearance as the pointer rests on it in a browser window.

Rollover image An image that changes in appearance as the pointer rests on it in a browser window.

Root folder *See* local site root folder.

Root-relative path A path referenced from a website's root folder.

Roundtrip HTML The Dreamweaver feature that allows HTML files created in other programs, such as Microsoft Expression Web, to be opened in Dreamweaver without adding additional coding, such as meta tags or spaces.

RSS (Really Simple Syndication) Regularly scheduled information downloads used by websites to distribute news stories, information, or announcements.

Rule A set of formatting attributes that defines styles in a Cascading Style Sheet.

Rule of thirds A design principle that entails dividing a page into nine equal squares and then placing the page elements of most interest on the intersections of the grid lines.

Sans-serif font A block style character used frequently for headings and sub-headings.

Scope creep When impromptu changes or additions are made to a project without accounting for corresponding increases in the schedule or budget.

Screen reader A device used by the visually impaired to convert written text on a computer monitor to spoken words.

Seamless image A tiled image that is blurred at the edges so that it appears to be all one image, or made from a pattern that, when tiled, appears to be one image, such as a vertical stripe.

Secure FTP (SFTP) An FTP option which lets you encrypt file transfers to protect your files, user names, and passwords.

Selector The names or tags in Cascading Style Sheets to which style declarations are assigned.

Semantic markup Coding to emphasize meaning.

Semantic web Refers to the way page content can be coded to emphasize the meaning to other programs accessing the information, such as screen readers and search engines.

Serif font A font with small extra strokes at the top and bottom of the characters; used frequently for paragraph text in printed materials.

Server A computer that is connected to other computers to provide file storage and processing services.

Server Behaviors panel The panel that is used to add, edit, and create server behaviors such as a login page.

Server-side scripting A script that processes a form on the form's host web server.

Shortcut (Win) An icon that represents a software program, folder, or file stored on your computer system.

Single-line text field In a form, a data entry area that is useful for small pieces of data such as a name or telephone number.

Site map A listing of all of the pages in a website.

Site usability test A process that involves obtaining website feedback from users who are not connected to the project.

Skin The bar at the bottom of a video with the control buttons.

Skype A video and audio communication service.

Smart Object A Photoshop file with layers that contain image source information to allow an image to be modified while retaining the original data.

Social networking Any web-based service that facilitates social interaction among users.

Split a cell To divide a cell into multiple rows or columns.

Spry Open source code developed by Adobe to help designers quickly incorporate dynamic content on their web pages; *also called* Spry framework for AJAX.

Spry effect Screen effects such as fading or enlarging page elements.

Spry framework for AJAX *See* Spry.

Spry menu bar A preset widget that creates a dynamic, user-friendly menu bar.

Standard mode A Dreamweaver mode that displays a table with no extra space added between the table cells.

Standard toolbar A toolbar that contains buttons for some frequently used commands on the File and Edit menus.

State On a menu bar, the condition of a menu item relative to the mouse pointer, such as Up, Down, Over, and Over While Down.

Static position A CSS property that places an element in order with the document flow.

Status bar A bar that appears under the Dreamweaver window; the left side displays the tag selector, which shows the HTML tags being used at the insertion point location; the right side displays the window size and estimated download time for the page displayed.

Streaming download video Similar to a progressive video download, except streaming video downloads use buffers to gather the content as it is downloading to ensure a smoother playback.

Style Rendering toolbar A toolbar that contains buttons that can be used to display a page using different media types.

Sub keyword *See* child keyword.

Submit To send the information on a form to a host web server for processing.

Swap Image behavior JavaScript code that directs the browser to display a different image when a mouse is rolled over an image on the page.

Swap Image Restore behavior JavaScript code that restores a swapped image back to the original image.

Synchronize To transfer the latest version of website files to a server.

Tab A CSS style that creates a method of organizing data on a page similar in appearance to a file folder tab; used for navigation above page content.

Tab group *See* panel group.

Table A grid of rows and columns that can be used to hold tabular data on a web page.

Table header Text placed at the top or side of a table on a web page and read by screen readers.

Tabular data Data arranged in columns and rows that are separated by a delimiter.

Tag An individual piece of HTML code that instructs the browser how each page element should be displayed.

Tag selector A location on the status bar that displays HTML tags being used at the insertion point location.

Target The location on a web page that the browser will display in full view when the user clicks an internal link.

Target audience The characteristics that make up the population that will be using a website, taking into consideration such factors as age, occupation, sex, education, residence, race, and computer literacy.

Template A Dreamweaver predefined page layout.

Template author The person who creates a template.

Terms of use Rules that govern how a user may use a website's content.

Text area *See* multi-line text field.

Text field On a form, a box in which a user can enter text. *See also* single-line text field and multi-line text field.

Thumbnail slider A sliding control that is used to change the size of the thumbnails being viewed in the Content panel.

Tiled image A small graphic that repeats across and down a web page, appearing as individual squares or rectangles.

Timeline A JavaScript feature that will cause an AP element to appear to move along a path, or change size, visibility, or position.

Top property (T) The distance between the top edge of an AP element and the top edge of the page or AP element that contains it.

Trademark Protects an image, word, slogan, symbol, or design used to identify goods or services.

Transparent background A background composed of transparent pixels, rather than pixels of a color, resulting in images that blend easily on a web page background.

Twitter A website where users post short messages, called "tweets."

Unordered list *See* bulleted list.

Upload To send a form or files to a host web server.

URL (Uniform Resource Locator) The address for a web page as an assigned series of numbers, separated by periods.

Validate markup To compare code against the current standards and identify code that is not compliant.

Vector-based graphic A scalable graphic built using mathematical formulas rather than pixels.

Vertical space Blank space on the sides of an image that separates the image from the text or other elements on the page.

Vertical symmetry Web page elements are balanced down the page.

Vidcast *See* vodcast.

Visited link A link that the user has previously clicked, or visited; the default color for a visited link is purple.

Vodcast A video podcast; *also called* vidcast.

Web 2.0 The evolution of web applications that facilitate and promote information sharing among internet users.

Web browser Software used to display web pages.

Webcam A camera used for video communication on the web.

WebDAV (Web-based Distributed Authoring and Versioning) A remote access option used with servers such as the Microsoft Internet Information Server (IIS) and Apache web server.

Web design program A program used to create interactive web sites.

WebM Google-developed open-source video format.

Web Open Font Format (WOFF) Describes fonts available through font libraries for embedding in web pages through the CSS3 @font-face property.

Web page A page in HTML format with text combined with images and media objects in various formats.

Web-safe color palette A color palette that displays colors that will display consistently in all browsers, and on Macintosh, Windows, and Unix computers.

Web server A computer that is connected to the Internet with a static IP address and software that enables it to make files accessible to anyone on the internet or an intranet; *see also* IP address.

Website A collection of related web pages.

White space An area on a web page that is not filled with text or graphics; not necessarily white.

Widget A piece of code that allows users to interact with the program interface.

Width property (W) The width of an AP element either in pixels or as a percentage of the page.

Wiki A site where a user can use simple editing tools to contribute and edit page content in the site.

Wikipedia An online encyclopedia where users can use simple editing tools to contribute and edit page content.

Wireframe A prototype of each page's content and relationship to other pages in a website.

Word wrap A command that keeps all code within the width of the Document window.

Workflow reports Reports that enable you to check the progress of a project, such as a report that will list all files that have been modified recently.

Workspace The Dreamweaver interface made up of the document window, the menu bar, toolbars, Property inspector, and panels.

Workspace switcher A drop-down menu on the Application bar (Win) or Menu bar (Mac) that allows you to quickly change between different preset workspace screen arrangements.

World Wide Web Consortium (W3C) An international community that develops open standards for web development.

WYSIWYG (What You See Is What You Get) A program such as Dreamweaver that displays web pages as they will appear in a browser.

XHTML (eXtensible HyperText Markup Language) The current standard language used to create web pages.

YouTube A website where you can view or upload videos.

Z-index property The property used to specify the vertical stacking order of multiple AP divs on a page.

Index